THE STATE OF THE WORLD'S CITIES 2004/2005

THE STATE OF THE WORLD'S CITIES 2004/2005

Globalization and Urban Culture

United Nations Human Settlements Programme

UN-HABITAT

London • Sterling, VA

First published by Earthscan in the UK and USA in 2004
for and on behalf of the United Nations Human Settlements Programme (UN-Habitat)

Copyright © United Nations Human Settlements Programme (UN-Habitat), 2004

United Nations Human Settlements Programme (UN-Habitat)
PO Box 30030, Nairobi, Kenya
Tel: +254 2 621 234
Fax: +254 2 624 266
Web: **www.unhabitat.org**

DISCLAIMER

The designations employed and the presentation of the material in this publication do not imply the expression of any opinion whatsoever on the part of the Secretariat of the United Nations concerning the legal status of any country, territory, city or area, or of its authorities, or concerning delimitation of its frontiers or boundaries, or regarding its economic system or degree of development. The analysis, conclusions and recommendations of the report do not necessarily reflect the views of the United Nations Human Settlements Programme, the Governing Council of the United Nations Human Settlements Programme or its Member States

HS/726/04E

ISBN: 1-84407-160-X (Earthscan paperback)
         1-84407-159-6 (Earthscan hardback)
         92-1-131705-3 (UN-Habitat paperback)
         92-1-131706-1 (UN-Habitat hardback)

Page design by Danny Gillespie
Page layout, figures and maps by MapSet Ltd, Gateshead, UK
Printed and bound in Malta by Gutenberg Press Ltd
Cover design by Susanne Harris
Cover photographs © Topfoto and Topfoto/The Image Works (bottom left, centre, top right)

For a full list of publications please contact:

Earthscan
8–12 Camden High Street
London, NW1 0JH, UK
Tel: +44 (0)20 7387 8558
Fax: +44 (0)20 7387 8998
Email: earthinfo@earthscan.co.uk
Web: **www.earthscan.co.uk**

22883 Quicksilver Drive, Sterling, VA 20166-2012, USA

Earthscan publishes in association with WWF-UK and the International Institute for Environment and Development

A catalogue record for this book is available from the British Library

Library of Congress Cataloging-in-Publication Data

The state of the world's cities : globalization and urban culture / UN-HABITAT.
       p. cm.
    Includes bibliographical references and index.
    ISBN 1-84407-160-X (pbk.) — ISBN 1-84407-159-6 (hb)
     1. Cities and towns. 2. Sociology, Urban. 3. Globalization. I. United Nations Human Settlements Programme.

    HT151.S644 2004
    307.76—dc22

                                                                      2004016349

This book is printed on elemental chlorine free paper

Foreword by the Secretary-General

This issue of *The State of the World's Cities* examines the cultural impact of globalization on cities – on how they are governed and planned, on the make-up and density of their population, and on the development of their cultures and economies.

Advances in communications technology and the increasing movement of people across national borders have given many greater freedom and opportunity. But, as this report shows, it has also contributed to a bleak situation in many cities. Many cities face pervasive and persistent problems, including growing poverty, deepening inequality and polarization, widespread corruption at the local level, high rates of urban crime and violence, and deteriorating living conditions.

The lives of international immigrants in many of the world's cities are physically, culturally and economically separated from the lives of other city dwellers. Many live in overcrowded slums and cannot afford adequate housing. They must deal with discrimination, insecure tenure and the exploitation of their labour. Their daily lives are all too often plagued by violence, poverty, and poor health. Yet their economic contribution to the cities in which they live is profound. So too is their contribution, through remittances, to their countries of origin. In short, urban culture today is marked by intensified cultural differentiation. This can enrich and strengthen cities; but it can also be a source of division and a basis for exclusion.

This report not only documents problems in the world's cities; it directs our attention to policies, programmes and projects that can help to create multicultural and inclusive cities. As the report emphasizes, if we are to create cities that are open to all and exclude none, we need to plan for *cities of difference*, and capitalize on the benefits of multicultural existence. This requires the engagement of all non-governmental and community stakeholders, on the basis of legislation that guarantees citizens' rights to the city, and judicial systems that enforce those rights.

By addressing the relationship between globalization, culture and poverty within cities, this report will help the assessment of progress towards the attainment of the Millennium Development Goals and Targets, particularly those relating to slums, water and sanitation. Its conclusions stand as a clear challenge to city planners and managers to nurture an urban culture of peace – one that supports the eradication of poverty and ensures that all urban dwellers, regardless of their race, sex, language or religion, are full citizens of the cities in which they live.

Kofi A Annan
Secretary-General, United Nations
July 2004

Introduction by the Executive Director

The aim of *The State of the World's Cities* report series is to provide information on urban conditions and trends around the world and, in doing so, on progress in the implementation of the Habitat Agenda and towards the realizations of the Millennium Development Goals and Targets on slums, water and sanitation. The first issue of the report, released in 2001, comprehensively reviewed urban conditions, emerging policies and best practices covering five main topics: urban shelter; urban society; urban environment; urban economy; and urban governance.

The present issue, the second in the series, adopts a thematic approach and focuses on globalization and urban culture. It discusses the socio-economic impacts of globalization on cities that are relevant to urban development, including cultural impacts, as well as metropolitanization, international migration, urban poverty, urban governance (focusing on safety and transparency) and urban planning. In particular, the report highlights the challenges of multicultural existence within cities, in the context of globalization, and the need for an urban culture of inclusion. I am therefore delighted to introduce this report as part of UN-Habitat's contribution to the Universal Forum of Cultures (Barcelona, 9 May–26 September 2004).

Throughout history, urbanization, economic growth and civilization have been mutually reinforcing, and cities have always been the loci for national as well as global cultural fusion and innovation. This report shows how cultural differentiation is becoming an important characteristic of globalizing cities and how this is largely attributable to international migration. But the report also looks at culture from another angle, that is the ways in which culture-driven strategies are being used by many cities to market themselves globally as 'cities of culture'.

Under globalization, the spatial structure of cities is changing as new economic production patterns require more horizontal integration between functions in different sites, and as cities shift their attention to external locations and activities, resulting in new geographies and a 'splintering' of earlier urban spatial patterns. The associated decentralization has major implications for the spatial configuration of cities, intensifying the process of metropolitanization and the related management problems.

The report shows how poverty is increasing in many cities and how this is partly an outcome of the uneven costs and benefits of economic globalization. In addition, the report shows how urban poverty has been increasingly concentrated in particular neighbourhoods that have, generally, become the habitats of the urban poor and minority groups: racial minorities in some societies, international immigrant groups in others.

The report also shows how urban governance is increasingly influenced by globalization, focusing on two specific issues: safety and transparency. On the one hand, urban safety is frequently compromised by transnational crime, such as smuggling and trafficking of drugs, firearms and human beings, all of which have been facilitated by opportunities arising from the globalization process and have had devastating impacts on many urban poor communities. On the other hand, transparency at the city level has been compromised by corruption, while the current solutions to this challenge are emerging from a context that may be described as the 'globalization of norms of good urban governance'.

Finally, the report examines the ways in which urban planning is responding to the impacts of globalization on cities, including the cultural impacts. It identifies the main characteristics of what may be described as a new urban planning culture, including the ways in which planning is becoming an innovative, learning process that addresses – in addition to its traditional land use concerns – environmental, social and economic concerns, as well as the challenges of urban multicultural existence and social inclusion.

While the primary purpose of *The State of the World's Cities* series is to describe urban conditions and trends, many of the experiences and best practices cited in this issue offer possible directions for planning and managing socially inclusive multicultural cities, within the context of increasing globalization.

Anna Kajumulo Tibaijuka
Executive Director, UN-Habitat
UN-Habitat Headquarters, Nairobi, July 2004

Acknowledgements

The State of the Worlds Cities 2004/2005: Globalization and Urban Culture is the culmination of the efforts and contributions of many individuals, as well as of a number of institutions and governments. The report was prepared under the general guidance of Donatus Okpala, Director of UN-Habitat's Monitoring and Research Division. Naison Mutizwa-Mangiza, Chief of the Policy Analysis, Synthesis and Dialogue Branch, supervised the preparation of the report. Joseph Maseland managed the preparation of the report in the early stages of the process and was succeeded by a team consisting of Iouri Moisseev and Christine Auclair. Naison Mutizwa-Mangiza and Iouri Moisseev were responsible for the editing and finalization of the report.

The overall direction of the report, in terms of structure and content, was guided by a special UN-Habitat Task Force consisting of the following staff members: Rafael Tuts, Wandia Seaforth, Tatiana Roskoshnaya, Christopher Williams, Lucia Kiwala, Christine Auclair, Roman Rollnick, Seyda Turkmemetogullari, Joseph Maseland, Iouri Moisseev and Naison Mutizwa-Mangiza.

UN-Habitat is particularly grateful to the following experts who prepared background papers for and draft chapters of the report: John Friedman (University of British Columbia, Canada); Michael Cohen (formerly with the World Bank and now at New School University, New York, US); Sharon Zukin (Brooklyn College and City University Graduate Centre, New York, US); Michael Lippe (a former senior staff member of USAID and Transparency International); Vittorio Piovesan (Università IUAV di Venezia, Italy); Guido Martinotti (Università Milano-Bicocca, Italy) and Willem van Vliet– (University of Colorado, US). Christine Auclair and Kathie Oginsky also prepared draft chapters. The short essays in the report were prepared by Reginald Yin-Wang Kwok, Theodore Levin, Corrine Archer, Paul Okunlola, Hilary Clarke, Rasna Warah, Askold Krushelnycky and Miloon Kothari. Wandia Seaforth and Christine Auclair prepared the report's best practice boxes. Design assistance was provided by Pouran Ghaffapour and Urs Ringler.

The report benefited from the detailed comments of several staff at UN-Habitat, including the Executive Director, Mrs Anna Tibaijuka, Daniel Biau, Donatus Okpala, Nefise Bazoglu and Jay Moor.

Antoine King, Henk Verbeek, Felista Ondari, Sriadibhatla Chainulu, Karina Rossi, Josie Villamin, Mary Dibo and Josephine Gichuhi provided financial administrative support during the preparation of the report, while Pamela Murage and Mary Kariuki provided secretarial and general office administrative support.

UN-Habitat is grateful for the assistance and guidance of the team at Earthscan involved in preparing the report for publication, particularly Jonathan Sinclair Wilson, Frances MacDermott and Andrea Service, and the entire team at James & James/Earthscan.

Special thanks are due to the governments of The Netherlands and Germany for their earmarked contributions to the United Nations Habitat and Human Settlements Foundation in support of the preparation of UN-Habitat's flagship reports.

Contents

Foreword by the Secretary-General   *v*
Introduction by the Executive Director   *vii*
Acknowledgements   *ix*
List of Maps, Figures, Tables and Boxes   *xiv*
List of Acronyms and Abbreviations   *xvii*

Overview   1
Changes and challenges in a globalizing world   2
New cultural strategies of urban development   4
Globalization, culture and planning inclusive cities   5

1   The Impacts of Globalization on Cities   9
The cultural dimension   10
    Overall impacts of globalization on urban culture   11
    Emergence of urban ethnic spaces   13
The economic dimension   15
The social dimension   19
Institutional and political dimensions   20
Spatial changes   21
The demographic dimension   24
Challenges for policy and management   25
    Creating multicultural, inclusive cities   25
    Maintaining stability, equilibria and balances in the face of exogenous change   26
    Building and strengthening capacities   27
    Establishing a longer time frame for decision-making   27
    Maintaining the physical world of infrastructure   28
    Financing investment and operations   28
    Mobilizing for sustainability   29
Defending the public interest in cities in an era of globalization   29

2   Cultural Strategies for Urban Development   31
Redevelopment of urban spaces   32
    Redevelopment of inner-city areas   33
    Preservation of cultural heritage   35
    Gentrification   37
Growth of cultural industries   38
The consumption spaces of globalizing cities   42
    Fusion in the design and architecture of consumption spaces   43
    Enclosure of consumption spaces   47
Towards an inclusive urban culture   47

3 Metropolitanization   **49**

Dimensions of metropolitanization   51
    The spatial dimension   51
    The social morphology dimension   52
    The institutional dimension   54
    The economic dimension   57
Twentieth-century trends: managing differences and externalities at different scales   58
    Fragmentation   58
    Differentiation, inequalities and polarization   58
    Spatial mismatch   59
Metropolitan development in an age of globalization   60
Trends in developing countries   62
    Asia and the Pacific   62
    Latin America and the Caribbean   64
    Middle East and Northern Africa (MENA)   67
    Sub-Saharan Africa   69
Trends in transition economy countries   71
Trends in advanced economy countries   73

4 International Migration: Socio-economic and Cultural Implications   **76**

Global overview   77
    Regional trends   77
    Economic impacts   79
    Social and cultural impacts   81
    Policy aspects   82
Developing countries   83
    Asia and the Pacific   83
    Latin America and the Caribbean   86
    Middle East and Northern Africa (MENA)   88
    Sub-Saharan Africa   91
Economies in transition   94
Advanced economies   96

5 Assessing Living Conditions: Focus on Urban Poverty   **101**

Slums and urban poverty   103
Developing economies   106
    Asia and the Pacific: an unprecedented decline in poverty   106
    Poverty, inequalities and slums in Latin America and the Caribbean   110
    Urban poverty in the Middle East and Northern Africa (MENA): progress hindered by
        conflicts and poor governance   113
    Sub-Saharan Africa: more urban poor in life-threatening conditions   116
Urban poverty in the transition economies   121
Homelessness in the advanced economies   124

6 Urban Governance: Safety and Transparency in a Globalizing World   **131**

Global overview   132
    Overall urban crime trends in the world   134
Regional trends in urban crime   136
    Asia and the Pacific   137
    Latin America and the Caribbean   138
    Middle East and Northern Africa (MENA)   142
    Sub-Saharan Africa   143
    Transition economies   149
    Advanced economies   151
Is there a way forward?   156

7   Globalization and the Changing Culture of Planning   **159**
Notable features of contemporary planning cultures   160
Planning cultures: a preliminary assessment   172
Principles of an emerging planning culture   174
   Planning as an innovative practice   174
   The expanded scope of planning   175
   Expanded and multiple scales of planning   175
   Planning for an endogenous development   176
   Planning for cities of difference   177
   The critical role of civil society   178
   A strategic focus for planning   180
   The governance of city planning   181
The future of spatial planning   182

References   *184*
Photo Credits   *192*
Index   *193*

List of Maps, Figures, Tables and Boxes

Maps

1.1 Rates of change in urbanization, 2000–2005   24
1.2 The world's largest cities, 2003   25
4.1 The world's international migrations, 2000   78
5.1 Urban slum incidence, 2001   106
5.2 Major armed conflicts in sub-Saharan Africa, 1995–2003   120
6.1 Control of corruption, 2001   136

Figures

4.1 Countries and areas with the largest number of international migrants and the highest percentage of international migrants in Asia and the Pacific, 2000   83
4.2 Countries and areas with the largest number of international migrants and the highest percentage of international migrants in Latin America and the Caribbean, 2000   86
4.3 Countries and areas with the largest number of international migrants and the highest percentage of international migrants in the Middle East and Northern Africa, 2000   88
4.4 Countries with the largest number of international migrants and the highest percentage of international migrants in sub-Saharan Africa, 2000   91
4.5 Countries with the largest number of international migrants and the highest percentage of international migrants in Central and Eastern Europe and Central Asia, 2000   94
4.6 Countries and areas with the largest number of international migrants and the highest percentage of international migrants in Northern America, Western Europe and the Pacific (advanced economies), 2000   96
5.1 Slum incidence and Human Development Index (HDI), 2000   104
5.2 Slum incidence and gross domestic product (GDP) per capita, 2000   104
5.3 Slum incidence and rate of urban growth in 2000–2005   105
5.4 Income poverty trends, selected countries, 1970–2000   108
5.5 Population in poverty and slums, selected countries   109
5.6 Income poverty and urban slum incidence   112
5.7 Corruption and slums   112
5.8 Slum incidence and government effectiveness   113
5.9 Income inequalities, selected countries   114
5.10 Slum incidence and child mortality   114
5.11 Rate of urban growth and slum incidence, 2000–2005   118
5.12 Poverty in sub-Saharan Africa, selected countries   119
5.13 Poverty levels comparison, selected countries   121
5.14 Female- and male-headed households below the poverty line   123

5.15 Urban population growth in selected countries, 1960–2025 — 123
5.16 15 per cent of EU citizens at risk of poverty — 128
6.1 Victimization rates by region for burglary, robbery, assault and threat in 1999 — 134
6.2 Contact crime by region, 1999 — 135
6.3 Percentage satisfied with police performance, by region, 1999 — 137
6.4 Overall gun ownership rates, 1996 — 139
6.5 Characteristics of young gang members in El Salvador — 140
6.6 Trust in institutions, Latin America, 2003 — 141
6.7 Percentage of victims of urban crime by city: selected sub-Saharan countries, 1990–1999 — 144
6.8 Percentage of respondents who were victims of different crimes at least once over the past five years, 1995–2000 — 144
6.9 People who felt very unsafe walking in their areas after dark in selected African cities, 2000 — 145
6.10 Changes in prevalence rates (% of population victimized) of most common crimes in cities in countries in transition 1992–2000 — 149
6.11 Perceptions of corruption among public officials, 2001 — 150

Tables

1.1 Economic importance of selected cities in proportion to their population — 16
1.2 Population size and growth, urban and rural — 23
4.1 Total population, international migrants, net migration and refugees: number and distribution, 2000 — 77
4.2 Countries with highest remittances received, 2001 — 79
5.1 Slums: five key dimensions — 103
5.2 Slum incidence and indicators of human development, 2000 — 105
5.3 Urban slum indicators and human development — 106
5.4 Income inequalities and slums — 107
5.5 Distribution of the world's urban slum dwellers, 2001 — 107
5.6 Key global indicators — 108
5.7 Reported homelessness in the advanced economies — 126
6.1 Corruption by sectors — 137

Boxes

1.1 Hip-hop: the universal music of youth? — 11
1.2 New York's Arab-American immigrants of a century ago — 14
1.3 Ethnic ghettos in Chicago, US, 1920s to 1930s — 14
1.4 Africans and Chinese in Dublin, Ireland — 15
1.5 *Funkeiros* in Rio de Janeiro, Brazil — 15
1.6 Concentration and decentralization of 'global city' functions — 21
1.7 Urban bilingualism in Miami, US — 26
1.8 Long-range vision: a framework for decision-making — 27
2.1 Plateau Beaubourg, Paris, France — 33
2.2 Glasgow, UK: culture as a new economic base in declining cities — 34
2.3 The Guggenheim Museum, Bilbao, Spain: a global district — 35
2.4 The Esplanade, Singapore: city-branding in the south — 36
2.5 Loft living in New York, US — 37
2.6 Zanzibar, Tanzania: preserving the historic Stone Town — 38
2.7 Kathmandu, Nepal: restoring a centuries-old water supply system — 39
2.8 Dakshinachitra, Chennai, India: using traditional crafts for global marketing of cities — 42
2.9 The role of finance and symbols in cultural industry: garment and 'dot.com' industries, New York, US — 43
3.1 Bangkok: challenges of governance in response to uneven levels of urban expansion — 64
3.2 São Paulo: massive urban expansion combined with absence of suitable urban policy yields increasing social and spatial inequity — 66

3.3 Abidjan: effective urban policy structure confronts expansion, but weaknesses exist   71
4.1 Migrant communities in cities   82
4.2 Covering local skills shortage: the Vietnamese immigrants in Cambodia   85
4.3 Efficiency of immigration policies in Singapore   85
4.4 Migration and cultural identity: Nicaraguans in San José de Costa Rica   87
4.5 Migratory flows between Uruguay and Buenos Aires metropolitan area   87
4.6 Transit immigration in Moroccan cities   90
4.7 Female domestic helpers in the Gulf region: the case of Bahrain   90
4.8 International migration and urban marginality in Abidjan   93
4.9 Managing diversity and informality: the case of Johannesburg's international communities   93
4.10 New Turkish communities in Polish cities   95
4.11 The challenge of integrating migrants within host societies: the case of Berlin   98
4.12 The importance of remittances: three stories of international migrants in London   98
5.1 Global trends in urban poverty during the last decade   102
5.2 Slum data   104
5.3 Dharavi: the largest slum in Asia   110
5.4 'One family, two systems': welfare reforms in urban China   110
5.5 Poverty and Space in São Paulo   111
5.6 When a house is not a home: girls working as housemaids in Morocco   115
5.7 Palestinian refugee camps   116
5.8 Sexual risk-taking in the slums of Nairobi   119
5.9 The toll of conflict in Africa: slums and refugee settlements   120
5.10 Refugee camps in the Democratic Republic of Congo   121
5.11 The Roma community   125
5.12 The feminization of poverty   125
5.13 Defining homelessness   127
5.14 Women's homelessness and domestic violence   127
5.15 Child homelessness   129
5.16 Homelessness and HIV/AIDS   129
6.1 Fear of crime   132
6.2 Globalization of governance norms   133
6.3 The Urban Governance Index (UGI)   134
6.4 Urban crime in Brazil   139
6.5 MV Bill rapping from a Rio *favela*   141
6.6 Violence against women: innovative search for a solution   147
6.7 Decline in frequency of bribery in Kenya's local authorities   148
6.8 Urban planning for crime prevention   156
7.1 Main elements of Santiago de Chile's strategic plan   163
7.2 Havana's 1998–2001 strategic plan   164
7.3 Urban planning in Abidjan, Côte d'Ivoire   165
7.4 Integrated development plans in South Africa   166
7.5 Urban planning in transition: the example of Moscow   167
7.6 Mumbai: the polarizing impact of international investment   177
7.7 Participatory budgeting in Porto Alegre, Brazil   179

List of Acronyms and Abbreviations

ADA	Israeli Anti-Drug Authority	
ADB	Asian Development Bank	
AE	advanced economies	
APEC	Asia and Pacific Economic Cooperation	
APHRC	African Population and Health Research Centre, Nairobi	
APNAC	African Parliamentarian Network against Corruption	
ASEAN	Association of East Asian States	
AU	Africa Union	
BMA	Bangkok Metropolitan Administration	
BRU	Bus Riders Union (Los Angeles)	
CAFSU	Montreal Women's Urban Safety Action Committee	
CARP	Cultural Assets Rehabilitation Project of Eritrea	
CBD	central business district	
CBO	community-based organization	
CHAIN	Community Health Advisory Information Network	
CIA	US Central Intelligence Agency	
CIC	citizen information centre	
CIDEU	Ibero-American Centre for Strategic Urban Development	
CIS	Commonwealth of Independent States	
CMDA	Calcutta Metropolitan Development Authority	
CoE	Council of Europe	
CPI	Corruption Perceptions Index	
CPTED	crime prevention through environmental design	
CSO	civil society organization	
CUNY	City University New York	
DDA	Delhi Development Authority	
DETR	Department of the Environment, Transport and the Regions	
DHS	demographic and health surveys	
ECPAT	End Child Prostitution, Child Pornography and Trafficking of	

	Children for Sexual Purposes in Bangkok
EMR	Extended Bangkok Metropolitan Region
EMU	European Monetary Union
ENHR	European Network for Housing Research
EPLF	Eritrean People's Liberation Front
EPM	environmental planning and management
ESDP	European Spatial Development Perspective
EU	European Union
FDI	foreign direct investment
FEANTSA	European Federation of National Organizations Working with the Homeless, Brussels
FMS	Russian Federal Migration Service
GBV	gender-based violence
GDP	gross domestic product
GNP	gross national product
GOLD	Global Observatory on Local Democracy
HASA	HIV/AIDS Services Administration (New York)
HDI	Human Development Index
HIC	higher-income country
ICO	Johannesburg Inner City Office
ICT	information and communication technology
ICVS	International Crime Victim Survey
IDP	integrated development plan
IDP	internally displaced person
ILO	International Labour Organization
IMF	International Monetary Fund
IT	information technology
IULA	International Union of Local Authorities

IUSSP	International Union for the Scientific Study of Population	SSPs	Danish school, social service and police committees
KMC	Kathmandu Municipal Council	SWOT analysis	Strengths-Weaknesses-Opportunities-Threats analysis
LAC	Latin America and the Caribbean	TE	transition economies
LCSC	Labour Community Strategy Centre	TFYR	The former Yugoslav Republic
LRSP	Vancouver Liveable Region Strategic Plan	TNC	transnational corporation
		TPLF	Tigray People's Liberation Front
MDG	Millennium Development Goal	UAE	United Arab Emirates
MENA	Middle East and Northern Africa	UBC	University of British Columbia
MERCOSUR	*Mercado Común del Sur*	UCLG	United Cities and Local Governments organization
MESA	Middle East Studies Association of North America	UGI	Urban Governance Index
MICS	multiple indicator cluster surveys	UK	United Kingdom
MIT	Massachusetts Institute of Technology	UN	United Nations
		UNCHS (Habitat)	United Nations Centre for Human Settlements (Habitat) (now UN-Habitat)
MTA	Los Angeles County Metropolitan Transportation Authority	UNCTAD	United Nations Conference on Trade and Development
MUR	mega-urban region		
NAACP	National Association for the Advancement of Coloured People	UNDP	United Nations Development Programme
NACAB	National Association of Citizens Advice Bureaux	UNECA	United Nations Economic Commission for Africa
NAFTA	North American Free Trade Agreement	UNECE	United Nations Economic Commission for Europe
NCC	Nairobi City Council	UNECLAC	United Nations Economic Commission for Latin America and the Caribbean
NCPC	Naga City People's Council		
NEPAD	New Partnership for Africa's Development	UNESCAP	United Nations Economic and Social Commission for Asia and the Pacific
NIC	newly industrializing country		
NGO	non-governmental organization		
NS	Dutch rail company	UNESCO	United Nations Educational, Scientific and Cultural Organization
OAU	Organization of African Unity (now AU)		
OECD	Organisation for Economic Co-operation and Development	UNFPA	United Nations Population Fund
		UN-Habitat	United Nations Human Settlements Programme (*formerly* UNCHS (Habitat))
PA	Palestinian Authority		
PC	personal computer		
PPGIS	public-participation global information systems	UNHCR	United Nations High Commission for Refugees
PPP	public–private partnership	UNICEF	United Nations Children's Fund
PRD	Pearl River Delta	UNICRI	United Nations Interregional Crime and Justice Research Institute
RDA	regional development agency		
RSFSR	Russian Soviet Federative Socialist Republic	UNODC	United Nations Office on Drugs and Crime
SADC	Southern African Development Community	UNU	United Nations University
SAPS	South African Police Service	US	United States
SCP	Sustainable Cities Programme	USSR	Union of Soviet Socialist Republics
SEWA	Self-Employed Women's Association	UTO	United Towns Organization
SO	street office	WHO	World Health Organization
SSA	sub-Saharan Africa	WTO	World Trade Organization

Overview[1]

The operative mode of poetic thought is imagining, and imagination consists, essentially, of the ability to place contrary or divergent realities in relationship (Octavio Paz).

This report does not stand in isolation but builds on the work of several earlier benchmark publications. *An Urbanizing World: Global Report on Human Settlements 1996* characterized cities around the world as places of opportunity and viewed them as engines of growth.[2] In 2001, *Cities in a Globalizing World: Global Report on Human Settlements 2001* directed attention to the implications of globalization for cities, emphasizing the uneven distribution of costs and benefits and advocating support for cities as agents of change.[3] The Millennium Development Goals (MDGs), adopted by United Nations (UN) member states in 2000 set out broad goals related to poverty reduction and environmental sustainability.[4] Target 11 of Goal 7, calling for 'significant improvement in the lives of at least 100 million slum dwellers by 2020', guided *The Challenge of Slums: Global Report on Human Settlements 2003*.[5] This report offered a further assessment of the global trends of poverty and inequality, with a focus on slums, providing a new operational definition, first ever global estimates of slums worldwide, and an examination of the antecedent dynamics of and policy responses to slums. The key message of *The State of the World's Cities 2001* reinforced the importance of establishing partnerships between local and national governments in order to address the existing urban challenges effectively.[6]

The current report extends the themes developed in these earlier publications. Its focus on the uneven socio-economic impacts of globalization on cities and on the need for an urban culture of inclusion and peace in the context of globalization confronts us with an important question: how can the daunting challenges found in cities around the world be realistically recognized, on the one hand, and hope for constructive problem-solving be still maintained, on the other?

The chapters that follow sketch an often bleak picture of cities. They report pervasive and persistent urban problems, including growing poverty in many regions, deepening inequality and polarization, widespread corruption, high levels of crime and violence, and deteriorating living conditions with inadequate sanitation, unsafe water and so forth. These are real problems with serious consequences for the daily lives of millions of people. These problems must be acknowledged and documented. Doing so is a necessary step towards their amelioration. The challenges are often overwhelming and resources are frequently insufficient to address them effectively.

Nonetheless, cities also function as engines of economic growth and an examination of promising practices around the world shows examples of low-income communities who mobilize successfully, often in partnerships, to improve difficult situations. It is important to draw lessons from these experiences and learn how approaches that work well in one place may be adapted in other places that share similar problems. Such knowledge exchange may take different forms and holds potential for positive development. It encourages hope for progress.

The Millennium Development Goals, adopted by the United Nations, set out broad goals related to improvement of living conditions

This report, therefore, acknowledges the multitude and magnitude of problems facing cities today, especially those associated with the impacts of globalization. But it also directs attention to policies, programmes and projects that instil hope and envision progress towards the creation of liveable cities, open to all and excluding none.

Towards this end, the following chapters take stock of the current state of the world's cities, focusing on salient issues within the context of globalization. This Overview presents the main observations made in these chapters and highlights the suggested directions of work that could contribute towards inclusive and liveable cities.

Changes and challenges in a globalizing world

Globalization is not a new phenomenon. However, global connections today differ in at least four important ways from those in the past. First, they function at much greater **speed** than ever before. Improved technologies enable much faster transportation of people and goods and the instantaneous transmission of information. Second, globalization operates on a much larger **scale**, leaving few people unaffected and making its influence felt in even the most remote places. Third, the **scope** of global connections is much broader and has multiple dimensions – economic, technological, political, legal, social and cultural, among others, each of which has multiple facets.[7] Linkages have proliferated to involve multiple, interdependent flows of a greater variety of goods, services, people, capital, information and diseases. Fourth, the dynamic and often unmediated interactions among numerous global actors create a new level of **complexity** for the relationships between policy, research and practice.[8]

In the urban context, globalization finds expression in developments that are described in this report. In this regard, at the city level, there are significant economic, social, political, spatial and demographic impacts. Throughout history, cities have played important roles in the economic well-being of nations. Urbanization, economic growth and civilization have been mutually reinforcing. Cities, especially large cities, typically mean larger per capita incomes. Urban-based economic activities account for more than 50 per cent of gross domestic product (GDP) in all countries and up to 80 per cent in more urbanized countries in Latin America, and more in Europe. Improved understanding of the multiple interactions between globalization and cities can, therefore, contribute to identifying new strategies for protecting and sustaining national economies.

Advances in communication and information technologies, improved transportation and deregulation of capital markets (but not labour markets) have enabled private investors to take advantage of national differences in tax rates, labour costs and environmental restrictions to maximize financial returns by moving development, production and marketing functions to the most profitable locations. Losers in this 'race to the bottom' have been, for example, female workers in many countries in East Asia, whose wage levels and working conditions have declined as a result of the dropping of barriers to footloose industries. In the more advanced economies, a consequence has been the rise in just-in-time and flex work, with the associated loss of benefits and decrease in job security.[9] A general trend is the 'informalization' of the urban economy, with increasing shares of income earned in unregulated employment. This trend not only affects workers, but also undermines the governance of cities, which obtain less revenue to provide needed public services.

The most obvious socio-economic aspect of the aforementioned developments is the growing diversity of urban populations. The outstanding characteristic of this increase in population differentiation is intra-urban inequality, reflecting the influence of bipolar job markets, migratory flows and practices of social exclusion. Effects manifest themselves not only in unequal income, but in the impact on household assets, as when coping strategies require relocation and sale of a home, causing disruption of support networks. Further consequences occur through spatial segregation and unequal access to urban services and infrastructure and, hence, life chances. At the societal level, inequality not only affects political and social stability, but also productivity and poverty levels.

In the political realm, the most significant impact of globalization on cities has been the weakening of national and local public institutions, relative to external private economic power. The privatization of public services in many cities is one outcome of this process, in which external investors 'cherry-pick' the more profitable services, further eroding urban revenues and leaving cities with the poorly performing services. At the same time, relinquishing responsibility for water supply, sanitation, waste collection, fire fighting, street maintenance and, occasionally, safety and social services has also meant losing important tools needed for the rehabilitation of existing areas and the guiding of new development.

Under globalization, the spatial structure of cities is changing as new economic production patterns require more horizontal integration between functions in different sites, and as cities shift their attention to external locations and activities, resulting in new geographies and a 'splintering' of earlier urban spatial patterns. The associated decentralization has major implications for investments in infrastructure development and maintenance. Such investments have been highly uneven, which, in turn, has significant impacts on access to the urban services necessary for liveability.

The effects of the aforementioned developments are amplified by demographic trends, which are characterized foremost by rapid growth in the cities of the developing economies. Research reported in Chapter 1 projects that by 2030 about 60 per cent of the world's population will live in cities, a trend that equals the addition of a city of 1 million residents every week. In dealing with these changes, accentuated and generated by globalization, urban policy-makers face several key challenges, which will be reviewed in a later section of this overview.

At the metropolitan level, important changes can be seen, as well (see Chapter 3). Subsumed under the label of 'metropolitanization', these changes have spatial, institutional and economic dimensions. One of the most visible aspects of recent metropolitan development has been its spatial expansion, spilling over into adjacent jurisdictions and incorporating them within the larger municipality of the central city. As noted above, decentralization of jobs (especially in the manufacturing sector) and people is an important element of this process, in many places leading to polycentric forms, with economic activities clustered around transportation nodes. In the institutional realm, spatial expansion has been accompanied by a proliferation of administrative entities with responsibilities for different aspects of metropolitan government, including, for example, municipal government, special functional districts for specific services such as solid waste collection, sectoral authorities (such as transport), metropolitan planning authorities and metropolitan government, all of which require a higher level of cooperation and coordination.

Taken together with the changes at the city level, described earlier, these developments are leading to greater fragmentation and differentiation, as well as growing inequalities and spatial mismatches between resources and needs. Assumptions about the economies of urban agglomeration as having a multiplier effect and leading to greater returns on investment for individuals, households, firms, production sectors and cities have not been borne out and urban liveability has fallen short of 'metropolitan expectations', as Chapter 3 explains.

Developments at the city and the metropolitan levels are situated in larger national and global contexts. International migration is an important aspect of these wider contexts. The review in Chapter 4 shows how globalization generates movement of people across national borders at a very large scale. The latest data indicate about 175 million international migrants, including refugees, but excluding undocumented migrants.

The increased population differentiation, noted above as an important characteristic of globalizing cities, is significantly attributable to international migration. Today's migration streams are much more diverse than those in the past, including underpaid manual and service workers, highly paid skilled professionals, students, reuniting family members, asylum seekers and refugees, and undocumented persons.

The more developed economies are the most notable destinations of these population flows (77 million), followed by the transition economies of Eastern Europe and the former Soviet Republics (33 million), Asia and the Pacific (23 million) and the Middle East and North Africa (21 million).

In many cases, newcomers live spatially segregated lives as a result of discriminatory practices, self-selection and lack of housing affordability, often in slums under inferior situations, enduring labour exploitation, social exclusion, insecure tenure, overcrowding, violence and other unhealthy conditions. Immigrants often work in segmented job markets in activities that tend to be refused by the indigenous population. Xenophobia has become a more salient issue, even though careful research does not support the popular view that immigrants are an economic burden.[10] For example, some developing countries have forcibly repatriated large numbers of foreigners, ostensibly in order to address rising urban crime. Similar tensions exist in other areas, including many border regions and 'Fortress Europe'.

However, immigrants make important economic contributions, not only to the urban economy of their host country, but also to the countries that they left. Remittances back home are second only to oil in terms of international money flows, providing an important and relatively reliable source of foreign exchange finance. In 2003, for example, the Indian Diaspora sent back US$15 billion, exceeding the revenues generated by the country's software industry.

The developments, briefly summarized above, set the stage for the daily lives of people in globalizing cities. They affect these lives in many ways. This report focuses attention on impacts related to poverty, crime and corruption.[11]

Slums are the physical manifestation of urban poverty. To monitor progress towards Target 11 of MDG 7, 'significant improvement in the lives of at least 100 million slum dwellers by 2020', an operational definition of slums has been developed that includes the following criteria: access to adequate drinking water; access to adequate sanitation; quality of housing as it relates to locational and structural characteristics; overcrowding; and security of tenure.[12] According to this definition, almost one third of the world's urban population lives in slums. This figure obscures large regional differences. As Chapter 5 demonstrates, at the low end, slum dwellers make up 5 and 10 per cent of the urban populations in the advanced and the transition economies, respectively. At the other end of the spectrum, the proportion of the slum population in the cities of the developing economies is 43 per cent, and in cities in the least developed economies it is 78 per cent. The multidimensional nature of urban poverty is especially evident in slums where people experience inadequacies in income, assets, shelter, public infrastructure, basic services, legal protections and political power.[13]

The probability of being a victim of crime is higher in cities than in non-urban areas (see Chapter 6). Despite large variations between regions, countries and cities, recent years show a widespread increase in urban violence worldwide, including homicide, assault, rape, sexual abuse and domestic violence. Although globalization has been linked to greater economic volatility, inequality and social exclusion – all of which have been associated with the occurrence of crime – there exists no evidence that globalization is a cause of the increase in crime. There is, however, evidence that globalization is accompanied by a rise in organized transnational crime.[14] Globalization has expanded illicit opportunity structures and created new ones. Crimes such as human trafficking, drug smuggling, illegal export of cultural property and animals, software piracy, money laundering and terrorism are all on the increase. In defiance of laws and in the face of indignant reactions, many thousands of children and women are being held in bondage under abominable conditions, suffering malnutrition and abuse at the hands of their captors.[15] In the wake of the tragedy of 11 September 2001, there has also been a sharply increased interest in the implications of terrorism for urban life and the form of cities, leading some to question the viability of prevailing paradigms for urban development.[16]

Corruption, lack of accountability and transparency are a different form of crime. They may be described as 'institutional and structural violence' because they relate to the institutions and structures of governance, including public- and private-sector agencies responsible for providing services and enforcing the law. Chapter 6 also shows the prevalence of corruption in many countries when citizens interact with officials in schools, clinics, land administration, tax offices, police and the courts on matters such as obtaining a birth certificate, enrolling their children in school or securing medical tests. The incidence of corruption undermines popular trust in public institutions and hampers democratic processes.

The changes and challenges associated with globalization briefly sketched above pose formidable problems in the planning, development and management of urban centres. There exists great variation in the responses of cities to these problems. However, an increasingly dominant theme permeating these responses relates to urban culture (see Chapter 2). Development approaches built around the cultivation of urban culture have been both enthusiastically embraced and harshly criticized. The final sections of this Overview summarize the nature of, and reactions to, the notion of urban culture and situates it in the wider perspective of the need for a culture of planning that promotes inclusive and peaceful cities.[17]

New cultural strategies of urban development

A recent publication proclaims that the era of globalization, like that of other economic doctrines from Marx to Keynes, has come to an end.[18] This obituary reporting the death of globalization is open to question. Although its goals and contents must change to produce more sustainable and equitable outcomes, vested and emerging interests enmeshed in worldwide interdependent networks and established technologies ensure that globalization will not vanish any time soon. Global capital has a great capacity to reconfigure itself.[19] In the face of this reality, cities around the world search for strategies that take advantage of their unique assets to strengthen their competitive position in the global economy.[20] Urban culture has emerged as an important ingredient of these strategies.[21]

Culture, in this sense, includes but goes beyond its traditional definitions. It comprises material aspects such as the physical infrastructure, public spaces, buildings and other artefacts of the urban environment. It also consists of nonmaterial aspects, such as the values, attitudes, beliefs and lifestyles of urban residents. In this meaning, urban culture has penetrated to the far reaches of the world. Chapter 2 broadens the meaning of urban culture to include the capacity of cities to adapt to change, specifically changes resulting from globalization.

The use of culture as a motor of economic growth reflects the transition from manufacturing to more flexible, design-, knowledge- and service-based activities, particularly in cities in the advanced economies. Under globalization, manufacturing activities in these cities have been relocated 'off-shore' to the developing economies whose lower labour costs, lower taxes and lesser environmental protections enable higher profits. This development has created unused space, which in many cities has been converted into new work–live spaces, as illustrated by the adaptive reuse of factory lofts by artists. In many places, local governments have supported this trend by, for example, enacting regulations to protect buildings from demolition and tax incentives to encourage restoration. Cities in the developing economies provide examples of this approach as well, as seen in Quito,[22] Ankara,[23] Havana,[24] Cartagena,[25] Pueblo,[26] Penang,[27] Vientiane[28] and Kampong Glam.[29]

Nor is it just local governments that seek to connect economic and cultural strategies. In countries where central government controls the management and budgets of cultural institutions, this confluence of forces leads to the pursuit of '*grand projets*' as seen in France (for example, the Beaubourg) and the commercial '*branding*' of cities.[30] At an international level, the European Union (EU) established an annual competition to select the European City of Culture that similarly serves to promote economic development through cultural strategies.

The case of Bilbao has received much attention as an instance of the economic development of urban culture,[31] although similar approaches can be seen in many cities around the world. The experience of Florence with art restoration indicates that urban cultural strategies can generate jobs, and may be accompanied by spatial restructuring of the urban fabric.[32] However, in a growing number of cities, the record shows that not everyone benefits.[33] Indeed, a recent review of several hundred projects in 20 nations and 5 continents concludes that the promoters of multibillion-dollar mega-projects systematically and self-servingly misinform parliaments, the public and the media in order to get construction approval. It reveals an unhealthy cocktail of underestimated costs, overestimated revenues, undervalued environmental impacts and overvalued economic development effects.[34]

The emergence of cultural themes in urban development must be seen in light of the dominance of a consumer culture that endows urban commodities and commercial experiences of the city, often in privatized public spaces, with symbolic values attached to images of 'the good life' characterized by affluence and consumption.[35] There is also a growing concern about the role of local and corporate entrepreneurs in the ascendance of commodified urban culture,[36] and the ways in which they influence local government through campaign contributions and other political activities that bypass democratic processes.[37] Waterfront developments have featured prominently among the signature projects geared to global place marketing.[38] Their uneven distribution of costs and benefits, with winners and losers, further calls into question the notion of the 'public interest' and the 'common good' in urban planning.

Not only is urban culture a tool of economic development whose benefits and costs are distributed unevenly, it can also be used as a political instrument in pluralistic societies to help define cultural identities, with important implications for languages used and permitted in schools, the courts and official documentation, placing certain population groups in positions of privilege, while disadvantaging or excluding others. In this connection, the development of planning for multicultural cities that are inclusive of diverse populations takes on special significance. Such planning poses difficult challenges, including those related to communicating across culture-based epistemologies.[39]

Globalization, culture and planning inclusive cities

Globalization intensifies population differentiation, which contributes to polymorphous and variegated urban cultures. Such cultures can enrich and strengthen cities; but they can also be a source of division and basis for exclusion.[40]

The advances in communication and transportation technologies that have facilitated globalization have also transformed urban communities. Whereas in earlier times, spatial constraints were a determining factor in the delineation of communities, today many more people are able to self-select their 'communities of interest'[41] based on shared values and objectives, rather than mobility restrictions. As a consequence, many communities do not coincide with neighbourhood boundaries and many neighbourhoods do not function as communities. Instead of being based on territory, communities are more often spatially extensive networks, consisting of channels through which resources flow – information, money and social capital. Population differentiation has intensified this development. Insofar as the outcomes of these processes result not from residential choice but from distortion and segmentation of housing and job markets, they help to produce patterns of residential segregation that create unequal access to services, education, employment and life chances, in general.[42]

In light of the 1999 United Nations Declaration and Programme of Action on a Culture of Peace[43] and of the International Decade for a Culture of Peace and Non-Violence for the Children of the World (2001–2010), planners have an opportunity and moral obligation to help nurture an urban culture of peace. Such a culture can be said to consist of the fusion of material and non-material factors that support practices of inclusion and rights to the city for *all*, without distinction of any kind, such as race, colour, sex, language, religion, political or other opinion, national or social origin, property, birth or other status. This inclusive formulation calls for cautious elaboration. It has been suggested that the world has gone through a century of 'premature universalism', as though there were one right way of doing things.[44]

However, it is necessary to recognize the great diversity that exists among the very many ethnic groups in the world. Each of these groups, no matter how small, has developed its own ways of dealing with difference. Accordingly, there exist numerous practices and processes to resolve conflict. As such, each of these groups is a resource for managing change. Their cultural diversity enriches societies and enhances their capacity for positive transformation. It is important, therefore, that urban cultures do not seek to eliminate difference, but value and celebrate it. Difference does not divide people in inclusive and liveable cities. Rather, such cities acknowledge diversity as a source of untapped development potential.[45]

To plan for pluralistic cities, rather than a hypothetical unitary public interest, acknowledging and supporting the full diversity of *all* population groups, planners must develop a new kind of multicultural literacy. An essential part of this is familiarity with the multiple histories of urban communities, especially since those histories intersect with struggles over space and place, with planning policies and resistances to them, with traditions of indigenous planning, and with questions of belonging and identity and acceptance of difference.[46]

Chapter 7 describes planning culture as the ways, both formal and informal, in which planning is conceived, institutionalized and enacted. Planning, in this sense, is inevitably embedded in national and local political cultures, which show great variation across countries and regions.[47] Thus, there are significant differences in the degree of decentralization and the division of responsibilities and resources between national and lower levels of government, the roles of civil society and the private sector, the prevalence of improprieties and corruption, and the focus on physical or other aspects of planning. These elements, in turn, are intertwined with different political and institutional contexts (for example, unitary and federal states, and multinational entities), different constitutional frameworks, and different levels of economic and urban development.

Notwithstanding their many differences, planning cultures around the world share in common the fact that they are constantly in transition, undergoing change in adapting to and anticipating internal and external circumstances. These changes have several recurring themes. For example, the developments reviewed in Chapter 7 show how, in all cases, the role of national governments in urban management is being weakened, while that of regional and local governments is being strengthened. There is also a trend away from planning conceived as a restraint on market forces (for example, through zoning legislation) to a kind of entrepreneurial planning that seeks to facilitate economic development through the market.

Another important development concerns the role of civil society in planning. In the wake of the adoption of rights-based policy platforms and international conventions during the world summits of the 1990s, and the concomitant globalization of associated norms for democratic decision-making and resource allocation, marginalized populations have become increasingly recognized as actors in their own right, with entitlements and potentials to affect their situation. The report provides positive examples that attest to the capacity of vulnerable populations to be proactive and underlines the significance of policies and programmes that support those abilities.

There are encouraging examples of opportunities for planning multicultural, inclusive cities. They are found in this report in the chapters on international migration, and newly emerging forms of governance and planning, as well as elsewhere. For example, there is work that builds on the functions of customary land tenure systems as an alternative to modern, formal cadastral land registration systems in order to assist access to land by the urban poor in African cities.[48] From Thailand to the US, there is also growing interest in the design of public space, its access and use by diverse groups, and its role in supporting citizen involvement in democratic processes of urban governance.[49] The rights of indigenous people are getting more attention, as in New Zealand, where a national mandate intended to redress human rights violations now requires local governments to prepare environmental plans and to support participation by indigenous people.[50] Planners also take a growing interest in the development of information technologies, such as public-participation global information systems (PPGIS), to develop tools suited to new forms of cross-border activism in this era of globalization, strengthening the grassroots efforts of marginalized peoples and communities who are working for social justice and environmentally sustainable livelihoods.[51] Community-based justice systems are spreading rapidly as they prove to be an effective approach to reducing crime in multicultural communities, 'bringing the court to the problem' rather than 'bringing the problem to the court'. These and other examples[52] illustrate the importance of a planning approach that nurtures multicultural pluralism in inclusive and liveable cities.

Against this background, a new culture of planning is emerging that goes beyond narrow professionalism and public institutions. Planning by and through the state is only one version among many, rather than the only version of planning. Today, not all professionally trained planners work as agents of the state. Increasingly, planners work for diverse local communities, including minority groups such as immigrants, in a dialogic relationship that goes far beyond advocacy. Planning as a profession has also expanded to include environmental policy, historic preservation, community development and poverty alleviation.[53] Planning in this more inclusive sense involves multiple actors from the public and private sectors and civil society. It is not only about comprehensive action or hierarchical coordination of master plans, but also entails interdependent processes concerned with the many dimensions of liveable cities – environmental sustainability, social justice and equity, and community and aesthetics. The new planning is being constructed as a learning process, and demands continuous monitoring and critical reflection on the part of planners and relevant publics. Its practice will vary according to local circumstances and will require institutional experimentation and innovation,[54] with further implications for professional education.[55] The new planning supports urban development 'from within' – endogenous development of the city's wealth-generating resources,[56] and 'civilizing' projects that expand the spaces of democratic practice and discourse and encourage diversity in everyday life.

The contours of the new planning culture, outlined in Chapter 7, also bring into sharper relief themes addressed in earlier chapters on urban culture, metropolitanization and international migration, particularly those concerning the contestation of public space in the face of increasing diversity. A key characteristic of the new planning in this regard is, therefore, the planning for cities of difference, which requires engaging civil society organizations based on legislation that guarantees, and a judicial system that enforces, citizens' rights to the city.[57]

Notes

1 This Overview was drafted with assistance of Willem van Vliet–, University of Colorado, Boulder, US.
2 UNCHS (Habitat), 1996.
3 UNCHS (Habitat), 2001a.
4 UN-Habitat, 2003a.
5 UN-Habitat, 2003a.
6 UNCHS (Habitat), 2001b.
7 For example, economic globalization can include growth of international trade as well as increases in foreign investment. Likewise, political globalization can be seen in greater cross-border cooperation between national governments, but also in the 'twinning' of municipal governments and in the rise of international networking of non-governmental organizations (NGOs) and civil society groups.
8 For a fuller discussion of these points, see UNCHS (Habitat), 2001a. See also Smart and Smart, 2003; and Savitch, 2002.
9 In an attempt to arrest the 'race to the bottom' in the form of steep declines in corporate tax rates during the 1990s, the European Union (EU) agreed on a code of conduct for business taxation and in 2001 the European Commission proposed to consolidate the activities of a company across all of its European activities: companies would no longer have to calculate the taxable profit earned in each member state, but only the total taxable profit earned in the EU as a whole (Devereux et al, 2003).
10 See, for example, Vernez and McCarthy, 1995.
11 These problems are by no means presented as a comprehensive inventory, and many other issues demand attention. For example, the decentralized, multiple-nuclei form typical of globalizing urban economies has direct implications for the development of transportation systems, which rely heavily on private automobiles with major ramifications for allocating public and household budgets, environmental pollution and public health, including the incidence of accidents. In a recent report, the World Health Organization (WHO) estimates 1.2 million traffic fatalities and 50 million injuries per year (Peden et al, 2004).
12 See UN-Habitat, 2003a; 2003b.
13 See Satterthwaite, 2002.
14 See Williams, 1999.
15 See, for example, West Africa: traffickers hold thousands of children, women in bondage, www.irinnews.org/print.asp?ReportID=37815; 'Rising count, dropping years – Summit on ending the curse of trafficking', *The Telegraph*, Calcutta, India, 24 March 2004; *Trafficking in Human Beings*, www.unodc.org/unodc/en/ trafficking_human_beings.html. See www.childlaborphotoproject.org/ for excellent photography of 'child labour in the global village'.
16 See, for example, Savitch, 2003; Savitch and Ardashev, 2001; Simpson et al, 2001; Swanstrom, 2002.
17 This orientation is not to negate other approaches, such as integrated spatial planning. Different approaches may co-exist. However, the focus here is on urban culture as a component of urban planning and development that has been touted as a source of revenue and urban rejuvenation, but that has received relatively less attention as a building block of inclusive cities.
18 Saul, 2004.
19 See, for example, Friedmann, 2002a.
20 See also UNCHS (Habitat), 2001a.
21 There are other important questions related to the effects of globalization on urban culture, as examined, for example, in a stimulating ethnographic study of how class and race mutually articulate youth cultures in an English town affected by post-industrial changes; see Nayak, 2003.
22 Middleton, 2003.
23 Erendil and Ulusoy, 2002.
24 Scarpaci, 2000.
25 Bromley, 2000.
26 Jones and Varley, 1999.
27 Teo, 2003.
28 Long, 2002.
29 Yeoh and Huang, 1996.
30 Evans, 2003.
31 See, for example, Plaza, 2000; Vicario and Monje, 2003.
32 See Lazzaretti, 2003.
33 See, for example, Newman, 2002; Spirou and Bennett, 2002.
34 Flyvbjerg et al, 2003.
35 Gottdiener, 2001. In a related vein, a recent analysis of the development trajectory of Asia-Pacific concludes that the support for 'creative service' industries is crucial to the planning response to globalization in that region (Hutton, 2004). In this case, and more generally, inclusion of stockbrokers, litigators and like professionals among the 'creative class' (Florida, 2002) raises questions about what exactly is being created by these professionals and whether use of the term creativity in this

connection does not set up an analytically anaemic cultural *passe-partout*.

36 Rantisi, 2004.

37 Judd and Simpson, 2003.

38 See Sandercock and Dovey, 2002.

39 For a fuller discussion of the challenges of participatory planning in culturally diverse cities, see Umemoto, 2001. For an examination of the challenges of a national policy of social mixing in disadvantaged neighbourhoods in The Netherlands, see Uitermark, 2003.

40 See the discussion of the 'quartering of the city' in Chapter 2 of UNCHS (Habitat), 2001a.

41 Newman, 1980.

42 See Shevky and Bell, 1955, for the first systematic analysis of residential differentiation as a socio-spatial reflection of larger societal processes. A fine discussion can also be found in Timms, 1971. For recent studies of residential segregation in the context of globalization, see Dupont, 2004; Forrest et al, 2003; Poulsen et al, 2002; and Simpson, 2004.

43 Resolution adopted by the United Nations General Assembly, A/RES/53/243, 6 October 1999, serving as the basis for the International Year for the Culture of Peace and the International Decade for a Culture of Peace and Non-Violence for the Children of the World.

44 Boulding, 1999.

45 Building on writings by Ezra Park, Louis Wirth and Herbert Gans, at a theoretical level, Claude Fischer (1984) proposed the sub-cultural theory to explain the potential for positive, as well as negative, urban phenomena as a function of a city's *critical mass*, which incorporates the effects of population composition as well as structural determinants.

46 See Sandercock, 1998a. For a thoughtful essay on the preparations that planners need for their roles in constructing pluralistic, multicultural cities, see Sandercock, 1998b.

47 Savitch and Kantor, 2003.

48 See, for example, Durand-Lasserve, 2004.

49 See, for example, Boonchuen, 2002; Day, 1999; Day, 2003.

50 See Berke et al, 2002.

51 See, for example, Sieber, 2003; Kyem, 2000.

52 For example, Burayidi, 2000; Qadeer, 1997; Edgington and Hutton, 2000.

53 See Sandercock, 1998a, for a fine discussion of the histories and practices of planning.

54 This may be especially so in cities in the transition economies whose institutions are being restructured as in the case of, for example, the pressures and constraints on real estate development in the context of globalizing investment patterns. See Keivani et al, 2001; 2002.

55 See, for example, Afshar, 2001.

56 See Chapter 7 for a description of the seven major resource complexes that constitute an urban area's productive assets.

57 Friedmann, 2002b. See also Harvey, 2003, and Purcell, 2003, both of whom treat 'rights' primarily at a theoretical level. For good recent coverage of aspects of housing rights in various countries, see Leckie, 2003.

Chapter 1

The Impacts of Globalization on Cities[1]

The cultural dimension	**10**
Overall impacts of globalization on urban culture	11
Emergence of urban ethnic spaces	13
The economic dimension	**15**
The social dimension	**19**
Institutional and political dimensions	**20**
Spatial changes	**21**
The demographic dimension	**24**
Challenges for policy and management	**25**
Creating multicultural, inclusive cities	25
Maintaining stability, equilibria and balances in the face of exogenous change	26
Building and strengthening capacities	27
Establishing a longer time frame for decision-making	27
Maintaining the physical world of infrastructure	28
Financing investment and operations	28
Mobilizing for sustainability	29
Defending the public interest in cities in an era of globalization	**29**

The assertion that processes of globalization have important and far-reaching impacts on cities is not controversial in the early days of the 21st century. Evidence of economic, political and cultural change is everywhere. From shopping centres selling global products to ubiquitous telephone call centres and internet cafés to the huge flows in people, information, goods and services, globalization is the household word of our time.

The extent to which local events and conditions can be attributed to globalization is not as important as the fact that globalization is used to explain patterns of change and many features of urban life. Heated debates occur about the meaning of these impacts, whether they are positive or negative, and whether they are subject to public policy and control. Debates in Cairo, New Delhi or Caracas are all enriched by the extraordinary diffusion of information, stories and experiences from one city to another, from one country to another. What is clear is that the interaction between globalization and cities is not unidirectional; it is not just that cities are affected by global forces, but that local economies, cultures and polities also affect global patterns. Global factors become embedded in local culture, practice and institutions.[2] This two-way process is clear, for example, in the Asian financial crisis of 1997. Local financial conditions in Thailand, Korea and Indonesia interacted with global financial practices and behaviours to produce the collapse of national and local financial institutions, with major economic consequences for the populations of those countries.

In the world of the internet, we know more and more, about more and more; yet, perhaps not surprisingly, our analytic tools and understanding can hardly keep up with the pace of change and the amounts of data we receive. The **challenge to understanding**, therefore, is an important part of the world's experience of globalization. This challenge is of more than academic interest because policy and action must be guided by understanding. The stakes are high;

millions of people are living in poverty. Effective policy and action is urgently needed.

This chapter examines the impacts of globalization on cities in terms of its multiple dimensions, presenting the forms of data and evidence that confirm these impacts. These include *cultural, economic, social, institutional, political, spatial* and *demographic evidence*. This chapter roots these impacts in the longer-term processes of economic and demographic change which underlie processes of urbanization, at the global, national and local levels. The chapter concludes by highlighting a set of national and local challenges for policy and management of cities in the 21st century.

With respect to cultural impacts, this introductory chapter addresses only the broader issues, including how international migration is shaping the social composition and spatial organization of cities all over the world. The ways in which culture has been used as a strategy for redeveloping and marketing cities globally are picked up in Chapter 2.

The cultural dimension

To speak of globalization and urban culture today risks making a double error – first, because the phrase suggests that cities have never before experienced periods of such intense global trade and migration, and, second, because it implies that cities produce a singular urban culture. Cities are always made by mobility – or, as in current parlance, by flows – of people, money, goods and signs. They combine, for this reason, paradoxical extremes of wealth and poverty, familiarity and strangeness, home and abroad. Cities are where new things are created and from which they spread across the world. A city is both a territory and an attitude, and perhaps this attitude is culture.

Every city in the world has its own rough-and-tumble attitude – as marked as its local accents and neighbourhoods. For example, New York City, like many other cities, is an unintended assemblage of constructions, a collage of collages, and a place where urban culture is hammered out, or negotiated, in public space: streets, parks, stores, cafés, the media. If there is a single measure of urban culture, it is this multiplicity of dialogues and interactions, but it is also – in both a material and a symbolic sense – a multiplicity of evictions, erasures and avoidances.[3]

Culture, of course, has many meanings. As a practical human activity, it is an inherent part of both individual and collective development, from the education of a single child to the finest artistic expression of entire peoples and nations. Closely related to both the achievements of the past (in the form of history) and of the future (in the form of innovation), culture suggests the capacity to survive, as well as to adapt to change. Especially in cities, culture takes material form in the built environment of palaces, temples, opera houses, art museums, places of entertainment, parks, memorials, marketplaces, shops and restaurants. These, in turn, become visual symbols of local identity.

Even during the 19th century, cities at the centre of media, financial and manufacturing networks, such as New York, London and Paris, were pre-eminent sites of cultural innovation.[4] From fine arts to fashions, the confluence of cultural production and consumption in these cities magnified their importance and spread their reputation throughout the world. Cultural innovations in those days spread by means of exports of new products and models and by images published in newspapers and magazines. It took weeks, and even months, for these images to reach distant regions. Today, innovations travel at much greater speed. Aircraft have replaced steamships and freight trains, and courier services guarantee overnight delivery across the planet. News and entertainment programmes arrive instantaneously via satellite television and computer.[5] Moreover, technology has made it possible for images to be broadcast in all directions, encouraging the development of communications networks – and cultural identities – in national, language and ethnic groups that have spread across regions of the world. Korean and Mexican soap operas are watched as eagerly in New York City as in Seoul or Guadalajara.

Culture takes material form in the built environment as symbols of local identities

Overall impacts of globalization on urban culture

Within the crucible of cities, globalization has had the effect of both diversifying and enriching cultures, sometimes leading to vibrant fusions. At the same time, the appearance of the 'strange' cultures of international immigrants has sometimes resulted in fear, racial tension and polarization in some cities, as is shown in Chapter 4. Another significant impact of globalization on urban culture has been standardization, as people all over the world increasingly have access to the same cultural products, such as music and films, through the internet and satellite television and radio.

DIVERSITY AND ENRICHMENT It is difficult to predict the effects of the rapid – almost instantaneous – global exchanges described above on urban identities, for all city dwellers' lives are more highly mediated than ever before. In earlier years, men, women and children moved between the relatively

BOX 1.1 **Hip-hop: the universal music of youth?**

Hip-hop has become one of the most popular forms of music among the world's youth. From Europe to South Africa, from Greenland to New Zealand, hip-hop has given a voice to underprivileged youth who rap about problems in their communities. African HIV-hop informs the public about AIDS. In Algeria, members of the group MCLP use rap to denounce both sides of the ongoing strife between Islamic rebels and the government. In New Zealand, the Maori rap about identity and pride in one's history. Similarly, Nuuke Posse, an Inuit group in Greenland, is credited with bringing back pride in the Inuit way of life. Hip-hop has become important worldwide for the mostly urban youth as a means of depicting the reality in poor communities, and almost all rappers talk about how hard it is to survive in their world.

Source: Habitat Debate, 2003.

Symbols of urban ethnic spaces

encourage urban residents to become polymorphous cultural consumers. This may make them, paradoxically, both more tolerant of strangers in their own community and more closely connected to a distant homeland. It is not yet known which attitude will prevail, in which place and when. But the uncertainty that surrounds the effects of wider access to cultural diversity is emblematic of a larger problem of globalization: does global culture – regardless of how 'strange' it initially is – displace the more familiar local?

FEAR AND POLARIZATION   Despite their cosmopolitan façade, city dwellers fear strangers moving in among them, settling down and establishing roots. This is hardly a new theme in urban culture. During the late 1800s, when Chinese sailors and workers came to New York and Vancouver, both cities demonized some aspects of Chinese culture and restricted Chinese settlement to 'Chinatowns'.[7] Unease with foreigners inspired much of the literature of modernity, including urban sociology. As observed by some sociologists, urban men and women often close ranks against the 'truant proximity' of strangers, especially those with a different ethnic past.[8] In recent years, closing ranks has included enlarging the metropolitan police force and hiring vast numbers of private security guards, mainly to control access to public space. In New York, Berlin, Budapest and other cities, public parks have been privatized by turning their management over to park conservancies, business associations or property owners who limit use of the park, especially by homeless people, or at night. In São Paulo, Cape Town and almost any city where there is new single-family housing construction, much of it is enclosed within gates and walls. All of these strategies were put in place well before the current upsurge in international terrorism.[9]

Globalization brings Senegalese to Atlanta, where they find work as taxi drivers; Pakistanis become greengrocers in Rotterdam; and the Dutch become flower-growing company managers in Nairobi. But current trends suggest that if one of the great strengths of cities is their openness to the economic functions that strangers fulfil, their great weakness is a slowness to absorb them in the micro-politics of everyday life, in both public spaces and private institutions.[10]

STANDARDIZATION   Continuous flows of immigrants, products and images are currently reducing absolute differences of space and time. The same music might be performed at a club in Kinshasa, Paris, and New York City – or in Los Angeles, Shanghai, Cincinnati and Kingston. In recorded form, it may be listened to on the same brand of portable CD player. From this point of view, all cities are

simple spaces of home, work and neighbourhood, all of which reinforced bonds based on ethnicity and social class. Networks and institutions of sociability, from mothers chatting at the corner grocery store or open-air market to children attending religious school at the local parish or mosque, directly formed local cultures. Today, urban residents commute through great distances to go to work, with poor migrants to the developing world city generally travelling much farther, from the edge of the city to the centre, in search of a livelihood (see Chapter 3). Through television, film and popular magazines, rich and poor alike see images of affluence and modernity and compare them with their own lives. For computer users, information is more likely to come from the worldwide web than from workmates or neighbours. The inability to escape these multiple images and sources of information may be disconcerting; but access to more images and information is generally enriching the cosmopolitan culture of cities.

Recent studies of media consumption, from satellite radio to the internet, show that users of one 'channel' also consume several others.[6] Access to so many different types of images and messages should

affected by globalization. The capacity of financial markets to shift capital rapidly around the world, the transfer of heavy manufacturing from the US and Western Europe to Asia, and the outsourcing of many skilled jobs, even in the services and computer fields, tie cities to the same projects and time line. And just as music and other cultural products become as global in their sources as 'global cars', so the cities where they are designed, assembled and sold lose some of their unique ethos by bending to the requirements imposed by a more specialized, but also more standardized, global market system.[11] This also broadens the menu of economic and cultural choices that are available to even relatively poor consumers.

The standardization of urban culture is significantly reinforced by the increasing multicultural nature of cities, which is itself a direct result of international migration. The principal outcome of this has been the emergence of what may be called *urban ethnic spaces* within cities, often in the form of ethnic ghettos, but also in the form of culturally distinct non-residential spaces, such as shops and restaurants. This, of course, has given rise to some fundamental challenges about how to manage multicultural cities.

Emergence of urban ethnic spaces

Although most cities have been officially multicultural since the current era of transnational migration began during the 1980s, they do not fully understand how to integrate ethnic 'minorities' without fear of losing their historic cultural identity. In fact, despite cities' presumed air of tolerance and real social diversity, they have always been flashpoints of ethnic hostility. The density of different minority populations makes it easy to target their homes and shops for persecution. During the early 20th century, riots by 'majority' populations, such as Nazis in Berlin and white homeowners in Detroit, contradicted the democratic civics lessons that countries thought they had learned from World War I. Even now, political candidates advocating a 'return' to ethnic homogeneity win votes in cities from Amsterdam to Marseilles, where some of the residents are afraid that their tenuous hold on hegemony will be taken apart by foreign cultures.

Neither is it easy to integrate immigrants into the indigenous or existing urban culture. Very often, their lack of money and knowledge of the local language both pulls and pushes them into ghettos with groups very much like themselves. In those places, they set up workshops that employ immigrants as cheap subcontracted labour, often working for co-ethnic managers and entrepreneurs; places of religious worship and instruction; and stores that cater to their special needs: kosher or halal meat, cafés with tobacco,

Immigrants expose their historic cultural identities in the urban environment

and newspapers from home. Often these new residents of the city are its true cosmopolitans (see Box 1.2).

In fact, ethnic ghettos in advanced economy cities have a long history, as illustrated in urban ecology studies of Chicago, US, during the 1920s and 1930s (see Box 1.3). It was during this period of significant international migration into US cities that ethnic ghettos such as Chinatown and Little Sicily in Chicago were formed.

Immigrants these days are both concentrated in ethnic ghettos and less limited to them. Although immigrants to the US still predominantly enter the country through New York and Los Angeles, they often settle in the suburbs of those metropolitan regions. They also live in much greater numbers than before in smaller 'gateway' cities, and form new concentrations in areas of the country that never had foreign-born populations but need them now in unattractive, low-wage jobs in industries such as meat, poultry and fish processing (see Chapter 4).

BOX 1.2 New York's Arab-American immigrants of a century ago

'We came as sojōurners', Moustafa Bayoumi writes of Arab-Americans who came to New York as immigrants more than 100 years before 11 September 2001, sold foods and rugs imported from the Middle East, and fanned out across the US as pack peddlers. 'After establishing ourselves in New York, we launched out, men and women both, around the country… From the beginning, then, our lives here have been about being on the move.'[i]

Note: i Thompson, 1967; Laguerre, 2004; Bayoumi, 2002, pp134–135.

New immigrant clusters of home, work and shop expand the visible symbols of the old inner city over a broader geography. The increase in Asian immigrants has given New York, for example, two new Chinatowns in the outer boroughs of Queens and Brooklyn, and many suburbs of Los Angeles are divided between Anglo, Mexican and Asian populations, where struggles over visible signs – quite literally, shop and street signs written in a foreign language – arouse intense political battles, with older majority populations mobilizing local political institutions against new immigrants.

Within some Western European cities, migrants from Eastern Europe, Asia and Africa now fill inner-city streets that have become visibly multicultural: their food shops, clothing stalls and long-distance

---

BOX 1.3 Ethnic ghettos in Chicago, US, 1920s to 1930s

Theories of city form that have been current in urban geography, until the post-modern paradigm shift during the 1980s, stem originally from the urban social ecology ideas of the 1920s and 1930s – collectively known as the 'Chicago School'. They lived in an urban environment where the inner city had largely been vacated by families who had moved outward to the suburbs in rings and wedges from the downtown centre, leaving the decaying inner city to the most disadvantaged groups. The Chicago School saw the internal spatial organization of cities as an outcome of 'ecological' competition for niches between social classes who behaved like different species in terms of their endowments and wants, and who would compete for different land uses, with the strongest groups taking the most desirable positions and the weaker groups occupying residual spaces. As society and transport technology changed, and as the circumstances of the groups altered or housing became inadequate, they would vacate particular areas for the suburbs, leaving them for new immigrants or social groups who would occupy them, forming – in their turn – ethnic ghettos: Little Sicily, Chinatown and the Black Belt.

Source: UN-Habitat, 2003a.

---

telephone calling centres seem uneasily placed in a different history, as illustrated by the presence of Africans and Chinese in Dublin, Ireland (see Box 1.4).

As in Dublin (see Box 1.4), Budapest's marketplace of cheap clothing and household goods has become a 'Chinese' public space. The word 'Chinese' 'is applied as a comprehensive ethnic label to all Asians, and it has also become a symbol of cheap goods sold at such marketplaces and also elsewhere'.[12]

As shown in Chapter 4, immigrants fit into the urban economy in either ethnic enclaves, where they cater to the needs of their own community, or ethnic niches, where they specialize in certain jobs and businesses in the mainstream economy, according to their training or as opportunities arise. Certainly, immigrants bring with them specific skills and experience; but they can only make a living by filling a need left open by market conditions and access to jobs and property within the city. Recent Chinese immigrants to Vancouver came with experience in manufacturing, but went into service businesses; new Korean immigrants came to New York with college degrees, but opened greengrocer shops and nail salons. Caribbean men who knew how to drive became 'dollar-van' drivers in Brooklyn because of inadequate public transportation. In Cambodia, Vietnamese immigrants are engaged in jobs that require some expertise – for example, fishing and fish processing, as well as machinery and electronic repair – filling a gap left vacant by Cambodians, while in South Africa, immigrants from the northern part of the continent range from highly trained professionals fulfilling the sudden need created by the collapse of apartheid, to domestic servants and street hawkers. These groups create an ethnic strand in urban culture by taking advantage of the city's economic opportunities.[13]

Immigrant groups take part in creating a wider, more diverse urban culture. Muslim halal butchers and Turkish and Moroccan restaurants literally feed cosmopolitan Amsterdam the way Indian and Pakistani 'curry houses' have done for many years in UK cities such as Bradford. But these ethnic spaces can be interpreted in two contrasting ways: for Muslims, the halal butcher shop is home; for ethnic Dutch people, it is foreign. By the same token, a traditional Dutch butcher shop that remains in a neighbourhood from earlier days can be interpreted as 'not halal', and therefore not safe, by Muslims, but 'as things used to be', and therefore safe, by ethnic Dutch. Indeed, any shop that is decorated in traditional Dutch style, or caters to elderly customers, or features intensive social interaction between owner or clerk and customers, preserves an older urban culture – and one that new immigrants, especially the children and teenagers who are demographically dominant among them now, may resist.[14]

Yet new immigrants serve the broad urban public, not only in 'ethnic' restaurants, but also in many mainstream stores and fast-food franchises. In New York, McDonald's deliberately hires new immigrants to work in ethnic neighbourhoods where they speak the customers' language. Most fast-food restaurants, especially those in central business districts with the most diverse customers, mix managers from different countries. These hallmarks of American culture are really crucibles of multicultural urbanity, although that multiculturalism is seriously compromised by the different positions into which different groups of immigrants are thrust in the ethnic and racial hierarchy.[15]

There is, in short, a large gap between the cultural and social spaces available to 'ethnic others'. Although immigrants and ethnic minorities achieve recognition for infusing new music and foods within urban culture, employers, the police and the broader public are often all too ready to turn against them. Particularly when ethnic minorities live in segregated zones, their music, slang or look may inspire fear, as illustrated by the experience of *funkeiros* in Rio de Janeiro, Brazil (see Box 1.5).

The economic dimension

The economic history of the world during the 20th century has dramatically demonstrated that the processes of urbanization and economic progress are mutually reinforcing.[16] The explosion of political and economic development in Africa, Asia and Latin America in the post-World War II period fuelled and was fuelled by the movements of peoples, knowledge, technology and wealth. As in earlier periods, much of this activity involved movement to cities and towns, or was itself based in urban areas.[17] The experiences of developing countries in all regions indicate that urbanization is closely associated with increasing levels of income and improvements in social indicators, such as life expectancy, literacy, infant mortality and access to infrastructure and social services.[18] Countries that urbanized earlier than others have higher incomes, more stable economies, stronger institutions and are able to better withstand the volatility of the global economy.[19] A study of 90 countries from 1960 to 1980 concluded that the urban share of population itself increases with national income per capita; the share is also increased by industrialization, trade orientation and foreign capital inflows.[20]

Aggregate data are supported by numerous country studies that accented, as Table 1.1 shows, the important role of individual cities in their national

accounts. These data and many supporting studies conclude that 'cities, especially bigger cities, mean higher productivity and higher per capita incomes. The results remain consistent for nations with different economic systems and cannot be simply explained by what some would call the unequal development patterns of (capitalist) free market economies.'[21] During the 21st century, regardless of ideology, cities are the loci and motors of economic and social change.[22]

Yet, despite this evidence, it is surprising that urban growth and the urban share of the national

---

BOX 1.4 Africans and Chinese in Dublin, Ireland

So many Africans have arrived since the 1990s that Moore Street, in Dublin, Ireland, is now called 'Little Africa' – although the street is sacred to the history of Irish independence because nationalist insurgents surrendered to the British army in a house there. The African grocery stores that are common on Moore Street are unfamiliar to Irish people. Their back rooms are set up for socializing rather than for commerce – they offer a place where Africans, in Dublin, can come together. The fact that so many Africans have established a community around the tenements and shops of Moore Street recalls what Bayoumi writes about earlier Muslim immigrants to New York: 'What we have always loved about this city is that we were never lost in it. By discovering each other, we found ourselves here.'

But Little Africa is also the home of new Chinese immigrants – so many, that people estimate half of Ireland's Chinese population lives on Dublin's Northside. Like Spanish in Miami, Chinese has replaced Irish as the second language of the city. The Chinese are more visible than other ethnic groups because of their restaurants, shops and market stalls.

Source: Spiller, 2001; McGuire, 2003; Bayoumi, 2002, p138.

BOX 1.5 *Funkeiros* in Rio de Janeiro, Brazil

In Rio, in 1992, the mass arrest of young people who caused a disturbance on the beach resulted in a massive condemnation of *funkeiros*, youths from the northern and western slums who crowd into the city's dance clubs on weekends to enjoy funk music. They were labelled as poor, black and unruly – their music a symbol of resistance to authority. Funk, like rap or any other modern music, can, indeed, be a sign of resistance; but in Rio, it is a specific rejection of the dominant urban culture, symbolized by the prominence of the samba in the image construction of carnival for tourists and controlled by the non-black middle class of the southern zone of the city. Urban cultures are primarily cultures of proximity and fusion. But even in multicultural Brazil, they are also sites for fighting proxy wars of power and exclusion.[i]

Note: i Yudice 2003.

TABLE 1.1 **Economic importance of selected cities in proportion to their population**

Urban area, country	Current city size (000,000)	(A) Population percentage of national total	(B) GNP percentage of national total	Ratio (B/A)
São Paulo, Brazil	17.9	8.6	36.1	4.20
Buenos Aires, Argentina	13.0	35.0	53.0	1.51
Santiago de Chile, Chile	5.5	35.6	47.4	1.33
Lima, Peru	7.9	28.1	43.1	1.53
Guayaquil, Ecuador	2.3	13.1	30.1	2.30
México, Mexico	18.7	14.2	33.6	2.37
All Cities, Mexico		60.1	79.7	1.33
San Salvador, El Salvador	1.4	25.8	44.1	1.71
Casablanca, Morocco	3.6	12.1	25.1	2.07
Abidján, Cote d'Ivoire	3.3	18.1	33.1	1.83
Nairobi, Kenya	2.6	5.2	20.1	3.87
All Cities, Kenya		11.9	30.3	2.55
Karachi, Pakistan	11.1	6.1	16.1	2.64
All Cities, India		19.9	38.9	1.95
Shanghai, China	12.8	1.2	12.5	10.42
Manila, Philippines	10.4	12.1	25.1	2.07
Bangkok, Thailand	6.5	10.9	37.4	3.43
Moscow, Russia	10.5	5.8	10.9	1.88
All Cities, Turkey		47.1	70.1	1.49

Note: City size data are for the year 2003; 'A' and 'B' column data recorded for years within the range of 1975–1995.
Source: UN Population Division, 2003; Freire and Polese, 2003.

economy, either as gross domestic product (GDP) or as locus of production, trade and exchange, is rarely recognized in global debates about economic and development policy. It has been known for more than a decade that urban-based economic activities account for more than 50 per cent of GDP in all countries, and up to 80 per cent in more urbanized countries in Latin America, or more in Europe.[23] The ten largest metropolitan areas in Mexico, accounting for one third of the country's population, generate 62 per cent of national value added.[24] This disproportionate economic contribution of cities – indeed, their importance to the economy as a whole – is normally ignored or overlooked. This neglect is dangerous because, as this chapter will show, cities and towns are not only the loci of production, but they are also the loci of the most important impacts of globalization and, hence, the places of change and expectations for the future. Undervaluing urban areas can unwittingly place the economic and social futures of countries at risk. Improving understanding of the multiple interactions between globalization and cities can therefore contribute to identifying new

strategies for protecting and sustaining urban economies, and, hence, national economies, over the longer term.

The transformation of the global economy during the last two decades is perhaps the most important dimension of globalization because it has supported the diffusion of global culture and provoked deep and broad adjustments within countries and cities. Flows of capital, labour, technology and information have supported the growth of world trade from US$579 billion in 1980 to US$6.272 trillion in 2004, an increase of 11 times.[25] Trade in goods has become an increasing share of the GDPs of national economies, rising from 32.5 per cent in 1990 to 40 per cent in 2001.[26] What began as trade in goods and services is now accompanied by the flow of capital and the exchange of currencies in world financial markets, which themselves are equal, on a daily basis, to the GDPs of many countries – more than all of Africa and Latin America combined. Information technology has allowed the birth of global interest rates and the increasing movement of capital to new opportunities for immediate and short-term financial benefits. Concerns about 'footloose industries' have given way to cyber markets for finance and investment. Events in East Asia are not only immediately felt in interest rates in Bangkok, but they change investment decisions in Barcelona, Boston, Brisbane and Buenos Aires. Investors and financial managers felt the impacts of the tequila effect during 1994–1995 (Mexican peso crisis), the Asian financial crisis in 1997, the vodka effect in 1998 (Russian economic crisis), the samba effect in 1999 and the tango effect during 2001–2002 Argentina's economic crisis).

These changes have been amplified by processes of trade and financial liberalization since the mid 1990s, as governments and multilateral institutions believed that 'open markets' would attract investment and foster growth. While these policy changes have benefited some countries, others have been unable to cope with the pace and scale of change.[27] Inequality of incomes between countries grew over this period, leading to the judgement by many economists that the 'fruits of globalization' were not equally enjoyed.[28]

The differences in attractiveness to investors between countries is reflected in the great concentration of foreign direct investment in a set of ten countries (including China, Brazil, Mexico, Indonesia and Thailand) and the almost total exclusion of others – largely, the poorest countries and mostly those in Africa.[29] This distribution of the 'fruits of globalization' reflects private-sector judgments about the expected financial returns to these investments, their security, and the economic and political environments in which they occur.

At the city level, the rapid entry of new, mostly foreign, investors and new capital led to changes in the composition of economic activity, particularly favouring financial services and those industries able to benefit from connectivity. The role of 'global cities' and global circuits of networked cities[30] led to 'new geographies of centres and margins'.[31] These spatial impacts will be discussed below; but they are also reflected in the change in the composition of urban employment and value added during the 1990s. Buenos Aires, for example, saw more than 50 per cent of its employment switch sectors, as many medium-sized enterprises closed in a process of de-industrialization, including more than 4600 enterprises from 1995 to 2000, or about two per day.[32]

Two major changes in the composition of employment occurred in many cities in both developed and developing countries over the last two decades. First, there have been greater financial returns to jobs in the financial sectors and those activities involved in access and management of information. These jobs, many requiring university-level education, have been part of the emerging pattern of interconnected global financial markets. At the national and local levels, they include international banks, insurance companies and a wide range of financial services previously not accessible to most urban residents around the world. They are knowledge-intensive industries in which technology and connectivity determine profitability and employment profiles.

At the same time, capital has been attracted by the high returns to these sectors and away from industrial production. The lowering of trade barriers in many countries, coupled with improved transportation networks and multinational production processes for many manufactured goods, has meant that differentials in wage costs have become much more important in global competition among products. This has, in turn, meant the flight of capital and jobs to locations with lower wage costs. This process has been evident in many previously productive urban industrial cities in the US, such as Detroit, Chicago, New York and San Francisco, which have lost large shares of their employment base as companies have moved to other countries, seeking lower wages and fewer labour and environmental regulations.[33] Even many *maquiladora* enterprises of northern Mexico have closed as their owners have moved the businesses to China in search of lower costs and higher profits. This process has been referred to as 'the race to the bottom'[34] and it challenges many of the asserted wage benefits of trade liberalization. There is strong evidence, for example, that female wage levels and working conditions have dropped in many countries in East Asia as a result of dropping barriers to footloose industries. Studies in other regions document similar processes.[35]

The 'race to the bottom' also occurs within individual cities, resulting in job loss where large segments of the labour force have to shift from one sector to another, often losing jobs with benefits and job security while having to compete for income-generating opportunities without such benefits. This leaves many people unable to obtain stable jobs and incomes, and, thus, unable to afford housing and other essential services. The consequent patterns of social exclusion vary across cities; but they often are reflected in other social cleavages as well, such as along racial and ethnic lines.[36]

This, in turn, accelerates and increases the process of 'informalization' of the urban economy, with increasing shares of incomes earned in non-formally regulated employment. Several economic processes converge to 'informalize' employment and other aspects of urban life. The closing of formal-sector enterprises often coincides with the downsizing of ancillary industries and services, resulting in further 'multiplier effects' in urban areas. For example,

SURGING URBAN DEVELOPMENT AND CULTURE ACROSS THE ASIA PACIFIC
Reginald Yin-Wang Kwok

Current debates on development and urbanization have led to the rediscovery of 'culture' as an important but often overlooked component of urban living. During recent years, the re-evaluation of indigenous traditions, native religions, ethnic identification and local art has seen a strong upsurge in the Asia-Pacific region. It is increasingly being realized that spatial arrangements should be shaped not only by economic development considerations but also by local cultural forces.

As the technological innovations of (post-) industrial production pervasively propelled economic and urban development in Asia Pacific, they brought a decidedly modernist, market-oriented, globally spreading culture – often referred to as Americanization. It is in the world's urban places where these global and local cultures first meet and start to interact. Dynamic, open-ended relationships are often the result; but complex and, at times, confrontational relationships have also now started to emerge in urban manifestations and spaces.

The Asia Pacific is now more deeply embedded that ever before in the global network of production and trade. Industrial-urbanization processes led by global corporations, however, have not only led to a new technological domination, they have also fostered a global cultural homogenization. While global culture is all too often readily adopted, the growth of Asia-Pacific wealth and confidence has also brought a new awareness of, and attention to, the survival of essential local culture and native identification. Asia-Pacific urbanization is at a point where cultural convergence and confrontation between the global and the vernacular meet. The conditions for, and the outcome of, these encounters between global and vernacular culture are crucial factors in the formation of urban space.

Asia-Pacific cities that received overseas capital and technology became world cities with global connections. These injections gave rise to a series of contests between foreign and local businesses that regularly resulted in the defeat of indigenous competitors. The dynamics of the Asia-Pacific city were caught in the throes of an intense struggle between foreign capital and local labour;

the state and society; traditional elites and transnationals; family enterprises and international corporations; and the rock guitar and the native reed. Within this economic, social, political and cultural context, globally connected cities experience continuous restructuring of urban spaces.

The interaction between local and global aspects in towns gives rise to an intense economic, political, social and cultural dualism between a global modern sector and the vernacular indigenous sector. But when global and vernacular systems meet and collide, the seemingly inevitable outcome is global economic, political, social and cultural domination. As Asia-Pacific cities became incorporated within the globalizing economy, they took the frontal brunt of global penetration and became frontiers of adaptation, as well as resistance, in the cultural conflict brought on by these global developments.

By accepting global economic integration, Asia-Pacific cities witnessed major social and political change. With rapid economic growth and improvements in living standards, production and community decisions became increasingly decentralized. Following rapid expansion in the information sector and its attendant body of professionals, newly burgeoning local middle classes started to seek national identity and an independent voice, and they began to demand political participation in order to better influence social policy. Concurrently, industry and information raised an army of underclass manual and service labour. By their sheer size, these labour masses, the chief users of vernacular space, imposed their claim on space, services and rights. The emerging civil society, however, was faced with state coordination of urban space and transnational corporations demanding prime urban and other locations. As states and civil society attempted to maximize their claims, power and status, they were subjugated to the overwhelming economic powers of transnational corporations, and localities frequently lost the battle. Cities, as stages upon which manipulation, bargaining and settlement development were acted out, had come to embody the battlegrounds of cultural conflict brought on by global development.

In large cities, the production conditions have drastically altered. Whereas manufacturing produces primarily physical goods, information produces non-physical services. Similarly, production plants for manufacturing are factories, those for information are offices. As manufacturing becomes transnational, information also becomes transnational. With technological progress transforming the dominance of manufacturing to information as the major urban economic activity, global production processes have made offices the new production spaces. This evolution fundamentally changed urban landscapes by enlarging central business districts (CBDs). As the architecture and urban design of expanding CBDs primarily served the needs of international commercial and residential interests, the global-vernacular confrontation became evident. Complex relationships of subjugation, co-option and cooperation between global production-related spatial demands and vernacular culture largely played themselves out in city centres; but they also permeated the larger metropolitan landscape. More offices and related building complexes had to be provided to serve transnational interests. Social habits and the lifestyles of vested interests and professional classes demanded ever-more international travel, recreation, community and cultural facilities. The new CBD and its related functions – as the hub of urban activity – started to expand into extensive spatial annexations.

Globalizing urbanization thus fundamentally re-orders economic and spatial demand and structures as global development introduces three different clusters of new urban activities. The primary cluster of international business services large numbers of transnational and local professionals and quickly outcompetes other sectors to reside in the modern international high-rise offices of CBDs. The secondary cluster services the primary cluster through real estate, hotels, high-income housing, restaurants, shopping and entertainment, and spreads over the modern sections of the city. The tertiary cluster focuses on international commerce and tourism, designating international airports and convention centres as the new urban landmarks.

Although the main impacts of globalization in urban development tend to concentrate on the CBD, it has an overall effect on the entire city and its surrounding metropolitan area. The greater the infusion of transnational capital, the quicker and the more intense is the takeover of the vernacular indigenous sector by the global modern sector. This process of economic, social, political and cultural appropriation displays itself in urban space as a phase of fast expansion, where physical planning and urban design become almost irrelevant to spatial organization and restructuring. The first victim is orderly and equitably spatial development.

Globalization also enforces a universal international style. The specific mode of economic penetration, the associated production technology, the real-estate demands and the prevailing modern construction methods and practices all contribute to determining a similar internationalized urban form for global cities, regardless of their cultural origins. CBDs' physical forms are dictated by efficiency for business and movement; but they often become impersonal and inhospitable in the process, creating environments entirely unfit for socialization. Physical planning theory and urban design practice abide by economic and technological logic to facilitate the production of this new and universal form of urban centres. But none can marshal sufficient justification to repel what has become the global norm.

However, growing demands of emerging local professional classes and the continuously 'upgrading' labour masses caused a revival of traditional religion, ethnic identity and native culture in many Asia-Pacific nations. The affirmation of the importance of indigenous parts of society helped to stimulate vernacular landmark restoration, concurring with global trends in increased demand for historical preservation. Native districts and buildings of architectural or historical significance are now more often being protected and adapted to new uses.

However, in Asia-Pacific global cities, there are two main unresolved and common contradictions, which consistently continue to perplex urban designers and planners. First is the environmental dilemma between globalization dictates and local concerns. Rigid economic demands of global industrial capital and the severe competition for limited central urban land leave little room for environmental improvement or social and humane purposes. Second, in the contending views of formal expression between vernacular and globalization, national identity is often seen as ideological and an attempt at political liberation from the dominance of globalization.

Global development demands acceptance of, and adaptability in, the local economy. As global development advances, it provides more choice and opportunity and it also provides ample grounds for contradiction and conflict. As the local economy moves deeper into global modes of development and acquires greater economic success, the state and society have to improve social flexibility, political reconciliation and the ability for multi-role playing in order to exploit untried possibilities.

The capability and dexterity to coordinate the extremes – modernity and traditionalism, globalization and the vernacular – must be recognized as the critical pre-condition for development. As global development takes hold of the economy, the capability to regulate competition, resolve controversy and balance opposition decreases. The urban tetrad of the state, the transnational, the professional and labour has to learn to adjust and accommodate, avoiding conflict and confrontation in order to co-exist under a new global regime. Accordingly, urban spatial development in Asia Pacific moves in the direction of assimilating, accommodating and synthesizing diverse and often conflicting elements and events. Cites must gradually become softer and more open, organic and dynamic – creating and accepting a complex spatial mosaic of assorted urban forms within local cultural contexts.

REGINALD YIN-WANG KWOK IS PROFESSOR OF ASIAN STUDIES AND PROFESSOR OF URBAN AND REGIONAL PLANNING AT THE UNIVERSITY OF HAWAII.

---

declines in one industry – light engineering – in Karachi, led to reduction in incomes in the city as a whole. Former employees were no longer able to purchase so many services on the street; hence, street vendors also suffer. Simultaneously, if utility tariffs increase, as they did in Karachi during the 1990s, other enterprises suffer and are forced to reduce their operations or close altogether.[37]

The twin processes of informalization and de-industrialization demonstrate how competition intensifies between and within urban labour markets. In a policy environment of few barriers to financial flows and investment, there is little to arrest the continued shifting of industrial investment and employment to sites of lower wages. The example of 'outsourcing' of major commercial functions, from accounting to medical analysis, to telephone calls from the US to India illustrates how the mobility of resources both connects and disrupts the economic lives of cities.

The social dimension

The economic impacts of globalization cited above also have a major social component: they accelerate the process of socio-economic differentiation in cities. The two major consequences of these economic changes are increased urban poverty and increased intra-urban inequality. As shown below, both also have particular consequences for women and children. While both urban poverty and inequality are treated in greater depth in Chapter 5, they also need to be understood as parts of this process of socio-economic differentiation.

A major 2003 report on urban population dynamics in the US concluded that the process of urban socio-economic differentiation is one of the major transformations of cities over the past two decades.[38] This differentiation is, in part, fuelled by demographic processes, including migration and integration of ethnic and racial groups, but also by the

Globalization has often reinforced long-standing urban patterns of inadequate access to basic infrastructure and housing

and housing, the creation and expansion of slums, and the environmental and health impacts faced by the urban poor in many cities. If the absorptive capacity of cities in terms of jobs and urban services was a problem during the 1970s and 1980s, this capacity was strained further by the rapid and immediate consequences of changes in employment and patterns of income generation. Studies of the socio-economic consequences of economic change during the 1990s in Budapest, Guayaquil, Lusaka and Manila demonstrated how changing job markets have coincided with cuts in public expenditures and rising prices of essential consumption items, such as food and health services. Together, these three channels of macro-economic change dramatically undermined the stability and upward mobility of families.[41]

Institutional and political dimensions

The major institutional impacts of globalization on cities have been the weakening of national and local public institutions relative to the face of external private economic power and information. The 1990s were a period of growing awareness of the weaknesses and limitations of the public sector in many countries.[42] The vigorous arrival of powerful, decisive and informed external private-sector companies in all parts of the world has added to the further weakening of public institutions. Companies arrive in cities, exploring the possibility of investing in a factory or shopping centre. They do not feel constrained by local building codes, zoning or environmental regulations. If their demands for tax holidays and other waivers of regulation are not accepted by local authorities, they simply move on to the next city. Local authorities, on the other hand, are desperate to attract private investment to create jobs and generate incomes in their cities. This produces an asymmetry in power and certainly in the negotiations.

The privatization of public services in many countries also contributed to both the shrinking of effective government power during the 1990s as specific services and functions were 'outsourced' from government to private companies. This process also reduced revenue and sources of finance. As expected, the most attractive and potentially profitable services in cities were frequently bought by external private investors – a process known as 'cherry-picking' – leaving governments with already poorly performing services. Governments were thus faced with the financial problems of weak performers; at the same time they were losing control of revenue-producing services, particularly infrastructure, which were also

diversity of household and individual coping strategies in the face of economic change. As employment opportunities shift towards jobs requiring higher levels of education, the returns to education increase markedly and set apart those individuals with the requisite training and credentials. At the same time, those who are losing in relative terms find that their assets are also at risk: they may have to sell their houses and other assets during periods of economic stress. They experience both income and wealth effects that convert them into 'the new poor', with new insecurity and vulnerability in the face of economic changes. The middle class in some countries, such as in Argentina during the 2001–2002 crisis, or in the transition economies of Eastern Europe and the former Soviet Union, suddenly find themselves lacking the skills for the new economy and fighting for lower-paying jobs in a severely constricted and competitive job market.

While the importance of inequality was not stressed for many years by the international community, recent studies, particularly of Latin American countries, have focused on the many forms and manifestations of inequality.[39] It is now understood that inequality itself undermines the rate and quality of economic growth. Great differences within societies have long been seen as major factors in determining political and social stability; but now there is an appreciation that inequality affects the productivity and allocation of resources within countries, as well.[40]

These socio-economic consequences of globalization reinforce the long-standing urban patterns of inadequate access to basic infrastructure

important symbols and constituent parts of state power.

The privatization of urban services, such as water supply, sanitation, waste collection, street maintenance and sometimes social services has meant that government has also lost the tools to guide development in newly urbanized areas and to rehabilitate areas needing revitalization. Mayors and city councils are forced to negotiate with private companies whose obligations are not only to provide services but also, and frequently more importantly from the perspective of the entity, to provide high financial returns to stockholders in their country of origin. It should not be surprising that privatized companies do not want to invest their profits in extending services to unserved slum or squatter areas in Latin American cities. They would rather send the profits back to their stockholders in Spain or France.[43]

If public institutions have weakened under the impacts of globalization, so too has citizenship. The process of privatization has transformed the nature of 'belonging' in a city. In countries lacking strong democratic institutions, people may find that their primary relationships to the providers of services are as 'clients', not as 'citizens', which implies less power and legitimacy in asserting grievances.[44] Indeed, urban residents, particularly in large cities with privatized services, can well wonder what the real functions of local government are.

This lack of effective control by politically legitimate institutions is one of the most commonly articulated feelings among local government officials. Investment decisions in their cities, employment opportunities and even the management of previously public services seem to have been transferred 'away' from local governmental jurisdictions. One of the

Demonstration on housing and welfare issues in the US

most remarkable examples of this transfer has been the Argentine case where the government's refusal to allow the Buenos Aires French-managed privatized water company to increase water tariff had to be resolved at board meetings of the International Monetary Fund (IMF) and the World Bank. An essentially 'local' issue, water price, had been globalized so that it had to be decided at a board meeting of a multilateral international institution.

Spatial changes

One of the most documented impacts of globalization has been the changes in the spatial organization of urban life as a result of new patterns of infrastructure and connectivity. The notion of 'global infrastructure' suggests that infrastructure has at least three purposes:

BOX 1.6 Concentration and decentralization of 'global city' functions

One of the most observed results of economic globalization has been the concentration of key 'command-and-control' functions within the modern financial sector and within transnational corporations. The concentration of financial-sector control in 'global cities' began during the 1980s and received specific attention during the early 1990s with the publication of *The Global City* (Sassen, 1991). Key cities of New York, Tokyo and London became the key sites for global financial transactions, strategy formulation and markets for new ideas and financial instruments. While other cities such as São Paulo, Frankfurt and, later, Shanghai also became important, they deferred to the concentrated functions in the

first 'global cities'. Simultaneously with this concentration was another process, the dispersal of production, assembly and distribution of various goods and services in other urban areas around the world. In these usually smaller national capitals and regional cities, new intra-urban spatial patterns developed around transportation and communication infrastructure networks, allowing a high degree of connectivity and mobility for these economic activities. The resulting intra-urban spatial patterns included a flight from central cities, establishment of special economic zones within and around cities, and highly concentrated suburban sites chosen and designed for specific economic functions.

Source: Sassen, 2001.

---

to serve local needs, to serve global needs, and to connect the local and the global.[45] These changes mark a significant transformation in both the theory and practice of infrastructure development from the 1990s, when both the international community and the national governments were arriving at similar conclusions about infrastructure: that infrastructure networks in many countries reflected a supply-side bias, were not consumer friendly, were too expensive, and required a better balance between investment and maintenance if they were to continue to perform their intended functions.[46] These studies suggested that more attention was needed on the demand side focusing on consumers and market research to ascertain the scale and composition of demand.

This work has demonstrated that infrastructure is an essential component of the productivity of countries. This was understood on the basis of the infrastructure experiences of major cities, including their blackouts, water main breaks and other infrastructure failures caused by natural disasters, such as earthquakes in Mexico City or flooding of cities along the Danube River in Central Europe. It was most appreciated in studies of the efficiency of infrastructure – for example, the port of Mumbai in facilitating trade, or city highway systems in alleviating traffic congestion in cities such as Bangkok, Cairo or Istanbul. Infrastructure, therefore, was an important aspect of the planning of new urban space.

While the infrastructure studies of the1990s were consistent with both planning theories and the administrative decentralization process in local governments – focusing on popular participation and the role of civil society in making decisions that affect infrastructure design and operations – they were quickly overshadowed by the globalization process and the local incorporation of global concerns and needs within the structure of the city itself.

Four major changes occurred in the spatial structures of cities as a result of the economic forces of globalization:

- First, cities began to shift their inward attention to external locations and activities. Economic and political actors became aware that new investment and employment opportunities required being aware of decisions taken outside the city boundaries. Indeed, this awareness was a necessary but not a sufficient condition for competitiveness in the global economy.
- Second, the dynamics of global economic production patterns required a shift from vertical integration of producers, suppliers, finance and distributors in one place and in one market, towards horizontal integration with other

geographical locations where these functions were performed.
- Third, in spatial terms, the location of industry and services was no longer determined by local markets and patterns of consumption – for example, in central business districts – but rather by types of logics that connected highly dispersed functions and actors.
- Fourth, this led to a splintering of earlier urban spatial patterns, creating new patterns that embodied new definitions of efficiency, land use and forms of access in which physical proximity was no longer the major decision variable. This splintering has been referred to as 'variable geometry'[47] or 'new geographies of centres and margins',[48] as mentioned earlier.

The splintering of earlier urban spatial patterns was reflected in changes in urban hierarchies, where the agglomeration economies of the largest cities were no longer essential for activities that were no longer based solely on local or domestic markets. The negative externalities of big cities such as congestion costs, air pollution or crime could be avoided by locating economic activities on the peripheries of big cities or in secondary cities, as long the necessary communications and transport infrastructure were available. The active debate of the 1980s and 1990s about the importance of secondary cities as an alternative to the growth of megacities with populations of over 10 million was being overtaken by thousands of decisions by individuals, households, firms and local governments as they surveyed the changing global economic landscape. It was not that people could work at home and then occasionally visit the office downtown; rather, their office was increasingly mobile and their markets and headquarters could not be reached by an hour's drive on the highway. Locating in Charlotte, North Carolina or Guadalajara, Mexico, might have been unthinkable two decades ago; but if back office operations are in Mumbai or Bangalore, front office decisions can be made anywhere.

New transnational urban spatial linkages were being established, bypassing neighbouring districts or regions, but seeking partners and complementary producers in locations that were simply unknown a generation ago. As these linkages are growing, national and local governments seek to develop infrastructure to attract these new economic activities. The cost of infrastructure requires that the needs of potential customers are identified and surveyed. This is actually the demand-side approach to infrastructure investment recommended by the studies cited above. All of these investments have helped to drive the process of decentralizing the functions of 'global cities'.[49]

In reality, the 'competitiveness' of cities in the global era has been closely linked to the quality and reliability of their communications and transportation infrastructure.[50] These requisites become widely advertised as ways of attracting new investment. Indeed, even in the well-established financial centres, if these infrastructure services are not reliable, firms are willing to relocate to more secure locations. The rapid decisions by some of the Wall Street firms to leave downtown Manhattan after 11 September 2001 were facilitated by their prior search for alternative sites in Connecticut and New Jersey.

This motivation has also led to the building of enclave zones to perform specific functions within the production chains of multinational firms. The financial functions of the Cayman Islands or Hong Kong have been replicated many times over in locations previously considered remote, such as islands in Indonesia or Malaysia. If these centres cannot yet be described as 'cities', they are rapidly becoming 'urban' in their economic activities, their levels of income and wealth, and their cosmopolitan character.

While the growth of these new urban spatial forms in response to the demands of globalized economic activity is clear, they are still small in terms of the population involved. In contrast, the growth of mega-urban regions in Asia – for example, from Bangkok to Seoul – has been a well-established pattern absorbing and employing millions of people for more than two decades.[51] Similarly, the growth of urban regions along the coast of China has also been a

spatial form combining vertical integration with new forms of communication and transport for China's growing global trade (see Chapter 3).[52]

If these new forms suggest the direction of future change, it is also important to note the present patterns of spatial inequality, which were suggested earlier in this chapter. While governments are preoccupied with establishing productive and profitable connections with actors in the global economy, they have, nonetheless, contributed to enormous differences in the quality of life within cities. Studies of intra-urban inequality during recent years show that the location of infrastructure investment is an important determinant in the quality of housing, education and other services. A study of infrastructure investment in Buenos Aires from 1991 to 1997 concluded that 11.5 per cent of the population received 68 per cent of investment, leading to the observation that the city is, in fact, five cities, each with different levels and quality of infrastructure and public services.[53]

Infrastructure investment is a good predictor of other urban indicators – for example, access to water supply correlates with health status in many cities. These studies demonstrate the wide differences within the same city. A non-governmental organization (NGO) in New York publishes an annual report on children in the five boroughs of the city, showing the strong correlations between various impacts of public policies, investments and behavioural outcomes.[54]

These cumulative impacts have also been demonstrated in econometric studies of 100 US cities.[55]

TABLE 1.2 **Population size and growth, urban and rural**

	Mid-year population size (millions)				Population growth rate (per cent)		
	1950	1975	2000	2030	1950–1975	1975–2000	2000–2030
Urban							
World total	751	1543	2862	4981	2.9	2.4	1.8
High-income countries	359	562	697	825	1.8	0.9	0.6
Middle- and low-income countries	392	981	2165	4156	3.7	3.2	2.2
Rural							
World total	1769	2523	3195	3289	1.4	0.9	0.1
High-income countries	219	187	184	139	−0.6	−0.07	−0.9
Middle- and low-income countries	1550	2336	3011	3151	1.6	1.0	0.2

Note: High-income countries have gross national income per capita of US$9266 or more based on World Bank estimates.

Source: National Research Council, 2003, p85.

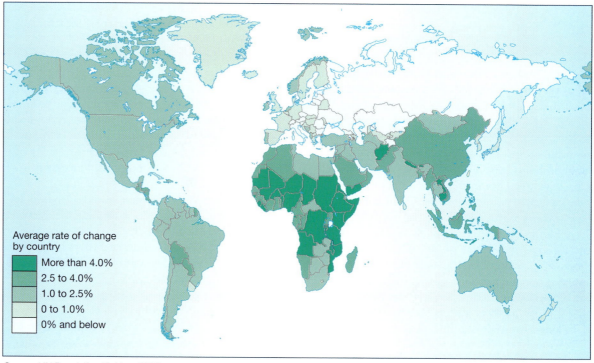

Source: UN Population Division, 2003.

MAP 1.1 **Rates of change in urbanization, 2000–2005**

The demographic dimension

The demographic dimension of the impact of globalization on cities cannot easily be separated from the broad patterns of urban growth. The review of United Nations' urban growth projections by the US National Academy of Sciences Panel on Urban Growth Dynamics is the most analytic and comprehensive report undertaken in recent years.[56]

The report confirms the scale of change projected by the United Nations, with the expectation that the world's urban population will grow from 2.86 billion in 2000 to 4.98 billion by 2030, of which high-income countries will account for only 28 million out of the expected increase of 2.12 billion.[57] As Table 1.2 illustrates, the world's annual urban growth rate is projected at 1.8 per cent in contrast to the rural growth rate of 0.1 per cent.

The report concludes that about 60 per cent of the world's population will live in cities. Most importantly, urban growth in middle- and low-income countries accounts for about 2 billion of this increase, suggesting that urban growth on a weekly basis will be close to 1 million persons, or a city the size of Hanoi or Pittsburgh each week. Much of this growth will be in cities over 1 million persons. The report notes that by 2003, there were 39 cities over 5 million in population and 16 over 10 million.[58] This pattern is accompanied by sustained growth of medium-sized cities below 1 million in population.

Some of the important implications of these patterns are the consequent impacts on health, reproductive health and fertility, and the availability of needed infrastructure, such as water supply and sanitation and social services, including education. Prior to the 1990s, there was an assumption that urban dwellers in most countries enjoyed an 'urban health advantage' as a result of higher incomes and more available health services. The increase in urban poverty, however, coupled with continued demographic pressure, the growing incidence of HIV-AIDS and many water-borne diseases in urban areas, suggests that this health advantage is not so prevalent as previously expected, even though urban dwellers are better off than the rural population.[59] All of these conditions are highly dependent on urban incomes. Poorer people live in areas with less infrastructure; they are more likely to suffer poor health due to both lack of food and environmental conditions; and they are less likely to have access to, or be able to afford, healthcare. As observed earlier, globalization has introduced a high degree of volatility in urban economies, often affecting most those industries and activities that are labour intensive and, hence, more likely to employ the poor. It is therefore plausible to infer that globalization, like economic change in earlier periods, is provoking negative health consequences for the poor, particularly in developing countries. The same case can be made for families in developed countries who have lost incomes through

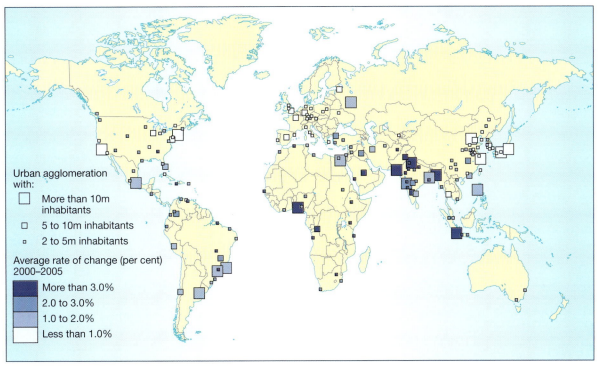

Source: UN Population Division, 2003.

MAP 1.2 **The world's largest cities, 2003**

Legend for map:

Urban agglomeration with:
- More than 10m inhabitants
- 5 to 10m inhabitants
- 2 to 5m inhabitants

Average rate of change (per cent) 2000–2005
- More than 3.0%
- 2.0 to 3.0%
- 1.0 to 2.0%
- Less than 1.0%

the flight of jobs to countries with lower wages and no benefits.

An aspect of these demographic dimensions is the shift in the age composition of urban populations. While life expectancies in developed countries have continued to grow only marginally, there is now a growing and important proportion of urban residents in developing countries who are elderly. This complements earlier data showing the relatively young urban populations in developing countries, and suggests the need for at least a bimodal social policy, with services for the young and the old. This is part of the social differentiation noted above.

Challenges for policy and management

The dimensions of change cited above are generating many new challenges for national and local policy and management. While many of these challenges are specific to local conditions, others can be found everywhere. Some of these are suggested below.

Creating multicultural, inclusive cities

As indicated earlier in this chapter, one of the outcomes of international migration is the intensification of the multicultural nature of cities,

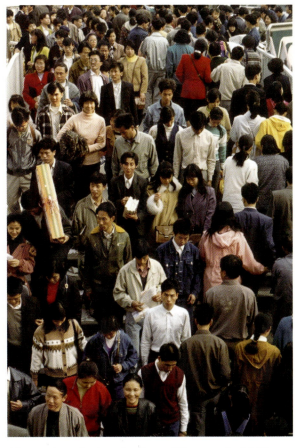

The number of urban dwellers will increase by 2 billion worldwide within 25 years

BOX 1.7 **Urban bilingualism in Miami, US**

In Miami, struggles emerged over the use of Spanish. The practical necessity of establishing an official policy of 'bilingualism' aroused considerable political opposition, and only the entry of Latin American immigrants, especially Cubans, into business leadership and political office legitimized a true multicultural approach. But multiculturalism has had a good effect on the city. The Latinization of Miami's culture has drawn from, and responded to, a continuous flow of capital from Latin America. The city, and its surrounding metropolitan area, has become the Latin American cultural capital, with corporate headquarters and avant garde studios creating cutting-edge fashions, music and art, and new media programmes. These changes have been amplified by the flow of media attention to, and capital investment in, the Art Deco hotel district of nearby Miami Beach for quite different reasons related to gentrification. All of this adds to the vitality and buzz of Miami's urban culture – but at the cost of driving up property values and housing prices, and with the support of American political and financial power. At the two ends of the American Sunbelt, and in the inner cities of Chicago and New York, marked by successive Mexican, Dominican and Puerto Rican immigrations, Latin Americans are gradually shaping a less hegemonic, but still global, urban culture.[i]

Note: i Horton, 1995; Portes and Stepick, 1993; Yudice, 2003; Davis 2000.

with different ethnic spaces emerging. While this juxtaposition of cultures can be enriching, it can also result in fear and polarization. Cities have to formulate clear strategies for addressing the anxieties of indigenous populations, while highlighting and taking advantage of the positive effects of urban multicultural existence. As is shown in Chapter 4, some cities have created specific municipal committees to address all issues surrounding the presence of immigrant communities. One specific issue that has to be addressed in creating peaceful multicultural and inclusive cities is language recognition. This is particularly important for cities with very large ethnic minorities. As stated earlier, language can become a divisive issue in urban politics. However, as illustrated by the experience of Miami (see Box 1.7), official policies of bilingualism can be successful, especially when accompanied by the entry of ethnic minorities into positions of political and business leadership.

Maintaining stability, equilibria and balances in the face of exogenous change

The multiple types of impacts of globalization on cities, as described above, imply processes of change that introduce considerable instability, disequilibria and imbalances into the lives of urban residents. Their jobs, consumption patterns and opportunities for social mobility are all influenced by external factors. These forms of instability can enter national and local contexts through at least four important channels:

patterns of investment, labour markets, prices and public expenditures. Each of these has different mechanisms, velocity, depth and scale of impact. Moreover, they occur in different locations within the city, creating patchworks of decay, renewal, economic revitalization and implosion. These processes, indeed, raise the very issue of what is equilibrium and stability, and how it is experienced, perceived and understood.[60] The challenge, therefore, for national and local authorities is to identify which kinds of changes are occurring, or better still, which types of changes might be anticipated, in order to consider whether there are measures to cushion or mitigate these impacts.

Three principles should be considered in this process:

1 Expect changes; therefore, set aside resources and capacity to deal with them.
2 Apply solutions to the immediate impacts of change in order to avoid the extension of change through multipliers.
3 Identify the groups most vulnerable to change and identify compensatory measures that may be required.

The first step in applying these principles is to anticipate that some processes are largely driven by outside forces – for example, the decision by a foreign firm to close down a local firm. But when this process begins, governments need to have the flexibility to move some of their own resources into activities to absorb labour – for example, by increasing construction or maintenance programmes. Anticipating this likelihood would help to create a modest safety net for the employees who face lay-offs. Examples include assuring that potential secondary earners, usually mothers, should have access to day care for children, thereby allowing them to go into the labour market. Similarly, assuring basic food supplements such as milk subsidies would help to protect the nutritional status of children. Both of these measures are more important than the municipality operating its full range of programmes.

These measures require financial resources. While all governments feel their budgets are severely constrained, they need to apply discipline to save some of their resources for these future needs. This is the opposite of borrowing, implying passing on debts to future generations. It means saving for the future. In reality, this saving is an insurance policy against future unknowns. Having such resources allows decision-makers to face the future more confidently and to smooth out the impacts of volatile changes in the global economy at large.

Building and strengthening capacities

One of the most important requirements to cushion external impacts is national and local capacity to recognize what is coming. This observation leads to the conclusion that public institutions need to train their personnel to be better informed, better connected and more forward looking in their work. In the era of globalization, this means having the capacity to recognize and interpret the patterns of change, economic transactions and new livelihoods that are developing around them. Investing in training may be more important than investing in the extension of new infrastructure or other services. This is probably more important in secondary cities than in capital cities where there is already more information and connectivity. Indeed, if the pace of demographic growth is likely to be faster in smaller and medium-sized urban centres, it would be particularly important to invest in capacity at that level than in making marginal additions to staff in the largest cities.

This is one area in which international networks of cities and the urban professions can play an invaluable role in disseminating best practice, experiences and the many debates about these issues. Knowing that there is not only one solution to a problem can be very helpful in an isolated community. The growth of the international organizations of cities – the International Union of Local Authorities, Metropolis and Cités Unies – has played an important role but could become more important in the future with regard to sharing information and experiences in dealing with problems incurred by globalization. This is likely to be facilitated by the increasing cooperation of such organizations, evidenced by the recent formation (by International Union of Local Authorities (IULA), United Towns Organization (UTO) and Metropolis) of the United Cities and Local Authorities, which has proceeded to launch the Global Observatory on Local Democracy (GOLD).

Establishing a longer time frame for decision-making

One challenge to policy and management is to introduce a longer time frame for decision-making. Some cities and citizen groups have begun initiatives to introduce this longer perspective – for example, the 2050 programmes in Buenos Aires, Barcelona and New York, each of which asks urban actors to consider the hopes and fears of citizens for their cities in 2050 and how short- and medium-term decisions would have an impact on the longer term. In each of these cities, the

framework is somewhat different: in Buenos Aires the initiative was started during the economic crisis in 2001 and, hence, asked citizens to think beyond the immediate solution to the crisis. In Barcelona the process will engage the municipalities beyond the old city, seeking to establish the basis for a 'metropolitan Barcelona' in the period leading up to 2050. In New York, the 2050 programme, a citizens' initiative endorsed by the city government in 2004, seeks to go beyond the intensive planning of Lower Manhattan after 11 September 2001 to reach out beyond the five boroughs to the metropolitan area as a whole.

Establishing a longer-term vision is much more than just physical planning. Indeed, the consultation process in these three cities has already demonstrated that citizens are concerned with a broad range of economic, social, environmental and political issues. They ask how economic and environmental justice can be protected in the face of new processes of change and actors from distant places. They worry about whether their locally elected institutions have the capacity to anticipate these changes. But what is clear is that popular participation that focuses on the future unleashes strong creative and imaginative energies that pose new questions for urban policy and management beyond the normal daily concerns of municipal authorities. In this regard, establishing a longer time frame can be a major asset in assuring the sustainability of the benefits of urban life, while at the same time anticipating new problems. As will be

---

BOX 1.8 Long-range vision: a framework for decision-making

The 2050 initiatives grew out of the experience of the exhibition *Buenos Aires 1910: Memoria del Porvenir*, which attracted more than 100,000 people in Buenos Aires in 1999, and later visited Washington and New York. The strong popular response to the exhibition showed people's fascination with what their ancestors thought about the future. This led to the decision in Buenos Aires, in 2001, to call for new ideas about the future, asking people to imagine what it would be like in 2050. University seminars and a municipal exhibition elicited more positive reactions. Most importantly, it encouraged people to think beyond their normal time horizons.

In New York this approach responded to the enormous focus on Ground Zero in the aftermath of the attack of 11 September 2001. Many citizens' programmes – Imagine New York, Listening to the City and others – mobilized popular interest; but this was overly focused on the 16 acres of Lower Manhattan. The Buenos Aires team suggested to their New York colleagues that it would be important to think at a broader, city-wide, metropolitan and regional scale and within a longer time frame. This led to the New York 2050 initiative.

A similar approach was discussed in Barcelona, whose mayor also saw the need to consider the future of that city in a wider metropolitan framework and within a longer time frame.

Source: www.NewYork2050.org.

shown in Chapter 7, this kind of visioning can be seen as a dimension of strategic urban planning.

Maintaining the physical world of infrastructure

One of the areas in which national and local authorities can act to cushion cities from the impacts of globalization is to ensure that the benefits of existing infrastructure networks continue to flow. Estimates of the stock of urban infrastructure in developing countries during the early 1990s, for example, amounted to US$3 trillion. This included all existing systems of urban water supply, sewerage, electricity, highways, street lighting, solid waste management systems and other services.[61] As we know, however, many of these systems do not receive the maintenance and rehabilitation that they require in order to function properly. Most infrastructure systems in the majority of countries are 'under-performers'. They rarely deliver the sustained level of service, or in economic terms, the benefits, which were promised by their designers.

In part to redress this situation, and in part to meet the service needs of growing populations, urban infrastructure continues to receive substantial shares of public investment. The flow of investment during the 1990s amounted to about US$150 billion each year, 95 per cent of which came from domestic sources. Local managers must find ways of improving the benefits of under-performing systems. For example, if local authorities were able to obtain an additional 5 per cent in benefits from the existing stock of US$3 trillion, they would be harvesting a gain of US$150 billion or an amount equivalent to annual new investment. If such benefits could be obtained from existing investments, rather than new investments and projects, they could avoid many of the financial, social and environmental costs of mobilizing resources for new projects. Clearly, the name of the game must be to 'get more from what you have already'.[62]

This implies shifting more resources to rehabilitation and maintenance of existing networks, fixing potholes before whole streets need to be re-paved, and ensuring that infrastructure systems continue to support the productivity of urban economies. Not to pay attention to the condition of these systems is to court disaster, as cities in developed and developing countries experience each year. The August 2003 electricity blackout of the northeast of the US and parts of Canada demonstrated the high costs of poor maintenance. The failure of infrastructure – for example, after the Mexico City earthquake in 1984 – demonstrated the high economic costs. Similarly, the flooding of the Danube in Central Europe had devastating costs to local economies. Yet it is also important to recognize that such infrastructure failures may be a result of poor initial design, and not only of poor maintenance.

The benefits of responding to this infrastructure challenge was well argued in important research during the 1990s in Lagos, Jakarta and Bangkok, where studies found that in the absence of public infrastructure services – water, sanitation, electric power, urban transport and solid waste management – small- and medium-sized enterprises had to provide their own services. This represented a significant share of capital investment and, hence, reduced profits and the ability of these enterprises to grow and to generate new employment.[63]

Financing investment and operations

The challenges of urban finance in the face of globalization are complicated and involve many levels of government and different types of actors within the private sector. On the private side, it is apparent that there are more actors and potentially more investors in local projects. The challenge of financial policy is to broaden and stabilize the public revenue base while directing and controlling the growth of expenditures through some form of public financial discipline. Growing urban populations require more services and constantly expanding governmental operations. While the need for more public expenditures is enormous, it is also important to channel these resources towards the highest-priority uses and not to attempt to finance an ever-growing range of programmes. Finding the balance between revenue and expenditures is a difficult task.

Achieving this balance is, of course, complicated by the multiple institutional levels that affect urban governance. This is particularly the case for metropolitan government, which also includes intergovernmental financial relations with provincial and national governments.[64] While analytic studies on urban finance have made significant progress over the last decade, leading to sound recommendations for municipal and sub-national governments,[65] it has been less easy to apply these principles in contexts of changing revenue bases and increasing demands for expenditures, in part driven by growing urban populations. Instability in national government finance, unclear and often changing rules for intergovernmental transfers, occasionally perverse incentives for sub-national governments, and a lack of accountability at the local level have all complicated the urban finance problem. All of these issues are affected by changes in the global economy and their consequences for national and local economies.

Mobilizing for sustainability

A final challenge for governments in the face of globalization is to improve the efficiency of their use of natural resources. This is an issue that affects patterns of investment as much as operations of urban services. For example, all cities in the world are experiencing increasing marginal costs for drinkable water. As Beijing, Los Angeles and Mexico City go greater distances to collect and transport water supplies to their already large populations, they are already using enormous financial and energy resources for this task. This fact suggests that it would be much wiser for cities to urgently improve how they use natural resources, such as water. Since the cost of infrastructure is a function of the length of networks and not their width – longer pipes cost more than wider pipes – any initiatives to reduce physical sprawl and spatial expansion will help to reduce infrastructure costs.

Applying some of the lessons and practices from cities such as Curitiba in Brazil would be a good start. Decision-makers in Curitiba have insisted for two decades that problems should not be addressed one by one, but rather in a holistic manner, allowing one government initiative to solve more than one problem at a time.

Defending the public interest in cities in an era of globalization

This chapter has demonstrated the complex and rapid changes that affect cities as a result of globalization. These impacts are multidimensional, often simultaneous and never homogenous in their consequences. The diversity of the city is being further differentiated as patterns of opportunity, loss, growth and deprivation create new identities, cultures and conflicts. Changes affecting individuals, households and neighbourhoods are reflected in new economic and social behaviours, as well as in spatial and physical patterns. All of these changes raise the issue of constantly redefining the 'public interest'. Who and what is the public? Is it local or does it include the connections to distant actors and locations, which also affect the city and have interests there? Who are the guardians of the public interest? Does the notion of governance at this time, with a multiplicity of actors, imply that government by itself is only one actor in determining what is acceptable behaviour in the city? These questions suggest that identifying and defending the 'public' interest, in contrast to the multiplicity of private interests, is now the central challenge for urban policy, as will be further explained in Chapter 7.[66]

Global changes require coherent global responses

This challenge, however, raises the issues of public values: of tolerance for differences, of social inclusion rather than exclusion, of participation and representation rather than centralized management, of transparency and accountability, and the need to make these values concrete and immediate by embedding them in daily public practice. This visibility is more important than ever. In a world of virtuality and technology, the virtual city should be turned into the city of virtue, where values are visible and clear.[67] The Greeks believed that conscience is in the eyes; only when the eyes see something is conscience activated.[68] This conscience is more important than ever in helping to guide the management of local processes and the impacts of globalization.

Notes

1   This chapter is based on drafts prepared by Michael Cohen, New School University, and Sharon Zukin, Brooklyn College and City University Graduate Centre, New York, US.
2   Appadurai, 2001.
3   In simple terms, 'symbolic economy' may be defined as the creation of wealth from cultural activities, including art, music, dance, crafts, museums, exhibitions, sports and creative design in various fields.
4   On New York, for example, see Burrows and Wallace, 1999.
5   Regional editions of the *Wall Street Journal* and *Financial Times*, as well as regional programmes on cable TV networks, such as the BBC, CNN and MTV, are partly received by satellite distribution from a central node and partly edited in local capitals. Al Jazeera's headquarters are in Dubai; but its coverage of news events in the Middle East reaches an audience in Dearborn, Dublin, Mumbai and Cape Town.
6   Papper et al, 2004.
7   Anderson, 1991; Tchen, 1999.
8   Simmel, 1950.
9   Zukin, 1995; Ellin, 1997; Caldeira, 2001; Sorkin and Zukin, 2002.
10 See Sandercock, 2003.
11 For a more positive view of losing ethos because of globalization, see Cowen, 2002.
12 Fejos, 2001, p88.

13 See the arguments in favour of economic context rather than ethno-cultural background in Kloosterman and Rath, 2001, and Rath et al, 2002.
14 See Blokland, 2001.
15 Talwar, 2002.
16 Black and Henderson, 1999.
17 Hall, 1998.
18 National Research Council, 2003.
19 World Bank, 2002a.
20 Moomaw and Shatter, 1996, see also Brockerhoff, 1999.
21 Freire and Polese, 2003, p6.
22 Hall and Pfeiffer, 2000a.
23 World Bank, 1991.
24 National Research Council, 2003, p303.
25 UNCTAD, 2003.
26 World Bank, 2003d, p312.
27 Rodrik, 2001.
28 Stiglitz, 2002.
29 World Bank, 2001a; 2002b; 2003a.
30 Sassen, 1991; 2001.
31 Sassen, 1994.
32 Cohen and Debowicz, 2001.
33 Pollard and Storper, 1996.
34 Brecher and Costello, 1994.
35 Jauch, 2002.
36 Beall, 2002; Abel and Lewis, 2002.
37 Hasan, 2002.
38 National Research Council, 2003, pp155–198.
39 de Ferranti et al, 2004; Thorp, 1998.

40 Birdsall, 2001.
41 Moser, 1996.
42 Ferreira and Khatami, 1996.
43 Cecchini and Zicolillo, 2002.
44 Catenazzi, 1999.
45 Graham and Marvin, 2001.
46 See World Bank, 1994, and US National Academy of Sciences, 1993.
47 Castells, 1996.
48 Sassen, 1994.
49 Sassen, 1991.
50 Graham and Marvin, 2001, p315.
51 McGee and Robinson, 1995.
52 Yeung and Chu, 2000.
53 Cohen and Debowicz, 2001.
54 Citizens' Committee for Children of New York, 2002.
55 Galster, 1998.
56 National Research Council, 2003.
57 National Research Council, 2003, pp82–83.
58 National Research Council, 2003, p87.
59 National Research Council, 2003, Chapter 6.
60 Simone, 2001.
61 Cohen, 1998.
62 Cohen, 1998.
63 Kyu Sik Lee et al, 1999.
64 Bird and Slack, 2003.
65 Bahl and Linn, 1992.
66 Kemmis, 1995.
67 Cohen, 1997.
68 Sennett, 1990.

Chapter **2**

Cultural Strategies for Urban Development[1]

Redevelopment of urban spaces   **32**

Redevelopment of inner-city areas   33

Preservation of cultural heritage   35

Gentrification   37

Growth of cultural industries   **38**

The consumption spaces of globalizing cities   **42**

Fusion in the design and architecture of consumption spaces   43

Enclosure of consumption spaces   47

Towards an inclusive urban culture   **47**

Chapter 1 addressed the overall impacts of globalization on culture within cities and highlighted the social dimensions of these impacts, especially in terms of ethnicity and its manifestation in urban space. This chapter takes a material perspective of urban culture, which, as stated in Chapter 1, focuses on the built environment of palaces, temples, opera houses, art museums and so on. During recent years, culture has taken on a more instrumental meaning. It now represents the ideas and practices, sites and symbols, of the symbolic economy. This new concept of culture is increasingly being used to shape city strategies in the face of globalization and global competition, on the one hand, and local resistance, on the other.

Many cities entered the 21st century committed to promoting a symbolic economy that produces information, designs and images, and aims to foster cultural creativity. Although some cities are still developing their industrial base – mainly by combining foreign investment with indigenous entrepreneurs and low-wage labour – and others are replacing their remaining factories with offices, hotels and leisure centres, culture is a common element in their thinking about future growth.

Each city wants to sustain itself – its population, buildings, infrastructure and culture, as well as its relative sphere of influence within a larger political territory, from the local state or province to the national state, as well as the regional and global levels. Meeting this challenge requires a city to find a viable role within the current international division of labour. But this task places every city in a dilemma, for it must open itself to free exchanges with other cities and

cultures while protecting residents from the erosion of local identities that these free exchanges often bring.

During the current era of globalization, the growth of the symbolic economy is reshaping the cultures of cities in distinctive ways. Most visibly, it is encouraging the *redevelopment of urban spaces* in terms of cultural capital. On the assumption that culture can be a motor of employment growth, it is directing investment toward *new cultural industries and cultural districts*. And the common denominator has been found in developing new *public spaces as spaces of consumption*, whose cultural amenities are intended to harmonize different social interests and improve the quality of urban life. Although each city presents its own cultural strategies as a way of distinguishing itself from other cities, demonstrating its social cohesiveness as well as its unique creative force, it should be remembered that these ideas and practices are worked out in a competitive framework. They reflect the competitive globalization of economic production and the equally competitive commercialization of culture.

This chapter discusses the ways in which culture, within the context of globalization, is influencing patterns and processes within cities all over the world. The first part addresses the most direct influence of culture on cities – that is, the ways in which cities are using culture as a central component of strategies for the *redevelopment of urban spaces* in ways that are designed to capitalize on the economic benefits of globalization.

The second part discusses trends in the emergence of *urban cultural industries*, focusing on the role of finance and cultural symbols in the development of urban 'cultural districts', or spatial concentrations of creative economic activities, such as fashion and clothing design.

Finally, the last part discusses the ways in which globalization is shaping the emergence and spread of new *urban consumption spaces*, often in the form of mixed-use complexes and malls containing globally standardized cultural amenities, shops and housing.

Redevelopment of urban spaces

Many city authorities and urban development agencies all over the world are increasingly using culture-related activities as tools of urban redevelopment, or revitalization.[2] This strategy has been used to promote the civic identity of cities, to market cities internationally and, in particular, to boost the economic fortunes of cities experiencing industrial decline. Current trends in many parts of the world suggest that culture will play an increasingly important role in the future of cities. Of particular significance among these trends have been the

Identity is an important feature of the symbolic economy

BOX 2.1 **Plateau Beaubourg, Paris, France**

Under President Georges Pompidou, the French government decided to create a new museum of contemporary art in the centre of Paris, a public museum that would follow the historic tradition of *grands projets* set 200 years earlier by the Louvre, and would also demonstrate that the country had not lost its creative edge. This strategy had an educational as well as a promotional goal. A multipurpose museum of contemporary art would reach out to young French people, especially those who had been most disaffected by the political protests of 1968, and foster their creativity. But it would also connect creativity to industrial design and encourage innovation in all fields, from the 'pure' to the commercial, and from atonal music to conceptual art. It was a foregone conclusion, in such a centralized system, that such a great museum would only be built in Paris.

Yet, the government envisioned the museum not only as revitalizing French creativity, but also as stimulating the redevelopment of a dilapidated part of the inner city. In fact, the buildings on the Plateau Beaubourg that were torn down to build the Centre Georges Pompidou were shabby and lacked modern conveniences. With its boldly modern architecture, and the crowds of young people, both Parisians and foreign tourists, who came to ride the external elevators and congregate outside, the spectacular museum that replaced them immediately infused this area of the city with new cultural capital. The Beaubourg quickly developed into a world-class tourist attraction. Its success was not identified with a permanent collection of art. Instead, the museum was identified partly with the Beaubourg's innovative programmes and initially free admission, and partly with Richard Rogers and Renzo Piano's signature high-tech building design. This image of the Beaubourg quickly became as potent a symbol of the city as the Eiffel Tower. It was featured in architecture and news magazines around the world and drew crowds

Global branding of cities

to the large, open space in front of the building, which became a gathering place for young people, street entertainers and tourists from abroad: a post-modern plaza. The Centre Pompidou's success in 'branding' Paris strongly suggested that big investments in flagship cultural projects could revitalize a city's economy and reputation – even though, or maybe especially if, the architects who built the project came from overseas.[i]

Note: i Mollard 1977; Evans 2003.

following: culturally driven redevelopment of inner-city areas; preservation of historic buildings as well as revival of traditional crafts for enhancing the global tourism potential of cities; and gentrification of inner-city residential areas.

Redevelopment of inner-city areas

During the 1960s, governments in Europe began to show an interest in redeveloping the centres of cities around cultural capital. Both the UK and French governments, like the administration in Washington, DC, passed new laws to support artists and historic preservation. The French felt that they needed to do something that would reassert France's prominence on the world stage – to devise a strategy that would respond to both economic competition with the US and cultural competition between New York and

Paris, as described in Box 2.1.

Other European cities did not fail to note the example of the Plateau Beaubourg.[3] Unlike in the US, where nearly all public museums and other cultural facilities are supported by local government and private donors, in many European countries the central governments generally control the management and budget of cultural institutions. When central governments became more involved in regional redevelopment during the economic crisis of the 1980s, they started connecting economic and cultural strategies. Indeed, the more socially devastated a region appeared, and the less likely to experience new industrial growth, the more governmental authorities turned to marketing cities as centres of culture in order to create a new business climate. This seemed ever more important with the growth of computer software, media and consumer products industries, which placed a priority on design

BOX 2.2 Glasgow, UK: culture as a new economic base in declining cities

In Glasgow, where traditional industries and ship-building had long since entered a terminal decline, local groups started an annual arts festival, Mayfest, and opened a new museum, the Burrell Art Collection, in 1983. The district council declared that Glasgow would find a new role for itself in business services, higher education, media industries and the arts. When the Scottish Development Agency hired McKinsey and Company, an international consulting firm, to devise an urban redevelopment strategy, they proposed building on these initiatives by promoting Glasgow as a cultural centre. The McKinsey plan aimed to attract multinational corporations and, like the Beaubourg, to stimulate residents of the city to show more creativity. Like the unplanned cultural strategy of gentrification, the plan was also connected to local business interest in revalorizing the centre of the city – by converting old warehouses and factories to a Scottish version of loft living, and building new luxury housing in the docklands.[i]

Note: i Gomez, 1998.

innovation and access to the latest cultural trends. This trend is illustrated by the strategy implemented by the then industrially declining Glasgow, Scotland, for marketing the city as a cultural centre from the 1980s (see Box 2.2).

Culturally based city-centre redevelopment strategies were intensified and broadened by the European Union (EU), which established an annual competition, in 1985, to select the European City of Culture. Each winning city sponsors a months-long festival that includes performances and exhibitions in various locations. Local governments take this as an opportunity to lobby for European Regional

BEST PRACTICE

CIUTAT VELLA PROJECT: REVITALIZATION OF THE HISTORIC CENTRE OF BARCELONA, SPAIN

Ciutat Vella is Barcelona's main historic, cultural and leisure centre, containing most of Barcelona's historic, cultural and artistic heritage. Despite this, the district was experiencing major deficiencies in education and healthcare delivery, housing and urban infrastructure, loss of economic activity, marginalization and unemployment. In response, the city council, in partnership with citizens and the private sector, formulated an integrated plan to rehabilitate housing, improve public infrastructure, promote local economic development and implement social welfare programmes. Work done includes the construction and renovation of museums, a public university, civic centres and a public hospital, over 2000 public residential dwellings and rehabilitation of 22,400 residential dwellings. Gentrification has been deliberately avoided through measures to guarantee the permanence of the resident population.

Urban redevelopment and social policies have improved the quality of life in the district, including educational levels, household income, economic activity and security. This has, in turn, reduced the economic and social gaps that existed within Ciutat Vella and between this district and the rest of the city.

Source: www.bestpractices.org.

Development funds, which they use to renovate and expand existing museums and concert halls and advertise their city around the world. The regional competition has enlarged the use of cultural strategies geographically: in 2000, nine cities shared the title. Significantly, two (Prague and Krakow) are in Eastern Europe and one (Reykjavik) is in a country that does not belong to the EU. Helsinki, also chosen to be a European City of Culture in 2000, connected festival events with ongoing plans to build new museums, cinemas, art bookshops and cafés, as well as new media quarters.

These redevelopment strategies have their own problems, however. The spread of Cities of Culture throughout Europe, and to the Americas, as well, attempts to justify each city's claim to cultural distinctiveness. But 'cultural cities' reproduce the same facilities in any number of places, echoing the globalization of industrial production, with its geographical dispersion of production and aggregation of consumption. Critics complain that the many competitions to host special events, including the Olympics, exhaust a city's resources in preparing endless bids. Winning cities take the major share of regional and national funds, depriving smaller cities of grants and favouring products and performances that will attract the largest possible audience. This, too, suggests a parallel between economic and cultural globalization, for global products and imports are often seen as more competitive than domestic art and culture that may appeal to a specialized audience. Moreover, the investment of so much money into the fixed capital of cultural facilities strikes an imbalance. Like gentrification and new luxury housing, it concentrates resources in the urban centre, while paying less attention to culturally underserved peripheries. In their own way, then, these cultural strategies create 'global districts' in big cities around the world, with their own modern art museums, luxury hotels, cafés, and shops – all promoting the same band of mobile architects, artists and designers.[4] Perhaps the best-known example of this to date is the revitalization of the waterfront in Bilbao by the Guggenheim Museum, joined by the Euskalduna Conference and Performing Arts Palace, hotels and a shopping centre (see Box 2.3).

The challenges facing Bilbao (highlighted in Box 2.3) also face Asian cities that have adopted cultural strategies of redevelopment, as the experience of Singapore (see Box 2.4) shows. Its cultural strategy was based on the development of a cultural complex of international reputation, the Esplanade.

Tokyo, which has even lost some multinational offices to the more modern Singapore, is facing the same problems as those experienced by Singapore (described in Box 2.4). In Tokyo, the metropolitan

BOX 2.3 The Guggenheim Museum, Bilbao, Spain: a global district

As in Glasgow (and Manchester, Sheffield and Liverpool, UK), the absence of new industrial growth to counter the decline of traditional industries in Bilbao led authorities to turn to building facilities for cultural consumption. Deliberately following in Glasgow's path, and influenced, no doubt, by the success of Barcelona, which hosted the 1992 Olympics, as well as by Seville's sponsorship of a World Exposition, Bilbao also developed a cultural plan. Local authorities would revitalize the centre in order to attract multinational business services, especially in banking and finance. They would invest in dramatic new infrastructure facilities that would create cultural images in their own right and pay not only for a new museum, but also for the art to fill it. The city hired famous architects from outside its borders: Norman Foster, to design stations for the new metro; Cesar Pelli, to draw up guidelines for the waterfront plan; Santiago Calatrava, to design the terminal at Sondika Airport and the Zubi Zuri bridge over the Nervion River; and Frank Gehry, to create the architectural design for what was to be the major draw on the other side of the river – the Guggenheim Museum. The new image of the city is intended to attract both tourists and corporations. As in Glasgow, these projects show 'the overriding presence of large emblematic schemes with a strong marketing dimension and an intense regard for aesthetics and design'; in other words, following the example of the Beaubourg, Bilbao's cultural strategies would intentionally create a globally recognized brand. This thinking matched the expansionary strategies of the Guggenheim itself, which under its director, Thomas Krens, had sought since the 1980s to become the first global museum – a museum whose brand name, signature architecture and contemporary art would cover many branches.[i]

Although Bilbao's failure to reverse the outward migration of young people and high rate of unemployment have been highlighted by critics, the cultural strategy of redevelopment has won the city a great amount of favourable publicity. From the moment the competition to

Outstanding museums have been used to market 'global cities of culture'

design the museum began, art and architecture critics flew to Bilbao to visit the site and write about it. At the museum's opening, in 1997, they returned to praise the beauty of Gehry's design and the audacity of his use of a new material – titanium – to construct a façade of flowing curves that radiate in the sun, a visual reference to Bilbao's modern roots in the ship-building industry and to the steel mills that are no longer in operation. Despite the overall admiration, social critics raised questions about the results of the cultural plan. Is it a positive development that this attraction brings affluent tourists to Bilbao, especially from abroad, but excludes jobs for most of the resident population? Does the city's new image counter the fact that the expected corporations have not come?[ii]

Notes: i Gomez, 1998; Zukin, 1995; Evans, 2003. ii Plaza, 2000; Ockman and Vidler, 2001; Rauen 2001; see also Friedmann, 1995a.

---

government also spends the major share of its steadily increasing cultural budget on large, mixed-use cultural and convention complexes, big theatres and art museums – without significantly developing urban cultural producers or stimulating artistic innovation.[5]

The idea of using culture as a motor of economic growth also reflects the transition from manufacturing cities to sites of more flexible design- and knowledge-based production. Beginning during the 1970s, the movement of factories out of cities in the US and Western Europe left unused space in older buildings and opened manufacturing districts where rents were relatively cheap for alternative uses. Although zoning laws and building codes prohibited using industrial buildings for housing, visual and performing artists began to convert manufacturing

lofts covertly into live–work spaces. The experience of New York City (see Box 2.5) illustrates this process well.

Preservation of cultural heritage

Culturally driven models of redevelopment are succeeding partly because of two interrelated changes: growth in the business services of cities, especially those supporting the symbolic economy in finance and media, and new perceptions of the value of older buildings. These new perceptions have manifested themselves in two distinct processes, the preservation of historic buildings (discussed in this section) and gentrification (discussed in the next section). The

Cultural heritage sites are playing notable roles in the symbolic economy

often paid for by federal government subsidies for urban renewal. Other downtown districts were abandoned as businesses moved to new 'campuses' in the suburbs. By the mid 1960s, however, a broad-based movement had formed to preserve historic buildings from demolition, especially in US and Western European cities. Community groups whose neighbourhoods were threatened by urban renewal plans joined more affluent elite groups who felt that the quality of life was jeopardized when historically significant buildings and districts were destroyed. For some people, this movement was a principled opposition to the bureaucratic modernism of city governments and planners; for others, it was a last-ditch effort to conserve their cultural heritage – that is, to retain the built forms of the city's collective memory.[6]

Like the support that New York artists mobilized for loft living, support for historic preservation depended on connections between elite patrons of the arts and architecture and public officials – in this case, both federal and local. New York was the first American city to pass a law to protect, or 'landmark', historic properties; but this law was swiftly joined by federal classification of such buildings through the National Trust and federal tax laws that encouraged preservation and restoration. Some noted activists for community preservation in New York City defended a mix of new and old buildings as necessary for the city's social and cultural vitality. They also argued that the low rents in old buildings allowed them to serve as incubators for small-scale artisans and businesses. This point, which is still only grudgingly accepted by property developers, has served as a springboard for many neighbourhoods' economic revival. The aesthetic and historic value of old buildings provides them with a kind of cultural capital.[7]

By the early 1980s, the movement for the preservation of cultural heritage buildings had spread to many developing countries. For example, during the mid 1980s, in Zanzibar, Tanzania, the Stone Town Conservation and Development Authority was established to plan and coordinate conservation activities in the Old Town (see Box 2.6). By the 1990s, with the growth of Cultural Heritage Tourism, more and more cities in developing countries were investing in the conservation of old historic buildings and thus tapping into their 'cultural capital' (see Box 2.7).

A variation of cultural heritage preservation, especially in developing country cities, has gone beyond buildings and has focused on the revival of traditional crafts, using this to attract international tourists. In Nairobi, Kenya, promoters of traditional textiles, jewellery and carvings have started using the internet for global marketing of their products. The Dakshinachitra crafts museum in Chennai, India,

former has been used by cities as a strategy for attracting international tourists (cultural heritage tourism), while the latter process has entailed renovation of run-down inner-city residential areas by middle-class residents of developed country cities.

By the 1960s, growth in the corporate sector and modernization had destroyed older districts of the city, especially in the US. Old buildings, whatever their use, had been torn down and replaced by corporate headquarters, high-class hotels and expensive housing,

BOX 2.4 The Esplanade, Singapore: city-branding in the south

Singapore, which during the 1990s committed itself to building the Esplanade, a new cultural complex on the waterfront for performing arts, focused on creating large-scale facilities that benefited touring foreign artists. But this policy neglected the city's own considerable pool of talent. Although they were active and energetic, native artists, musicians and theatrical performers lacked products that would attract a big, multinational audience. Singaporeans were expected to support blockbuster exhibitions at the art museum and imported attractions such as the Cirque du Soleil. They would profit eventually, city officials believed, from a new and broader climate of cultural consumption; like the art galleries of SoHo, two decades earlier, or the European cultural capitals, Singapore would attract the attention of multinational media and, eventually, would also attract more regional offices of multinational corporations. Although criticism of this import-oriented policy persuaded the city government to prod cultural institutions and international artistic groups to hire and train Singaporeans, the 'hardware' of the new cultural infrastructure tended to support local citizens' cultural consumption, rather than their cultural innovation and production.

(described in Box 2.8) illustrates this approach in global marketing of developing country cities on the basis of cultural heritage.

Gentrification

Within the advanced economies, appreciation of the aesthetic and historic value of old houses also drew new middle-class residents to older districts of the city, especially from the 1970s onwards. With a university education, and often working in media industries such as publishing and advertising, human services such as social work or teaching, or jobs connected with the arts, these men and women settled in areas of the city among working-class and ethnic communities. Though the new residents were not usually rich, they could afford to pay higher prices for housing than most of the residents who were already there. Moreover, they brought new patterns of socialization and cultural consumption into these communities, as well as a markedly different aesthetic.[8] 'Gentrifiers', as sociologists in the UK have termed them,[9] preferred to socialize in their homes rather than on the streets, called on their friends for help rather than on their neighbours, and restored the original architectural features of their houses rather than modernized them. Their preference for bookshops rather than betting parlours, and for wine bars and cafés rather than pubs, gradually changed the character of the streets and removed places where the older residents had forged class or ethnic solidarities. Their demand for the housing stock, after they demonstrated how to improve it, also raised rents, driving out many low-income tenants. It encouraged individual property owners to sell out for what they considered windfall prices, helping both to increase the population of gentrifiers and to raise property values. Together with the more limited model of loft living, gentrification signalled that the symbolic economy could produce a new type of urban space in older, de-industrializing cities – a space with cultural capital.

Strictly, neither gentrification nor loft living was a planned strategy of redevelopment. Because they depended on self-financing through savings, personal loans and sweat equity, they seemed to legitimize the gradual withdrawal of governments from building new public housing. In the US, they also partly compensated for middle-class 'flight' from cities to new housing in the suburbs, and slowed the racial turnover in cities (apart from in public housing) from European or white ethnic groups to African-Americans and Latin Americans. Most important, however, was the way in which they reshaped the symbols and spaces of the city, both displacing social problems connected with the inner-city poor and

BOX 2.5 **Loft living in New York, US**

New York, where 'loft living' became fairly common during the 1970s, was pressed to legalize the situation by the hundreds of artists who moved into lofts, aided by the close relations these artists had with socially prominent patrons. When two industrial districts of Lower Manhattan were rezoned to permit artists' housing in SoHo, and residential reuse, in general, in Tribeca, the city government cast its vote for an 'artistic mode of production' that would complement a post-industrial renewal of the local economy. This direction seemed to be justified by the flowering of art galleries and performance spaces, and eventually restaurants and design stores, in these areas. Cultural production bloomed not only because American artists migrated to Lower Manhattan, but also because artists, actors and musicians came to New York from other parts of the world, notably Europe and Asia. They created artwork, opened galleries and performance spaces, and were written up in newspapers and magazines in other countries. This media coverage maintained the city's reputation as the place to be – the global capital – for cutting-edge cultural creation.

During the depths of the city's fiscal crisis, in the late 1970s, the media promoted loft living as a comfortable and sophisticated urban lifestyle, stoking interest in lofts as a new and distinctive means of cultural consumption. Under these conditions, and with a steady movement of production out of state and overseas, the supply of lofts increased to meet rising demand. While other housing markets were saturated with new, and relatively small, apartments, individuals with some savings to invest and little connection to the arts began to renovate lofts for both rental and purchase. Their entrepreneurial success, in turn, attracted professional real-estate developers. Within a few years, loft living sparked both a residential and a commercial revival of Lower Manhattan and raised property values to historic heights.

Source: Zukin 1989; Guilbaut 1983.

BEST PRACTICE
ATELIER 231: STREET ART IN SOTTEVILLE, FRANCE

Atelier 231 is located in a former French railways building, rehabilitated to accommodate artists involved in the production of plays, synchronized dancing, poetry, paintings and sculptures. It forms part of the historical features of the predominantly railway town. Weekly fairs are organised to showcase street arts. This has been made possible because of a cultural policy in favour of promoting street arts, which have now become popular and accessible to all since they are featured free of charge in an open arena. Consequently, it was essential to establish an appropriate system of rehabilitation. The street arts project motivated the different departments of the town council to get involved in the initial opening of the festival, as well as in all subsequent events. The whole philosophy of this project was to initiate a cultural project in a city that had no prior experience and to make it sustainable. This has helped to build and strengthen the social fabric of the city.

Source: www.bestpractices.org.

BOX 2.6 **Zanzibar, Tanzania: preserving the historic Stone Town**

The Stone Town is the centre of the greater city of Zanzibar and houses much of the island's commercial and government activity. It is famous for its traditional coral stone buildings, intricate balconies, massive carved doors and narrow bazaar streets. With the rapid population growth in Zanzibar town, lack of maintenance and uncontrolled new constructions, the fabric of the Old Stone Town has been under increasing pressure. Not only are many historic buildings very dilapidated – some even collapsed – but in some instances residents in traditional buildings have partitioned, altered, added onto, or demolished and replaced the traditional buildings with new structures. Realizing the need to preserve the Stone Town in Zanzibar, the Stone Town Conservation and Development Authority was established in 1985, and the Stone Town Conservation Plan was approved in 1994. The plan, designed to coordinate the conservation initiatives in the Stone Town, lays out a general planning framework, and establishes the broad conservation and development policies for the Stone Town. The plan proposes controls on the use and development of land, measures to protect individual buildings, street elements and open areas, and measures to develop and improve parcels of land and other larger spaces in the central area, including methods to improve parking and circulation of vehicular traffic in and around the Stone Town. As a result of the concerted efforts of the

The cultural heritage conservation movement has spread all over the world

Stone Town Conservation and Development Authority and its partners, several buildings in the Stone Town have been gazetted as monuments, while numerous others have been repaired and restored and 80 per cent of the streets in the Stone Town have been paved.

Source: Siravo, undated.

infusing these neighbourhoods with a gritty, self-conscious glamour.

Similar processes of change have occurred, to some extent, in central areas of Paris, London and other European cities, whose historic districts also suffered from a combination of abandonment, demolition and terrible new construction – notably, on the waterfront and around the sites of wholesale food markets that had moved to the outskirts of the city. More educated residents, especially university graduates and graduates of art schools, moved into live–work spaces in these areas, entranced as much by the authenticity of the buildings and the districts' historic aura as by relatively low rents. These qualities also attracted young people, university students and social activists, some of whom (notably, in Berlin, Amsterdam and Copenhagen) took advantage of half-vacant space by occupying it in illegal squats. For the same reasons as in New York, these central areas of the city developed a new kind of cultural capital.

Growth of cultural industries

Cities have the greatest concentrations of political power, trade, rich consumers, entertainment and cultural creativity. Creativity is not just an artistic concept. Developing creativity implies not only that a city can place new products on global markets, but that it can quickly respond to changing competition and demand. Although the immediate result may be to enrich a narrow group of private factory owners, designers and marketing entrepreneurs, the long-term public goal is to provide a new industrial base that ensures employment for the broader urban work force. Creativity is reflected in the urban imaginary that – through literature, media representations and film – confirms a city's reputation. A creative city is one that has learned how to use its cultural capital to attract innovative businesses and services, as well as members of the mobile 'creative class'. It respects the city's social and architectural heritage, provides amenities from bicycle lanes to pavement cafés, and encourages environmentally sensitive buildings and technologies. These material and symbolic factors are interrelated. Just as the culture of the city pervades product design, so design creates the image of the city.[10]

Setting such a dynamic in motion has become incredibly important to local public officials – at least, rhetorically, in terms of 'branding' the city as creative. Since massive industries such as steel and automobiles based on standardized mass production have fallen in many developed country cities, one by one, to competition from cities with lower costs located in developing countries, attention has focused on flexible industries that value knowledge, information and technology. Officials and planners look at regional clusters of industry leaders – such as California's Silicon Valley and Hollywood – and dream about creating the same kind of place identification in their own town. But flexible industries are difficult to master. In Silicon Valley or Hollywood, they thrive on a polarized social structure of highly paid founders, managers and engineers (or studio owners, producers and stars) and low-wage manufacturing and craft workers. When these areas become heavily urbanized – with air and water pollution, traffic congestion and overburdened public services such as schools – companies move to, and new companies prefer to locate in, other cities where industry is less entrenched. Moreover, globalization encourages flexible industries to separate parts of the production process in regions around the world and coordinate them, in real time, by email, faxes and jet planes. This allows managers to pick and choose among local labour markets and political conditions – or among pools of different experience, skills and wages. So far, they have tended to keep the more design-oriented, innovative parts of the business in their home cities within the advanced economies, while shifting less skilled work to the developing world. Yet, although new industries reshape urban cultures around their needs, they are too geographically fragmented to dominate a city as the textile, steel, automobile and even computer industries used to do.[11]

The fact remains, however, that most cultural industries are located in cities.[12] A dense population and concentration of skills allow them to draw upon tangible human resources, and a city's usual history of tolerance and social diversity offers intangible resources of inspiration and experimentation. Because modern urban culture is so intertwined with publicity and marketing, a city location also pushes cultural innovators to think about selling their work and provides many sites for them to do so. These conditions make it impossible to see cities only as either producers or consumers of culture. One of a city's most important roles is to consume, as well as to produce culture – and to demonstrate, in the urban imaginary, how cultural products should be consumed. This is uniquely confirmed by the global cities (New York, London and Tokyo) that dominate the contemporary urban imaginary, as well as by smaller global cities such as Miami, Hong Kong, Rio de Janeiro and Lagos.

BOX 2.7 Kathmandu, Nepal: restoring a centuries-old water supply system

In 1997, the Kathmandu Municipal Council (KMC) established the Heritage and Tourism Department to spearhead the cultural conservation activities of the city. Since then, the department has been developing several strategies for heritage conservation, including education and awareness programmes for an informed public, heritage tours for school children, media (radio and television), community participation, public–private partnerships and financial incentives. One of the projects undertaken by KMC, in collaboration with UNESCO, is the restoration of the centuries-old water supply system of sculptural 'stone spouts' and wells. The stone 'spouts', scattered all over the city, were once the centre of community life and were initially developed to serve the people as places to collect drinking water and to bathe. Although the city no longer depends upon them, the restoration of the water spouts not only helps to preserve a unique living heritage, but also contributes to the improvement of the water supply and drainage system in a city that suffers from chronic water shortages.

Sources: Global Development Research Centre, 1999; UNESCO, undated.

Cultural industries influence urban development

Globalization footprints are seen in cultural consumption spaces

Western-style discount shopping to countries with much lower wages. Shopping has also been enhanced by the proliferation of credit cards. Most important to governments, however, is the fit between shopping and their social and cultural goals. In Singapore, the government decided in 1996 that shopping presents the ultimate modern image that the city-state needed to project to multinational corporate investors. In China, shopping represents modernity, access to world markets, and an opening of both domestic markets and cultures. And shopping in the US, it has been observed, represents a patriotic effort to support the economy, especially in the face of political and financial anxieties – an important point in a country where two-thirds of gross national product (GNP) depends upon consumer spending.[19]

Intensification of shopping today also reflects the strategic expansion of global brands. Luxury products are no longer just works of individual artistry and collective artisanal skill; they are names that get their value from association with a famous designer, and they provide value to the corporation that sells them, in various forms and at various prices, as a portable display of social status. Changing luxury goods into brands requires that companies intensify their promotions, and building new stores in major shopping districts around the world is one of the most effective forms of advertisement. Multinational luxury goods corporations hire the same multinational architects who design the mixed-use and cultural districts and are no less eagerly courted by city governments than the cultural districts.[20] Indeed, in the major redevelopment of Potsdamerplatz in the centre of Berlin, the reunification of East and West Germany takes material form in a shopping, office and entertainment centre.

Teenagers and young adults are the most enthusiastic shoppers. Since shopping is, after all, a way of trying on identities, young people naturally gravitate towards this activity. Shopping is also a means of socializing, and for the current young generation that is hardly involved in politics or labour unions, it offers a way of entering the public sphere. But this is not the public sphere of the *café du quartier*, the marketplace or other forms of traditional local culture. Shopping for products that are globally recognized as signs of youth, such as jeans, shoes and music, is a means of resisting the traditional public sphere. As one writer says of young people in Singapore, they draw fashions from a 'globalized "image bank"' that is familiar from movies, TV and music videos, and consume these as a form of protest. Shopping for global products, then, signals rejection of a politics that is identified with traditional or local culture.'[21]

However, it has also been observed that the consumption spaces that are most identified with

represents a way in which everyone can 'buy into' the symbolic economy, pursuing his or her private dreams in a public space. Like the cultural districts that are built for performance and display, these new, mixed-use shopping developments are spaces where residents of the city can perform the role of modern – or global – consumers and display their knowledge and wealth. This space is not, as many critics charge, 'American' so much as it is 'modern' and 'global'. Or, rather, it really began in the US, but it has been re-territorialized in every city of the world.

Many countries have recently experienced a long wave of intensified shopping. This does not just reflect the fact that, with economic development, consumers have more leisure time and spending money. Shopping has been intensified by the concerted action of an institutional network of retail stores, manufacturers, marketing experts, display designers, advertising agencies and independent critics who write reviews of products and styles; it is shaped (or stimulated) by government policies on wages and taxes and, increasingly, by multinational treaties on trade and free-trade zones. The global intensification of shopping is also encouraged by governmental decisions to lower entry barriers to foreign-owned retail stores, which have negotiated to open more stores in some developing countries, bringing

globalization are really polyvalent. Like the fusion spaces of culture and capital, these consumption spaces *become* a part of local urban culture. The space of a McDonald's is useful for young people doing homework outside of their small apartments in Singapore and for elderly men in Taipei who want an inexpensive place indoors to sit and chat. In a survey in Beijing, young women said that they liked McDonald's more than Chinese fast-food restaurants because they received equal treatment there – which they would not receive in a traditional Chinese restaurant. When McDonald's is used to satisfy these needs, it develops into a local institution.[22]

Enclosure of consumption spaces

Global-type consumption spaces increasingly share a sense of enclosure that is new to traditional urban cultures. This enclosure is technical, social and cultural, and it facilitates the privatization of public space. Many of these indoor spaces have introduced air conditioning – which really requires closing the windows and doors. In the shopping malls of São Paulo, the consumption spaces protect shoppers from fear of being robbed by building a wall. In Barcelona, they make a surprising turn away from the streets by creating an indoor shopping mall. And in Shanghai, a development consortium of Hong Kong investors and North American architects have created a self-contained district of shops, cafés, and restaurants – the trendy Xintiandi – by reusing the old stone buildings of an earlier colonial-Chinese architectural style. Yet, in the US, shopping malls are a part of suburban rather than urban culture, as shown in Chapter 7. Only during recent years have big cities such as Chicago and New York experimented with indoor malls; smaller cities, however, have easily built underground passages or skyways of shops that avoid the streets, as in Nagoya, Japan. While enclosed consumption spaces are not a historic part of urban culture, with globalization, they are becoming a universal expression of privatized public space. The danger in this kind of globalization is that enclosed public spaces represent a more limited form of citizenship.

The quest to create various objects of consumption creates spaces of cultural fusion

Towards an inclusive urban culture

The flows of people and money which pass through global cities continually replenish the supply of potential creators. But to nurture creativity, a city must have a generous and inclusive culture; it must have 'an attitude'. What, in the end, creates the culture of New York City, for example? A fashion critic recently observed that New York has excelled as an originator of style because it has 'moxie [courage, energy, audacity, nerve]…a broad racial dispersion…and an unquenchable thirst for the new'.[23] Often this combination of nerve, racial diversity and an impatient desire for new things explodes into an astoundingly uncivil society, characterized by oppositional cultures in which men and women speak frankly of their differences and struggle openly to protect their rights. This, however, is the price that today's global cities have to pay for creativity and cultural inclusiveness.

Notes

1 This chapter draws primarily on a background paper 'Globalization and Urban Culture' prepared by Sharon Zukin, Brooklyn College and City University Graduate Centre, New York, US.

2 See, for example, Griffiths, 1995.

3 Bianchini and Parkinson, 1993; Kearns and Philo, 1995.

4 Evans, 2003.

5 Chang, 2000; Sasaki, 2001.

6 Zukin 1989, Berman 1982.

7 Jacobs, 1961; Bourdieu, 1984.

8 Smith and Williams, 1986.

9 Glass, 1964.

10 Hall, 1998; Landry and Bianchini, 1995; Molotch, 1996; Scott, 2000; Florida, 2002.

11 Saxenian, 1994; Bielby and Bielby, 1998; Nevarez, 2003.

12 Scott, 2001, p8.

13 Adapted from Sanagata, 2002, p20.

14 Pratt (in press).

15 Scott, 2000.

16 Coe, 2000; Miller et al, 2001.

17 The name of this architect is Jon Jerde, whose firm is based in Santa Monica, California.

18 'Projects Taking Shape in China', *Architectural Record*, March 2004, p112; see Hanningan, 1998.

19 On shopping as an institutional field, see Zukin, 2004; on Singapore, see Chua, 1998.

20 Frank Gehry has designed an Issey Miyake store in Tribeca in Lower Manhattan; Rem Koolhaas, a Prada store in SoHo; and Herzog and de Meuron, who transformed an unused power station in London into Tate Modern, the 'Prada epicenter' in Tokyo.

21 Chua, 1998; on Latin America, see Garcia Canclini, 2001.

22 Yan, 2000.

23 Trebay, 2001.

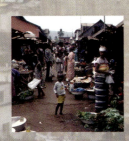

Chapter 3

Metropolitanization[1]

Dimensions of metropolitanization	**51**
The spatial dimension	51
The social morphology dimension	52
The institutional dimension	54
The economic dimension	57
Twentieth-century trends: managing differences and externalities at different scales	**58**
Fragmentation	58
Differentiation, inequalities and polarization	58
Spatial mismatch	59
Metropolitan development in an age of globalization	**60**
Trends in developing countries	**62**
Asia and the Pacific	62
Latin America and the Caribbean	64
Middle East and Northern Africa (MENA)	67
Sub-Saharan Africa	69
Trends in transition economy countries	**71**
Trends in advanced economy countries	**73**

In every country, there are 'metropolitan expectations'. Whether in Monterey or Mumbai, Dacca or Dakar, cities have more people and cover more land. They offer more and different kinds of employment and ways of making a living. Their social forms are more complex, whether inside the evolving forms of the household, neighbourhood or borough. The range and diversity of people's appearances and behaviours have grown. And there are increasing numbers of institutions that presume to play a role in what has been described as 'urban governance'.[2] And yet, 'the metropolitan project' is an under-achiever.

Demographic growth, spatial expansion, economic differentiation, social complexity, cultural diversity and institutional fragmentation would all suggest that metropolitan forms and frameworks should emerge to respond to the many challenges that accompany these processes. Enormous problems of poverty, inequality and dangerous levels of air pollution in many cities are begging for solutions. But even with the added pressures of globalization that are commonly perceived as increasing the concentration of urban populations in metropolitan areas,[3] there are few cities which claim to have created sustainable metropolitan frameworks for managing their affairs.

This is surprising because most analyses of urbanization processes during the post-World War II period have suggested, implicitly or explicitly, that cities and towns will grow to become 'metropolitan' in scale, territory and complexity, including their institutions. Economists developed 'metropolitan expectations' based on their assumptions of economies of agglomeration through which greater economic returns will be generated for individuals, households, firms, sectors of production and urban economies. These economies of agglomeration assumed proximity and density as necessary conditions for facilitating urban economic multipliers. In short, from an urban economic perspective, bigger was not only inevitable, – it was also better.

This perspective seemed to be justified by the important economic role of metropolitan areas. For example:

- São Paulo's 75 miles' wide girth and seemingly unending population growth are seen as evidence of its economic productivity and unrealized potential as a source of income and employment.
- Mumbai's (Bombay's) power in generating one sixth of the gross domestic product (GDP) of India confirms the synergy of private entrepreneurs and investment in a single location, despite insufficient infrastructure.
- During the late 1990s, the GDP of Seoul, Republic of Korea, equalled the GDP of Argentina, while that of Mexico City equalled

Thailand, and Rio de Janeiro and São Paulo together equalled the Andean countries.

These examples support the conclusion of research showing that the sharpest rates of urban growth occur within countries below US$2000 per capita income. Metropolitan concentration is a central feature of that growth.[4]

Demographers also developed 'metropolitan expectations'. In developing countries, rural to urban migrants have been attracted to cities by high wages.[5] Larger cities, with higher productivity resulting from agglomeration economies, have higher wages – hence, migration flows were thought logically to be channelled first to the larger cities. When natural increase replaced migration as the primary source of urban growth in highly urbanized regions, such as Latin America or Europe, larger populations would replace and increase themselves *in situ*. These analyses led to predictions of many megacities in all regions. During the 1970s, demographers were predicting that Mexico City would reach 30 million people by the year 2000. In fact, Mexico City stopped growing much beyond 20 million, as migrants began to search for better opportunities in other cities such as Guadalajara, Monterey and other locations. This reduced pace of metropolitan growth, not just in Mexico City, but in cities such as Calcutta and New York, suggested that not all was well with 'metropolitan life', including its costs, congestion and crime.

As migrants learned, metropolitan scale brought with it many new problems. More people needed to produce more to generate surpluses that could be used to purchase and consume more goods and services. There are many complicated positive and negative consequences – externalities – of that process which themselves need to be managed. This, in turn, requires new rules and institutions to govern behaviour at the metropolitan scale and to ensure that behaviour and activities at the municipal and urban scales are not disruptive or costly at a higher scale. These new rules and institutions introduce new forms of hierarchy, complementarity and interdependence within spaces governed by multiple jurisdictions. Multiplicity requires complicity, even when a formal public metropolitan institutional framework exists.

However, even with this rationale for metropolitan governance, the articulation and implementation of this 'metropolitan imperative' has not always proven to be predictable. The multiple interactions of scale, territory and complexity have given rise to new institutional forms, often without the public policies or resources needed to give them weight and power. The new metropolitan institutions have frequently been directed in the short term to mitigating and/or resolving the impact of negative externalities. But in the medium and longer term, they have proven to be under-performers. For many cities, 'metropolitan expectations' have been disappointed and frustrated.

These disappointments have not only been institutional or political, with real impacts; they have also occurred at the level of policy and analysis. Metropolitan forms cannot work in the real world if they are not adequately described and analysed. This observation is reflected in the following recent assessment of US cities:

> *It is becoming a commonplace that established representations of the city and the suburbs do not hold. Our capacity to describe or theorize the social and spatial organization of the contemporary metropolis is manifestly inadequate to what we know of the metropolitan experience.[6]*

This chapter describes the process of metropolitanization in terms of its spatial patterns, jurisdictional and institutional forms, and new demographic and social dynamics. It examines the gap between metropolitan expectations and performance in terms of the institutional and financial constraints found in most cities. The chapter further explores the differences between metropolitan experiences up to the year 2000 and the new pressures facing 'the metropolitan project' in an era of globalization. It ends with a description of metropolitanization trends in different regions of the world.

Dimensions of metropolitanization

The spatial dimension

As suggested above, one of the most dramatic aspects of metropolitan areas is their spatial expansion. Urban areas in all countries and in all regions have grown beyond their municipal borders to extend into surrounding jurisdictions. Two phenomena have occurred. First, populations have grown and spilled over into neighbouring administrative and political units, such as municipalities on the periphery of big cities. Second, these previously independent units have been incorporated within the larger municipality of the central city. These processes are best captured in individual cases described later in this chapter (see Boxes 3.1 and 3.3). Bangkok, for example, grew from 67 square kilometres during the late 1950s to 426 square kilometres by the mid 1990s.

A study of Latin American cities during the late 1970s found that nine of the ten largest cities were all

experiencing rapid growth on the periphery of the cities, with the periphery rising faster than the city as a whole.[7] At the same time, large cities have also increased in density. This pattern was evident by the 1970s when observers noted that while some of the large Latin American cities had continued to expand spatially, they were also substantially increasing the density of their downtown or central areas. São Paulo, for example, increased its density from 1380 persons per square kilometre in 1950 to 4005 by 1970; similarly, the density of Mexico City increased from 16,225 per square kilometre in 1950 to 21,074 by 1970.[8] Over time, the density gradients for the Latin American cities have declined; but, interestingly, in both Latin America and North America, smaller cities had steeper density gradients.[9]

One aspect of this process has been the decentralization of employment growth away from downtown central cores and towards peripheral centres of metropolitan areas.[10] This pattern has been identified in cities in all regions, from Shanghai, where one third of its workers were rural in 1991, to Johannesburg, where manufacturing decentralized out of the city centre.[11] By the late 1990s, central business districts in

Rapid growth of city peripheries has been evident from the 1970s

cities in developing countries had only between 10 and 20 per cent of all metropolitan employment.[12] As manufacturing jobs move out of the centre, they are replaced by service-sector jobs.[13] This process has taken on what is called a 'polycentric form', with a number of employment centres being created on the periphery of growing cities.[14] What were initially called 'bedroom communities' during the 1950s have gradually been transformed into what have been called 'edge cities' (see Chapter 7).[15] These cities frequently clustered sets of vertically integrated industries, with both blue- and white-collar jobs. In the US, the examples of Tysons Corner in suburban northern Virginia and Walnut Creek, California, to the east of San Francisco and Oakland illustrated how economic activity clustered around transportation nodes. In analytic terms, what were called 'monocentric cities' have evolved into 'polycentric cities'.[16] The latter pattern has the following major characteristics:

- Sub-centres are prominent in both new and old cities.
- The number of sub-centres and their boundaries are quite sensitive to definition.
- Sub-centres are sometimes arrayed in corridors.
- Employment centres help to explain surrounding employment and population.
- Sub-centres have not eliminated the importance of the main centre.
- Most jobs are located outside centres.
- Commuting is not well explained by standard urban models, either monocentric or polycentric.[17]

This latter point is particularly important due to its major impact on infrastructure and mobility patterns. In the US, commuting studies show that centralization of employment increases commuting; but in Bogotá, Colombia, average distances to work remained relatively constant, even though population had grown by 40 per cent, because of the decentralization of employment.[18] The role of transportation, therefore, remains very important in predicting land-use patterns. Lower density cities also appear to have higher dependence on private cars. Interestingly, efforts to reduce transport by planning communities to have residential and employment areas have not proved to be particularly successful, as jobs are frequently found outside the planned community.[19] A summary of these studies concluded that development patterns in cities in both developing and industrial countries with market-based economies had similar patterns of decentralization of people and jobs.[20]

However, when globalization is added to the mix, these new polycentric cities are increasingly shaped and 'sized' by their relationship to exogenous economic activity – that is, by their connectivity with globalized firms, as suggested in Chapter 1. Not all firms, however, compete at the global level; many continue to compete in the local and regional markets in which they exist. The differences between these two kinds of firms are captured in a debate about the characteristics of competitiveness and how this evolves over time. Earlier notions of industrial clustering have given way to the understanding that there are more dynamic changes going on that constantly position and reposition firms in relation to global and local markets.[21]

The social morphology dimension[22]

A second dimension of the process of metropolitan growth has been the changing social morphology of cities. Recent analyses of the social dimension of metropolitanization have identified four types of population that are associated with different generations of cities and metropolises, as well as with specific forms of mobility:[23]

1 *inhabitants*, who dominated the *traditional, pre-industrial city*;
2 *commuters*, who are associated with the emergence of the *first-generation metropolis*;
3 *city users*, associated with the *second-generation metropolis*; and
4 *metropolitan business people*, who are closely associated with the *third-generation metropolis* and with globalization.

THE TRADITIONAL CITY: CITY INHABITANTS AS CITY WORKERS   The traditional city was one and the same with its inhabitants. Since the very beginning of urbanization, city dwellers understood themselves as being in a distinctive situation, as opposed to the rest of the world. This difference carries over to the language associated with urban living, with terms such as 'urbane', 'civic' and 'civilization' used to distinguish urban from rural attributes.

The social morphology of the traditional city largely depended upon the division of labour in the community. During pre-industrial times, this rested on corporations, guilds or *stände*, which defined the local social structure, often with visible distinctions through dress prescriptions and rituals. Despite the existence of impoverished neighbourhoods, the pre-industrial town was not particularly segregated. The Industrial Revolution introduced important changes in the social and physical structure of traditional cities. A new social institution, the factory, became the strategic ordering factor of the shape of urban space and of its social morphology, as well. Factories were increasingly large, noisy, polluting and tended to cluster in special areas of the city, often in the periphery – although this has always been a relative and temporary zone, in view of the progressive expansion of industrial cities such as Paris, London and Milan.

THE FIRST-GENERATION METROPOLIS: SUBURBAN COMMUTERS

While one *enters* the traditional city, in the first-generation metropolis one can only *arrive*. The latter is an entity with no precise borders and is characterized by a strong diffusion and heterogeneity of settlements, as well as by a maze of transportation infrastructures. The social morphology of the first-generation metropolis is largely determined by the territorial division of labour between its functional components, *core* and *fringes*. First-generation metropolises tend towards social segregation, with populations different in income and ethnic traits clustering in different geographical parts of the city. The specific patterns of this territorial differentiation, however, vary according to different historical conditions.

In all cases, nevertheless, it is the availability of mass transportation, both public and private, that produced the first-generation metropolis and led to the creation of a new population beside that of the inhabitants – namely, the 'commuter population' – common by the middle of the 20th century. Commuting was made possible by the enormous diffusion of transportation, particularly the private car, but, more generally, mass transportation systems. Contrary to what is usually thought, information technology also had its impact. The ready availability, especially in the large North American conurbations, of intra-office communication via telephone and, up to a point, air mail, favoured the concentration of productive and administrative functions in large establishments in central locations.[24]

This pattern developed in many major cities of the world: from New York (with its subway), to London (with its tube), to Paris (with its metro), as well as in Moscow, Tokyo, Mexico City, Johannesburg and São Paulo. The daily exchange of flows between the central business district (CBD) and the fringes of the metropolitan area became the major daily urban dynamic that shaped the cityscape and determined the enormous amounts of resources invested in mobility infrastructures. Lifestyles regulated by daily and weekly time frames became the prevailing mass pattern.

SECOND- AND THIRD-GENERATION METROPOLIS: CITY USERS AND METROPOLITAN BUSINESS PEOPLE

The increased mobility of individuals, combined with higher income levels and greater leisure time, particularly in the second half of the 20th century, allowed the differentiation of a third population: *city users*. This population is composed of individuals going to a city primarily to use its private and public services, such as shopping, movies, museums, restaurants, health and educational services. This is a swelling population that is radically affecting the structure of cities and that actually uses localities in a rather uncontrolled way.

But the population of city users is not limited to leisure or shopping. The city provides other services that can be used, such as those connected with mass education or health. The type of metropolis that is growing out of the heightened gravitation of city users is the one most common today and has been defined as the *second-generation metropolis* or *mature metropolis*.

Yet a fourth metropolitan population is forming. This is the very specialized population of *metropolitan business people*: people who go to central cities to do business and establish professional contacts, or business people and professionals who visit their customers, conventioneers, consultants and international managers. This fourth population is relatively small but growing. It is characterized by having access to considerable private and corporate money. It is a population of 'expert urbanites' who tend to know their way around and who are very selective in terms of shopping and hotel and restaurant use, as well as in the use of high-end cultural amenities, such as concerts, exhibitions and museums, but also sauna and gym facilities.

This fourth population increasingly constitutes a transnational middle class living not in *a city*, but rather *in cities* or *between cities*. This affects the morphology and functions of all large cities well beyond the group's numerical weight. This still emerging metropolis has been called the *third-generation* (or *late*) *metropolis*.

During the 1980s, with the diffusion of a new mass-produced machine in the home (the PC hit *Time Magazine* cover in 1983), it was generally assumed that the pressure for physical transportation, particularly the home-to-work journey, would abate to the point of rendering the concentration of activities in dense areas called cities obsolete. Early prophecies of the disappearance of cities were frequent, not only in the popular press, but also in theoretical studies in which concepts of 'de-urbanization' were leading.[25] It turned out that far from reducing the need for physical movement, information computer technology (ICT) was, in a sense, actually boosting it. ICT and transportation have actually tended to dilate the urban edges to a point at which the edges themselves acquire new forms of centrality.[26]

Today, there are cities that have very small populations of *inhabitants*, slightly larger populations of *commuters*, but vast populations of *users*. Venice is a typical case. It has a *resident* population (which is shrinking) of about 70,000, has a working population composed almost entirely of *commuters*, and on certain days has a population of visitors (*city users*) as large as its resident population. The density of people becomes so high that Venice probably is the only city in the world that has pedestrian traffic lights. Venice is an extreme case; but many other cities of the world, and not only the so-called 'cities of art', experience this phenomenon.

Cities such as Singapore have more visitors than inhabitants and are entirely geared to consumption.[27] They are not different in many ways from New York, London or Milan (where, for example, about 300,000 Japanese visit the Last Supper as well as the fashion 'golden triangle' every year). Cities such as Panama City or Bangkok, also attract large populations of shoppers, and the number of such cities is rapidly growing. Nor is the list limited to cities with only mercantile attractions. In 2000, the Jubilee in Rome attracted millions, while Mecca, Varanasi, Santiago de Compostela and many others are the destinations of pilgrims, giving rise to the important business area of 'religious tourism'.

The emergence of the third-generation metropolis has important implications for urban democratic representation and participation. The presence of mobile populations in the new metropolis is part of the periodical crises that affect local governments the world over. This specific aspect of the crisis refers to a *de facto* political disenfranchising of local voters. In other words, local representatives are elected by inhabitants, but increasingly have to respond to transient populations because the urban economy depends to a greater extent on the spending of external populations. But there is a larger implication. For centuries in Western culture, the link between democratic practices and the physical place in which public debate occurred has been taken for granted: '*la piazza e' il cuore della citta*', in the words of an Italian analyst.[28] Today this condition is disappearing in many places. Urban politics seems to be getting more rather than less complex. The striking example of a mass protest movement, stretching from Seattle, to Pôrto Alegre and to Mumbai, almost exclusively created through online contacts, provides evidence that the globalization process widens the reach of power players; but it also offers opportunities for the coalescence of social movements.[29]

The emergence of the third-generation metropolis also has significant implications for metropolitan finance systems. The central issue in handling the metropolitan finance system is the question 'who pays what for what?' In the presence of a relatively stable population, it was easier to impute the weight of collective goods and services used by the community, although it goes without saying that debate on the sharing of this burden has always been common. Today, however, with a metropolitan system composed of various 'nomadic' populations, there are compounded difficulties. More recently, the main issue hinges around some kind of 'commuter taxes', such as those imposed in London, Singapore and New York. The final impact of these provisions is not yet clear. However, it can be safely said that the presence of transient populations is a new phenomenon and that the public finance sciences have not yet adapted their conceptual apparatus to this new situation.

The institutional dimension

A third dimension of the process of metropolitan growth has been the growing numbers of administrative institutions and jurisdictions with responsibilities for various functions of metropolitan governance. A well-known study of New York during the 1950s showed that its metropolitan area had 1400 local government bodies.[30] These institutions fall into several categories:

- municipalities;
- special functional districts for specific services, such as solid waste collection;
- sectoral authorities, such as for transport or water supply;
- metropolitan planning authorities;
- metropolitan government, with overarching authority for multiple municipalities;
- state or provincial government units with responsibilities that frequently overlap those of the institutions listed above.

The appearance of new municipalities in expanding cities is not surprising. As new land is urbanized, new units of local government are added to meet various community needs, whether in infrastructure, security, education or health services. Because most of these communities are poor, it is also not surprising that these new municipalities are expected to provide services; but they lack the revenue base to do so effectively. They frequently enter into relationships with neighbouring municipalities to provide such services, particularly those that are the most costly, such as health. While the new municipalities are results of citizen and community needs, their representative and political functions are not typically as important as their service roles at the outset. Thousands of municipalities have been created over the last several decades.

A similar process has occurred with the establishment of special functional districts for the provision of specific services, such as solid waste management or water supply. The various steps in the management of waste, for example, from collection to transfer to disposal, necessarily cover a large spatial area. Waste from the central city is normally transferred to peripheral disposal sites or landfills. It is not unusual for the co-operative agreements covering and managing these arrangements to exist between municipalities at a level above the municipal but below the metropolitan level.

At the next level are sectoral authorities responsible for managing and providing a service for all units within the metropolitan area. These often include water supply – for example, the Metropolitan Manila Water Supply and Sewerage Authority, or the Metropolitan Water Authority in Bangkok. These authorities have responsibility for managing the services, including protection of the natural resource, investment, service provision, operations and maintenance, and financial management. While these metropolitan institutions frequently conflict with local municipalities, their functions are relatively clear and they provide the important opportunity of rationalizing the management of critical services.

One of the most popular institutional innovations during the 1960s and 1970s in Asia was the establishment of many metropolitan planning and development authorities. Cities such as Bombay, Calcutta, Delhi, Karachi, Madras and Manila all created powerful planning agencies that soon added development functions.[31] Agencies such as the Calcutta Metropolitan Development Authority (CMDA) took on metropolitan-wide responsibilities for planning, investment, programme and project design, and implementation. They received financial and technical support from the World Bank and other multilateral agencies and became the primary guides of metropolitan development in their cities. While effective, these development authorities frequently found themselves in conflict with state and provincial authorities, as well as with the more numerous local units: the municipalities. They also ran into difficulties when they planned sectoral investments and policy, such as transport in Bombay, where other jurisdictions responsible for implementing those policies and programmes on a daily basis sought to retain their responsibilities and power.

In addition to the specialized metropolitan institutions described above, other cities adopted metropolitan government as a whole. Following the model of Paris, some Francophone African cities such as Abidjan and Dakar established metropolitan governments that had overarching responsibility over a number of municipalities. As shown in Box 3.3, each of the municipalities had elected mayors and city councils, as well as varying levels of technical capacity and resources; but the responsibility for managing and coordinating the municipalities as a group remained at the metropolitan level.

This pattern has taken on a special form in Santa Cruz, Bolivia, where a metropolitan directorate oversees policy, but a 'commonwealth' or 'mancommunidad' is technically responsible for coordination among municipalities, execution of projects and operations. It is supported by technical teams in various areas of infrastructure and public service.[32]

As urban populations grow and the occupied areas of cities spread into state and provincial territories, it should not be surprising that urban jurisdictions should also find themselves overlapping state and provincial government jurisdictions. This happens in cities such as Buenos Aires or Rio de Janeiro, where the states, with the same names, have direct operational responsibilities for providing security, infrastructure, environmental management, education and other services to populations living just outside municipal borders. In some cases, the municipalities on the periphery of these cities depend upon the states for financial transfers and legal supervision of their operations. The public services provided in metropolitan Buenos Aires legally depend upon the provincial government in La Plata.

City centres are losing some power to new peripheral local authorities

THE POWER AND THE HEARTBEAT OF WEST AFRICA'S BIGGEST URBAN JUNGLE

Paul Okunlola

In a region where unprecedented urbanization rates have brazenly outstripped the global average, Nigeria's former capital, Lagos, remains an enigma to both visitors and those charged with the management of Africa's most populous city.

Misunderstood by many but passionately loved by its citizens, Lagos has always been the subject of extreme emotions. Some call it 'an urban jungle', others see it as an explosive place that is losing the battle to catch up with itself. But hate it or love it, stay or leave it, Lagos is the engine room driving national and regional growth, a place to which more migrants flock than any other city in the entire sub-region.

Sitting on 3577 square kilometres of coastal plain along Nigeria's southwestern Atlantic seaboard, the settlement has always possessed a peculiar appeal, even from the time when it became a British colony in 1861. Over the years, it became Nigeria's earliest central business district (CBD), spreading from the Marina-Broad Street (Ehingbeti) district, taking in Lagos Harbour, the European Piers, the financial market, the seat of colonial government, and the location of major local and foreign conglomerates and transnational corporations.

One-and-a-half centuries later, although Lagos remains the smallest of Nigeria's 36 regional administrative states, it is, at the same time, the most populous. Covering barely 5 per cent of the country's land area, the state has always been home to between 5 and 8 per cent of the total population. The metropolitan area, home to more than 75 per cent of the state's population, also accounts for more than one third (36.8 per cent) of Nigeria's urban residents.

But well beyond its demographic characteristics, Lagos has remained the country's economic powerhouse, accounting for some 65 per cent of Nigeria's industrial infrastructure and contributing more than half of national economic development.

While urbanization in sub-Saharan Africa has generally occurred without a commensurate industrial and economic growth, the dominant role of Lagos as the heartbeat of both the Nigerian and regional economy has established its position as the destination of choice for most job seekers, migrants and itinerant traders. With a population growth rate put at between 6 to 8 per cent yearly, Lagos's population is believed to be growing ten times faster than New York or Los Angeles, and today it is more populous than 32 African countries.

From a 5 square kilometre patch inhabited by barely 50,000 people in 1910, researchers say that, by the year 2000, Lagos had grown in both spatial and population terms by a factor of up to 100, and now accommodates up to 2600 loosely defined settlements. Other estimates indicate that even the pre-independence population density of Metropolitan Lagos was up to 45 per cent less than what it is today, while over the last 25 years alone, the metropolitan area has at least tripled in spread and in the density of active, fully built-up neighbourhoods.

Although much of this growth has occurred on its northern axis towards Ibadan and Abeokuta and on the western axis along the Badagry Expressway, the easterly Lagos-Epe axis has recently recorded almost unprecedented development activity, fuelled by a fresh investment boom for upper-middle and higher-income housing projects and communities. The Lekki corridor, a spin-off from the highbrow Victoria Island, is already estimated to be growing at up to 16.6 per cent yearly.

A city best known for the survival instincts of it residents, floundering economic fortunes over the years have left the central role of Lagos in the national socio-economic landscape untouched. Consequently, by 1980, when city administrators were designing a development plan that would be valid until the year 2000, the yearly growth rate was already estimated at about 300,000 people, or 34 additional people every hour. Although the last national head count in 1991 put the population of Lagos at 5.7 million, the city has continued to swell rapidly, rising to 13.4 million people in 2000.

By 2002, when Lagos became one of sub-Saharan Africa's first mega-urban regions as it crossed the 10 million population mark, yearly growth had doubled over 1980 estimates to 600,000 additional persons each year, or 1644 people daily.

Today, with the current population estimated at about 15 million residents, spread as densely as between 3746.2 to 20,000 persons per square kilometre depending upon the district, Metropolitan Lagos perches on the verge of what officials have termed 'a grave urban crisis'.

The basis for concern is visibly etched on the city's streets. Unsightly heaps of waste are testimony to the logistical nightmare of clearing over 10,000 tonnes of refuse generated daily in an urban area that enjoys only 40 per cent sanitation coverage. Endless traffic snarls expose the challenge of managing a vehicular density of 222 automobiles per kilometre against the national average of only 11 per kilometre.

To most residents, the consequences of a 40 per cent access rate to potable water are particularly critical. The most prevalent diseases – malaria and diarrhoea – could be curbed by better sanitation. Also lurking in the background, an HIV/AIDS prevalence rate of 6.6 per cent, higher than the national average of 5.4 per cent, portends a looming danger to Lagos residents.

Daily, city managers confront the challenge of slashing maternal and infant mortality rates estimated at 8 per 1000 and 84.6 per 1000, respectively. The infant mortality rate, though lower than the national average of 107 per 1000, remains higher than that for any other region in the world, and considerably exceeds the global average of 57 per 1000.

In the schools, administrators are compelled to cope with the challenge of an average pupil-to-teacher ratio of 150:1, which falls far short of both the government target of 50:1 and the United Nations Educational, Scientific and Cultural Organization (UNESCO) target of 25:1.

Despite its relatively more buoyant economy, and although Lagos boasts of more than 10,000 commercial concerns with over 250 financial institutions and some 29 industrial estates, one major challenge is how to precipitate the creation of some 250,000 new jobs each year over the next five years. This, according to experts, must also happen at a sustained economic growth rate of at least 12 per cent yearly if the state is to halt and reverse prevailing poverty levels which show that today, two out of every three Lagos residents are officially classified as living beneath the poverty line.

For the politicians, administrators and community leaders who have to manage this complex, heaving mass of urban humanity, therefore, the quantum of decaying infrastructure, widespread urban poverty, massive unemployment, pervasive security inadequacies, emerging slums, and, overwhelming, environmental decay have become the major characteristics that progressively define the city's fortunes. These, the authorities say, have become an even more critical challenge of urban governance. Estimates project that by 2015, Lagos would become the third largest city on Earth with up to 24.3 million residents.

'There is a remarkably intense network of urban rumours about Lagos, about the dangers it represents. They begin at the airport, continue along the highway, the bridges, the buses, into every neighbourhood', said the Dutch architect Rem Koolhaus in a 2001 lecture after a six-year study of the city.

Culturally, Lagos has always been well known for its unique cosmopolitan tendency, ever since its emergence as seat of the British colonial administration for the amalgamated union of Nigeria's Northern and Southern Protectorates in 1914.

Lagos became the regional administrative centre for the colonial administration in 1914. By 1967, seven years after the nation's independence, Lagos assumed the additional status of a regional administrative centre when it was carved out as one of the then 12 states in the federation. Coming at a time when the country was moving from a predominantly agriculture-based economy into one that derived its revenue essentially from crude oil,

Lagos easily became the destination of choice for the emerging generation of school leavers and unemployed. Many migrants also came from the West African coast, particularly Ghana, and from across Nigeria's northern borders with Niger and Chad.

Some experts have noted that from available data, the population of Lagos doubled twice within two decades: first between 1965 and 1975, and again between 1975 and 1985. However, the numerous layers of culturally diverse ethnic templates have on no fewer than three occasions during the past five years formed a deadly mix with the high population densities to precipitate severe inter-racial conflicts that have resulted in significant loss of lives. A police–citizens ratio of 1:1000 against the United Nations recommended target of 1:100 has not helped the situation.

Administratively, as with most mega-urban regions in sub-Saharan Africa, Lagos is run by a multiplicity of administrative units or local government areas, each headed by an independent council under the overall coordination of a state governor.

Traditionally made up of five divisions – Lagos, Ikeja, Ikorodu, Epe and Badagry – the state structure comprised 20 local council areas, of which 17 were located within the metropolitan area. In 2002 it was further subdivided into 57 local council areas. This implies that, technically, although the federal constitution makes provision for one state governor, there could be as many different political programmes in operation for the 57 council areas as there are political parties elected into office.

However, the state government, going by constitutional provisions, retains the responsibility for providing oversight functions for running the state. The mobilization of revenue to meet the huge shortfalls in service provision is one hurdle that city administrators are yet to scale. The situation is further compounded by the influx of

refugees from war-ravaged neighbouring West African countries and persons displaced locally from regions of ethnic strife. These hordes of daily migrants consist largely of young school leavers, unemployed artisans and graduates. To survive, therefore, the safety net for most has become the informal economy, which already accounts for up to 70 per cent of all productive activity in the state.

But the drawback is that much of the resources required to finance infrastructure provision, housing and other social services are shut outside the formal economy, resulting in significant shortfalls in tax revenue. In Lagos state, for instance, barely one third of anticipated internally generated revenue for the year 2000 was realized, although improved collection mechanisms may have been responsible for an increase in the proportion to just over half by 2001.

Hence, while Johannesburg, for instance, South Africa's largest city, has only one sixth (2.5 million) of the population of Lagos (15 million), it operates a yearly budget of US$1.2 billion, which is four times that of US$300 million for Lagos.

'Lagos seemed to be a city of burning edges. Hills, entire roads were paralleled with burning embankments. At first sight, the city had an aura of apocalyptic violence; entire sections of it seemed to be smouldering, as if it were one gigantic rubbish dump', said architect Rem Koolhaus:

> What was stunning, and only visible from above the city, was that those processes were taking place at scales that were almost unimaginable in any other city. What seemed, on ground level, an accumulation of dysfunctional movements, seemed from above an impressive performance, evidence of how well Lagos might perform if it were the third largest city in the world.

PAUL OKUNLOLA IS AN ASSISTANT EDITOR WITH THE NIGERIAN NEWSPAPER THE GUARDIAN.

The economic dimension

Projections of future metropolitan growth are supported by data on urban industrial structure and on the importance of the proximity of labour, capital and technology in generating jobs and incomes. Within the past decade, export facilities for globalized production and trade have also become important perceived factors in metropolitan concentrations (see Chapter 1). These processes have resulted in new forms of production as well, such as increasing shares of 'delocalized output', with individual localities providing specific intermediate products and value-added which contribute to larger products that assemble inputs from diverse locations.

These changing patterns of production also affect the creation of new jobs on the peripheries of cities, usually close to transportation connections and corridors. Patterns of job creation involving downtown incubators and subsequent suburban investment found in Colombia and Korea during the 1980s, have shifted towards the periphery of metropolitan areas, where lower land costs, better infrastructure and associated industries in close proximity all contribute to agglomeration economies and the new locus for job creation.

These economic dimensions are also shaped by changing demographic dynamics of urban growth, particularly increased female education and female labour force participation. The latter has provided a relatively lower cost of labour for many new industries. All of these forces contribute to increasing urban concentrations with startling shares of total population and total urban population living and working in metropolitan areas. In the US, 80 per cent of the population lives in metropolitan areas. In Northern America, Latin America and Eastern Asia, for instance, more than 40 per cent of the urban population (50.1, 44.6 and 43.3 per cent, respectively, in 2000) lives in cities with over 1 million persons.[33]

Twentieth-century trends: managing differences and externalities at different scales

The institutional complexity of metropolitan areas described above has largely resulted from the growth of population and urbanized areas. These various institutions are responses to specific kinds of needs and citizen demands. They are intended to manage externalities such as environmental pollution from high population densities or to coordinate the provision of services such as transport. These services, as illustrated in Boxes 3.1–3.3, are necessary and important.

But these institutional forms are also ill suited to addressing the complexity of metropolitan processes that are going on in these cities. A 1997 study of the Chicago metropolitan area identified processes that can also be found in cities in all regions of the world, whether in rich or poor countries.[34] These include fragmentation, differentiation, growing inequalities, poverty concentrations, decentralization, polarization and 'spatial mismatch', where problems are found in jurisdictions lacking the resources to solve them.

Fragmentation

The process of fragmentation of metropolitan areas is driven by economic and social processes; but, historically, its first indicator has been institutional. When communities and their local government units no longer perceive that their 'natural' links are with the metropolitan core, the process of fragmentation begins. Jurisdictional affinities become closer to non-central institutional units, to provinces or neighbouring units of different sizes. These institutional leanings reflect economic and social realities. During the late 1980s, this process was described in Brazil as 'de-metropolitanization'. Examples included the communities on the periphery of Rio de Janeiro and along the transport corridor towards São Paulo; they no longer looked to downtown Rio de Janeiro but, rather, were more concerned with how their infrastructural lifeblood would be managed and how growing traffic and trade in the direction of São Paulo would influence local production, municipal services and incomes. The Rio de Janeiro metropolitan area was literally breaking down, on its periphery. Similar examples occurred in São Paulo, as its economic hinterland in São Paulo State became much more important than activities located on the downtown Avenida del Paulista.

This process is well underway in Buenos Aires, with a population of 12 million, of which only 3.5 million individuals live in the *Capital Federal*. The remaining 75 per cent live in municipalities that depend upon the province of Buenos Aires under the control of a governor who frequently has different political affiliations from that of the mayor of Buenos Aires. If the downtown holds the valued patrimony of the past, the province is clearly the locus of the future, its aspirations, technology and investment. This is similar to Chicago, Los Angeles or Manila.

As noted in Chapter 1, this process is compounded by globalization, where the markets for goods and services are beyond the city and even the metropolitan boundaries. For some enterprises, the most important location in the city is the port or the airport. These locational shifts reflect economic realities and are evident in the extraordinary growth of factories, depots, offices and hotel facilities near transport nodes.

Differentiation, inequalities and polarization

A second process is differentiation within metropolitan areas. Commonly held public perceptions of the great differences in income between neighbourhoods, *barrios*, *quartiers* and other areas in cities such as Abidjan, Nairobi, Karachi or Caracas can now be supported by rigorous studies on the distribution of infrastructure investment, social services, poor households, youth violence and other indicators.[35] Studies in Abidjan, for example, show enormous differences between the well-endowed neighbourhoods of Cocody and Deux-Plateaux with the growing areas of Abobo-Gare. These kinds of differences are found in Paris and New York, as well as in Hong Kong and Jakarta.

Pockets of wealth and poverty within metropolitan areas reflect the consolidation of economic and social power and its translation into political power, as well. These patterns are thus also spatial. Shortages of basic infrastructure such as water supply, electricity, sanitation, transport and housing impose heavy private costs on urban households at the periphery of metropolitan areas. A study in Ciudad Juarez, a busy and growing city on the Mexican–US border, found that households living on 'the poor side of town' spent 29 per cent of their income on transport to work. A study in Davao, the Philippines suggested a 'concentric theory of income distribution', with the richer households living in the centre, often with the difference between rich and poor being the opportunity for a secondary wage earner in the household to take advantage of central locations. Residential location is a powerful predictor of socio-economic status and future earning potential.

Over time, these patterns have become cumulative inequalities. The costs of metropolitan life determine levels of welfare, as well as social mobility. For growing numbers of the urban poor, the city no longer promises a better life for one's children. Rather, in the absence of skills and health, a low-wage future is the only alternative. Worse still are growing numbers of children washing car windscreens at city traffic lights. Programmes to provide only basic education and skills rather than high-quality training for the poor contribute, in some sense, to the problem: in order to compete, young people must have skills that can add quality to the production of goods and services. Yet, providing such quality services is prohibitively expensive in most cities. Only where strong family and community incentives exist, as in some Asian cultures, can these opportunities become vehicles for upward social mobility.

If the studies of Chicago show the predominance of poverty on the city's south and west sides, they also reveal growing numbers of poor households in other parts of the city as well, including in the previously white suburbs. While this poverty is not as evident as in the *bustees* of Calcutta, these areas are, nevertheless, concentrations of poverty in Chicago, just as such concentrations are found in London, Berlin or Istanbul. They are reinforced by poor schools and

transport services. They are compounded by social disorganization, crime, declining property values and closing down of business. Evidence from Los Angeles shows that most banks have moved out of poorer districts of the city, leaving only automatic teller machines for populations unable to have access to such facilities. In 1998, the US government estimated that 300,000 monthly welfare checks in Los Angeles were sent to commercial addresses where poor households pick them up; their residential addresses are neither secure nor permanent.

It is not surprising that these spatial and institutional patterns generate social polarization between rich and poor, between long-time residents and recent arrivals, and between racial and ethnic groups. Social behaviour mirrors perceived material interests. They exist not only in developing countries – for example, between Malays and Chinese in Malaysia – but also in New York between African-Americans and Koreans. Growing differences and competition that are reflected in residential location, social mobility and quality of life all tend to increase segregation. This segregation is manifest in the quality of schools, concentrations of poor children, crime and unemployment, and in fundamentally different land-use patterns.[36]

A 1998 study of 100 cities in the US provides some of the first rigorous econometric analysis of this process.[37] It shows that shocks to labour markets in specific cities are reflected in individual and aggregated social behaviours, such as the rates of crime, school dropouts and female-headed households that, in turn, magnify the initial shock. This affects the metropolitan opportunity structure because these elements are mutually interactive. Labour and housing markets respond to changes in crime, drop-outs and incidence of female-headed households. Differences, therefore, are heightened over time. This supports the 1998 findings of a study that, historically in Latin American countries, macro-economic growth has had a disproportionately strong impact on urban poverty, with poverty increasing during periods of recession and being slower to decrease when growth resumes.[38]

Spatial mismatch

Finally, it is also clear that there is a 'spatial mismatch' between the problems cited above and the availability of resources and capacity to deal with them. Richer, more advantaged districts, usually in the suburbs of some developed country cities, tend to have financial resources and technical capacity to address these problems, while inner-city areas do not. This mismatch is serious because each jurisdiction tends to jealously guard their own resources and capacities to

Affluence and poverty juxtaposed

address their own problems, ignoring the fact that problems of neighbouring jurisdictions 'spill over' their boundaries and quickly become their problems as well. These externalities are the essence of metropolitan life; but metropolitan and municipal institutions are not well suited to deal with them.

Together, these processes illustrate the complexity of metropolitan change. While some processes are the consequences of the evolution of policy and institutions, others are largely socio-economic and exist outside the realm of public municipal responsibility. Together, they reinforce the phrase by which Los Angeles describes itself: 'a world of differences'.

Several conclusions emerge from this analysis, which summarize the status of metropolitanization until the year 2000:

- First, some aspects of metropolitan diversity that contribute to the economic and cultural vitality of cities can also undermine social cohesion, economic productivity and, eventually, social mobility and opportunity. Differences can easily become barriers.
- Second, there is a growing tension between the promise of metropolitan growth in economic terms, both at the urban and national levels, and the growing economic and social differences between individuals, households and communities.[39]
- Third, short-term economic differences are becoming structural as they are reflected in patterns of residential investment and neighbourhood quality of life. Spatial and physical differences deepen social and economic differences and inequalities, and thus increase polarization.
- Fourth, these structural differences are reflected in radically different perceptions of politics and social justice across neighbourhoods.
- Fifth, it is not surprising that inward-looking behaviours are occurring at all income levels, with one indicator being the spectacular rise of gated communities in many countries.
- Finally, these impacts have not received the policy and institutional attention they require if the 'metropolitan expectations' described earlier are to be achieved.[40]

Metropolitan development in an age of globalization

While the processes described above are present to varying degrees in cities in both developed and developing countries, they are what might be described as consequences of earlier evolving forces and patterns. And yet, as the 21st century begins, it is also apparent that these processes have taken on new forms and dynamics as global forces become embedded in local spaces and socio-economic realities. They therefore require new modes of analysis and understanding.

This phenomenon is well illustrated in the case of New York. Before 11 September 2001, New York's economy had grown to generate almost US$360 billion a year. This gross domestic product (GDP) made New York the ninth largest 'economy' in the world. Its population, at close to 17 million, had already made the metropolitan area the 49th largest 'country' in demographic terms.[41] The New York economy had exemplified the process of de-industrialization experienced by many cities in both developed and developing countries: manufacturing jobs had left the city, replaced by an increasing proportion of employment in the service sector. Unlike most cities, however, the position of Wall Street and the financial sector had completely dominated the economy of New York. While this is a matter of degree when compared to other cities, in New York, 66 per cent of municipal revenue came from taxes on the financial sector.[42] The economic downturn starting in 2001 was accelerated by the loss of US$110 billion to the metropolitan economy as a result of 11 September.[43]

But the most significant aspect of this transformation is demographic. It is now apparent that about 300,000 people leave the five boroughs each year for other destinations. Most are white families, fleeing the high cost of living in New York, moving either to the suburbs or to other cities in the US. However, they are replaced by 200,000 immigrants each year, with major flows coming from the Dominican Republic and China. According to a very recent analysis, projections for New York City's population show that the city is becoming increasingly Hispanic and South Asian, with large numbers of immigrants from India, Pakistan and, more recently, Bangladesh (see Chapter 4 for more detail).[44] This analysis shows, moreover, that the pattern is replicated in the first ring of counties adjacent to New York City, in New Jersey and New York states. Communities on the metropolitan periphery have become as ethnically mixed as New York City, reflected not just in national origins, but in the myriad restaurants, businesses, cultural facilities and schools. The comment 'No one speaks English in Brooklyn' now also applies to some of the communities in New Jersey. While this is certainly an exaggeration, it captures the intensity of the international ethnic mix in the metropolitan area.

How then can these phenomena be understood? A helpful typology of recent metropolitan studies suggests the following six perspectives:[45]

1   **The restructured metropolitan economy**: Urban economies have undergone significant industrial restructuring during the last four decades, losing manufacturing jobs and gaining in new service functions. This process has changed spatial patterns, leading to clustered employment opportunities on the peripheries of metropolitan areas, while also increasing income disparities within and between industries.
2   **The globalization of city space**: Globalization has contributed to industrial restructuring by offering opportunities for footloose industries to leave cities altogether. But it has also increased the connections and linkages between economic production, consumption and investment across and between cities and countries. As a result, metropolitan areas are part of new geographies of power.

Metropolitan development in an age of globalization has many new meanings

3   **The restructuring of urban form**: Metropolitan areas have expanded to outer cities, edge cities and peripheral settlements, changing the economic and social character of central areas.
4   **The appearance of the fractal city**: Patterns of economic and social differences, identities and inequality are replicated in many communities who make up the metropolitan area.
5   **Violence and conflict in metropolitan space**: These differences and changing patterns of dislocation and relative inequality have led to growing crime and violence, which is managed through increasing numbers of urban jails, gated communities and other efforts to provide security in insecure metropolitan environments (see Chapter 6).
6   **Sim cities and the urban imagination**: These changes have provoked intensive discussion about the impact of technology on metropolitan form and social behaviour, captured in computer simulations and games.

Together, the six perspectives provide new descriptive and analytic lenses through which to observe the metropolitan phenomena of the 21st century. What the perspectives do not provide, however, are the normative answers in policy terms. Each has implications for economic or social policies; but these have not yet been elaborated in systematic terms. Interestingly, however, many provoke a discussion of the role of public space.

All of these descriptive and analytic debates about the form and functions of metropolitan economies lead to the question of whether the metropolis is coming together or breaking apart. It is difficult to describe the whole, because the parts themselves are in motion. They are restructuring and reconstituting themselves, with new economic activities, different kinds of people and new forms of cultural expression. It is not surprising that public institutions lag behind and are not able to evolve as quickly; but it is clear that they face important challenges of representation, legitimacy and efficacy as they seek to guide, if not actually manage, increasing levels of 'metropolitan complex-city'.

Trends in developing countries[46]

Asia and the Pacific

Demographic and urban transformations are tremendous in Asia. Asia now holds 61 per cent of the global population and its share of the global urban population has risen from 9 per cent in 1920 to 48 per cent in 2000 and is expected to rise to 53 per cent by 2030.[47] The latter is more than double the projected 2030 urban population of the entire Western world. Currently, Asia holds more than half of the world's cities with more than 10 million people, and that number is rapidly rising.[48] However, national trends and figures vary considerably, given the many diverse countries, ranging from rich to poor and from large to small.[49]

Nevertheless, the growth of Asian cities is astounding, with many doubling their population every 15 to 20 years. Dhaka, for instance, from a mere 417,000 inhabitants in 1950, is currently the world's ninth largest urban agglomeration, with 12.5 million inhabitants. Within a decade, it will grow to become the world's second largest metropolis, with 22.8 million people.[50] Many Asian urban systems show comparable growth and, by 2015, Asian developing countries will hold three of the world's five largest urban agglomerations: Mumbai, Dhaka and Delhi. The urban *systems* emerging from recent Asia-Pacific hyper-urbanization can contain more than 100 million people.

Asia is now about halfway through its urban transition. As the combined outcome of demographic growth, global economic reorganization and changes in state–society–capital relations, parts of Asia-Pacific are experiencing hyper-urbanization never before seen in world history.[51] Whereas London took 130 years to grow from 1 to 8 million,[52] Bangkok took 45 years, Dhaka 37 years and Seoul only 25 years.[53] Recent Asian urbanization is occurring mostly *outside* formal urban boundaries. A distinguishing contemporary urban feature, particularly in Asia-Pacific, is urbanization far *beyond* metropolitan borders and the

formation of enormously extended urban–regional configurations that develop along infrastructure corridors, radiating over long distances from core cities. As an outcome of global economic reorganization, mega-urban regions (MURs) have multiplied in Asia and growth projections indicate that, during the 21st century, Asian MURs may contain 10 to 30 million people each, with some even comprising more than 100 million inhabitants.[54]

The late 20th century de-industrialization of North America and Europe saw industries shifting towards developing countries. Competing for these industrial investments, a group of newly industrializing countries (NICs) emerged around the world from among the countries that offered conducive entrepreneurial environments. Decisive factors included availability of a large low-wage labour force; good infrastructural facilities; stable political and labour regimes; and negotiated benefits, such as corporate tax holidays and lowered environmental standards. While there have been many NIC 'boom–bust' stories, the rise of Japan and the Asian dragon economies was a sustained process, steadily including more Asia-Pacific nations in the core global economy. With Western corporations moving their labour-intensive industries, Asia-Pacific NICs received huge investments in urban-based branch plants, replacing existing local import substitution with export-oriented industries. This resulted in persistently high rates of urban-industrial and economic growth, and triggered accelerated urbanization as new urban-industrial employment opportunities drew rural labour into urban and peri-urban manufacturing.

From the 1980s onwards, however, transnational corporations (TNCs) started to withdraw from production-related direct investments, focusing, instead, on global control of production factors and leaving actual manufacturing processes to subcontracts and franchises. Investment in local industrial development was left to governments and local private-sector interests, who had gradually become more inclined to investing in the built environments demanded by global business interests. Thus, by the late 1980s, several Asian NICs became major regional investors in their own right, and, as their economies evolved, they too started to relocate low-wage manufacturing within the region.[55] To continue capturing ever-larger shares of the global manufacturing and services markets, huge investments were sunk in commerce-inducing infrastructure, varying from international airports to trunk highways, light rail systems and ICT. With the creation of infrastructure corridors radiating from core cities, peri-urban and rural areas were rapidly opened up for the development of urban-industrial and residential functions beyond urban peripheries.

While seemingly repeating 20th-century advanced economies' urbanization experiences, Asia-Pacific urbanization was different. Rather than the urban-centred urbanization of the advanced economies that drew rural populations into urban concentrations, Asia-Pacific urbanization largely occurred as 'regional urbanization', with combinations of rural–urban migration and the absorption *in situ* of populations along ribbon developments, spreading far into rural hinterlands. Regional urbanization processes, much more than city-based urbanization, tend to create huge, amorphous spatial forms of urban frog-leaping along infrastructure corridors without boundaries or a set geographic extent. The resulting spatially extended urban form – referred to as the mega-urban region (MUR) – comprises one or more core cities, metropolitan fringes, peri-urban developments, urban developments along transport corridors, satellite towns and outer zones in a complex mix of urban and rural functions and uses.[56] In functional terms, they create huge regional–urban economic platforms with industrial parks and residential satellite towns – often at mega scales – and at considerable distance from, but nevertheless integrated with, the metropolitan core.

The emergence of Asian MURs closely reflected the chronology of national economic restructuring. The Tokyo–Osaka MUR evolved first, followed by Seoul, Taipei, Hong Kong and Singapore. These were soon followed by Bangkok, Jakarta, Kuala Lumpur and Manila.[57] It is expected that, by 2020, two-thirds of the entire Association of East Asian States (ASEAN) urban population will live in only five MURs: the Bangkok-centred MUR (30 million); the Kuala Lumpur–Klang MUR (6 million); the Singapore Triangle (10 million); the Java MUR (100 million); and the Manila MUR (30 million).[58] However, Southeast Asian MURs will be relatively small, compared to those in East Asia, such as the Tokyo–Osaka–Kyoto–Kobe–Nagoya MUR (60 million), the Hong Kong–Shenzen–Guangdong MUR (120 million) and the Greater Shanghai MUR (83 million).[59] With the Shanghai MUR extending over 6340 square kilometres and the Beijing MUR covering an area of 16,870 square kilometres, East Asian MURs are introducing urban issues on geographic scales never before experienced.[60]

Because of different positions in the globalization process, South Asian urban agglomerations, such as Delhi, Dhaka, Karachi, Kolkata and Mumbai, are fuelled less by economic dynamism and more by rural poverty and continued high fertility.[61] Therefore, they are less prone to regional–urbanization processes and commensurate spatially extended urban configurations. Their apparent declining growth rates apply to very large

Asian cities accommodate 43 per cent of the world's urban population

population figures, so these agglomerations will continue to grow rapidly in absolute terms. Their respective projected populations for 2015 are 20.8, 22.7, 16.2, 16.7 and 22.6 million, respectively.[62]

Welfare indicators of Asian cities show that dwellers of large cities have considerable economic advantage over their rural counterparts.[63] Although urbanization and industrialization often lead to rising incomes and reduced population below the poverty line, such benefits are generally geographically concentrated, inequitable and achieved at high cost.[64] The inability of market-driven urbanization to translate short-term interests into long-term social, political and environmental sustainability is a major issue facing many cities in Asia.[65] This is exacerbated by the fact that MURs typically comprise many disjointed, traditional urban and rural jurisdictions without a single authority responsible for overall management, while applying traditional urban planning practices to MURs is proving hopelessly ineffective. A further complicating factor is that Asian urbanization is becoming as much an international as a national process, with MURs spilling over national borders, as is the case with the Singapore Triangle, which includes parts of Malaysia and Indonesia, or the Bohai Rim between China and South Korea. Such transborder agglomerations are not only difficult to manage because of their sheer size, but also because of territories extending beyond national control.[66]

To date, four types of area-wide governance arrangements have emerged in Asia:

BOX 3.1 **Bangkok: challenges of governance in response to uneven levels of urban expansion**

The Extended Bangkok Metropolitan Region (EMR), which consists of 17.5 million people and makes up 28 per cent of the country's total population, has long been the focus of Thailand's economic development. The city core of 8 million is governed by the Bangkok Metropolitan Administration (BMA), which has a staff of over 82,000 but limited power. Water and electricity services, for example, are under the control of national agencies. Outside the core, there are estimated to be over 2000 local government authorities, serving primarily small villages. There is no effective system of coordination. Provinces control most of the planning and no overall plans exist for the EMR.

During the 1980s, major increases in foreign direct investment and export-oriented manufacturing led to one of the fastest urban economic growth rates – 17.5 per cent – from 1990 to 1996. This economic expansion led to rapid outward sprawl from the city, expanding not only the population but the size and territory of the metropolitan region itself. This expansion led to increased traffic congestion,

environmental pollution and infrastructure problems. Among other difficulties, a substantial proportion of the population lived in substandard housing or slums. No adequate system of governance emerged that could tackle these problems in a coordinated manner.

The lack of coordinated governance became even more apparent when the 1997 economic crisis hit. Within a year, Bangkok's product dropped 50 per cent, unemployment increased from 1.4 to 5.1 per cent, and the slum population in the BMA grew from 1.2 million to 1.5 million in two years. Social conditions deteriorated for several years. Finally, various economic factors and public works projects sparked a turnaround. In order to adapt and encourage the recovery, the government of Thailand was forced to speed up its administrative decentralization to the local level, despite the weak institutional capacity. The BMA now faces the challenge of balancing decentralization with capacity-building in the local units, as well as establishing better overall coordination and planning for the expanding metropolitan region.

Source: National Research Council, 2003.

1 autonomous local governments, with most authority lodged in local governments;
2 confederated regional governments, with local governments entering into co-operative agreements for area-wide functions;
3 mixed systems of regional governance, with higher levels of government sharing powers with local levels of government (as in the case of Bangkok shown in Box 3.1); and
4 unified regional governance, where the MUR is under one regional entity.[67]

Mostly, however, they have tended to be inefficient due to complex administrative mixtures of governance philosophies, constitutional frameworks, statutory enactments, court decisions and strategies aiming at controlling urban growth.[68]

Latin America and the Caribbean

In 2000, 75.4 per cent of the Latin America and Caribbean (LAC) population – about 400 million people – lived in urban areas. Urbanization was highest in South America (77.2 per cent), followed by Central America (68.2 per cent) and the Caribbean (63.1 per cent). 31.6 per cent of the total LAC population and 41.8 per cent of the urban population lived in the region's 50 cities exceeding 1 million inhabitants, while 15.1 per cent of the total LAC

population and 61.5 per cent of its urban population lived in cities exceeding 5 million people. The region has seven such metropolises: Mexico City (18.1 million), São Paulo (17.9 million), Buenos Aires (12 million), Rio de Janeiro (10.6 million), Lima (7.4 million), Bogotá (6.8 million) and Santiago (5.5 million). In 2000, the first four ranked 2nd, 3rd, 11th and 15th respectively among the world's 15 largest urban agglomerations. By 2005, São Paulo and Mexico City will be in second and third positions, with 19.5 and 18.9 million inhabitants, respectively.[69]

LAC region-wide growth analysis of its cities with over 1 million people (as of 2000) over the period 1950–2010 generally shows a consistent trend of declining average annual urban growth rates. It also indicates decreasing urban primacy indices during the 1990s. But as these declining growth rates applied to increasingly larger *absolute* urban populations, it did not always translate into slowed absolute urban growth rates. During both the 1980s and 1990s, 17 of the region's cities with over 1 million people (34 per cent) combined declining urban growth percentages with increasing absolute growth rates. These cities will continue to have increasing absolute growth rates during the decade to 2010.[70]

While the region's larger cites are seemingly not following the urban growth predictions of the 1970s and 1980s, their overall urban-demographic and spatial development is far more complex and varied than simple decreasing growth rates. As the outcome of deliberate decentralization policies, strategies to relocate economic and residential functions, land market forces and spontaneous settlement formation, LAC urbanization, over the past few decades, has been changing in nature. Analysis of metropolitan spatial development trends reveals that urban-regional dynamics have become more prominent and that significant shifts from city-centred to regional forms of urbanization are currently taking place. The greater metropolitan regions of Buenos Aires, Mexico City and São Paulo, for instance, all show growth in and beyond their larger metropolitan areas through incipient polycentric urban development and the emergence of multi-nodal, urban regional systems rather than growth of the metropolitan core *per se*.[71] As urban growth data generally does not include extra-metropolitan developments, the true spatial and urban-demographic profile of LAC is incomplete without taking these new forms of urbanization into account.

Simultaneously occurring agglomeration and dispersion tendencies create pressures for metropolitan de-concentration and intensification of inter-urban and intra-urban mobility. This is increasingly leading to urbanization forms that concentrate on urban conglomeration systems around 'seed' metropolises. Although these processes have not yet been sufficiently studied, it would appear that the cities that are presently gaining the most are the medium- and smaller-sized municipalities located in the commutable vicinity of metropolitan agglomerations and along the development corridors that radiate from them.[72] In other words, the growth predictions of the 1970s and 1980s have not been entirely misguided. Rather, urban growth dynamics have shifted from city to region-centred configurations through spatial restructuring processes neither fully foreseen nor understood 30 years ago.

During the 1980s, the 50 LAC cities that were predicted to have over 1 million inhabitants by 2000 experienced declining population growth rates within their respective boundaries due to the decentralization of industries and population beyond their metropolitan borders. These cities stabilized during the 1990s when they regained, to some extent, their relative economic positions through expanding tertiary and quaternary sectors. The urban centres of over 5 million inhabitants, in particular, experienced persistently lower growth rates within their formal boundaries. Simultaneously, however, they became the cores of rapidly expanding regional urban configurations and emerging extended urban regions; as such, they continued to grow vigorously, albeit on a regional rather than city-centred basis.

The formation and consolidation of extended metropolitan areas was precipitated by the move of

In the 1980s, the process of spatial restructuring was intensified in many cities

industries and population to the outskirts of urban centres from the 1970s onwards and through expansion of road and other networks, incorporating ever-more new territories into urban zones. It created sub-centres in the metropolitan vicinity with relatively independent social and employment patterns, but, in functional terms, highly integrated with the dominant, nearby urban centre. Resulting from these trends, many LAC nations saw a steady diversification of their urban systems away from concentration in primate cities and with larger national areas taking on complementary roles in urbanization and the national economy. Although this tendency towards more polycentric spatial development and regional spread of urbanization is largely being considered a positive trend, because it reduces problems associated with economic polarization and urban primacy, many LAC countries are also experiencing problems resulting largely from insufficient consideration of urban development, globalization, structural adjustment and the new international division of labour in the formulation of holistic macro policies. In LAC's mega-urban regions, changes in spatial distribution therefore increasingly reflect deepening economic crises, rising

Periphery development in Cairo, MENA's largest metropolitan area

Damascus, Fez, Gaza, Istanbul, Sana'a and Teheran, all of which rapidly developed large pockets of concentrated urban poverty. Large urban slums emerged, packed with the poor – many below the age of 20.[94]

Impoverished and youthful urban populations have become the region's central urban issue. With one foot in conservative tradition and the other in modernity, large numbers of estranged youngsters started to search for societal alternatives. Better educated than their parents, they often left their rural origins for crowded cities in search of economic and social opportunities that were mostly not there. During the past few decades, it has become clear that most MENA governments had neither prepared for spiralling urban employment demands, nor for the housing and services needs of the escalating household formation rates associated with young urban populations.

The last population censuses taken in Egypt, Algeria, Morocco and Tunisia show a relative stabilization of growth of large metropolises and a steadier growth of the small- or medium-sized towns[95] in a trend that is believed to be occurring throughout most countries in the region. However, the region's urban agglomerations continue to show rapid absolute growth. In 2000, the MENA region had 16 cities of over 1 million inhabitants, with only Cairo, Istanbul and Teheran exceeding 5 million. In 2005, there will be 19 cities of over 1 million, 3 of over 5 million and 1 of over 10 million. By 2010, there will be a minimum of 24 cities of over 1 million within the region. It is forecast that by 2015, six cities will be larger than 5 million, with Cairo and Istanbul both exceeding 11 million. Teheran and Baghdad will remain the third and forth largest cities, with 6.9 and

4.8 million people, respectively, behind Cairo and Istanbul. Riyadh and Jeddah will grow to 7.5 and 5.2 million, respectively, by 2015.[96] These six largest cities are all transforming into metropolitan urban regions, albeit in different stages of development.

The population of MENA's largest agglomeration, the Cairo metropolitan area, has increased from 2.4 million in 1965 to about 10 million today and is predicted to reach 11.5 million by 2015.[97] Population densities within the city are some of the highest in the world and the urban area is now more than 400 square kilometres in extent. Cairo's development into a metropolitan region is largely the result of its location along the Nile River. Although Cairo and Alexandria are about 200 kilometres apart, the spread of low-density residential developments south of Alexandria and north of Cairo is well underway. The merging of both cities into a single and huge Nile Delta metropolis is a very real possibility.

Istanbul, as Turkey's largest city and commercial capital, has for decades been the destination of a continuous national migration process. Istanbul's annual urbanization rates since 1950 have persistently exceeded 3 per cent, with a peak of 5.12 per cent annually during the 1970–1975 period, making Istanbul Europe's most rapidly growing city. Today, its population exceeds 8 million and although its annual urbanization rate seems on the decline, Istanbul nevertheless continues to grow rapidly in absolute terms and is expected to reach a population of 11.3 million by 2015.[98] Istanbul's development region in Asia is penetrating well into the Kocaeli and Bursa provinces, with the cities of Izmit (0.22 million) and Bursa (1.2 million) gradually becoming part of a contiguous metropolitan area centred on Istanbul. Simultaneously, European Istanbul is expanding to the north and west, slowly enclosing the entire Sea of Marmara. The rapid urban growth of Istanbul is mostly spontaneous, without significant control by local or regional authorities, while there is also no serious metropolitan development plan.[99] At present, more than half of the population of Istanbul lives in slums.

During the crucial completion phase of its urban transition, the MENA region now needs to implement serious socio-economic reforms and urban policies. From being 25 per cent urban during the 1960s, it rapidly moved to a current urbanization level of 58 per cent. It will be 70 per cent urban by 2015, with hyper-urbanization processes now taking place in about half of its nations. With an urban future for the MENA states inevitable, the region's fate will hinge on its urban areas and cities that exceed 1 million, in particular. The challenge is to reshape its social and related urban policies in order to support effective economic policy for sustained economic growth and adequate living conditions for the rapidly expanding numbers of young and poor people.[100]

Sub-Saharan Africa

Despite its accelerating urbanization, sub-Saharan Africa (SSA) remains the least urbanized of the major global regions. Whereas the advanced economies and Latin America have largely completed their urban transition, and while the MENA region is now more than halfway through this process, SSA has only recently started its demographic transition, leading to an urban majority around 2030.[101] But despite SSA's comparatively late urban transition, the sheer speed of urbanization is posing serious problems and clear patterns of metropolitanization, as well as the emergence of several mega-urban regions, are already fact. In 2001, only Congo, Djibouti, Gabon, Mauritania and South Africa had urban majorities;[102] but by the end of the current decade, no less than nine SSA nations[103] will pass the 50 per cent urban mark.[104]

SSA urbanization is exceptional in the sense that it is occurring largely without industrial and economic growth. This is a unique phenomenon even across poor countries and poor economic performers. Although manufacturing became a locally noteworthy and diversified sector in some SSA countries, industrialization stalled with import-substitution production and did not lead to any significant export production. This was in contrast to other developing regions that saw industrial import substitution gradually developing into export manufacturing. Consequently, SSA is now facing very rapid population growth and accelerating urbanization without the economy to produce the public and private resources necessary for housing, infrastructure and urban employment at the scales required. To understand the reasons, a short historical perspective is required.

Under colonialism, many SSA societies were organized as extraction economies with low (if any) industrial and infrastructure development other than those that served external economic interests. Secondary- and small-town development was largely non-existent, as was comprehensive national infrastructure coverage. Urban populations typically formed in one or two primate cities that were important to the colonial economy. As a result, many SSA nations were highly under-industrialized and under-urbanized during independence.

In the early independence years, urban development remained a low-priority issue in most SSA nations because other political and economic priorities took precedence in these predominantly rural countries. National coordination was generally translated into power centralization and authoritarian, state-centred development models. The major SSA cities, as seats of the new governments and the national focus of economic activity, retained their central role at independence and started to grow very rapidly from the 1950s onwards. This was due to rapid demographic growth and the proliferation of public-sector employment in the primate cities, but also because independence released decades of latent rural–urban migration pressure. As a result, SSA's primate cities expanded very rapidly.

Both under colonialism and during the early independence decades, the rural populations of many SSA countries had largely been excluded from the modern national economy. Because wage employment was overwhelmingly concentrated in the urban areas, rural–urban migration increased rapidly. Frequent natural disasters, conflicts, rapid rural population growth and rural poverty further encouraged large and persistent rural–urban migration flows. The average SSA primate city typically experienced persistent annual urban growth rates of 5 to 6 per cent, while some cities saw annual growth rates in excess of 10 per cent, implying population doubling every decade. Whereas in 1960 Johannesburg was the sole SSA city exceeding 1 million inhabitants, in 1970 there were four (Cape Town, Johannesburg, Kinshasa and Lagos). By the late 1980s, the list also included Abidjan, Accra, Addis Ababa, Dakar, Dar es Salaam, Durban, East Rand, Harare, Ibadan, Khartoum, Luanda and Nairobi. By 2010, SSA will have at least 33 cities of more than 1 million inhabitants, with two exceeding 5 million and one (Lagos) having more than 13 million inhabitants.[105]

By the late 1960s it was becoming clear that political and economic centralization, combined with lack of secondary and tertiary urban development, were further reinforcing undesirable urban primacy patterns. Under-regulated, under-funded, under-skilled and under-empowered city management in SSA increasingly fell behind in the provision of employment, housing, services and infrastructures for spiralling concentrations of poor people. Although the need for decentralization soon became widely acknowledged, it rarely went beyond political rhetoric, and where it was actually implemented, decentralization was rarely successful because it was largely *ad hoc* and neither part of a coherent national urban policy, nor integrated with other macro-level policy decisions. Urban decentralization efforts typically became exercises in problem and responsibility devolution without simultaneous transfer of revenue-generation capacities. Thus, urban development processes became increasingly deficient

Trade-off between urban commercial and liveability considerations

and informal as increasing supply–demand gaps in land and services provision for the rapidly swelling urban populations led to uncontrolled urban growth through informal and often illegal developments. As a result, SSA cities are rapidly joining the ranks of the world's largest urban agglomerations with about 72 per cent of their urban dwellers living in slums.[106]

Lagos, Nigeria, is perhaps indicative of urban growth in SSA. In 1995, Lagos became the world's 29th largest urban agglomeration, with 6.5 million inhabitants. In 2000, it was the 23rd largest, with 8.8 million people. Lagos became one of SSA's first mega-urban regions when its metropolitan population reached 10 million inhabitants around 2002. Lagos continues to grow and by 2015 it is envisaged to become the world's 11th largest urban system, with 16 million inhabitants.[107] Major urban management issues of Lagos include its spectacular spatial expansion, now covering an area of well over 1000 square kilometres, its fragmented metropolitan governance, massive urban unemployment, a huge housing supply–demand gap and inadequate or erratic services provision.

South Africa is host to SSA's second largest mega-urban region. Metropolitan Johannesburg, with its 3 million inhabitants,[108] is the headquarters for most of South Africa's large corporations, banks and other financial and business activities. It is the central focus of an extended urban region of over 7 million people known as Gauteng. Besides Johannesburg, Gauteng comprises Pretoria,

Vereeniging, Benoni, Krugersdorp and their surrounding areas,[109] with a total of 23 municipalities.[110] It is estimated that by 2020, Gauteng will be an urban region of 20 million people. The main challenge for Gauteng in the foreseeable future is to create a functioning whole out of an agglomeration beset by huge internal imbalances. The most urgent issue – apart from creating a non-racial urban context and providing acceptable residential alternatives and employment for some 2 million informal settlement residents – is to create a more compact urban region. However, a common spatial development framework is now in place for dealing with Gauteng's problems that prohibits urban development beyond the current regional urban area, with similar restrictions around established nodes, such as Pretoria, Centurion, Sandton, Johannesburg and Randburg. However, it is unclear how the plan will cater for the residential needs of large numbers of low-income residents and how it will reverse the current departure of companies from the region's central business districts.

Kinshasa, capital of the Democratic Republic of Congo, is expected to join the world's 30 largest agglomerations in the next few years; by 2015, it will have risen to 23rd place, with some 10 million inhabitants.[111] This primate city (more than five times larger than the second largest) is rapidly developing into a huge urban agglomeration. From 50,000 inhabitants in 1940, Kinshasa is anticipated to become a 10 million agglomeration by 2015.[112] But the country has no long urban tradition and Kinshasa is a symbol of how difficult creating an urban society can be without structures to facilitate the necessary transformations. Decentralization efforts since 1977 have fragmented already deficient urban governance over levels whose roles and authority are not clearly defined.[113]

The governance implications of rapidly growing SSA urban entities in a context of poverty and increasing gaps between capacities, funding and needs are considerable. Governments are being compelled to devote ever-more attention to converting cities into globally competitive economic entities that can attract investment. Although this is one of the primary functions of governments and city managers, the promotion of cities often carries high social, political, environmental and urban liveability costs. In the urban trade-off between commercial and liveability considerations, the latter often loses.[114]

Worldwide, the first step in addressing mega-growth is creating workable mechanisms for metro- and region-wide planning, coordination and development control. This should be the first step for SSA, as well. Two major challenges are currently facing contemporary SSA metropolises:

BOX 3.3 Abidjan: effective urban policy structure confronts expansion, but weaknesses exist

Abidjan is the largest city of Côte d'Ivoire, with an estimated population of 3.3 million and taking up 627 square kilometres in 2000. Côte d'Ivoire has historically had one of the highest levels of urban development and most elaborate urban policy systems of any Francophone African country. Abidjan represents 40 per cent of the country's total urban population and 75 per cent of its formal employment. By taking a calculated and proactive approach to urban policy, the national government succeeded in coping with problems that come with urban expansion. In 1978 the president initiated a process of decentralization that involved restoring commune (municipal) status to major cities and smaller towns throughout the country. This action notably involved ten communes in Abidjan and the amalgamation of these ten Abidjan communes into a government body called the 'City of Abidjan'.

The simultaneous acts of devolving real power to the local councils through free and contested municipal elections, and strengthening central administrative systems to provide required administrative and technical support enabled effective coordination of an expanded metropolitan area. The city of Abidjan comprises a two-tier city government – one tier including the ten local communes' elected councillors and mayor, and the second tier composed of only the ten mayors and four representative councillors from each commune. This

upper tier is responsible for waste disposal and management; public lighting; sanitation; traffic regulation; maintenance of roads, parks and cemeteries; and town planning. The communes administer markets, allocate land for public uses, deal with schools and clinics, operate community centres and share functions with other levels of government with respect to pollution and hygiene. Private companies regulate electricity and water, under surveillance by the municipal or national government. While problems with revenues exist, as well as serious inequalities in spending among communes, this system has functioned for 20 years.

Some of the major problems identified include the national government's lack of willingness to devolve certain functions to the city of Abidjan, despite their inclusion in the city's legal mandate. These functions include inspection of construction sites, issuing of drivers' licences and control of fire-fighting and rescue operations. In addition, the city has little direct influence over its finances, as taxes go directly to national government and are then remitted to the local levels. Another problem this administrative structure presents is that the mayor of the city is not elected at large; rather, he or she is chosen by the mayors of the constituent communes. As a result, this individual does not have an independent political base from which to strategically promote metropolitan-wide policies.

Source: National Research Council, 2003.

---

1 decentralizing the public sector, with local intra-metropolitan governments acquiring more responsibility for administering public works and services, (see Box 3.3); and
2 addressing complex processes of socio-spatial segregation that result in substantial differences in household incomes between sub-areas of a metropolis, in the types of services demanded and in the quality of those services.

The interconnection between these two challenges is particularly clear in housing, where intra-metropolitan local governments face the need to upgrade irregular settlements and to rehabilitate the now well-consolidated but increasingly distressed self-help urbanization that began some 50 years ago.[115]

Although the past decades have not been easy for SSA, with sharp population increases, an unfavourable economic climate and multiplying conflicts, the region is changing, modernizing and urbanizing. For some years now economic growth has been stronger than population growth in some of the region's nations. Although SSA has massive problems, it is also brimming with possibilities and is endowed with major natural and human resources awaiting exploitation by African nations in a globalized environment.[116]

Trends in transition economy countries

By 2000, the geographical region of the former USSR and its satellite states was 68.3 per cent urbanized – up from about 17 per cent a century earlier. However, this average urbanization figure hides considerable intra-regional variations and strongly lopsided population distributions among and within the transition economies. Of the transition economies' 31 cities with over 1 million inhabitants in 2000, 25 are located in Europe.[117] Although the urban transition of the past century is generally expected to continue, leading to an anticipated 75 per cent average urbanization level around 2030,[118] recent developments in the Commonwealth of Independent States (CIS) warrant a closer look at this projection.

Moscow city centre reflects the region's long urban cultural history

The region's exposure to world market forces, severe political instability, declining economic output and recent widespread increases in poverty have had considerable impacts on demographic trends that may lead to far-reaching changes in regional urban growth. Between 1987 and 1994, for instance, marriage rates in the former Soviet Union fell by 25 to 50 per cent, divorce rates in some CIS nations rose by 25 per cent, while birth rates declined by 20 to 40 per cent.[119] As a result of the lifting of restrictions on internal migration, most of the 1990s saw a reversal of a decades-long trend of rural out-migration with rural areas regaining population in some of the CIS republics.[120] They also witnessed significant ethnic-based migration, partly due to deteriorating urban living conditions or economic and social stress, and partly as the outcome of growing nationalism.

For most of the 20th century, the cities of the Soviet republics have operated under a centralized planning system with government decisions rather than market forces determining the nature, scale and spatial distribution of economic activity.[121] Urbanization under such non-market conditions generated different spatial configurations. Limitations to private housing markets and emphasis on mass-produced housing estates imposed a different logic on the form of cities, as did centralized decisions on the

spatial distribution of industries.[122] As the outcome of the absence of land markets, many Soviet cities grew in concentric rings rather than along infrastructure corridors radiating from city cores.[123]

In 2000, seven cities exceeded 2 million people: Bucharest (2 million) Tashkent (2.2 million), Warsaw (2.3 million), Kiev (2.5 million), Katowice (3.5 million), St Petersburg (4.6 million) and Moscow (8.4 million).[124] The two large Russian cities display the most distinct city region formation.

The size of Moscow and St Petersburg relative to the other major cities reflects the long history of Russia as a centralized state. Moscow hosts half of Russia's banking activities, more than one fifth of its retail and one third of the national wholesale trade. But, with a mere 5.8 per cent of Russia's total population as of 2000, Moscow – although unquestionably a large city – is a primate city in economic rather than in relative population terms. Its economic primacy has not declined during the post-1989 period. Rather, Moscow has increased its 'global city' status by monopolizing the relations between the federation and the world economy at large. Moscow has also played a leading role in the USSR's political and economic decline because the urban embodiment of Soviet power broke down in its own governance processes.[125]

Between the 1970s and early 1980s, the growth of Russia's biggest cities proceeded largely unchecked. Faced with chronic urban housing shortages, pollution and escalating traffic congestion, authorities *did* attempt to control migration to the major cities while simultaneously encouraging development of small- and medium-sized cities. Nevertheless, the scope and tempo of big-city growth continued with combinations of natural growth and considerable illegal and undocumented labour migration. Whereas in 1970, 6 Russian cities had populations of over 1 million, by 1990 there were 12.[126] Due to the strong concentration of economic and political power in Moscow and Leningrad, metropolitanization and urban region formation did not become a feature of many Russian cities. Only the two cities with federal status, Leningrad and Moscow, grew to become regional cities with populations of 4.6 million and 8.4 million inhabitants, respectively, for the city proper, and total urban region populations of 6.3 and 15.2 million, respectively.[127] The reasons for this are illustrated below using the specific example of Leningrad.

Countries around the world have sought to gain control over their urban environments by influencing cities' economic, social, cultural and physical contexts. In only a few nations have central interventions gone deeper than in the USSR. In 1918, land ownership and private property in cities was abolished. Through nationalization and establishment of central command over cities' physical and economic planning, the Soviet state had – at the end of the first Five-Year Plan period (1928–1932) – seized control of virtually all urban housing and land, and administrative responsibility for these assets was entrusted with the local soviets.[128]

With respect to planning and management, a chain of control was devised. It was structured along sectoral lines, where instructions from the planning agency, *Gosplan*, flowed through national ministries to ministerial representatives at the regional level. An interesting aspect of this administrative organization was the linking of territorial and sectoral planning, where municipal managers were not only in charge of physical planning, but also served as industrial and social executives responsible for the local realization of goals and objectives set by Moscow-based ministries and other central institutions.[129]

Moscow and Leningrad, as federal cities, were entirely dominated by the regional, *oblast*, administration. Regional authorities of the Moscow and Leningrad *oblasts* controlled not only the region, but also the cities within them. The Moscow and Leningrad *oblasts* thus emerged as the institutions with power over both regional and municipal developments. In the case of Leningrad, this meant integrated management of a region that would grow to 83,908 square kilometres, including 29 municipal regions, 111 municipal districts, 9 cities and numerous smaller towns in 1986.[130] The regional administrative structure of Moscow and Leningrad created, by coincidence, the very type of metropolitan and urban region-wide governance that would emerge as a key urban management issue during the late 20th century. The dominance of regional institutions in the management of the greater urban regions of Moscow and Leningrad created possibilities for continued regionally integrated expansion of physical, economic and social planning strategies. Towns across the USSR were required to follow Leningrad's comparatively successful urban–region management lead and establish similar all-encompassing plans from the mid 1970s onwards. But with their special federal status and related shares of the state budget, Moscow and Leningrad had, unlike other USSR cities, predictable and assured budgets that enabled them to engage in long-term planning in a manner that did not apply to other Russian cities.[131]

As Russia is seeking forms of urban governance that allow market forces and smaller governmental units to assume more prominent roles, its cities have to find ways to redefine their positions in the international arena.[132] The choice is largely between continued centralized regional governance and planning or governance fragmentation, but with greater individual freedoms associated with poly-nucleated urban developments.

There are clear signs that city region formation is now also occurring in Katowice, Poland. Although a fairly small municipality of 400,000 people, it is the core of a 1250 square kilometre urban field of 15 cities,[133] with a combined population of 3.5 million people. Eight municipalities have populations in excess of 100,000. Since all of these are independent legal jurisdictions, the need for regional urban management will soon become evident. Polish authorities have taken tentative steps in this direction with the formation, in 1994, of a Union of Municipalities designed to initiate region-wide cooperation. Similar urban–region development is under way in Dnepropetrovsk, Minsk and a host of other cities.

Trends in advanced economy countries

Metropolitanization trends in the advanced economies became more visible during the middle of the 20th century. The most important change was initially observed in 1961, pointing to a newly emerging type of urban configuration involving the interweaving of cities in relatively close proximity within functionally integrated urban regions. Due to their unprecedented size, both in territory and population, such urban agglomerations were referred to as 'megalopolises'.[134]

In accommodating increasing populations and economic activity, cities sprawled onto peri-urban and adjacent rural lands. Mounting agglomeration diseconomies in many city cores (congestion, pollution, rising real-estate costs, etc) further fuelled the urban sprawl through the migration of middle classes and commercial activities to the new suburbs and other settlements in the commutable metropolitan region. From 1960 to about 1975, a clear trend of suburbanization with fast population growth rates in rural, urbanizing rural and suburban municipalities became the norm in Northwest Europe, North America and Japan.[135] With steadily more suburban housing estates being created along or beyond the urban periphery and further facilitated by expanding road and other infrastructure networks, formerly separate satellite towns, designated urban growth poles and smaller towns surrounding larger cities became steadily more integrated. Other suburban communities were not physically absorbed, but developed into separate sub-centres of large metropolitan functional systems. A clear pattern of polycentric urban regions started to develop in the advanced economies. Despite 'growth centre policies' that sought urban de-concentration and that attempted to steer urbanization away from ever-growing main urban centres, the polycentric metropolitan region became one of the defining characteristics of the advanced economies' urban landscape.[136]

Market forces are among the major factors influencing concentration of people and jobs

Rapid growth in the size and complexity of urban regions led to a search for optimum levels of urban management. This was particularly the case in Europe, where local governments also experienced strong growth as providers of statutory services and played an important role as an arm of central government in the expansion of the welfare state. Many reform experiments implemented by central governments were aimed at rationalizing urban management by integrating separate urban local authorities or by adjusting their boundaries. By the mid 1980s, reshaping territorial politics had become a never-ending process in many of the post-industrial countries, a trend now also echoed in oriental Europe. A first wave of attempts at forging effective urban governance for polycentric metropolitan systems took place in the UK, France, Scandinavia and The Netherlands. Mostly based on authoritarian functional approaches, the earlier reform efforts often focused on reducing the powers of cities by partitioning or merging municipalities. But the rapidly rising political and economic power of cities and city networks had been underestimated, and reform issues were frequently criticized for lacking legitimacy. During the following reform waves, top-down styles were replaced by negotiation and partnership. Perceived lack of legitimacy was, in some cases, addressed through consultations by providing referenda. Referenda spectacularly failed in, for instance, Amsterdam and Rotterdam precisely because residents refused to allow city powers to be broken up.[137] Similarly,

Metropolitan Helsinki created a collective of its municipalities to fight off the threats of rural interests and the state. These experiences indicate that, despite changes in urban scale, the European metropolitan centre is likely to remain important. In metropolitan and urban regions, local governments have not disappeared, but are being transformed to collectives for public policy delivery and strategic thinking. However, there is an obvious need for re-centralizing some political power to address region-wide issues.

There were clear parallels in the contemporary patterns and issues of urban areas on both sides of the Atlantic. Similar and simultaneous urban transformations occurred in North America, albeit with wide disparity in intensity of distributional problems. Government continues to affect patterns and problems in urban areas on both continents, despite the fact that the policies in the European Union (EU) and the US are very different. At the risk of oversimplifying the issues, in general terms it can be said that the EU stresses 'hard' urban policy instruments – housing and physical infrastructure, such as transportation networks – whereas the US stresses 'soft' instruments – welfare grants, education and health. Both, however, recognize the dominance of market forces in influencing location and concentrations of people and jobs, as well as the desirability of individual freedom of choice. At the same time, they recognize that there is a case to be made for a stronger role for governments in steering local-level changes in economic and social patterns through urban policies. In the US and Canada, major urban issues parallel those in Europe: unemployment; disparities in job creation; loss of central-city populations; social exclusion; poverty; sprawling cities; urban de-concentration; city region power fragmentation; and significant socio-economic differences between cities and suburbs.

Urban policy on both sides of the Atlantic, however, largely focuses on the functional city scale rather than the much larger metropolitan, regional, national or supranational scale.[138] In order to exploit the planning potential of polycentric urban regions, active support for regional organizing capacity is needed to shape the competitive advantages of polycentric urban regions. In practice, there are few successful examples of this. Evidence from polycentric urban regions in Northwest Europe shows that building of regional organizing capacity is conditioned by a number of spatial, functional, political-institutional and cultural factors that transcend the perceived functional city scale. Major constraints include institutional fragmentation, an internal orientation of key persons and the lack of identification with the region at large.

Notes

1 The first part of this chapter is based on a draft prepared by Michael Cohen, New School University, New York, US.
2 Ruble et al, 2000.
3 Hall and Pfeiffer, 2000b.
4 World Bank, 2001a.
5 Harris and Todaro, 1960.
6 Bender, 2001, p1.
7 Ingram and Carroll, 1978, p11.
8 Ingram and Carroll, 1978, p10.
9 Ingram and Carroll, 1978, p14.
10 Kyu Sik Lee, 1989.
11 Ingram, 1997, p7.
12 Ingram, 1997, p8.
13 Ingram, 1997, p9.
14 Anas et al, 1998, p1426.
15 Garreau, 1991.
16 Anas et al, 1998, pp1434–1444.
17 Anas et al, 1998.
18 Ingram, 1997, p11.
19 Ingram, 1997, p14.
20 Ingram, 1997, p25.
21 Malmberg et al, 1996.
22 The following section is based on a contribution by Guido Martinotti, University of Milan-Bicocca, Italy.
23 Martinotti, 1996.
24 Fischer, 1994.
25 Berry, 1986.
26 Crawford, 1992.
27 Bonazzi, 1996.
28 Cattaneo, 1972.
29 Martinotti and Pozzi, 2004.
30 Wood, 1959.
31 Sivaramakrishnan and Green, 1986.
32 Salmon, 1999.
33 United Nations Population Division, 2002a.
34 Orfield, 1997.
35 National Research Council, 2003.
36 It is perhaps not as vivid as the descriptions of apartheid from South Africa, but it is not surprising that an urban study published in the US during the 1990s was entitled American Apartheid. See Massey and Denton, 1993.
37 Galster, 1998.
38 National Research Council, 2003.
39 Polese and Stren, 2000.
40 Downs, 1994.
41 US Department of Commerce, 1997.
42 World Bank, 2002c.
43 Parrott, 1999; City of New York, 2001, piii.
44 Report by Joseph Salvo, see Cheng, 2004 for detail.
45 Soja, 2000.
46 This and the following sections of this chapter are based on drafts prepared by Jos Maseland of UN-Habitat.
47 United Nations Population Division, 2002a.
48 Jones, 2001.
49 UNCHS (Habitat), 2001a.
50 United Nations Population Division, 2002a.
51 Douglass, 2000.
52 Pendakur, 1995.
53 United Nations Population Division, 2002a.
54 Webster, 1995.
55 Douglass, 2000.
56 McGee and Robinson, 1995.
57 Rimmer, 1995.
58 McGee, 1995.
59 Wo-Lap Lam, 2002.
60 Hu, 2003.
61 National Research Council, 2003.
62 UN-Habitat, 2003a.
63 Jones, 2001.
64 Rimmer, 1995.
65 Douglass, 1995.
66 Douglass, 1995.
67 Laquian, 1995.
68 Laquian, 1995.
69 United Nations Population Division, 2002a.
70 United Nations Population Division, 2002a.
71 UNECLAC, 1998.
72 Carmona, 2000.
73 'Brazil, Migration and Urbanization', http://lcweb2.loc.gov/cgi-bin/query/r?frd/cstdy:@field(DOCID+br0035).
74 UNECLAC, 2000.
75 Carmona, 2000.
76 UNECLAC, 1998.
77 National Research Council, 2003.
78 National Research Council, 2003.
79 Cohen, 1997.
80 Brennan, 1995.
81 See http://parole.aporee.org/.
82 Ward, 1996.
83 Ward, 1996.
84 Benna, 2002.
85 United Nations Population Division, 2002a.
86 UN-Habitat, 2003a.
87 United Nations Population Division, 2002a.
88 See www.canberra.edu.au/crs/urban.htm.
89 See http://edc.usgs.gov/earthshots/slow/Riyadh/Riyadhtext#note1.
90 Fuccaro, 2001.
91 UN-Habitat, 2003a.
92 http://ist-socrates.berkeley.edu/~mescha/famabstracts/altorki.html.
93 Cordesman, 1999.
94 See www.csis.org/intern'forum398c.html.
95 Kharoufi, 1996.
96 United Nations Population Division, 2002a.
97 United Nations Population Division, 2002a.
98 United Nations Population Division, 2002a.
99 Pérouse, 1998.
100 Cordesman, 1999.
101 United Nations Population Division, 2002a.
102 Excluding small island states.
103 Botswana, Cameroon, Equatorial Guinea, Liberia, Nigeria, Sao Tome and Principe, and Senegal.
104 United Nations Population Division, 2002a.
105 United Nations Population Division, 2002a.
106 UN-Habitat, 2003a.
107 United Nations Population Division, 2002a.
108 United Nations Population Division, 2002a.
109 Piermay, 1997.
110 See http://parole.aporee.org/work/.
111 United Nations Population Division, 2002a.
112 United Nations Population Division, 2002a.
113 Piermay, 1997.
114 Douglass, 2000.
115 Cohen and Debowicz, 2001.
116 See http://www.unesco.org/education/esd/english/activities/map.shtml.
117 United Nations Population Division, 2002a.
118 United Nations Population Division, 2002a.
119 National Research Council, 2003.
120 National Research Council, 2003.
121 National Research Council, 2003.
122 National Research Council, 2003.
123 Cohen and Debowicz, 2001.
124 United Nations Population Division, 2002a.
125 UNCHS (Habitat), 1996.
126 United Nations Population Division, 2002a.
127 See www.RussiaVotes.org.
128 UNCHS (Habitat), 2001a.
129 Ruble, 1990.
130 See www.leontief.ru/rnsc/eng/nwregions/nwr5.htm; Gramberg, 2003.
131 Ruble and Blair, 1990.
132 National Research Council, 2003.
133 See http://www.unhabitat.org/programmes/sustainablecities/katowice.asp.
134 Gottmann, 1961.
135 National Research Council, 2003.
136 Kloosterman and Musterd, 2001.
137 See www.mfo.ac.uk.
138 See Rifé, undated, www.ub.es/graap/WP0900_Termes.PDF.

Chapter **4**

International Migration:
Socio-economic and
Cultural Implications[1]

Global overview   77

Regional trends   77

Economic impacts   79

Social and cultural impacts   81

Policy aspects   82

Developing countries   83

Asia and the Pacific   83

Latin America and the Caribbean   86

Middle East and Northern Africa (MENA)   88

Sub-Saharan Africa   91

Economies in transition   94

Advanced economies   96

International migration is becoming a worldwide issue and is gaining increasing attention among both policy-makers and the public. As a consequence of globalization, immigrants and refugees have become in many parts of the world much more visible in their differences and numbers. This flow affects both states of origin and host states in their economic activities, especially in cities, and with respect to the very fabric of their societies. Migrants are more than simply workers in their host state: they interact with local populations and contribute in many ways to the 'flavour' of the communities in which they live.[2]

Global overview

It is difficult to quantify the proportions of international migration directed to rural or urban areas due to the increase in undocumented migration and lack of data, especially in developing countries. However, there is considerable empirical evidence that, worldwide, cities are attracting more foreign people than in the past. According to the most recent data,[3] the total number of international migrants[4] in the world is approximately 175 million, which includes refugees[5] but does not capture undocumented migrants, who escape official accounting. In 2000, international migrants represented some 2.9 per cent of the world population – 6057 billion.[6] This percentage has been rising steadily over the past 25 years. Advanced economies (Western Europe, Northern America, Japan, Australia and New Zealand) have the largest number of international migrants (about 77 million), followed by transition economies (Eastern Europe and former Soviet republics, with 33 million), Asia and the Pacific (23 million), and Middle East and Northern Africa (MENA) countries (21 million).

Regional trends

The scale of migration varies significantly among world regions; but almost everywhere cities are becoming the primary destination for migrants who may be escaping violence, human rights violations, poverty or low-developmental environments. Table 4.1 shows that net migration represents a significant contribution to population growth in the developed

TABLE 4.1 **Total population, international migrants, net migration and refugees: number and distribution, 2000**

	Total population		International migrants			Refugees		Net migration (average annual) 1995–2000	
	Number (000)	Distribution (%)	Number (000)	Rate (%)	Distribution (%)	Number (000)	Distribution (%)	Number (000)	Rate per 1000
World	6,056,715	100.00	174,781	2.9	100.00	15,868	100.00		
Developing economies	4,791,393	79.11	64,643	1.3	36.99	12,469	78.58	–2001	–0.4
Asia and the Pacific	3,307,773	54.61	23,442	0.7	13.41	4786	30.16	–1218	–0.4
Latin America and the Caribbean	518,809	8.57	5944	1.1	3.40	38	0.24	–494	–1.0
Middle East and Northern Africa	345,334	5.70	20,926	6.1	11.97	4624	29.14	–105	–0.3
Sub-Saharan Africa	619,477	10.23	14,331	2.3	8.20	3021	19.04	–184	–0.3
Economies in transition	411,909	6.80	33,391	8.1	19.10	986	6.21	–186	–0.5
Central and Eastern Europe	338,021	5.58	27,372	8.1	15.66	598	3.77	130	0.4
Central and Western Asia	73,888	1.22	6019	8.1	3.44	388	2.44	–315	–4.3
Advanced economies	853,408	14.09	76,747	9.0	43.91	2414	15.21	2186	2.6
Asia and the Pacific	150,012	2.48	7175	4.8	4.11	66	0.42	159	1.1
Northern America	314,113	5.19	40,844	13.0	23.37	635	4.00	1394	4.6
Western Europe	389,283	6.43	28,728	7.4	16.44	1712	10.79	633	1.6

Source: United Nations Population Division, 2002b.

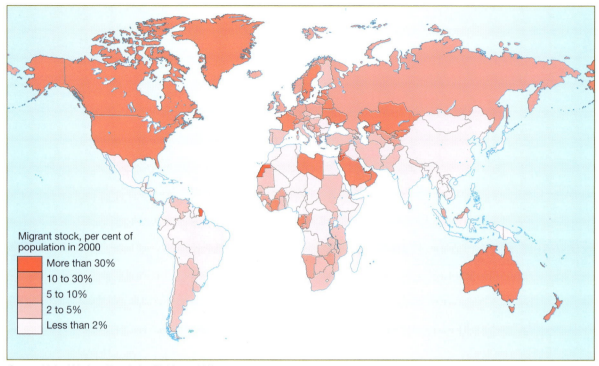

Migrant stock, per cent of
population in 2000

More than 30%
10 to 30%
5 to 10%
2 to 5%
Less than 2%

Source: United Nations Population Division, 2002b.

MAP 4.1 **The world's international migrations, 2000**

*Of the world's 15.9 million refugees, 78.6 per cent are
from developing countries*

countries, while its impact on population growth in
the developing countries is negative.[7]

Among advanced economies, which account for
about 77 million international migrants, or 44 per
cent of the world total, traditional migrant nations
such as the US, Canada, Australia and New Zealand
still attract migrants. The US continues to have the
highest number of foreign migrants, about 35 million.
However, since the 1990s, migrant populations in
Germany and France have increased due to inflows of
people from Central and Eastern European, African
and Middle Eastern countries. Migrants are becoming
the major source of population growth in both
European and Northern American societies, and their
presence is higher in urban areas.

Asia and the Pacific is largely a sending rather
than a receiving region: its migrants (about 23 million,
or 13 per cent of the world total) constitute the major
source of workers in Middle East and Northern Africa
(MENA) countries; but their presence is also
significant in North America. India and Pakistan
account for the largest numbers of international
migrants resident in the region, while the highest rates
are concentrated in Southeast Asian countries (notably
Malaysia and Singapore). In Asian cities such as
Karachi, Mumbai or Bangkok, international migration
is frequently linked to poor living conditions, spatial
and social segregation and labour exploitation.

Some of sub-Saharan Africa's international
migrants (about 14 million, or 8 per cent of the

TABLE 4.2 **Countries with highest remittances received, 2001**

Country	Total remittances ($ million)	GDP ($ million)	Total population	Total remittances as percentage of GDP	Total remittances per capita
Lesotho	209.0	796.7	1,852,808	26.2	112.80
Vanuatu	53.3	212.8	192,910	25.0	276.14
Jordan	2011.0	8829.1	5,153,378	22.8	390.23
Bosnia and Herzegovina	860.1	4769.1	3,922,205	18.0	219.29
Albania	699.0	4113.7	3,510,484	17.0	199.12
Nicaragua	335.7	2067.8	4,918,393	16.2	68.25
Yemen	1436.9	9177.2	17,479,206	15.7	82.21
Republic of Moldova	223.1	1479.4	4,431,570	15.1	50.34
El Salvador	1925.2	13,738.9	6,237,662	14.0	308.64
Jamaica	1058.7	7784.1	2,665,636	13.6	397.17
Dominican Republic	1982.0	21,211.0	8,475,396	9.3	233.85
Philippines	6366.0	71,437.7	81,369,751	8.9	78.24
Uganda	483.0	5675.3	24,170,422	8.5	19.98
Honduras	541.0	6385.8	6,357,941	8.5	85.09
Ecuador	1420.0	17,982.4	13,183,978	7.9	107.71

Source: IMF, 2003.

world total) originate from refugee movements, and there is generally no reliable data. Labour migrants are higher in some richer economies, such as South Africa, Côte d'Ivoire or Gabon, and tend to be concentrated in urban areas: one out of four people in Abidjan come from other West African countries. In the main cities of South Africa, international immigration is increasing, particularly after the collapse of apartheid.

In Latin America and the Caribbean, which accounts for about 3.5 per cent of the world's total international migrants (about 6 million), people tend to migrate to other continents (particularly Northern America). Intra-regional migration is relatively small and limited to some countries. In this region, major international flows are changing in character, and are becoming more urban oriented due to reduced job opportunities in agriculture. Moreover, Central America (and Mexico, in particular) currently receives transit migrants trying to enter the US.

MENA countries attract significant numbers of international migrants (21 million, or 12 per cent of the world total), who are mainly composed of workers coming from Asia or poorer Arab countries. They are predominantly employed in Gulf-region oil economies, where they arrive under a strictly regulated sponsorship system called the *kafeel*. However, strategies for the employment of nationals are reducing job opportunities for international migrants.

At the urban level, migrants work in various oil-related activities and services (which are normally located in the capital cities).

In the transition economies (TE) of Eastern Europe and former Soviet republics, international migration represents a relatively new phenomenon; but it is gaining importance, considering that it accounts for 33 million people, or 19 per cent of the world's total migrant population. The region is affected by both international and transit migration, with some urban impacts in Russia, the Baltic and Central European states.

Economic impacts

Labour migration has reached an unprecedented scale with the reduction of international travel costs and labour shortages in countries experiencing rapid economic growth. In particular, increasing segmentation of labour markets is becoming apparent in migrant destination areas. Whole sectors are becoming characterized by low income, low prestige, poor conditions of work and insecurity, and are consequently eschewed by local populations, even at times of high unemployment. This is particularly true of low-status manual occupations. The expansion of contract labour migration is facilitated by networks of recruiters, agents and travel providers.[8]

segregation. On the contrary, it may derive from a process of self-selection, with new arrivals preferring to be among their community and close to the places that can give them the special assistance they need (which is difficult to receive from local institutions).[11] This is the case with Nicaraguan immigrants who meet each other in Parco de La Merced in San José de Costa Rica to share information about job opportunities and housing, or just to eat their traditional dishes together.

Chinese from well-defined regions constitute local networks in Italian cities, sometimes providing within their community basic services such as education or health. Senegalese street vendors rely on local Senegalese communities, who assist them in accessing jobs in almost all French-speaking African capitals.

Of course, migrants generally tend to live in poor urban areas, often characterized by lack of basic services, unhealthy living conditions, insecure tenure, overcrowding and social violence. There are many cases of slums formed around an ethnic immigrant core. This tendency started first in the highly industrialized countries, and now it is present in developing world cities, too. Harlem (in New York City) is the best known example, with a very high majority of black immigrants (strictly not international migrants, but from the southern states) or Puerto Ricans. Similar situations are reported in the main French cities with Algerian *banlieues*, or in the Brixton area, in London. But spatial segregation is growing even in the developing countries: in Dharavi,

in Mumbai, which is considered the world's largest slum, Tamil is spoken as the main language; in Bangkok, Burmese migrants primarily live in the slum of Klong Toey; many Palestinians still live in very poor conditions in the refugee camps of Amman; Hillbrow, a squatter settlement of Johannesburg, has a population largely consisting of Nigerian and French-speaking African immigrants; the people living in the informal settlements (*asentamientos nuevos*) of San José de Costa Rica generally come from Nicaragua.[12]

Addressing the growing presence of international migrants, and related issues of spatial segregation and poverty, requires a capacity for managing multiculturalism and diversity. In fact, it is not enough to address only the migrants' side; the recipient context has also to be taken into account in order to avoid intolerance. Today, cities are changing faster, becoming more ethnically diverse than ever before, and in many countries with no multicultural background, this produces anxiety, fear and xenophobia. Hence the importance of public campaigns on integration issues, explaining social costs and opportunities of integration, but also underlying the rights and duties of both migrants and hosting communities.

Policy aspects

Migration policies are becoming increasingly important, especially in receiving countries. In general

---

BOX 4.1 Migrant communities in cities

Social networks are becoming the basis for the formation of residential clusters or fully-fledged ethnic neighbourhoods, where migrant social spaces are based on ties of kinship, language and common heritage. In the highly industrialized countries, some inner-city areas have received successive waves of immigrants: the Lower East Side of New York City, the Kensington Market area of Toronto and numerous suburbs in the Los Angeles metropolitan region. Several cities (especially New York, San Francisco and Vancouver) have well-established Chinatowns, while other US cities have developed new ethnic neighbourhoods in the past generation. Miami's Little Havana or Brighton Beach, known as Brooklyn's Little Odessa because of its Russian immigrants, are just two examples among many that might be cited. Some of these ethnic neighbourhoods are both residential and commercial, but others are strictly commercial. For example, Indian immigrants in New York are residentially dispersed; but the Jackson Heights area of Queens serves as the core of their

commercial life and social exchange. By contrast, in the Washington Heights area of New York, where Dominican immigrants both live and work, there are between 1500 and 2000 visible Dominican-owned enterprises. In Berlin, the Kreuzberg area, otherwise known as Little Istanbul, is a commercial and residential centre for the approximately 200,000 Turkish immigrants in that city, and a place where they have developed a stronger affiliation than to Germany as a whole. In Paris, the inner-city Goutte d'Or area is dominated by immigrants from North and West Africa. This pattern of ethnic enclaves can also be observed in developing countries. Significant international communities are present in Abidjan (mostly from West African Francophone countries); in Johannesburg (from Southern African countries and Nigeria); in Bangkok (from Myanmar, Cambodia and China), in San José (from Nicaragua) and in some Gulf capitals (from Southeast Asian countries).

Source: Brettell and Kemper, 2002.

---

terms, there is no doubt that the management of migration flows should not be unilateral. It should include international, national and local bodies.

Coordination among national governments should be improved. In fact, in the case of the European Union (EU), no institutions other than the sovereign member states have the technical means and the legitimacy to control international immigration, though it affects several countries, some of them as the entry door and others as the final destination of migratory flows. Also within the North American Free Trade Agreement (NAFTA) area, migrant flows from Mexico to the US involve economic, political and social factors inherent to both countries. Nonetheless, there are no common bilateral policies and effective measures for reducing illegal entries into the US or labour exploitation in the *maquilladoras* of Mexico. It is only very recently that the US has shown signs of moving in this direction.

A similar situation exists in Asia and Africa. Within the Asia and Pacific Economic Cooperation (APEC) countries, national governments tend to focus the agenda strictly on economic issues, giving less importance to social issues. It is only recently that migration has gained importance, since working opportunities for Asians have decreased in the Gulf States, with a consequent growth of international flows within APEC countries. Within the Southern African Development Community (SADC), labour migration policies lack coordination. For instance, some member countries have failed to recognize the increasing polarization between economically versatile member states such as South Africa, Botswana and Namibia, and the rest of the weaker ones. In particular, entry regulations are often too complex, and it can be more difficult travelling between any two SADC member states than to a third state.[13]

In contrast, *Mercado Común del Sur* (MERCOSUR) and the Andean Community have made some strides in ensuring the social, economic and labour rights of migrant workers. In the context of labour legislation, trade unions have formed a special committee for assessing the dynamics of the labour market, with special emphasis on migration. Moreover, in July 2002 the Andean Community governments adopted the Andean Charter, one section of which deals with the basic measures required to protect migrant workers and members of their families.[14]

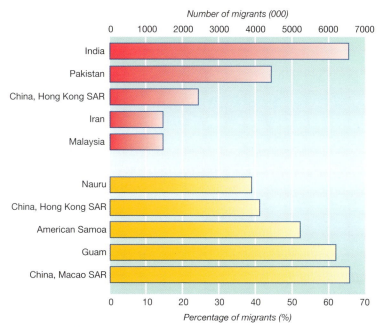

Source: United Nations Population Division, 2002b.

FIGURE 4.1 **Countries and areas with the largest number of international migrants (thousand) and the highest percentage of international migrants in Asia and the Pacific, 2000**

Developing countries

Asia and the Pacific

International migrants in the Asia and Pacific region total about 19 million and the rate of migrants, as a percentage of the total population, at 2.3 per cent, is very low. There are different migration patterns, generated either for economic or political reasons. In Southeast Asia, the percentage of foreigners is the highest in the region (about 5 per cent), with very significant percentages in Singapore (33 per cent) and Malaysia (7 per cent). This is probably associated with the rapid industrialization that has occurred during the last few decades. In South-central Asia (India, Pakistan and Bangladesh), the rate is quite low (1.5 per cent), even though the sub-region has the highest number of international migrants (about 12 million), mainly of people moving from Afghanistan to Pakistan and from Bangladesh and Nepal to India. In general terms, cities of the Asian and Pacific countries do not receive significant numbers of international migrants because people tend to migrate to other continents (Europe, Northern America, Australia and Arab States) or to rural areas (as in Thailand, Malaysia or India).

Labour outflows from the region to the oil-producing countries in the MENA region still involve

Many migrants in Asian cities reside in illegal squatter areas

large numbers of migrant workers, even though, since the 1980s, the mobility of people seeking temporary employment within Eastern and Southeastern Asia has become increasingly important. The high rates of industrialization have generated significant urban growth (more than 3 per cent during the last five years), in some cases sustained by international migrants. In cities such as Bangkok and Kuala Lumpur, their presence remains modest (and often unknown due to illegal and undocumented migration); but in small countries or city states, such as Singapore, their presence is much higher and visible. The financial crisis in 1997, which hit many countries in Eastern and Southeastern Asia, immediately tightened the labour market and the demand for foreign workers. While the crisis led some labour-sending countries to experience a renewed interest in overseas labour migration, the impact of the economic downturn on labour importation in labour-receiving countries was temporary, given the persistent demand for migrant workers in certain sectors.[15] Moreover, in some cities such as Bangkok, international migration continued to be sustained by an increasing flow of Burmese refugees.

The precarious situation of newcomers in Asian cities, where marginalization and urban poverty are growing,[16] is one of the many concerns of both national and municipal authorities. During the past, immigration policies have been tardily implemented, with these countries requiring only temporary labour. In many cities, social cohesion between the local population and foreign communities is becoming a political issue, and governments often give priority to restrictive rather than inclusive policies. For instance,

in 2002, Malaysia deported hundreds of thousands of illegal migrants back to Indonesia and the Philippines. Immigrants and their families (mainly located in urban areas and employed in industry and service sectors) made up some 10 per cent of Malaysia's total population, and, after a surge in crime, Malaysian authorities decided to repatriate most of them.[17] A similar situation is reported in India, where illegal migration to Delhi and Mumbai is becoming a key concern of some political parties. Integration and xenophobia are becoming significant issues, not only in the main cities of the country, but in border regions – such as Assam – where international migration generates social and religious conflicts. In Assam state, there is a very high level of migration of Muslim people from Bangladesh into both the capital city, Guwahati, and the rural areas. Illegal migration is high, and it is facilitated by the difficulty in distinguishing between immigrants and Muslim Indian citizens.[18] However, an estimate of international migrants is difficult in almost every country because of growing numbers of illegal immigrants and refugees. For instance, in Bangkok, some recent studies suggest that there are no reliable data on international migration, though migrants are estimated to be more than 2 per cent of the population (about 150,000 people).

Even though international migration is probably underestimated, there is evidence that, for Asian urban migrants, it is difficult to be integrated within receiving societies. There are differences in language and culture, as well as of understanding, interaction and communication between migrants and local people. Discrimination against migrants has mixed dimensions and is based on race, class and gender. Certain races are discriminated against – for example, Burmese in Thailand or Nepalese in India. Migrant women are more vulnerable to exploitation, even though the feminization of migration flows is growing in many Asian cities: Filipino women go to Kuala Lumpur, Bangkok or Brunei, usually to work as domestic servants; Burmese and Laotian women follow their husbands to Bangkok. Higher levels of discrimination and abuse are reported among migrant sex workers, who represent an increasing proportion in the Thai capital. The level of integration may vary according to specific situations: in Singapore, foreign migrants reportedly have the same rights as local people; Laotians seem to integrate more easily within Thai society due to their similarities in culture, language, physical features and, to some extent, ethnic traditions; and Vietnamese migrants in Cambodia may face more obstacles due to the historical and political rift between the countries, and the social resentment of their higher wealth.[19]

BOX 4.2 Covering local skills shortage: the Vietnamese immigrants in Cambodia

New waves of Vietnamese immigrants began to come to Cambodia during the 1990s, after the Peace Accord between the two countries. There is no account of the number of Vietnamese immigrants; but according to some approximations, there should be about 1 million persons (about 8.7 per cent of the population) of Vietnamese origin in Cambodia. While the major impetus for the Vietnamese to come to Cambodia has been a 'push factor' (Viet Nam presents the paradox of a country having relatively high skills, and yet a low capacity to fully utilize them), in effect there has been a 'pull factor' operating within Cambodia, since the nascent Cambodian economy lacked (and, to an extent, still lacks) some critical skills. Cambodians do not possess these at an adequate scale since substantial skill among the local population was lost during the protracted war. This migratory flow is directed to both urban and rural areas; but in Phnom Penh the higher expertise of the Vietnamese is particularly required. They are engaged in fishing and fish processing, construction (about 80 per cent of the small contractors and supervisors are believed to be of Vietnamese origin) and trade, and they work as skilled workers in machinery and electronic repair workshops and in wood-processing enterprises. Moreover, they are found working in bars, massage parlours, dance halls and in other such 'entertainment' businesses. The earning differential is an important bone of contention between the Khmer and Vietnamese communities. For example, a small-scale Vietnamese fisherperson could earn US$2 to $3 per working day, which is more than the average prevalent earning for such work in Cambodia.

Source: Acharya, 2003.

In Asian cities, the living conditions of migrants are poor and include overcrowded and unhygienic housing. They normally reside in illegal squatter areas. For instance, in Bangkok there is a very high concentration of Burmese migrants in the slum of Klong Toey; in Karachi there are about 1.5 to 2.5 million illegal immigrants (Bengalese, Afghan and Burmese), mostly in the unplanned areas (known as *katchi abadis*) of Baldia and Orangi.[20] Their marginal conditions are also worsened by difficult access to social services, including health services – they tend to seek treatment only when illnesses are more serious. But sometimes they do not know their rights, too. In Thailand, legal migrants who pay for the state health insurance scheme do not have access to such services because they have little understanding of it.

Asian countries are both sending and receiving countries; but governments tend to give priority to emigration policies in order to increase the employment of national workers abroad and their remittances. For instance, about 50 per cent of Southeast Asian countries have a policy framework sustaining emigration, particularly to the Gulf region.[21] Immigration policies are not developed, both at the national and local (urban) levels. Only Singapore has developed an urban immigration policy

BOX 4.3 Efficiency of immigration policies in Singapore

Singapore constantly needs to import foreign manpower at all levels to augment the local work force and support economic growth. According to the 2000 census, foreigners working in Singapore comprise about 600,000 individuals, or 29 per cent of the work force. The majority (more than 50 per cent) have below secondary education, and three out of four are employed in unskilled jobs. Only a few have managerial tasks. It is not easy to migrate to Singapore and illegal migration is very limited due to the severe entry norms. But once in the country, migrants enjoy the highest social and economic conditions in the region. Singapore has a policy of equal treatment for local and foreign workers under its laws. The Employment Act, the principal legislation stipulating the basic terms and conditions of employment, applies equally to foreign and local workers. Foreign workers covered by the act are entitled to prompt payment of salaries, payment for overtime work and other statutory non-wage-related benefits. Foreign workers, like local workers, are also covered under the Workmen's Compensation Act, and are compensated in the same manner as local workers if they are injured at work. Finally, they enjoy free access to all social facilities, including medical, transport and recreational facilities. They are allowed to gather at public places for recreation, and have access to the high standards of medical care enjoyed by Singaporeans at the same subsidized rates. There is a special Foreign Workers Unit at the Ministry of Manpower, set up to address the grievances of foreign workers. Conciliation and advisory services are offered free of charge to foreign workers.

Source: OECD, 2002.

framework, which has been facilitated by its city-state character. In other urban contexts, immigration policies are adopted to face some specific situations (such as presence of refugees, prostitution, female labour migration and assistance to marginal groups) and are often stimulated by local non-governmental organization (NGO) activity. In Bangkok, for example, some migrant groups receive help from private organizations, which aim to raise their awareness of relevant laws, policies and labour rights through publications or radio programmes broadcast in the migrants' own languages. Unfortunately, these actions are not always effective, for several reasons:

- too few employers or migrants know about the policy;
- employers are unwilling to pay registration fees and surety;
- migrants and employers do not want the Thai authorities to collect information about them; and
- employers find it cheaper not to register their migrants.[22]

Latin America and the Caribbean

Nearly 20 million Latin Americans and Caribbeans live abroad, especially in the US, and only a small proportion (about 5.9 million) migrates within the region.[23] International migration still retains some of its traditional features, particularly migratory flows for seasonal harvesting; but this now occurs on a smaller scale due to the decline in the attractiveness of the main countries of destination (Argentina and Venezuela). However, this trend is partially balanced by international migration to urban areas, which is growing in many countries (particularly in Costa Rica and Dominican Republic), where migrants tend to be concentrated in marginal areas.

In Central America, international migrants total 1 million, or 2.6 per cent of the sub-regional population. More than half of them live in Mexico, where they represent a modest 0.5 per cent of the national population. Costa Rica has the highest percentage of migrants (7.7 per cent or 300,000 people) and Belize also has a very high percentage (7.5 per cent), but they total only 12,000 people.[24] Mexico is affected by transit migration, as the major conduit for migrants seeking entry into Northern America. This flow is primarily to some Mexican border cities (Tijuana, Mexicali, Ciudad Juarez and Matamoros) that attract both national and foreign migrants as part of the *maquiladoras* phenomenon – that is, manufacturing plants located in northern Mexico, producing parts for assembly in the US. Migrants live in very poor conditions in these cities (even those who work) because labour in the *maquiladoras* is low paid, while the cost of living in border towns is often 30 per cent higher than in southern Mexico. Therefore, many *maquiladoras* workers are forced to live in shantytowns surrounding the factory cities, which typically lack electricity and water supply. Another significant flow into southern Mexico is the migration of poor people from Guatemala. During the past, it was mainly a circular migration with rural destinations; today it is becoming increasingly urban oriented. In 2002, for instance, there were more than 200,000 undocumented migrants into the southern state of Chiapas, mainly to the border cities of Tapachula and Ciudad Hidalgo. In Belize, rural migrants are still dominant: Belmopan and Belize City absorb only 33 per cent of total foreign immigration; but this percentage is growing, as is the marginality of migrants living there. In fact, the large majority of international migrants in Belize City (Nicaraguans, Hondureans and Salvadorians) live in the degraded neighbourhood of the south side area.

Nicaraguan migration to Costa Rica is one of the most significant in Central America. Like the region's other migration flows, it has deep historical roots in agricultural transient labour, even though this flow is becoming more urban oriented. Today, the San José metropolitan area holds large numbers of Nicaraguans (about 25 per cent of total migrants in the country). They go there as a consequence of political and economic upheaval in their homeland

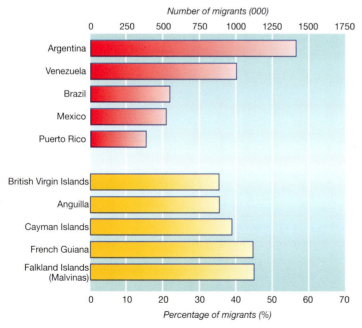

Source: United Nations Population Division, 2002b.

FIGURE 4.2 **Countries and areas with the largest number of international migrants (thousand) and the highest percentage of international migrants in Latin America and the Caribbean, 2000**

and are drawn by higher wages, as the Costa Rican minimum salary is three to four times higher than the Nicaraguan and there are more generous social benefits. During the last ten years, due to the diminishing job opportunities in agriculture, employment has shifted towards urban occupations and has become very gendered and informal: women work overwhelmingly in the domestic and informal marketing sectors, while men predominate in the construction sector.[25] As a consequence of the massive concentration of international migrants, informal settlements (called *asentamientos nuevos*) are increasing in San José: in El Zancudo, Barrio Nuevo, Cristo Viene and La Carpio, Nicaraguans are the large majority population.[26] Their increasing spatial and social segregation should be one of the main concerns of the municipal authorities; but there are no specific policies at present. In some respects, this is not necessary: the poverty subsidy (*bono familiar de vivienda*) is, for example, given to everyone eligible, independent of nationality. But in other cases, being an alien can be a problem: for instance, it is difficult to obtain a housing loan if one of the spouses is not Costa Rican.[27]

In the Caribbean, emigration (mainly to the US and Canada) is much higher than intra-regional migration. According to the official statistics, international migrants within the sub-region are a mere 400,000 (although this figure underestimates the illegal flow of Haitians to the Dominican Republic) or 6.7 per cent of the regional population. On some islands, the percentage of foreigners is very high (10 per cent in the Bahamas and Barbados); but their absolute number remains modest. The only significant concentration of

international migrants is reported in the Dominican Republic, which hosts about 500,000 Haitians (about 6 per cent of the total population) due to both Haiti's political instability and difficult economic conditions during the 1990s. These migrants mainly live in the capital city, Santo Domingo, or in the secondary towns along the eastern coast. Whereas in the past they were mainly employed in agriculture, today they work in various informal activities, including street vending, temporary work or prostitution, or in the tourism sector. In all cases, migrants live in marginal conditions, receiving lower wages and suffering job

---

BOX 4.4 Migration and cultural identity: Nicaraguans in San José de Costa Rica

Among the various effects of Nicaraguan immigration in Costa Rica is the development of a 'tico-nica' or Costa Rican–Nicaraguan culture in many family units, in particular in San José, where the concentration of Nicaraguan immigrants is higher. According to a household survey carried out in San José in 2000, Costa Ricans and Nicaraguans live together in 5 per cent of all households, which may be labelled as being 'intercultural'. Nicaraguan immigrants, on the other hand, have gradually created opportunities to preserve their traditions. The celebration of the *gritería*, on 8 December, is an example of this. Furthermore, they have attained a presence in the media with programmes such as *La Voz Nica*, the *Revista Notíciosa Nicaragüense* and *Nicaragua y Usted*. In the sports arena, numerous Nicaraguans participate in local baseball tournaments and boxing matches. Zadidas, which is a traditional disco located in downtown San José, organizes special events on Sundays – for example, broadcasting baseball games from the Nicaraguan tournament.

Source: IOM, 2003.

BOX 4.5 Migratory flows between Uruguay and Buenos Aires metropolitan area

Argentina is attracting less immigrants than in the past due to the recent national economic crisis, and return migration of workers from Peru, Chile and Bolivia has started during the last few years. Nevertheless, interaction between Buenos Aires and Uruguay is still reported, facilitated by geographical, economic and cultural proximity, so that the Argentinean capital still maintains a substantial concentration of Uruguayan immigrants. Movements to and from Uruguay (mainly Montevideo) represent some 40 per cent of the total entries and exits of persons in the Buenos Aires metropolitan area. The persons in question stated that the reasons for their journeys were visits to friends and relatives, the use of services and commerce, and work connected with business and government activities, and many of them said they travelled very frequently. A smaller flow to Uruguay – mostly from

Buenos Aires – is reported, too. This information gives grounds for formulating the hypothesis that traditional migratory movements, involving poorer and long-term migrants, are only a part of the intense mobility observed. Leaving aside tourism, which follows long-established circuits, the new feature is that there is a close association with the functioning of social, business and institutional networks operating in both territories, which extend across national borders and mainly involve highly qualified workers. How far these new forms of mobility are encouraged by formal integration processes, and how far they simply represent the continuation of existing dynamics, are open questions. What is clear is that, with increasingly low transport costs, these movements allow some persons to attain objectives that could previously only be achieved through traditional migration.

Source: Piovesan, pers comm.

insecurity due to their undocumented and illegal status. Moreover, the Dominican Republic also pays a price, as the large supply of cheap Haitian labour lowers the wages of its unskilled nationals, reduces incentives for improving productivity and increases social conflicts.[28] There are other smaller flows within the sub-region that have some urban impacts: Puerto Rico represents a major destination for migrants from the Dominican Republic and Cuba, where they work in industry and urban services. The Bahamas, with its higher standard of living based on tourism and off-shore financial services, has been a major destination for migrants from Jamaica, Haiti and the Turks and Caicos Islands.[29]

Latin America has the highest number of international migrants in the region (3.7 million), but they represent only 1.6 per cent of the sub-region's total population. Only Venezuela and Argentina have more than 1 million foreigners (or 4 per cent of their national populations). Brazil has a significant 500,000 migrants, although immigration is rapidly decreasing (the figure was double just ten years ago).[30] Some traditional destination countries (Brazil and Venezuela), were strongly affected by the economic crisis of the 1990s, lowering job opportunities in non-urban sectors such as agriculture in Argentina or oil production in Venezuela. In many cases, this situation has increased informal urban migration: for example, in Venezuela, where foreign immigrants (mostly Colombians and Caribbean nationals) tend to

concentrate in cities, especially in the Caracas metropolitan area. This has aroused government concern about illegal migrants in urban areas, who were not so many in the past. In fact, up to some years ago, there were three different types of migrants:

1 fairly permanent migrants settling in urban regions, where work was predominantly in industry, trade and services;
2 permanent migrants settling in border regions, working in farming and stockbreeding, or in urban-type jobs; and
3 seasonal transborder immigrants at harvest time.[31]

The recent economic crisis is progressively lowering the number of foreign immigrants, and those who stay are becoming poorer. In Argentina, for instance, immigrants from Chile, Peru, Bolivia and Paraguay are returning to their home countries; but some of them (people who have lost their jobs and are actually unable or unwilling to leave the country) are concentrating in Buenos Aires, where they live in very marginal conditions. Some poor migrants are clearly visible in the streets, begging in the traffic.

Even though migration issues are debated within the framework of the *Mercado Común del Sur* (MERCOSUR) and the Andean Community – and according to the latest analysis,[32] at least half of Latin American and Caribbean countries have some migration policies – there is no evidence of any specific regulation at the urban level. Where international urban migration is very high, migrants tend to create their own local networks, often with the assistance of local NGOs. In San José de Costa Rica, for instance, Nicaraguans have formed a forum, *Foro sobre población migrante*, in order to highlight migration issues within the political debate, with particular reference to housing problems.[33]

Middle East and Northern Africa (MENA)

The MENA region hosts about 21 million migrants or 6.1 per cent of the region's total population. However, migratory patterns are quite different in each sub-regional area. In the Gulf states, the percentage of migrants is higher (more than 50 per cent of the population), and in some countries international migrants constitute 80 to 90 per cent of the labour force. In the Middle East, there is a large number of migrants (12 million) due to considerable numbers of refugees resulting from decades of conflict; in Northern Africa there is no significant and stable presence of international migrants (they are less than 2 million, or a modest 2.5 per cent of the sub-region's population), even though transit migration is growing,

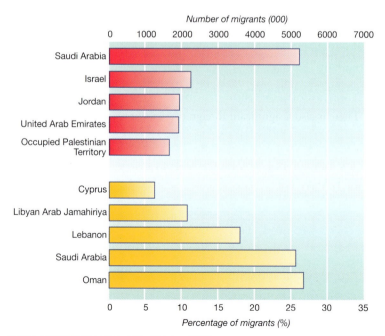

Number of migrants (000)

Source: United Nations Population Division, 2002b.

FIGURE 4.3 **Countries and areas with the largest number of international migrants (thousand) and the highest percentage of international migrants in the Middle East and Northern Africa, 2000**

and many cities of the sub-region are becoming the gateway to Europe for poor sub-Saharan migrants.[34]

In each sub-region, international migrants are mainly urban, where they work in the service sector, or in various industrial activities related to oil production. Their concentration in cities reflects a regional tendency (urbanization level is about 60 per cent), and it is facilitated by efficient employment networks, especially the *kafeel* system, which enables employers to engage migrants while they are still in their home countries. For this reason, illegal immigration is almost non-existent, particularly in the Gulf states. However, migrant conditions are not easy – especially at the beginning – because they must pay high 'sponsorship' fees to a local agent. Sponsorship is a profitable business and labour brokerage offices are a common sight on the streets of Arab cities. In Bahrain for instance, of the US$3200 charged for an ordinary visa, only about $1000 is used for official government fees, and often the *kafeel* can extract additional funds for renewal after some years.[35]

In the Gulf region, high rates of urban population and international migration are strongly correlated. The biggest migrant community is located in Saudi Arabia (more than 5 million), where urban population is 86 per cent, but also in Kuwait and Qatar, where international migration is significant in percentage terms (58 per cent and 73 per cent, respectively) and urban population is very high (97 per cent and 92 per cent, respectively). The very large majority of foreigners are concentrated in the capital cities, and since the 1970s they mainly consist of Southeast Asians, who have overtaken intra-MENA migrants due to their much lower wage demand level, better working expertise and discipline and higher English proficiency (which is useful for technical posts). In addition, Asian workers were preferred when Gulf monarchies started to realize that large-scale immigration from other Arab countries also implied importing radical socio-political ideas, including pan-Arab ideologies and Arab nationalism. Non-nationals (both Arabs and Asians) are not eligible for either permanent residence status or citizenship in the Gulf states, except for a foreign woman marrying a national. There is a general lack of methods to integrate immigrant populations within the receiving societies. Immigrants arrive there mainly to work, not to live permanently and generally do not bring their families.[36] Today, the tendency of hiring foreign workers is changing and most of the Gulf governments are taking a second look at labour immigration, given the rapid increase in the local population and their increasing preference for nationals in the allocation of skilled jobs. However, these 're-nationalization' policies do not seem yet to be effective. Many Gulf states still do not have enough

Number of illegal or undocumented migrants is unknown

people with adequate practical skills and expertise, and private employers still prefer migrant workers as they are considerably more flexible in terms of working hours and wages. At the urban level, any notable responses to international migration seem to be linked to wider issues. In Kuwait, for example, since the 1990s, the government, in an attempt to change the concentration pattern and relieve overcrowding in Kuwait City, has invested in the new secondary towns at Subiya and Al-Khiran in order to attract a large number of workers and investors.

In the Middle East, apart from some specific situations such as those in Israel and Palestine, there are high rates of international migrants in Jordan and Lebanon: 40 per cent and 18 per cent, respectively, with Palestinian refugees making up the bulk of the international migrants in both countries and in Syria, too. There is also a significant foreign presence in Turkey (about 1.5 million).[37] In this country, in particular, cities are becoming an entry door for both legal and illegal migration to Europe. About 200,000 undocumented migrants transit through Turkey each year, stopping for various periods in Istanbul or in the secondary towns of the Aegean Coast. These people come from various Asian or African countries (such as Afghanistan, Bangladesh, Iran, Iraq, the Democratic Republic of the Congo, Egypt and Ghana) and are either economic migrants re-routed after failed attempts to enter the EU countries or asylum seekers. In addition, there are many eastern European immigrants looking for work in Turkish cities, often entering illegally or ending up in illegal situations.[38] Istanbul is also the terminal of a complex migratory network of cities in the Arab States. In fact, for the last two decades, a migration movement has developed

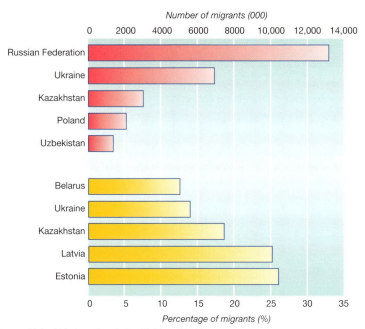

Source: United Nations Population Division, 2002b.

FIGURE 4.5 **Countries with the largest number of international migrants (thousand) and the highest percentage of international migrants in Central and Eastern Europe and Central Asia, 2000**

them in the care of tenants. This has contributed to overcrowding because tenants often sublet at lower rentals.[53]

In general terms, migration policies in Africa are very scarce, both at the national and urban level: immigration policies are evident only in 2 per cent of African countries, while half of them have no specific policies at all.[54] When authorities have been unable to face increasing illegal migration, they have often resorted to massive forced repatriations, which normally produce social conflicts and political tensions among countries. Despite this negative situation, there is evidence that where programmes or strategies have been implemented, some positive results have been obtained. In South Africa, for instance, the Johannesburg and Durban municipalities

(respectively through the *Inner City Street Trading Management Strategy* and the *Department of Informal Trade and Small Business Opportunities*) are trying to integrate foreign informal street traders.[55] Moreover, some migratory flows are related to strong transurban networks, which involve many cities in their routes (the Maputo or Beira corridors in Mozambique; the Atlantic urban corridor running from Cape Town to Douala; the Southern African Development Community urban corridor from Dar es Salaam to Johannesburg; and some historical Sahelian routes, such as the Kano-Khartoum trading route).[56] All of them have remarkable economic potentials. Strengthening these networks (which remain mainly informal), and linking them to local, national and bilateral policies, could be an effective way of promoting social integration and economic development at the urban level.

Economies in transition

Since 1989, the countries with transition economies (TE) have witnessed a dramatic increase in population movements, due to social changes that occurred with the collapse of their political system. Most migration flows are to the advanced economies, consisting of people looking for both jobs and asylum; but there are significant movements within the region, too. There are 33 million international migrants, or 8.1 per cent of the regional population, mainly located in Eastern Europe and Russia. The slackening of border controls, the deterioration of local economies and some local conflicts have forced large numbers of people to move, even though there is no clear picture of the distribution of international migration. According to the latest reports,[57] in many countries (for example, Russia, Poland and the Baltic states) there is evidence that international migration is largely to urban areas, which now account for about 70 per cent of the region's total population. Urban international migration in TE countries is frequently associated with the increasing role of the informal sector, and with a general impoverishment of these societies, as evidenced by unemployment, inequality, deterioration of public services and a fall in the provision of educational services.[58] In terms of migratory flows, Russia remains by far the most important destination country in Eastern Europe and Central Asia, with more than 13 million immigrants (about 9 per cent of its population), followed by Ukraine, Kazakhstan and Belarus. The Baltic republics have the highest percentage of foreign population (in Estonia, 26 per cent; in Latvia, 25 per cent; and in Lithuania, 9 per cent). Most of them live in the main cities (with an increasing number of illegal immigrants): for instance, in Lithuania their main destinations are the three major cities of Vilnius, Kaunas and Klaipeda, which together attract over 80 per cent of the foreign labour force.[59] Moreover, populations in the Trans-Caucasus region are continuing to leave their countries, migrating to the richest TE countries (Russia, Poland and the Baltic republics) and to Western Europe (mainly Germany). Finally, an increasing immigration trend is occurring in some Eastern Europe capitals – such as Warsaw, Prague and Budapest – due to the new political and economic roles of their nations, as most of them will join the EU in the next few years.

Russia is the main receiving country among the TE countries and although access to labour markets is more difficult than during the Soviet period, historical ties, habit, language and proximity make it easier for migrants from the Trans-Caucasus and Central Asia to work in Russia. The first major flow of both migrants and refugees into Russia occurred in 1988 and 1989, when Azerbaijanis and Armenians (mainly the latter) fled the conflict in Nagorno-Karabakh and when people fled Uzbekistan following a massacre in 1989. During the same period, a significant return migration of Russian people was reported from the Baltic republics, particularly to St Petersburg. These flows found Russian cities unprepared: in 1992, the national government established its first agency for dealing with such conditions, the Federal Migration Service (FMS); but the service has generally been under-funded and understaffed. Given the FMS's limited resources and the very bad living conditions of migrants, several international social and charitable organizations are active in aiding migrants, especially in Moscow, where they constitute slightly more than 10 per cent of the urban population.[60] Moscow and St Petersburg are among main poles attracting migrants from the former Soviet republics. However, Asian migration is primarily to the cities along the Russian–Chinese border or to Vladivostok. In particular, this city is hosting a growing number of Chinese, Vietnamese and Northern Korean citizens, who are mainly illegal, resulting in some negative consequences, previously unknown: growth of crime and prostitution, underemployment and worsening of the social climate.

Since a few decades ago, Eastern European cities have become points on two main transit routes of illegal migrants coming from the Balkans, Russia or Asia, which pass through Poland. It is estimated that up to 15,000 people illegally cross the territory of Poland every year. The first route is the 'Balkan trail', used by Romanians, Bulgarians and citizens from former Yugoslavia who enter legally because regulations allow a one-month stay without a visa. Then they try to cross into Germany illegally. The second emigration trail via Poland runs from the Lithuanian border to Germany and it is mainly used by people from

Illegal migrants put themselves at risk

Afghanistan, Iran, Iraq, India, Pakistan and Sri Lanka. As a result, cities such as Warsaw, Lodz, Prague, Budapest and Sofia host transit migrants, who can find jobs only in the informal sector due to their illegal status in the country. But in some cases, even seasonal or temporary migration is reported. Some citizens of Russia and Ukraine come to Poland for very short periods (from three to seven days or some weeks), mainly for the purpose of trade.[61]

International migrants tend to move finally to Western Europe, even though people who remain in TE countries are increasing. In particular, this happens among those nationalities that establish solid local networks and large national communities. Their numbers are not always known; but according to some

---

BOX 4.10 New Turkish communities in Polish cities

The total number of Turkish immigrants staying in Poland (compared with other groups of migrants, such as Vietnamese or citizens of the former Soviet Union) is not large enough to stir up the attention of official institutions and initiate the monitoring of Turkish residents in Poland. Furthermore, due to their peculiar strategy of settlement, the total number of Turkish in Poland (some several thousand) is underestimated and data concerning the same topic (for example, the number of Turkish citizens crossing the border illegally) collected by different public institutions seem to be rather incoherent. Over the last decade, Poland has seen a wave of Turkish immigrants, which exemplifies a specific pattern of chain migration. Unlike in Germany, Turkish migrants coming to Poland have not had access to jobs as low-skilled industrial workers, but have had to actively look for an economic niche for themselves. They started as small traders and wholesalers; today, they have become successful businessmen and investors who bring from Turkey potential partners or engineers, not just poor family members. The majority of them live in Warsaw or in the vicinity; but small communities of Turks are reported in Poznan, Gdansk and Lodz.

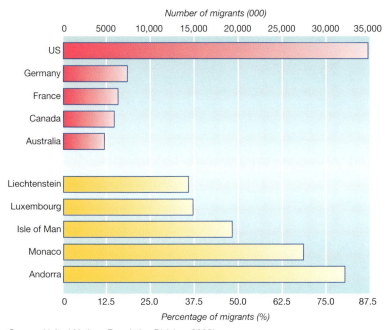

Source: United Nations Population Division, 2002b.

FIGURE 4.6 **Countries and areas with the largest number of international migrants (thousand) and the highest percentage of international migrants in Northern America, Western Europe and the Pacific (advanced economies), 2000**

estimates, there are more than 10 per cent in Prague, between 5 and 10 per cent in Warsaw and about 5 per cent in Budapest, where migrants from other TE countries and the Far East are present. As in other urban contexts, Chinese immigrants are generally employed in the growing restaurant business in Prague or Budapest; Ukrainian people work as unskilled labourers in the construction sector; Vietnamese work in Warsaw and Prague as market traders, selling clothing and electronics; and Armenians work in the informal street-market trade. East European migrants work as unskilled or semi-skilled employees, while Asians prefer self-employment or working in activities managed by their own nationals. In both cases, illegal workers are the majority, due to the high level of undocumented migration. Access to jobs follows different routes and it depends upon nationality. Inside their internal networks, exploitation is very high; but for an illegal migrant, this is normally the only way to obtain work. Sometimes these networks are very visible, such as the illegal 'people markets', well known to foreigners and local employers (a notable one is in the *Moskva ter* area in Prague). Not many communities are integrated within the hosting society, even though there are some exceptions. For instance, the Vietnamese in Polish cities seem to be well organized socially, and they are usually not involved much in crime and other negative activities. They send their children to Polish schools, learn the Polish language,

read Polish papers and watch Polish TV, and most of them aim to stay permanently in the country.[62]

In general terms, to this day TE countries have neither systematic migratory legislation nor specific policies for managing urban international migration. For this reason, immigrants use existing legislative inadequacies to their advantage and are compelled to violate other laws. It is only recently that some countries are beginning to introduce proper regulations for managing international migration; but priority is given to entry procedures. For example, since 2002, Russia has added new requirements in order to limit immigrant flows. However, little is done to lower illegal transit migration to Western Europe.

Advanced economies

The advanced economies (AE) have the largest number of international migrants, about 77 million, or 9 per cent of their total population. Northern America (Canada and the US) has the largest number of migrants at 41 million, and Oceania (Australia and New Zealand) has the largest percentage (24 per cent of the total population). Europe stands in the middle, with 28 million international migrants, or 9 per cent of its total population.[63]

In Europe, migrants are concentrated in Germany (7 million), France (6 million) and the UK (4 million), even though the country with the highest percentage of immigrants is Switzerland (25 per cent of its total population). Cities receive the majority of flows of international migrants, particularly the main European capitals. For example, the proportion of foreigners in the total population is almost 27 per cent in the London area and 26 per cent in the Brussels area, 14.5 per cent in Stuttgart and almost 17 per cent in Vienna. And this percentage is at least double the national average in the Paris area (13.9 per cent) and Madrid (5.7 per cent). The Greater London Metropolitan Area accounts for almost half of the country's foreign population, whereas its demographic weight does not exceed 13 per cent.[64] With the increase of international migration, major urban centres such as London, Paris, Frankfurt and Berlin have become multicultural metropolises; but ethnic diversity is also significant in some other cities. Marseilles is a gateway city for immigrants from Northern Africa, as is Lyon; Amsterdam is becoming both a gateway and a place of permanent residence for people from Northern Africa, the Middle East and the Caribbean; and finally some southern European cities, such as Rome and Barcelona, are witnessing significant migration flows from developing countries, with an increasing percentage of undocumented and illegal migrant residents.

This trend has produced significant economic and social impacts and requires new migration policies, which should involve both local and national governments. At the city level, migrants are involved in an increasing number of economic activities, both formal and informal, as employees or small entrepreneurs. For example, in some neighbourhoods of Marseille (Vieux-Port, Saint-Charles and Joliett), there is a very high concentration of informal trade managed by African and Southeast Asian migrants, which is considered the first step of migrants into the labour market.[65] Other ethnic groups are involved in more formal activities: Chinese are shifting from their traditional core business (food) to a wider set of retail products, not only in the biggest European capitals, but also in secondary towns of Italy, France and Spain. Their presence is becoming higher and more evident as well, producing highly visible social and cultural impacts – for example, in the way they use urban spaces, reproducing their own living habits. As a result of migration from Arab countries, Islamic communities (mainly located in cities) are spreading in many European countries and Islam is now the second most significant religion in Europe: Germany and France have more than 3 million Islamic inhabitants each, the UK more than 2 million, and significant communities are reported in Spain, Italy and The Netherlands.[66]

To face the different issues related to international migration, many municipalities are formulating strategies for socially integrating, and reducing the marginalization of, migrants. In Stuttgart, where 24 per cent of the 565,700 inhabitants are foreigners, priority is given to inclusive policies. The participation of migrants in municipal affairs has a long tradition, and since 1983, the Aliens Committee of the Municipal Council (an institutional body of the Municipality of Stuttgart representing aliens) has, since its creation, made important proposals to promote understanding between the various groups within the population.[67] A similar experience is occurring in Birmingham, where, since 1990, foreign communities can rely on the Standing Consultative Forum, which enables them to be consulted and engaged as recognized city actors by the municipality.[68] In many other cities, immigrants' issues are inserted in broader policy frameworks, involving social marginality, as a whole, or international communities, in particular. For example, at the end of the 1990s, the municipality of The Hague launched an urban and social renewal policy in its southwest districts, aimed at improving housing conditions and the provision of services. That action was not targeted specifically at migrants, but rather at disadvantaged neighbourhoods that happened to also have the largest concentration of migrants in terms of

Northern America is a traditional destination of international migrants

percentage (more than 25 per cent of the local population – mainly Turks, Moroccans and Surinamese).[69] In France, a similar policy has been implemented with a special fund, *Fonds d'Action Sociale pour les Travailleurs Immigrés et Leurs Familles*, allocated specifically for migrants living in distressed areas.[70]

Northern America is a traditional destination of international migration and has the highest number of migrants in the world: about 40 million, or 15 per cent of the total population.[71] Each year, Canada and the US receive legal as well as undocumented and illegal migrants, mainly from Central and Latin America (more than 50 per cent) and Asia, who have replaced the previous European migrants. They are primarily concentrated in large cities such as New York, Miami, Los Angeles, Toronto and Vancouver. About 93 per cent of the foreigners born in the US live in cities, compared with only 73 per cent of the native born. International migration often sustains cities' population growth. For example, while more than 1.2 million people left Los Angeles County during the first half of the 1990s, immigration and the

BOX 4.11 The challenge of integrating migrants within host societies: the case of Berlin

Like many other cities in Germany, Berlin faces the problems associated with a growing immigrant population. Berlin's present situation as an immigrant destination can, in many ways, be compared to other large European cities. Immigrants are the fastest growing group in the population. More than 500,000 out of 3.4 million people living in the capital today do not speak German as their native tongue, and in 2010 they will be over 630,000. Berlin is the largest Turkish city outside Turkey, with more than 180,000 people of Turkish origin. Most immigrants are blue-collar workers and poorly qualified for a labour market with high skill demands, a mismatch that can be found in other European cities as well. Since 1981, a commissioner for migration and integration has been in charge of some key functions, such as:

- formulating policies and addressing questions concerning migration and integration issues in Berlin;
- providing information to all residents and campaigning for and publicly promoting integration, tolerance and intercultural dialogue; and
- cooperating with partners at the European and national levels, as well as with the countries of origin of migrants living in the city.

As a result of this institutional innovation, Berlin is now seen as a prototype for integration policies. What is crucial in its success is that this public body did not focus its activities solely on the migrant population, but also directed them to local people. In this regard, Berlin's experience illustrates the importance of addressing local fears and anxieties when dealing with integration.

Source: IOM, 2003.

BOX 4.12 The importance of remittances: three stories of international migrants in London

The phenomenon of migrant workers sending money home is not new. What is new is the scale and importance to developing countries and their increasing visibility in higher-income country (HIC) societies, particularly within cities. The effect on some smaller and poor countries is remarkable, where the impact of remittances on gross domestic product (GDP) ranges from 10 to 30 per cent. Besides problems of social integration, illegal immigration and criminality (which normally attract higher political attention), migrants are playing important consumer and labour roles in the hosting countries, as well as making significant development contributions to their countries of origin through remittance networks. For example, 'non-resident Bangladeshis from the UK send home far more than the equivalent amount of UK aid through official and unofficial sources; they contribute almost a third of foreign exchange earnings', says Murad Qureshi, who leads the British Bangladeshi Professional Association campaign on the issue.

The Bangladeshi curry house bosses

Curry house owners have channelled thousands of UK pounds into building schools in needy areas. Shahid Abul Kalam, who runs the Raj Boy Restaurant on London's Commercial Road, funded the refurbishment and extension of a 900-pupil secondary school in his parent's home village of Gohorpur, in Bangladesh. He raised UK£16,000 and went back at the beginning of this year to see the works commence. 'Almost everyone in the British Bangladeshi community does this. Interestingly, it has moved on from sending money to families,

to funding useful social projects', says Murad Qureishi of the British Bangladeshi Professional Association.

The nanny from the Philippines

What may seem an unconventional marriage is, in fact, a relationship that provides vital aid for a community. Elli, 34, is from a rice-growing village in the Philippines. For years she had a pen-friend relationship with a London musician who earns money as a builder. They married after he flew out to meet her. In London, Elli is a live-in nanny earning around UK£300 per week, seeing her husband at weekends. The husband does not drink or smoke and they live cheaply. Some of their money is saved to buy a home; the rest is spent on 'foreign aid': 'My village suffers; they get very little from the government. Some of my family live in Canada; we all help.'

The waitress from Bogotá

Martina, 29, is bending the rules. She comes from Bogotá, Colombia, and has been in London for two years on a student visa. Her progress is monitored by the Home Office, but what they do not know is that Martina works illegally, getting up at 4.30 am four days a week to serve breakfast in a hotel. She earns about UK£160 a week, pays no rent or bills, and sends more than UK£100 each month to her mother, who has just bought a small farm outside Bogotá. Her mother borrowed from the bank and needs to pay the debt off quickly. Colombia is one of the most violent places in the world and Martina has no immediate plans to return.

high birth rate associated with migrants resulted in a net gain of more than 960,000 people.[72] In many Northern American cities, there is a significant presence of particular nationals or ethnic groups: 40 per cent of the residents of Los Angeles County are Hispanic, primarily Mexican; Dade County in Miami is home to the majority of Cuban immigrants in the US; most Dominicans and half of the Russian immigrants have settled in New York; while Chinese immigrants are concentrated in Vancouver and San Francisco's Chinatowns, as well as in New York City's Lower East Side. In addition, some foreign migrants are settling directly in smaller towns across the heartland of the US, especially where there are better employment opportunities.[73]

The presence of foreign migrants is stimulating urban economic development, sustaining investment in marginal areas, and contributing to the revitalization of inner-city areas. For example, in Canada, several neighbourhoods in Vancouver have been revitalized by immigrants, particularly by the Chinese, with changes evident in both the financial and social fabric of the city. Research shows that native residents in urban centres with a large foreign-born population fare better economically than residents in other areas, suggesting that city economies benefit from the expansion attributable to the presence of immigrants. Moreover, there is some evidence that most immigrant groups achieve earning parity with the local population within about ten years of their arrival in the US. It is notable that the household income of Asian-Americans, many of whom are first-generation immigrants, exceeds that of the native-born population. Of course, economic and social marginality is still present among international communities, especially among the Hispanics, who have incomes well below the average primarily because their formal education is more limited. In some cities (such as Los Angeles or Miami), their condition is a matter of concern for public authorities because increasing numbers of young Hispanic migrants are involved in local crime, which is making peripheral neighbourhoods violent and insecure.

Australia and New Zealand are two major traditional immigration countries and accommodate about 5.5 million international migrants, or 24 per cent of their total population.[74] In Australia, migrants are much more concentrated in cities and represent about 30 per cent of the urban population in Sydney. They primarily comprise skilled or semi-skilled Southeast Asian workers, who have replaced – as in Northern America – the European migration of the 1950s and 1960s. Even though the employment status of some migrants is precarious (especially those with non-English-speaking backgrounds), in Australian and New Zealand cities there is generally no significant spatial segregation of migrants (in contrast to some Aboriginal urban communities), at least according to the way in which the term is used for urban concentrations in the US or the UK.[75]

In Japan, international migration is encouraged by the decline in fertility rates and the appearance of socio-demographic disparities, as the national population is becoming older and as local people now generally refuse low-level employment requiring unskilled labour. The percentage of foreigners is low (1.3 per cent, or 1.6 million individuals), and urban international immigration is a relatively new phenomenon, considering that until the 1960s, Tokyo was largely a destination of Japanese rural–urban migrants. It was only during the late 1980s that significant immigration from other Asian countries started. However, during the last decade, illegal international immigration has been growing: illegal migrants are currently estimated to be about 300,000. As in other advanced economy metropolises, this phenomenon is generally associated with labour exploitation, spatial segregation and social violence. In Tokyo, Asian immigrants are transforming some inner-city areas (such as Shinjuku and Ikebukuro) into multi-ethnic communities, where tensions among different nationalities are widely evident. A similar situation is also reported in Toyota City, the centre of Japan's automobile industry, where there is a concentration of *Nikkeijin* workers: South American nationals with Japanese ancestry.[76]

Notes

1 This chapter is based on 'Transnational migration and globalization', a paper prepared by Vittorio Piovesan, Università IUAV di Venezia, Dipartimento di Pianificazione.

2 De Varennes, 2003.

3 United Nations Population Division, 2002a.

4 'Transnational migrants', or 'international migrants', or 'migrant stock' (the term used by the United Nations Population Division) refers to 'the mid-year estimate of the number of people born outside the country. For countries lacking data on place of birth, the estimated number of non-citizens. In both cases, migrant stock also includes refugees, some of whom may not be foreign-born' (United Nations Population Division, 2002a).

5 'Refugees' refers to 'persons recognized as refugees under the 1951 Convention Relating to the Status of Refugees or the 1969 Organization of African Unity Convention Governing the Specific Aspects of Refugee Problems in Africa; those granted refugee status in accordance with the United Nations High Commissioner for Refugees (UNHCR) Statute; and those granted humanitarian status or temporary protection by the State in which they find themselves. Also included are Palestinian refugees registered with the United Nations Relief and Welfare Agency (UNRWA)' (United Nations Population Division, 2002a).

6 International migrants, or 'migrant stock', expressed as a percentage of the total population (United Nations Population Division, 2002b).

7 Hugo, 2003.

8 Hugo, 2003.

9 'Remittances' refers to 'current monetary transfers made by migrants who are employed or intend to remain employed for more than a year in another economy in which they are considered residents' (United Nations Population Division, 2002a).

10 Contreras and Johnson, 2004.

11 OECD, 2002.

12 UN-Habitat, 2003a.

13 Mulenga, 2000.

14 Boye, 2002.

15 United Nations Population Division, 2003.

16 UNCHS (Habitat), 2001a, 2001b.

17 IOM, 2003.

18 Saikia, 2002.

19 Asian Migration Centre, 2002.

20 UN-Habitat, 2003a.

21 United Nations Population Division, 2002a.

22 Asian Migration Centre, 2002.

23 United Nations Population Division, 2002a.

24 United Nations Population Division, 2002a.

25 Mahler, 2000.

26 Morales, 2002.

27 IOM, 2003.

28 UNCHS (Habitat), 1996; IOM, 2003.

29 IMF, 2003.

30 United Nations Population Division, 2002a.

31 Pellegrino, 2000.

32 United Nations Population Division, 2002a.

33 IOM, 2003.

34 United Nations Population Division, 2002a; UNCHS (Habitat), 2001a.

35 United Nations Population Division, 2002a.

36 IOM, 2003.

37 United Nations Population Division, 2002a.

38 IOM, 2003

39 IOM, 2003.

40 Evans, 1999.

41 IOM, 2003.

42 United Nations Population Division, 2002a.

43 Boubakri, 2001.

44 Zohry, 2002.

45 McCormick and Wahba, 2002.

46 United Nations Population Division, 2002a.

47 United Nations Population Division, 2002b.

48 United Nations Population Division, 2002a.

49 IOM, 2003.

50 IOM, 2003.

51 IOM, 2003.

52 Oucho and Peberdy, 2001.

53 IOM, 2003.

54 United Nations Population Division, 2002a.

55 IOM, 2003.

56 UN-Habitat, 2002a,b.

57 IOM, 2003; OECD, 2003.

58 UNCHS (Habitat), 2001a.

59 UN-Habitat, 2003a.

60 UN-Habitat, 2003a.

61 Iglicka, 2001.

62 Iglicka, 2001.

63 United Nations Population Division, 2002a.

64 OECD, 2003.

65 OECD, 2003.

66 IOM, 2003.

67 UNCHS (Habitat), 1996.

68 United Nations Population Division, 2002b.

69 UN-Habitat, 2003a.

70 OECD, 2003.

71 United Nations Population Division, 2002a.

72 OECD, 2003.

73 Brettell and Kemper, 2002.

74 United Nations Population Division, 2002a.

75 OECD, 2003.

76 United Nations Population Division, 2002a.

Chapter 5

Assessing Living Conditions:
Focus on Urban Poverty [1]

Slums and urban poverty   103

Developing economies   106

Asia and the Pacific: an unprecedented decline in poverty   106

Poverty, inequalities and slums in Latin America and the Caribbean   110

Urban poverty in the Middle East and Northern Africa (MENA):
progress hindered by conflicts and poor governance   113

Sub-Saharan Africa: more urban poor in life-threatening conditions   116

Urban poverty in the transition economies   121

Homelessness in the advanced economies   124

TABLE 5.6 **Key global indicators**

	Year	Data
World's population living in urban areas	1970	36.8%
	2000	47.2%
	2030	60.2%
Urban population in the less developed regions (urbanization level)	1970	25.1%
	2000	40.4%
	2030	56.4%
Urban population in the more developed regions (urbanization level)	1970	67.7%
	2000	75.4%
	2030	82.6%
World's population growth	2000 to 2030	0.97%/year
World's urban population growth	2000 to 2030	1.8%/year
Urban population growth in the less developed regions	2000 to 2030	2.67%/year
Rural population growth in the less developed regions	2000 to 2030	0.1%/year
Population living below US$1 a day (extreme poverty)	1990	29%
	1999	23%
Share of the world's poorest quintile in total consumption	2000	2%

Sources: UNDP, 2002; World Bank, 2003c; UN Population Division, 2002a.

Ujung Pandang. Such high levels of acute malnutrition are usually only detected under emergency or disaster conditions and indicate a serious lack of food at the household level.[17] Water pollution in some locations has increased since the crisis began, as firms have exploited weaker government efforts to monitor and enforce regulations.[18] It further points to the strong

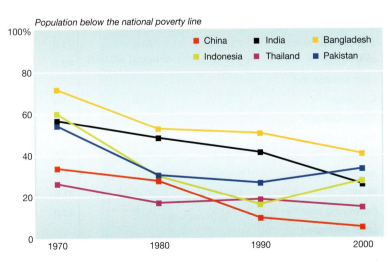

Population below the national poverty line

Source: World Bank, 2003c.

FIGURE 5.4 **Income poverty trends, selected countries, 1970–2000**

possibility that illegal dumping of toxic wastes has also increased. This has posed a serious health threat to slum areas that are more likely to be located near to dumping sites.

The South Asian experience shows that without satisfactory growth, wealth distribution and poverty worsen and pro-equity, anti-poverty transfers become unsustainable.[19] Studies in Indonesia, Malaysia, Thailand and the Philippines have shown that most of the decline in poverty rates has been attributed to economic growth rather than to improved distribution.[20] However, growth alone can produce undesirable distributional outcomes even when reducing poverty. A number of recent regional trends indicate disturbing increases in inequality across several dimensions, affecting certain economic population strata along the lines of class, caste, religion and ethnicity. This may be the result of 'policy packages' where liberalization measures have not been accompanied by sufficient redistributive policies. In China, where large-scale poverty reduction has been achieved,[21] inequality has deepened, with income distribution now in favour of urban areas and coastal regions. It is also expected that further increases in income inequality will deepen the rural–urban and inter-provincial disparities in China.

Although there has been remarkable progress in reducing poverty in Asia over the last 25 years, the continent still accounts for two-thirds of the world's poor, affecting about 800 million people;[22] 240 to 260 million of them reside in urban areas.[23] Nearly one third of the urban poor have no access to safe water and more than two-thirds do not have access to adequate sanitation.[24] The majority of the urban poor are concentrated in Bangladesh, India, Indonesia, Pakistan and the People's Republic of China. Six megacities in the region – namely, Beijing, Mumbai, Kolkata, Jakarta, Shanghai and Tianjin have the largest concentrations of urban poor.[25] Figures indicate that huge challenges still exist in the fields of basic education, gender equality, child health, maternal mortality and environmental sustainability before the Millennium Development Goals (MDGs) are attained.[26]

The overall urbanization trends, characterized by a rapid urbanization in a still fragile socio-economic context, pose serious challenges for poverty reduction and slum improvement efforts. The regional average urban growth rate, of about 2.68 per cent per year,[27] is about 6.5 times higher than for the developed regions, with the absolute number of total Asian urban residents being almost triple that in the highly industrialized countries.[28] The expansion of urban-based economic activities has led to massive rural–urban migration, which has put pressure on urban housing and other services, leading to the development of slums.[29]

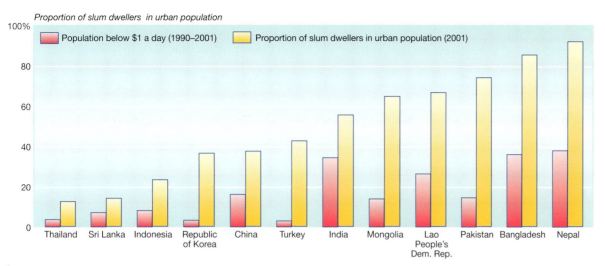

Proportion of slum dwellers in urban population

Legend:
- Population below $1 a day (1990–2001)
- Proportion of slum dwellers in urban population (2001)

Countries (left to right): Thailand, Sri Lanka, Indonesia, Republic of Korea, China, Turkey, India, Mongolia, Lao People's Dem. Rep., Pakistan, Bangladesh, Nepal

Sources: UN-Habitat, 2003b; World Bank, 2003c.

FIGURE 5.5 **Population in poverty and slums, selected countries**

Recent estimates of the numbers of slum dwellers in Asia and the Pacific also reveal that inequalities in terms of living conditions are still sharp. It is estimated that about half of the world's urban slum dwellers live in Asia and the Pacific. In 2001, 38 per cent of the region's 3.7 billion people were living in urban areas,[30] with 43 per cent of its 1.2 billion urban residents living in slums. India and China alone accounted for 65 per cent of the overall Asian urban slum population. The region's group of least developed countries had an urban slum incidence of about 72 per cent, about 30 per cent more than the regional average. Challenges in those countries are great, as they are subject to sustained high urbanization rates[31] and huge financial constraints in delivering adequate services.

In their transition from being predominantly rural countries to mainly urban ones, large numbers of migrants have flowed into the slums of attractive cities in search of new employment and educational opportunities. While the large Asian slums appear to be the main recipients of migrants, as with the famous example of Dharavi in Mumbai (considered to be the largest slum in Asia), many slums exist at a smaller scale in the forms of *encroachments* on the regular city areas, absorbing the labour needed to maintain the richer neighbourhoods. In most countries, slums host important informal-sector activities and are seen as intermediate locations for new migrants. They often turn into more permanent neighbourhoods with long-term informal activities, the latter becoming part of the main urban economy.

Available data are not sufficient to show the determinants of being a slum dweller or to reveal the differences in terms of living conditions between slum and non-slum neighbourhoods, in both urban and rural areas. However, some recent health studies on

Despite remarkable progress in poverty reduction, there are about 250 million urban poor in Asia

BEST PRACTICE
ARTISTRY THAT SHAPES DESTINIES: SELF-EMPLOYED WOMEN ASSOCIATION (SEWA), LUCKNOW, INDIA

SEWA's objective was to organize women who were engaged in handicrafts to gain direct access to markets. This was achieved through skills upgrading, a viable system of production, market development and paying higher wages. Strategies included reviving and improving craftwork and sensitizing artisans on the benefits of a collective approach. Craftwork has been revived and artisans have been placed in a strong position for individual and collective bargaining. Economic well-being has improved the quality of life, especially with regard to better nutrition, healthcare, breaking the debt cycle, improving shelter and, most importantly, raising the status of women in the household. Since women send their children to school, they are not forced into labour. Planned parenthood is becoming visible through a quiet revolution in which poor women are the key decision-makers.
Source: www.bestpractices.org.

BOX 5.3 Dharavi: the largest slum in Asia

More than half of the 12 million residents of Mumbai live in slums – on once-vacant lands, along railway tracks, on pavements and along the sea shore. They occupy 4 to 6 per cent of the total land area of the city. Dharavi, often qualified as the largest slum in Asia, is spread over 175 hectares and shelters about 1 million people. It is located between Mumbai's two main suburban railway lines, Western and Central Railway, which are the virtual lifelines of Mumbai, transporting thousands of people from one end of the metropolis to the other. People have found ways of getting water, even if water is not supplied, to build houses even when there is no security of tenure and no financial help, and to find work. Every year, the poor in Mumbai suffer incredible hardships during the monsoons. Their settlements – usually located in low-lying areas – are awash in rivers of sewage and rainwater that gush through their congested lanes. For days on end, the muck does not clear. The worst off are those who have perched precariously on hillsides or along water pipes. Despite their precarious existence, however, in many slums, enterprises and industries flourish, even though they are deemed 'illegal' because they do not conform either to industrial location norms or to working conditions required of such units.

Source: Sharma, 2001a, 2001b.

children have compared conditions between urban and rural slum areas. They have shown that slum children under five years of age suffer more and die more often from diarrhoea and acute respiratory infection than rural children. On average, slum children are also more likely to be underfed. The crowded conditions of slums, lack of clean water and sanitation facilities, and severe air pollution contribute

to the poor health status of urban slum children. In Ahmedabad, for example, polluted air, compounded by the use of cooking fuels inside crowded, unventilated dwellings, contributes to the prevalence of acute respiratory infection,[32] with infant mortality rates on average twice higher in slums than in the rural areas. Slum immunization rates are half those of rural children, and slum children experiencing diarrhoea receive oral dehydration therapy half as frequently as rural children.[33] Infant mortality rates in Manila's slums are triple those of non-slum areas. There is also evidence of a high incidence of tuberculosis, diarrhoea, parasitic infections, dengue and severe malnutrition affecting slum children.

Poverty, inequalities and slums in Latin America and the Caribbean

It is a general opinion amongst the Latin-American populations that in the sharp contrasts arising from globalization, the negative aspects dominate...to the extent that it has effectively meant the globalization of poverty (Mexican Catholic Cardinal Norberto Rivera).[34]

Looking back at the period of 1960 to 1980, the Latin America and Caribbean region enjoyed long-lasting and exceptional economic growth. Human development indicators were among the best compared to the other developing regions. The

BOX 5.4 'One family, two systems': welfare reforms in urban China

Economic and welfare reforms in Chinese cities have changed the pattern of job opportunities, the returns of labour and access to social services for the urban population. The state sector offers fewer opportunities than before. The private sector offers increased wages for highly skilled people, but wages for low-skilled people are low. Social security for state employees is being scaled down, while in the rapidly growing private sector few have access to social security. Urban Chinese households have adapted differently to the changes – adaptations that translate into marginalization and poverty for some and prosperity for others. The spectrum of opportunities is as follows:

■ *Old insiders*: households totally reliant on state or collective-sector employment. Employed members work for the state or in the collective sector; they receive low wages but good welfare coverage.

■ *New insiders*: households totally reliant on formal private-sector employment. They receive high wages, but are not eligible for social welfare coverage.

■ *New outsiders*: households where one or more members are laid off (*xia-gang*) or unemployed. The households have little or no wage income and reduced welfare benefits.

■ *Old outsiders*: people with rural residence permits (*hukou*), working for low wages in the private sector with few rights to social welfare.

■ *One family, two systems*: households with members employed in both state and private sectors. They enjoy the best of two worlds, good welfare coverage and increased wages from the private sector.

Source: Kristin Dalen, Norwegian Institute for Applied Social Sciences, pers comm 2003.

average index of human development, which stood at 0.465 during the 1960s, doubled to 0.824 two decades later, a truly impressive outcome.[35] However, since the 1980s, progress in human development has been very modest and has stalled in some countries. The 1980s were described as a 'debt-crisis decade', or a 'lost decade', because of massive external indebtedness, huge public-sector deficits, high inflation – reaching four digit levels in several countries – slow growth, the loss of global competitiveness in important sectors, the explosion of social problems and crime, and the deterioration of services.

From the end of the 1980s and throughout the 1990s, Latin America carried out market-oriented reforms, including far-reaching privatization programmes in many sectors, in the hope of attaining renewed economic growth in the global economy. From 1990 to 1997, the region experienced a cycle of moderate economic growth, cutting poverty by 5 per cent. Since 1997, the situation has worsened, primarily as a result of the Asian crisis, which severely hit the Latin American economies, as commodity export prices fell due to a lack of world demand. The more recent economic crisis in Argentina in 2001 seriously weakened the region's economy as a whole. By the beginning of the millennium, there was little doubt that the region was facing its worst economic crisis since the Great Depression of the 1930s.[36]

The crisis not only involves the economy, but every facet of social life. Progress in overcoming poverty has ground to a halt during the last five years, with poverty and indigence rates remaining practically constant since 1997. The sole exception was 2000, when better economic performance brought with it a reduction in the volume of poverty by more than 4 million people.[37] In 2002, the number of Latin Americans living in poverty reached 220 million (43.4 per cent), of which 95 million (18.8 per cent) were indigents. The general trend has been a relatively stable poverty level, except in Argentina and, to a lesser degree, Uruguay, both of which suffered severe declines in living conditions. In Argentina's urban areas, poverty rates almost doubled from 23.7 per cent to 45.4 per cent, while indigence grew threefold, from 6.7 per cent to 20.9 per cent.

Poverty levels were expected to rise further in 2003, due mainly to the lack of growth in per capita gross domestic product (GDP)[38] and generally in urban areas, where most of the current population growth is taking place. While the number of urban poor has tripled during the past three decades, from about 44 million in 1970 to about 138 million in 2000, the number of rural poor has remained stable. Today, out of six new poor, five appear to be in urban areas. Economists predict that in order to halve the Latin American and Caribbean poor population, the

region needs an average economic growth of 4 per cent per year and 7 per cent growth annually in the poorest countries.[39] However, analysts warn that economic growth alone is not likely to curb poverty and the stark inequalities that characterize the region.

Latin America's inequalities are the most extreme in the world. In 1999, Gini coefficients for all countries in Latin America were higher than the world's average of 0.4, and several countries – such as Brazil (0.64), Bolivia (0.60), Nicaragua (0.59) and Guatemala (0.58) – registered values close to 0.6.[40] Whereas the richest tenth of the people in the region earn 48 per cent of the total income, the poorest tenth earn only 1.6 per cent.[41] Inequalities are omnipresent in almost every aspect of life. A poor Guatemalan family has, on average, three children, whereas a rich household has 1.9 children. In the former household, 4.5 people live in each room, compared to 1.6 in the latter. The former household has a 57 per cent chance of being connected to the water main network and a 49 per cent probability of having access to electricity. The corresponding probabilities for the latter household are 92 and 93 per cent, respectively.[42] Furthermore, these inequalities are persistently driven by race and ethnicity in Latin America, particularly for indigenous and Afro-descended people who are *at a considerable disadvantage with respect to whites*.[43] Indigenous men earn 35 to 65 per cent less than white

---

BEST PRACTICE

ART + SOCIAL ORGANIZATION: DEVELOPMENT OF CULTURAL COMMUNITY CENTRES IN BOULOGNE, ARGENTINA, 2002

The programme developed by Art + Social Organization aims at fighting social exclusion and using culture as a source for social life, where participation is promoted and access to culture is considered a right. It is implemented in very poor communities, from the *shanties* and *villas miserias* of Boulogne, through cultural community centres training people in artistic activities, particularly through theatre. The project has been implemented in partnership with business corporations, and academic and cultural centres. The experience has spread to other neighbourhoods.

Source: www.bestpractices.org.

BOX 5.5 **Poverty and space in São Paulo**

The informal settlements, called *favelas*, in São Paulo are located as follows:

- 49.3 per cent on river banks;
- 32.2 per cent on land suffering from periodical flooding;
- 29.3 per cent on steep slopes;
- 24.2 per cent on land being eroded;
- 9 per cent on waste tips or landfill sites.

Source: Smolka, 2002.

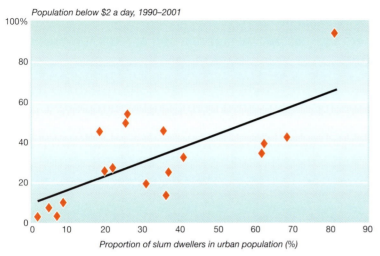

Population below $2 a day, 1990–2001

Proportion of slum dwellers in urban population (%)

Sources: UN-Habitat, 2003b; World Bank, 2003c.

FIGURE 5.6 **Income poverty and urban slum incidence**

men.[44] In Brazil, for instance, men and women of African descent earn about 45 per cent of the wages of their white counterparts. Race and ethnicity may also constitute important factors in spatial urban polarizations and slum formation. In Guatemala, Bolivia and Brazil, three countries where ethnic and racial categories are significant, over 50 per cent of households headed by white men or women have access to sewerage, compared to 30 per cent for those headed by indigenous men and 37 per cent for those headed by indigenous women. Among Brazilians, 50 per cent of households headed by white women have sewerage, versus 40.5 per cent for non-white males and 45.1 per cent for non-white females.[45]

In a general context of economic stagnation, sometimes coupled with poor governance, urban services have become largely insufficient to cope with the dramatic population increase in cities. In 50 years,

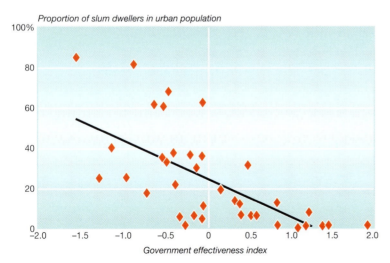

Proportion of slum dwellers in urban population

Government effectiveness index

Sources: UN-Habitat, 2003b; Kaufmann and Kraay, 2003.

FIGURE 5.7 **Corruption and slums**

Latin America's population has multiplied by three, increasing from 167 million in 1950 to 519 million in 2000. During the same period, the region's urban population grew more than five times, increasing from 70 to 391 million, imposing a heavy strain on cities. Three-quarters of the region's population now resides in just six countries: Argentina, Brazil, Columbia, Mexico, Peru and Venezuela. Latin America's four largest cities – Buenos Aires (12 million), Mexico City (18 million), Rio de Janeiro (10.7 million), and São Paulo (18 millions) – have reached sizes that are out of hand in many respects, posing great challenges in terms of infrastructure, basic social services and urban safety, thus providing the ground for increasing slum incidence.

Furthermore, given the continued rural–urban migration, as well as higher natural urban growth, land will be scarcer in future. Growing demand for space is likely to lead to increasing land prices, particularly in the absence of appropriate regulatory systems, and illegal or pirate lot subdivision for the low-income groups is likely to increase. In congested cities, the cost of infrastructure development will also be high, affecting the ability of the poor to improve their living conditions.

The region hosts a large slum population. In 2001, one third of the urban population (32 per cent) was living in slums, representing 128 million people and 14 per cent of the world's urban slum population. Behind this overall figure, slum incidence varies tremendously from one country to another. Central America (excluding Mexico), the least urbanized sub-region (52 per cent) but experiencing the highest urban growth, shows the highest slum prevalence, at 42.4 per cent in 2001. The Caribbean sub-region enjoys a lower prevalence, with 21.4 per cent, showing better overall performance in terms of access to basic services. In South America, where urbanization has reached a very high but relatively stable point of about 80 per cent, the proportion of slum dwellers was 35.5 per cent in 2001.

Separate measures of urban slum attributes show that the lack of improved sanitation is often the central determinant of slums in the region, the worst scenarios being in Haiti (86 per cent of urban slums) and Nicaragua (81 per cent) – the two least developed countries of the region. Central America (excluding Mexico), which has the highest slum prevalence, also has the lowest human development performance, with the lowest Human Development Index (0.679), compared to the other sub-regions and the overall regional average (0.762). Countries most affected by income poverty generally demonstrate higher slum incidence rates (see Figure 5.6).

Today, the question of how globalization and free-market reforms have affected the conditions of the poor, in terms of inequality, is the object of considerable scrutiny. Linked to this question is also the extent to which the proliferation of slums has been exacerbated by globalization. It is clear that, with the structural changes in the economy (not only changes resulting from globalization), some have gained and many have lost, especially since there has been insufficient creation of jobs in comparison to the expansion of the work force.[46]

However, new strategies have emerged at the community level that have led to innovative solutions, particularly in cities where governance has improved. In the past, public responsibility for social services has often been narrowly interpreted in terms of direct public provision of social services. But there is a lot of evidence to show that greater supply does not automatically translate into improved access for the poorest. As the Porto Alegre experience shows, democratic reforms that give greater voice to citizens and hold local governments accountable in budget allocations have done a lot to accelerate progress.

Figures 5.7 and 5.8 show that urban governance and the way in which slums grow are undoubtedly highly correlated; good governance implies improved access of populations to basic services, and better planning of urban settlements and their infrastructure, as well as better management of resources, especially land. Reduction of corruption can have an enormous positive impact on the way in which land is allocated and, therefore, on the people's security of tenure. In addition, a more effective local government is more likely to deliver water and ensure sanitation to slum areas.

Urban poverty in the Middle East and Northern Africa (MENA): progress hindered by conflicts and poor governance

With the ongoing Gulf and Middle East crises, the Middle East and Northern Africa (MENA) region seems to be playing an increasingly important role in today's overall global development. This becomes particularly apparent when the impacts of the 2003 Iraq war on the global economy and the uncertainties that it has generated in its aftermath are considered. However, the effects of the two consecutive Gulf crises were perhaps felt more keenly in the Arab States in terms of the direct death toll and destruction in Iraq and its neighbouring countries.

Cities have suffered significantly in the region, with Jenin, Baghdad and Basrah being dramatic examples of vast material and irreparable social and psychological damage. In Jenin, in the West Bank, military bulldozers brought down hundreds of refugee homes, leaving a large scar in the middle of the camp.

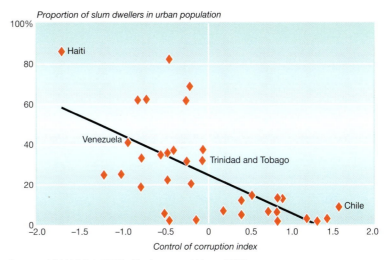

Sources: UN-Habitat, 2003b; Kaufmann and Kraay, 2003.

FIGURE 5.8 **Slum incidence and government effectiveness**

Around 2000 people were left homeless and with little hope of getting a new home. The rebuilding of Jenin was, and continues to be, plagued with difficulties as hostilities continue between the Israeli army and militants in the area. In Basrah, the first city to be hit by the Iraq war, and the third largest Iraqi city, about 1 million people were lacking water in March 2003, with only 2 litres a day per person, ten times less than the vital minimum. As a consequence, diarrhoeal diseases soon started to take a deadly toll. In April 2003, the city reached a refugee crisis, with thousands of people, mostly families, leaving the city. The situation has been restored in some parts of the city; but most people are still lacking basic services. In Baghdad more than half the population was entirely dependent upon the monthly food rations at the beginning of the war. In August 2003, for instance, taps ran dry after an explosion in northern Baghdad blew a hole in a water main. At the same time, petrol queues still stretched for hundreds of metres in the city.[47] As of today, Baghdad's 6 million inhabitants are in dire need of electricity, water, energy, telecommunications and security. They still do not have any of these in sufficient supply.

As a result of the Iraq war, economic growth has been severely hit in a number of MENA countries. Iraq and its neighbours have been the most affected;[48] but non-oil-exporting countries in the region, such as Jordan,[49] Egypt, Morocco, Tunisia, Lebanon and Syria, have also suffered from general loss of confidence and uncertainty in the region. Prior to the first Gulf crisis in 1991, Arab countries had made considerable economic progress. However, there were still large pockets of poverty and high unemployment. With the onset of the crisis, their economies have been dramatically shaken. The sudden exodus of more than 2 millions workers and their families from Iraq

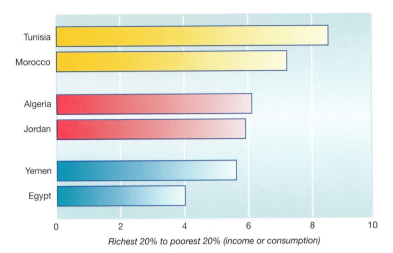

Source: UNDP, 2003.

FIGURE 5.9 **Income inequalities, selected countries**

While the Iraq and the Israeli–Palestinian conflicts, as well as several unresolved political tensions in Algeria, Syria and Lebanon, severely hinder the development of the region, some other factors keep large sections of the MENA region's population in poverty, in spite of the huge economic potential that nations in the region have. Without exception, MENA countries are currently facing many economic challenges, and poverty has increased in most countries.[50] Globalization processes, economic adjustment programmes and the short-term effects of economic reform are adversely affecting basic services, education and employment, and slowing progress towards gender equality. In a context of rapid urbanization and changing migration patterns, living conditions are deteriorating for large numbers of people and poverty has increased, especially among women and girls.

One of the most crucial problems of the MENA states is unemployment, with a regional average of 15 per cent, which is on the increase in almost all of the region's countries. The region's young population – 38 per cent of the population is under 14 – does not have sufficient access to educational and training opportunities, especially women who still lag behind in terms of school attendance and literacy. Another major obstacle is the general lack of democratic and efficient governance. Recent studies show that the MENA region has the lowest indicators in the area of governance, lagging behind sub-Saharan Africa with respect to accountability and the quality of public-sector administration.[51] The absence of sound governance systems in most countries hinders governments' abilities to respond to the demand for better services, either through maintenance, or improvement and expansion of existing infrastructure. However, there are stark differences between countries

has been disastrous, resulting in huge income losses, rising unemployment and increased pressure on government expenditures on social and municipal services in order meet the needs of the returnees. This has led to declining living conditions through the deterioration of basic services. For Kuwait, the invasion of Iraq has also been devastating, as a significant part of the country's infrastructure was destroyed, including basic water and sewerage systems. About half of the population left Kuwait at the same time. The Iraqi economy, already affected by the war with Iran, was devastated, unable to finance its own reconstruction and then paralyzed by the sanctions. The oil-for-food programme, implemented since 1997, started to have effects on social statistics by the beginning of the millennium, before being reversed by the second Gulf crisis.

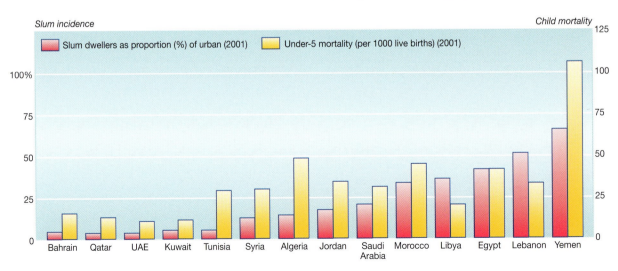

Sources: UN-Habitat, 2003b; UNDP, 2002.

FIGURE 5.10 **Slum incidence and child mortality**

in the region, with the lowest performing being the high-income oil economies, as their high incomes depend less upon a good environment for business activities.[52]

It is estimated that 23.3 per cent of the region's population live in poverty, with less than US$2 per day,[53] a modest proportion if compared to Asia or sub-Saharan Africa.[54] The region shows the lowest regional incidence of extreme poverty, with less than 2.5 per cent of the population living below US$1 per day, and it has, on average, one of the most equal income distributions in the world, with an average Gini coefficient of 0.364 (during the 1995–1999 period), which has been falling over time.[55] Comparison of the income share of the richest 20 per cent against the poorest 20 per cent of the national population in a number of countries confirms this picture (see Figure 5.9).[56] Available figures suggest that income distribution may be improving, explained by the unusually strong cohesive social system in the region and the fact that redistribution constitutes a priority policy in Islamic economies. This is best illustrated by the *zakat*, which requires people to donate about 2.5 per cent of their earning to religious bodies, and some strong and early social redistribution policies. This enables large segments of the population to escape the poverty trap.

Social safety nets are particularly needed, especially in light of the urban explosion that the region has experienced during the last 20 years. Two decades ago, only 30 per cent of the MENA population lived in cities. Today, about 60 per cent of the population is urban. By 2020, an estimated 70 per cent of the region's population will live in urban areas – half of which will be children below the age of 18 years. Urban growth rates are still high today, in spite of the rapid decline in fertility, and as rural–urban migration continues at a significant rate. This is triggered by social changes, climatic or political factors, as well as economic opportunities offered by large- and medium-sized cities. Data suggests that the average annual growth rate of the urban population during the 1990–2000 period was 3.3 per cent, as opposed to a 2.3 per cent natural population increase during the same period.[57]

Considering the pattern of high urban growth, increasing poverty and poor governance in the region, the slum population is likely to increase in MENA cities, already hosting about 30 per cent of the urban population, whether in the *mudun safi, lahbach, brarek,* or *foundouks* of Rabat; the *carton, safeih, ishash, galoos* and *shammsa* of Khartoum; the *tanake* of Beirut; or the *aashwa'i* and *baladi* of Cairo. Although the average urban slum incidence in the region (30.7 per cent) is close to the world's average (31.6 per cent), it varies dramatically across the region. Highest slum rates are prevalent in the poorest countries, such as Yemen

---

BOX 5.6 **When a house is not a home: girls working as housemaids in Morocco**

The large majority of *khadema*, or *petites bonnes*, work in the Moroccan cities. Below 15 years old, they are often recruited through middlemen who approach the parents from poor rural backgrounds, and who will then, in most cases, receive the wages directly. As girls grow older, they are more likely to keep their own wage. Contracts are seldom formal, and the conditions under which the girls work vary. Some attend evening school after work and are allowed to visit their parents. Others do not have this chance and are even subjected to punishments. The *petites bonnes* raise difficult policy issues in the goal to provide education for all, while reducing poverty. About 1 million girls do not attend school in Morocco and many girls are available for recruitment as housemaids.

Source: Jon Pedersen, Norwegian Institute for Applied Social Sciences, pers comm 2003.

(65.1 per cent), the Occupied Palestinian Territories (60.5 per cent) and Iraq (56.7 per cent).[58] About one third of the urban population lives in slums in Egypt, Libya and Morocco, with respective rates of 39.9, 35.2 and 32.7 per cent. Most Gulf countries (Kuwait, Bahrain, Qatar, United Arab Emirates, together with Tunisia) – which are also the most urbanized – show the lowest rates, having situations similar to those of the developed countries. Algeria, Jordan and Saudi Arabia have a moderate incidence of slums, with 11.8, 15.7 and 19.8 per cent, respectively.

The MENA region has 15 of the 22 countries identified by the World Bank as below the water poverty line of less than 1000 cubic metres per person per year. This obviously determines people's access to water in urban areas. The chronic lack of water affects all segments of the population, but hits the poor more severely, especially when it is coupled with the lack of adequate sanitation.

In spite of this general picture, there are also some grounds for optimism in the region, as evidence has shown progress in many fronts. In Tunisia, cities have recently made spectacular progress in providing basic services. Egypt has also seen its infrastructure dramatically improved in many urban areas. Some countries have shown notable progress in improving their governance, as evidenced by the new, effective municipal management system in Aden, or the launch of local elections in Lebanon,[59] both providing more guarantees for better inclusion and paving the way for poverty alleviation.

becoming less common. But poor communications between slum dwellers and the authorities have led to mounting tension within slums. According to Odindo Opiata, a lawyer with Kituo Cha Sheria, a legal aid non-governmental organization (NGO) based in Nairobi, the lack of information flow between the authorities and slum dwellers threatens to polarize residents even further and to result in more disputes in Kenya's major cities.

Slum life already has a profoundly destabilizing effect on families, often leading to a vicious circle of broken homes, crime and prostitution. Growing polarization and exclusion can further contribute to this destabilization, making slums a potential source of national, regional and global insecurity. Evidence around the world has shown that cities which are unable to bridge income inequalities and manage social integration are likely to be more violent and insecure than those which are less polarized.

Participatory, pro-poor policies addressing informal settlement issues can go a long way in alleviating current conflicts. At the macro level, however, governments need to implement economic policies that reduce urban income disparities.

Some of the most respected professionals in developing countries started their lives in slums and low-income settlements. Kenya is no different. Young teachers, lawyers or journalists are often forced to rent a room in a low-income area, probably sharing bathrooms with several people and dreaming of the day when they can own their home – an aspiration that is as distant as access to the mortgages that are beyond the reach of most people.

But slums and low-income settlements are a function of urban poverty, failing economic and urban management and, all too frequently, lack of political will. No slum improvement scheme can be successful without a strong commitment on the part of national and local governments to fight urban poverty. For this, they need to start making effective inroads into failing systems of housing markets, credit provision and wealth distribution.

RASNA WARAH, A FREELANCE WRITER AND JOURNALIST BASED IN NAIROBI, IS THE AUTHOR OF TRIPLE HERITAGE: A JOURNEY TO SELF-DISCOVERY, AND FORMER EDITOR OF UN-HABITAT'S QUARTERLY MAGAZINE, HABITAT DEBATE.

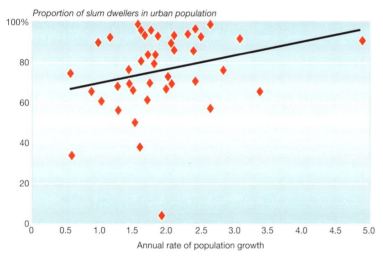

Proportion of slum dwellers in urban population

Sources: UN-Habitat, 2003b; United Nations Population Division, 2002a.

FIGURE 5.11 **Rate of urban growth and slum incidence, 2000–2005**

recent studies show considerable variations between people living in slums and those living in non-slum areas. For instance, while 11.3 per cent of the children in Nairobi's slums die before reaching the age of 5 years, only 0.78 per cent die before the same age in non-slum areas. Such studies also show the dramatic differences between urban slums, non-slum areas and rural settlements. Using the same example, under the age of 5 mortality rates and morbidity rates in slum areas equal or exceed those of rural areas.[64]

The lack of improved sanitation is the most important feature of slums in the African urban context. About 57 per cent of urban Africans do not have access to improved forms of sanitation. In some countries, this figure exceeds 80 per cent of the population, as in Niger (88 per cent), Sierra Leone (82 per cent) and Mali (81 per cent). The lack of improved water supply appears to be the second most important determining factor, affecting about one fifth of urban Africa.[65] The lack of sufficient living space or overcrowding is the third most important factor, widely varying from one country to another. The worst scenarios, where more than 80 per cent of the population live in slum-like conditions, are found in Western Africa: that is, in Sierra Leone (96 per cent), Guinea Bissau (93 per cent), Niger (92 per cent), Mali (86 per cent) and Mauritania (85 per cent).

Not taken into account in the available slum estimates is the vulnerability of slum dwellers to eviction, which defines their security of tenure. Eviction is still widely practised in Africa because of converging factors linked to poor governance, conflicts and insecurity. Studies show that forced evictions are often violent, and include a variety of human rights abuses beyond the violation of the right to adequate

BEST PRACTICE

MATHARE YOUTH SELF-HELP AND CLEAN-UP PROJECT, KENYA

The Mathare Youth Sports Association began in 1987 as a self-help youth project linking slum environmental clean-up with sport. Youth football teams participate in neighbourhood clean-up projects that earn them points in their league. Each completed waste-collection project earns a team six points, while a match victory earns the team three points. The association has grown to a membership of 24,000 youths aged 11 to 18 years who participate in over 800 boys' and 250 girls' teams, playing over 10,000 matches a year. Since 1994, over 300 young boys and girls have received training on HIV/AIDS prevention and have, in turn, reached out to over 100,000 youths with this critical information.

Source: www.bestpractices.org.

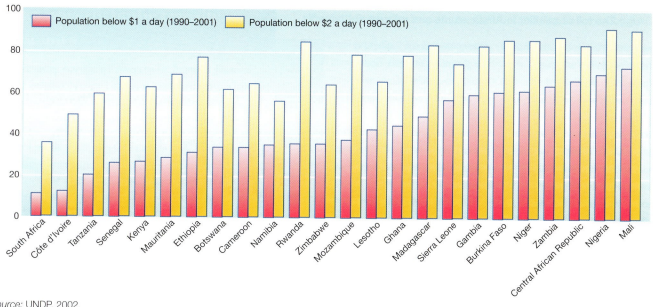

Source: UNDP, 2002.

FIGURE 5.12 **Poverty in sub-Saharan Africa, selected countries**

housing. Furthermore, evictees tend to end up worse off than before the eviction. Finally, forced evictions most negatively affect women and children.[66] Before eviction itself, which constitutes the ultimate shift, the threat of eviction, real or generated by the general lack of security of occupation, constitutes a real impediment to human development and an additional factor that pushes populations into the poverty trap.

In Africa, an estimated 29.4 million people are infected with HIV/AIDS. The worst of the epidemic clearly has still to come – notably, in Southern Africa where the pandemic is currently rampant. Studies reveal that HIV-induced declines in GDP levels in sub-Saharan Africa are severely undermining poverty alleviation efforts. The pandemic may currently shave off up to 2 per cent of annual economic growth in the worst affected countries. Some countries are likely to see their gross national product (GNP) shrink by up to 40 per cent within the next 20 years. On the whole, Africa's income growth per capita is being reduced by about 0.7 per cent per year because of HIV/AIDS.[67]

Ongoing economic recession aggravates transmission of HIV/AIDS through increased migration, which disrupts rural families and increases their risk levels. High poverty levels and the widening rural–urban gap in incomes and services have generated large seasonal or long-term population movements to cities in Africa. These population flows heighten the potential of the spread of HIV/AIDS at both ends. When lack of information about HIV/AIDS and diminished elder authority are combined with the customary practice of polygamy, labour migrants, for instance, are particularly at risk of contracting HIV in cities and rapidly spreading it

through their rural homelands.[68] Largely dependent upon massive road-transportation systems throughout the continent, the convoys of trucks traversing Africa have been dubbed the 'AIDS Express' and constitute a formidable force in the spread of HIV/AIDS through the trucker–prostitute contacts that occur along the major transportation routes.

Recent studies also show that the situation of extreme deprivation in cities, particularly in slums, traps residents into engaging in risky sexual behaviour for economic survival. Data reveal that slum residents

---

BOX 5.8 **Sexual risk-taking in the slums of Nairobi**

Research conducted by the African Population and Health Research Centre (APHRC) shows that slum women are more vulnerable to HIV/AIDS infection than their non-slum counterparts. Women who live in slums become sexually active about three years earlier. The difference in the median age at first intercourse between slum and non-slum residents who grew up in a city is five years. Young women (15 to 24 years' old) and married women in slums are 6.4 and 3.7 times more likely to have multiple partners than their non-slum counterparts. Data also show a marked difference between slum and non-slum residents in the perception of the best ways to avoid contracting the HIV virus. Slum women are less likely to practice abstinence, stick to one partner and use condoms. Slum dwellers' low average age for commencement of sexual activity and greater number of partners are largely the result of the extreme deprivation that prevails in slums. High levels of unemployment, unstable sources of income and the predominance of low-paying jobs push many women and children into prostitution to supplement household incomes. Furthermore, slum parents' authority over their children's sexual behaviour is greatly undermined by the lack of parents' privacy in crowded single-room accommodation.

Source: Zulu et al, 2002, pp311–323.

---

further decreased employment opportunities within advanced economies, as some skilled jobs are now also being transferred to low-wage countries. The outsourcing of information technology (IT) services and certain business processes, such as customer service, to India, the Philippines and other low-wage countries is seen as a big cost-saver in corporate boardrooms in the US and Europe, but is giving rise to mounting concern among the labour unions of these countries.

There has been a persistent level of unemployment in many European nations during the last decade or so, in spite of their virtually stagnant populations.[87] However, more recently, unemployment has slightly decreased in some of the European Union countries. Meanwhile, in Northern America, unemployment increased from 4.8 per cent in 2001 to 5.6 per cent in 2002 in the US and from 7.2 per cent to 7.6 per cent over the same period in Canada. Besides, hidden unemployment is reported in a number of recent studies,[88] as well as increasing precariousness of working conditions, because a significant share of the long-term poor are, in fact, 'employed'.

cities. Since the 1970s, employment in the manufacturing, construction and goods transport and warehousing industries has contracted and the demand for unskilled manual workers has fallen sharply. At the same time, there has been a growing demand for managerial, professional and other technical skills. The recent trend of relocating industrial and some service activities to the South has

Since the late 1980s, poverty has also been linked to the state's decreasing capacity to provide, to the majority of citizens, the minimum conditions for entry to the market. Today, safety nets are failing some of the most vulnerable sections of European societies. The urban poor who end up homeless become, at some stage, unable to mobilize social capital in the form of family, networks, community bonding and shared values. Stripped of their capacity to compete in a market economy, deprived of state welfare support and devoid of social capital, most of those who fall into the trap of homelessness are people whose vulnerability has been exacerbated by health, drug and alcohol problems, as well as by physical and sexual abuse.[89]

Homelessness in the advanced economies has changed significantly over the past decade. 'The old, derelict "wino" on the park bench has been joined by younger men, unemployed and destitute; by the confused and mentally ill, frightened by the pace of surrounding activity; by women and children, escaping violent and destructive domestic situations; by young people, cast off by families who can't cope or don't care.'[90] Furthermore, homelessness stories do not relate to individuals only, but to families in ways that suggest the failure of traditional welfare systems to adapt to today's changed social and family circumstances.

Families become homeless for many complex and often inter-related reasons: debt, rent arrears, unemployment, relationship breakdown and domestic violence, mental illness, substance abuse and disability, which can create a cycle of instability,

TABLE 5.7 **Reported homelessness in the advanced economies**

Country	Latest homeless figures	Year
Australia	147,000 (homeless service users)	1996–1997
Austria	21,000 (homeless service users)	1998
Belgium	18,880 people	1998–1999
Canada	35,000–40,000	2000
Denmark	7365 people	2000
Finland	10,000 people	2001
France	201,000 people	2001
Germany	500,000 people	2000
Greece	10,000 people	2002
Ireland	5234 households	1999
Italy	17,000 people	2000
Luxembourg	362 women, 365 children	2000
Netherlands	26,175 people	2002
Portugal	1300 people in Lisbon/1000 people in Porto	2000
Sweden	8440	1999
UK	England: 113,590 priority need people/ Scotland: 34,040/Wales: 4171	2000–2001
US	about 3.5 million people (1.35 million children)	2000

Note: These figures should be interpreted with caution, as they are based on different national definitions. As such, they cannot be used for international comparison.
Source: Various; European data assembled by the FEANTSA, 2002; Urban Institute, 2000 (US).

BOX 5.13 Defining homelessness

The *operational definition* of homelessness adopted by the European Federation of National Organizations Working with the Homeless (FEANTSA) provides a simple but robust definition of housing vulnerability as individuals experiencing one of the following situations:

- **Rooflessness:** defined as rough sleeping. This is the most visible form of homelessness. People with chaotic lifestyles or unsettled ways of living may be disproportionately represented among the roofless population. Successful resettlement for rough sleepers may be contingent as much upon the availability of appropriate support as upon the availability of temporary and permanent housing.

- **Houselessness:** refers to situations where, despite access to emergency shelter or long-term institutions, individuals may still be classed as homeless due to a lack of appropriate support aimed at facilitating social reintegration. People who are forced to live in institutions because there is inadequate accommodation (with support) in the community to meet their needs are thus

regarded as homeless. In this context, homelessness refers as much to the lack of housing as it does to the lack of social networks.

- **Living in insecure housing:** (insecure tenure or temporary accommodation) this may be a consequence of the inaccessibility of permanent housing. It may equally reflect the need for support to enable people to successfully hold a tenancy. The provision of appropriate support can be critical in helping people have access to permanent housing under their own tenancy. This category also includes people who are involuntarily sharing in unreasonable circumstances and people whose security is threatened by violence or threats of violence (for example, women at risk of domestic abuse, racial violence or harassment).

- **Living in inadequate accommodation:** includes people whose accommodation is unfit for habitation or is overcrowded (based on national or statutory standards), as well as those whose accommodation is a caravan or boat.

Source: Edgar et al, 2002.

BOX 5.14 Women's homelessness and domestic violence

My husband came home one night with another woman. He dragged me downstairs – I was five-and-a-half months pregnant. So I left (Mona, age 54).

Domestic violence is the main cause of homelessness among women in England. A report by the charity Crisis found that 63 per cent of homeless women aged between 30 and 49 said domestic abuse was the key reason they had lost their homes. Over half of these women had slept rough, the majority on more than one occasion – despite the fact that this made them vulnerable to rape and abuse. Several resorted to drugs and alcohol to blot out the dangers. Other reasons why women

said that they had become homeless were family breakdown, severe mental health problems and childhood abuse. Many avoided night shelters because they were deemed dirty, violent and unsafe. And a large proportion ended up staying too long in hostels. One woman had spent over 20 years in hostels. Some said hostel life was making them ill and several were on anti-depressants or were using drugs and alcohol. Many said they wanted to work, but felt it was not worth their while giving up housing benefit when the cost of hostel accommodation was so high. The majority of women said that they would welcome greater provision of move-on accommodation so they could free up places in hostels. And they wanted more support to make the transition away from homelessness.

Source: The report *Out of Sight, Out of Mind?* (FEANTSA, 2002) interviewed 77 homeless women across the UK in an effort to find out why, when homelessness was decreasing in general, the number of women in hostels or on the streets was increasing.

causing families to become homeless time and again as problems remain unresolved and local and national agencies fail to intervene effectively. In many large cities, rising rents, severe shortages of public housing and increased demand for crisis

accommodation have meant that thousands of young people, families and elderly people are being turned away from housing services and left to fend for themselves on the streets because there is nowhere else for them to go. The dwindling of employment

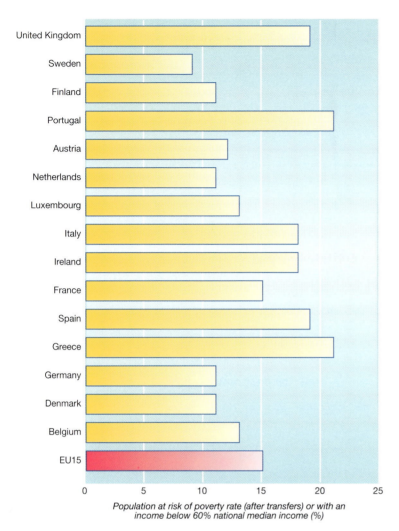

Population at risk of poverty rate (after transfers) or with an income below 60% national median income (%)

Source: Eurostat, 1999.

FIGURE 5.16 **15 per cent of EU citizens at risk of poverty**

In a wealthy street

opportunities for people with a secondary school education or less is contributing to the widening gap between the rich and the poor. In some countries, for example the US, the removal of institutional support for people with severe mental illness and drastic reductions in the use of long-term hospitalization for the mentally ill are leaving many individuals with few housing options. In addition, racial, ethnic and class discrimination in housing, along with local zoning restrictions that exclude affordable housing alternatives, persists in many urban areas.[91] Delays in assessing housing benefits have also aggravated the very problem the system was designed to avoid, and a number of people have lost their homes because of 'chronic delays' in housing benefits.[92] Families have also increasingly been placed in unsafe, ill-equipped bed-and-breakfast hotels, sometimes far away from their original home and social or other support networks.

Another new facet of homelessness is the rise of short-term homelessness, as opposed to chronic homelessness. Beside the more visible *rough sleepers*, camping in caravans, cars or *squats*, or sleeping on the spare beds or sofas of friends and relatives, are now the most common conditions of the 'new' homeless. Even when homelessness is experienced as a short episode of one's life, triggered by a change in income, mental and physical health, it is often devastating.[93]

There seems to be an increasing awareness of homelessness among the youth, as part of the general problem of homelessness, in a number of advanced economies.[94] Those at high risk of homelessness are children in foster care or substitute youth care institutions, those living in conflict-burdened family environments or abusive families, and children of homeless families. Young adults having to make their transition to independence, implying finding income, self-sufficiency and setting up a new household, are also experiencing problems in the context of unemployment. Figures show a more prolonged dependence of young adults on their parents, some of it associated with the extended duration of studies and the postponement of first employment. Housing markets in Europe also show a prevalence of home-ownership and a shortage of affordable rental housing for single young people.[95]

Finally, globalization has also produced a larger number of homeless international immigrants, whether asylum seekers, refugees, economic or labour migrants or undocumented immigrants. The EU reports a growing number of homeless immigrants who request and make use of homeless services. This sharp rise has taken place over the last decade and is projected to continue at a steady rate. Homeless immigrants tend to concentrate in urban areas, as big

BOX 5.15 **Child homelessness**

The multiple scenarios that homeless children endure go from 'crude' homelessness in the form of rough sleeping to various forms of temporary accommodation. They are especially harmful during the earliest years of childhood. School-age homeless children often face barriers to enrolling and attending school, including transportation problems, residency requirements, inability to obtain previous school records and lack of clothing and school supplies. Homeless children have been found to suffer bullying, unhappiness and stigmatization, and infrequent and late attendance of school is common. Frequent moves and changes of school lead to lower educational results and to lower educational attainment. A study in Birmingham found that only 29 per cent of homeless children were attending mainstream school. 73 per cent had been attending school before they became homeless.

Sources: Shelter, 2002a; Drennan et al, 1986; Jones et al, 2002; Shelter, 2002b; *Where's Home, Children and Homelessness in Bristol* (FEANTSA, 2002); Shelter NCVCCO, 1995; Vostanis et al, 1999.

Homeless encampment

BOX 5.16 **Homelessness and HIV/AIDS**

One out of four people living with HIV in New York City is homeless or marginally housed.[i] A Los Angeles study found that two-thirds of people with AIDS had been homeless.[ii] Depending upon who is counting and where, HIV infection rates in homeless communities run from 8.5 per cent to as high as 19.5 per cent in the US. People with HIV/AIDS are more likely to become homeless as their incomes are drained by the costs of healthcare. Also, homeless people are more likely to contract HIV/AIDS as a result of their living conditions. Many homeless adolescents find that exchanging sex for food, clothing and shelter is their only chance of survival on the streets. In turn, homeless youth are at a greater risk of contracting AIDS or HIV-related illnesses. Few homeless individuals are aware of their HIV status. Only a handful of homeless are informed about HIV treatment options, and even fewer are able to access such care.[iii] Tragically, individuals with HIV/AIDS are likely to die before they receive housing assistance.

Notes: i Data from the year 2000 of the Community Health Advisory Information Network (CHAIN) at Columbia University's School of Public Health. This figure seems to be on the rise. The recent New York City Council hearing on the HIV/AIDS Services Administration (HSSA) highlighted the city's increase in homelessness among people with AIDS. ii Shelter Partnership, Inc, 1999. iii Curry, 2000.

cities offer more employment opportunities and already host the immigrant communities among whom the newcomers seek support.[96] At the same time, recurrent racial, religious and cultural resistance continues to lead to the formation of 'ethnic slums' in cities, in addition to the new gated communities and enclosed shopping malls for the most affluent. The challenge goes beyond combating homelessness; effective responses to the spatial construction of poverty that is currently taking place, as well as the trend towards social segregation arising from inadequate urban policy, have to be found.

BEST PRACTICE
TANGENTYERE COUNCIL: INDIGENOUS URBAN SETTLEMENT, AUSTRALIA

The Tangentyere Council is a voluntary organization that was formed to address the needs of Aboriginal people living in town camps on the fringes of Alice Springs in central Australia. The dislocation of people from their traditional homelands has brought a range of different cultures together in an environment where factions and rivalries are common outcomes. In addition, countervailing pressures of Aboriginal and European cultures on

town campers occasionally cause extreme tension. Tangentyere Council provides social support services in housing, infrastructure, employment, training, education and other social services. It encourages and relies upon community involvement in activities designed to create a safer and more stable living environment for town camp residents.

Source: www.bestpractices.org.

Notes

1 This chapter is based on a draft prepared by Christine Auclair, UN-Habitat.

2 World Bank, 2000a.

3 UN-Habitat, 2003a, p52.

4 Stiglitz, 2002.

5 The definition may be locally adapted according to the situation in a specific city. For example, in Rio de Janeiro living area is insufficient for both the middle classes and the slum population and is not a good discriminator. It could either be omitted, or it could be formulated as *two or more* of the conditions such as overcrowding and durability of housing.

6 The UNDP Human Development Index (HDI) includes four sub-indices based on life expectancy, adult literacy, school enrolment and GDP per capita.

7 COHRE, 2003, p12.

8 ADB, 1999.

9 Between the early and late 1990s, the countries of Asia and the Pacific, as a whole, are estimated to have reduced the overall incidence of income poverty from 34 to 24 per cent; UNESCAP, 2003.

10 UNESCAP, 2003.

11 UNESCAP, 2003, based on national poverty lines.

12 UNESCAP (2003) argues that successful countries in poverty reduction put a great deal of emphasis on agriculture or on export-oriented, labour-intensive manufacturing, or a combination of the two, in order to achieve steady increases in employment, wages and agricultural incomes.

13 Smith and Timberlake, 2002.

14 Seong-Kyu Ha, 2002.

15 Chia Siow Yue, 2003.

16 Fry et al, 2002.

17 *Indonesia Crisis Bulletin*, 1999.

18 Afsah, 1998.

19 Jayasuriya, 2002.

20 Pangestu, 2000.

21 About 400 million people have been lifted out of poverty at the US$1 a day expenditure level; World Bank, 2003f.

22 Based on US$1 a day poverty line, 1990–1998. UNESCAP, 2003.

23 ADB, 2002.

24 ADB, 2002.

25 ADB news release, 31 May 2001 (www.adb.org).

26 UNESCAP, 2003.

27 For the period of 2000–2005. United Nations Population Division, 2002a.

28 UNCHS (Habitat), 2001b, p14.

29 UNESCAP, 2003, p258.

30 United Nations Population Division, 2002a.

31 Bangladesh, 4.7 per cent; Bhutan, 5.2 per cent; Nepal 5.6 per cent; Cambodia 5.8 per cent; Lao People's Democratic Republic 5.8 per cent; and Solomon Island 6.3 per cent (1980–1997).

32 *Environment and Health Project Brief*, 2003.

33 Fry et al, 2002.

34 74th Plenary Assembly of the Mexican Bishops Conference, November 2002.

35 Thomas, 2003.

36 Thomas, 2003.

37 UNECLAC, 2003.

38 UNECLAC, 2003.

39 González, 2002.

40 ECLAC, 2002.

41 World Bank, 2003d.

42 World Bank, 2003b, Chapter 1, p2.

43 World Bank, 2003b.

44 The study focused on seven countries: Brazil, Guyana, Guatemala, Bolivia, Chile, Mexico and Peru.

45 World Bank, 2003b.

46 Latin America's average unemployment rate rose from 6.7 per cent in 1980 to 8.8 per cent in 1999.

47 Rodgers, 2003

48 Provisional estimates suggest that GDP per capita in Iraq has declined by two-thirds, from US$3700 per person in I980 to US$1200 in 2001.

49 The World Bank announced that Jordan would be the worst hit, with the country's economy shrinking this year compared with previous growth estimates of up to 6 per cent.

50 UNFPA, 2003.

51 UNDP, 2003.

52 World Bank, 2003d.

53 68 millions people or 23.3 per cent of the total population in the MENA region lived below US$2 a day in 1999; see World Bank, 2002a.

54 50.1 per cent of the population of East Asia and Pacific and 74.7 per cent for sub-Saharan African lived below US$2 a day in 1999; see World Bank, 2002a.

55 Adams and Page, 2001.

56 UNDP, 2002.

57 Arab Urban Development Institute, Children and the City Conference, 11–13 December 2002.

58 This figure does not take into account the last war.

59 UNDP, 2002.

60 Population below US$1 per day in 1993 purchasing power parity terms; see World Bank, 2003d.

61 Estimates from NEPAD, UNECA Conference of Ministries, 1 June 2003.

62 UNCTAD, 2002.

63 UN-Habitat, 2003a.

64 APHRC, 2002, p91.

65 This proportion is based on a rather limited sample of cities as data are not widely available for this definition of 'access to water'.

66 The topicality of this issue has been stressed by the Global Campaign for Secure Tenure, www.unhsp.org/campaigns/tenure/tenure.asp.

67 UNAIDS and World Bank, 2001.

68 May 2003.

69 Grootaert and Braithwaite, 1998.

70 Stiglitz, 1999.

71 Braithwaite, 1995.

72 Dixon and Mason, 2000.

73 WHO, 2002.

74 From Commissars to Mayors: Cities in the Transition Economies, The World Bank, September, 2000, pp. 1,16

75 Grootaert and Braithwaite, 1998. Figures are based on household expenditure and income data for transition economies data sets (HEIDE). The poverty rate or the proportion of households below the poverty line was calculated as equivalent to two-thirds of the mean household expenditure per adult. The poverty gap is the poor's average shortfall in expenditure from the poverty line.

76 For instance, transitional Russia is going through a 'mortality crisis' that started with approximately 2 million additional deaths recorded between 1990 and 1995. The death rate from homicide in Russia is now about 20 times higher than in Western Europe and is among the highest recorded anywhere in the world. Shkolnikov and Cornia, 2000; Chervyakov et al, 2002.

77 UNFPA, 2002.

78 Pichler-Milanovich, 2000.

79 Wegelin, 2003.

80 Ghosh, 2003.

81 FEANTSA estimates in Ghosh, 2003.

82 Urban Institute, 2000.

83 Pohl, 2001. According to Murphy (2000), there were about 35,000 to 40,000 homeless in Canada in 2000.

84 OECD, 2002.

85 They increased from 1.4 million in 1979 and 4.4 millions in 1997. According to European Community Household Panel (1996) data, almost 25 per cent of children live below the poverty line. Other data show that 39 per cent of children were poor at least once over a five-year period – more than twice the child poverty rate for a single year (see Bradbury et al, 2002).

86 Bradbury et al, 2002.

87 ILO, 2004.

88 Beatty et al, 2002.

89 Interview with Freek Spinnewinjn, Director of the European Federation of National Organisations working with the Homeless (FEANTSA, Fédération Européenne d'Associations Nationales Travaillant avec les Sans-Abri) in Ghosh, 2003.

90 Murphy, 2000.

91 Burt, 2001.

92 'Benefit delays cause homelessness', BBC, 25 May 1999. A survey conducted by the National Association of Citizens Advice Bureaux (NACAB) in England and Wales found that more than one in five people had been threatened with eviction because of benefit delays.

93 Murphy, 2000.

94 Avramov, 1998.

95 Avramov, 1998.

96 FEANTSA, 2002.

Chapter 6

Urban Governance: Safety and Transparency in a Globalizing World[1]

Global overview   **132**

Overall urban crime trends in the world   134

Regional trends in urban crime   **136**

Asia and the Pacific   137

Latin America and the Caribbean   138

Middle East and Northern Africa (MENA)   142

Sub-Saharan Africa   143

Transition economies   149

Advanced economies   151

Is there a way forward?   **156**

This chapter addresses two urban governance issues that are increasingly influenced by globalization: safety and transparency. On the one hand, urban safety is increasingly compromised by transnational crime, such as smuggling and trafficking of drugs, firearms and human beings, all of which have been facilitated by opportunities arising from the globalization process. On the other hand, transparency at the city level has been compromised by corruption, while the current solutions to this challenge are emerging from a context that may be described as the globalization of norms of good urban governance.

Just as the formal economy is expanding internationally along with the globalization of markets, criminal enterprises are likewise seeking to expand their organizations and illicit activities at the international level. Such organizations do so by taking advantage of discrepancies between legal systems of countries in different parts of the world in order to gain access to these new markets.

Organized crime is thus becoming increasingly transnational and the number of globally linked criminal groups, such as mafia and drug cartels, is increasing. Many countries with lower levels of development have the highest levels of organized crime, the explosion of which is particularly notable in countries whose economies are in transition. The impact of organized crime on cities can be very damaging, especially among urban poor communities. This is particularly the case with respect to drug trafficking, as will be shown later in this chapter. High urban crime levels generally increase fear among all urban citizens and constrains their movements (see Box 6.1), while at the same time keeping away productive investment.

Global overview

Transnational organized crime includes smuggling of firearms, drugs and human beings. The seriousness of these problems is reflected in the United Nations Convention against Transnational Organized Crime and its two complementary protocols: the Protocol against the Smuggling of Migrants and the Protocol against the Trafficking in Persons. The convention and its two protocols were adopted at the United Nations Millenium General Assembly in 2000 and promote close international cooperation among signing countries to take measures against transnational organized crime. The convention and its protocols formally entered into force in September 2003, while a third Protocol against the Illicit Manufacturing of and Trafficking in Firearms, their Parts and Components and Ammunition is currently under development.

Human smuggling by transnational crime organizations and networks takes advantage of overall increased international migration patterns, particularly from developing countries and countries in transition to developed countries. Criminal organizations involved in smuggling benefit from weak legislation or differences in legislation between countries and are therefore able to reap huge profits at a lower risk of detection, prosecution and arrest, compared to other types of transnational organized crime. Illegal migrants are taking higher risks and are increasingly dependent upon criminal networks to smuggle them into destination countries, in light of the implementation of more restrictive immigration policies and improved monitoring of border crossings by many of these countries. The illegal status of migrants most often puts them at the mercy of their smugglers, who force them into illegal employment to pay off their transportation debts. In 1999, Interpol launched Project Bridge in an attempt to facilitate more efficient collection of information on organized crime groups involved in human smuggling and to promote collaboration among international law enforcement agencies to strengthen the fight against smuggling through prevention and investigation.[2]

Human trafficking is conducted specifically for the purpose of exploiting the migrant, often through forced labour and contemporary forms of slavery or prostitution. The United Nations Office on Drugs and Crime (UNODC) has recently begun to gather statistics on human trafficking around the world and

---

BOX 6.1 **Fear of crime**

Safety from crime is not only a necessary ingredient for overall economic and social stability and the growth of cities, it is also essential for citizens' quality of life. Urban crime affects people's levels of fear and influences their movements and social activities, how they use certain areas of their city and transport, and perceptions and behaviour towards others.

Fear of crime can be both justified and exaggerated. Public distrust or dissatisfaction with the police and criminal justice system, and mass media's particular focus on the gravest crimes, can unduly increase public perception and fear of crime so that they are not in proportion to the real risk of victimization. For example, while fear of burglary somewhat matches actual risk, feelings about street safety are not consistently related to actual levels of street crime. This lack of relationship between fear and risk of street crime has been evident in findings of the International Crime Victim Surveys and has serious implications for how much people restrict their day-to-day lives and routines.

Furthermore, insecurity – whether real or perceived – is a key factor increasing citizens' demand for weapons, including firearms. For example, fear of armed robbery may increase demand for firearms for self-defence, even if armed robberies actually may be low or decreasing. The desire to carry a weapon for self-defence or status can partly indicate the level of insecurity in a community.[i]

Note: i Arms Management Programme, 2002.

estimates that 700,000 to 1 million people are being trafficked annually. Trafficking of women and girls for sexual exploitation is a multibillion-dollar industry, valued at over US$7 billion annually,[3] with relatively low risks compared to trafficking of drugs or arms.[4]

The United Nations estimates that one quarter of a much higher 4 million people trafficked each year are exploited in sex industries.[5] According to an unreleased report by the US Central Intelligence Agency (CIA) in 1999, up to 50,000 women and children per year are trafficked to the US alone.[6] Victims are most often the most vulnerable of society, especially women, children and migrants recruited from poor countries in Asia, Central and Eastern Europe, Latin America and Africa. Women and children are most often trafficked into developed countries in Western Europe and Northern America to work as prostitutes, abused labour or servants. A significant proportion of children also find themselves trafficked into Asia, where the sexual exploitation of children has become a massive industry due to the support of tourists from industrialized countries.[7]

Post-conflict countries often become the source of large numbers of illegal weapons and hubs for weapons smuggling to neighbouring countries. Although there are exceptions, violent crime and homicides are generally higher where arms are widely and easily available.[8] The presence and proliferation of illicit weapons not only increases the likelihood of continuing violence and more violent crime, but also disrupts humanitarian efforts in conflict and post-conflict countries.

Corruption and fraud facilitate the growth of organized crime, particularly in countries where public administration is less oriented towards serving citizens than to exercising power over them in defence of state interests, and where there are inadequate political, legal and ethical frameworks to ensure accountability and transparency in decision-making.

While corruption[9] is still a major problem in many countries and cities, there has generally been an increase in transparency and in the globalization of good governance norms, and this is also highlighted in this chapter.

A low level of transparency in political and financial affairs is often the precursor to a lack of accountability. While the presence of transparency is no guarantee that accountability will follow, its absence can easily create conditions leading to corruption. Transparent governance is based upon such important values as openness, trust and good ethics. At the local level, where trust must be nurtured if governance is to improve, corruption is often the worm inside the apple. Corruption can undermine and eviscerate everything that is done to improve services for urban residents. Unchecked corruption can undermine the very trust between citizens, civil society and governments that is essential for good governance.

The past several years have seen an increasing number of important events at the international and regional levels concerning the fight to improve transparency and governance, events that are expected over the years to play a role in improving governance at the local level and to reduce corruption. These events mark an increasing tempo in the globalization of good governance norms, and some of the more important ones are shown in Box 6.2. The link between economic globalization and the increasing standardization of governance norms is striking. While

---

BOX 6.2 Globalization of governance norms

- The United Nations Treaty against Corruption was approved and signed in December 2003 in Mexico.
- Regional conventions against corruption are in effect in the Organisation for Economic Co-operation and Development (OECD) states and the Americas, with the first rounds of monitoring taking place.
- The Africa Union (AU) Convention on Preventing and Combating Corruption was approved by the AU Heads of States in 2003. The Southern Africa states, through the Southern African Development Community (SADC), have already agreed on their own convention.
- The Council of Europe Criminal Law Convention on Corruption has reached the required number of ratifications for its entry into force.
- The United Cities and Local Governments organization (UCLG), a result of the unification of the International Union of Local Authorities and the United Towns Organization, was formed and commenced operations in 2004, one of its objectives being to promote good governance at the local level.
- International NGOs such as Transparency International, and foundations such as the Open Society Institute, are increasingly involved in good governance issues at the local level.
- Bilateral and multilateral donors, including the United Nations and the World Bank, have focused substantial resources on developing models and supporting the globalization of good governance norms.

it might be explained, in part, by improvements in information technology, the more important and fundamental reasons have to do with decisions that are being made on where to place international investments, as well as an increasing acceptance by world and national leaders that transparency and other indicators of good governance need to be observed in the community of nations (see Box 6.2). Much credit is deserved by the international and bilateral financial institutions that have fostered this trend, international campaigns, including UN-Habitat's Global Campaign on Good Urban Governance (see Box 6.3), and the increasingly important role of non-governmental organizations (NGOs), such as Transparency International, which led the early efforts to make transparency a factor in international lending and governance programmes.

Overall urban crime trends in the world

While crime and victimization occur in all countries of the world, the probability of being a victim of crime is substantially higher in urban areas. As a world average – two out of three inhabitants of cities are victimized by crime at least once over a five-year period. Globally, one in five people are likely to be victimized by a serious contact crime such as robbery, sexual crime or assault.[10]

Overall, recorded crime rates may be stabilizing or even decreasing in the North; but they still remain higher than they were 30 to 40 years ago. Furthermore, not all types of crime have decreased; although property crime has decreased or stabilized in several industrialized countries, the risk of being a victim of violence is at least one in five.[11]

Rates of crime and insecurity tend to be highest and are increasingly serious threats in developing economy countries, particularly Latin America and sub-Saharan Africa, where they further compound other factors, such as poverty and social exclusion, which already limit quality of life. Furthermore, corruption and fraud, which are higher in developing countries and countries in transition, further threaten economic and social well-being.

Crime can vary widely across regions and even among countries of similar income. Asian countries with developing economies, particularly West Asia, show low crime levels, while crime levels in Africa are quite high. Murder rates tend to be fairly constant in most places, with lower rates in highly industrialized countries and much higher rates in Latin American countries – although there are exceptions in countries such as South Africa and Jamaica where guns, social disruption and drugs are more common.

Despite decreases in some types of crime, urban violence – including homicide, assault, rape, sexual abuse and domestic violence – has continued to rise in cities worldwide. Although there are large variations between countries and cities, on average urban violence has grown by between 3 and 5 per cent over the past 20 years and has come to make up at least 25 to 30 per cent of urban crime in many countries.[12]

Violence has traditionally been linked to poverty levels, although it is now increasingly realized that the phenomenon is just as much correlated with inequality and social exclusion.

The increased availability and use of firearms heavily influences levels of urban violence, both fatal and non-fatal. Murder rates can be much higher in cities where weapons are easily available compared to national averages for fatal violence. It is also important to remember that there are even far more non-fatal violent assaults than murders.

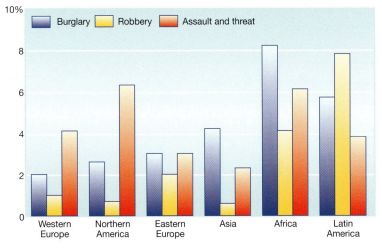

Source: Alvazzi del Frate, 2000.

FIGURE 6.1 **Victimization rates by region for burglary, robbery, assault and threat in 1999**

Adolescents are the most common group involved in offending and young offenders are most often victims themselves. Youth are becoming involved in offending at increasingly young ages, some as young as 12 years of age. Risk factors that influence youth becoming involved in offending include family problems, such as violence and poor parenting; poverty; inadequate housing and health conditions; poor schooling or lack of education; peer pressures; discrimination; and lack of training and work opportunities.

Along with increasing poverty, child and youth homelessness and the numbers of street children have been increasing in many countries, particularly those in developing regions whose urban centres cannot keep up with urbanization. Youth are at a higher risk both of becoming involved in, as well as being victimized by, crime, particularly when they are excluded from participating in and benefiting from school, employment, public space, health, safety and economic prosperity enjoyed by the rest of mainstream society's population. Youth involvement in offending is becoming particularly apparent in the growth of youth gangs, especially in Latin American and African countries where rapid urbanization is straining families' ability to meet the social and economic needs of youth.

It is particularly difficult to obtain accurate estimates on the prevalence of violence against women in its many forms due to its hidden nature, primarily occurring behind the closed doors of households and deeply rooted in social, cultural and traditional practices. Violence against women occurs across all socio-economic classes, and religious and ethnic lines.[13] According to the 2000 International Crime Victim Survey (ICUS) of 17 industrialized countries, women victims personally know the offender in about half of all sexual crimes. When considering assaults and threats, women were found to be more likely to know the offender than men.[14] Studies in 40 countries indicate that 20 to 50 per cent of women are victims of physical violence by their partners or ex-partners and that the same perpetrators also sexually abuse 50 to 60 per cent of these women.[15] Furthermore, 40 to 60 per cent of known sexual assaults within the family are committed against girls aged 15 and under, regardless of region or culture.[16]

According to the survey for the last decade, a large majority – 76 per cent of respondents in Northern America and the Pacific advanced economies – were satisfied with police control of crime. In Western Europe and Asia, 54 and 58 per cent, respectively, were also satisfied. However, almost comparable percentages of citizens in Africa (52 per cent) and countries in transition (40 per cent) report

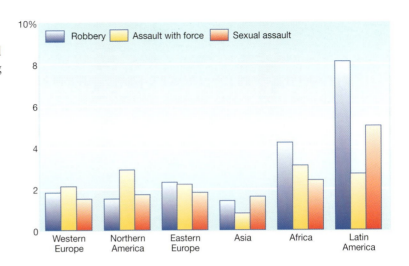

Source: Zvekic, 2000.

FIGURE 6.2 **Contact crime by world region, 1999**

More than a million people trafficked each year are exploited in sex industries

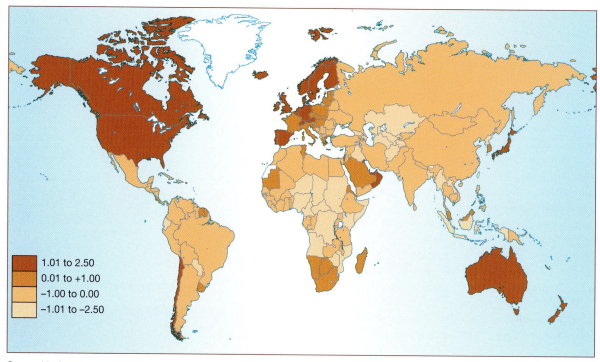

Source: Kaufmann and Kraay, 2003.

MAP 6.1 **Control of corruption, 2001**

not being satisfied. In Latin America, as many as 70 per cent reported not being satisfied.[17]

Partly linked with pubic satisfaction with police in controlling crime, street safety is perceived to be highest by citizens in Asia, followed by those in Western Europe and Northern America. According to the United Nations Interregional Crime and Justice Research Institute's (UNICRI's) 1996 International Crime Victim Survey (ICVS), citizens in countries in transition feel least safe compared to other world regions.[18] Slightly less than 60 per cent of citizens in Africa feel safe, while almost 50 per cent of citizens in Latin America feel very or fairly safe when walking alone after dark.[19]

With respect to corruption, the advanced economies continued to have the lowest levels of corruption, occupying most of the top 25 to 30 positions in the 2003 Transparency International Corruption Perceptions Index.[20] Governance indicators for these richer countries are generally excellent.[21] This does not mean that there is no corruption. Rather, it means that there are systems in place that ensure greater transparency and accountability at all levels. At the other end of the scale, the transition economies and the developing economies' nations are well represented. Many of them are poor, although some have great oil and mineral wealth. Governance indicators for these countries are generally lower. There is little evidence to suggest that corruption at the local level does anything other than parallel these overall findings in most countries. There are seldom multiple systems in place to promote transparency and accountability.

The rest of this chapter reviews urban crime trends in the world by region. Each regional section starts by describing overall crime trends of particular concern, such as youth involvement in crime and youth gangs, violence against women and corruption. It then highlights types of organized crime that are increasingly facilitated by globalization and whose resolution requires international cooperation, such as drug trafficking, and trafficking in firearms and human beings. The general overview of urban crime trends provides the overall context within which 'international' or 'globalized' crime, and its impact on cities in that region, may be better understood.

Regional trends in urban crime

Victimization data from the developing regions of Asia, Africa, and Latin America shows that Asia consistently ranks lowest for all types of crime, especially violent crime. Asia has the lowest rates of contact crime and violence, while Latin America and Africa have the highest rates. 'Contact crime' as measured by UNICRI's ICVS includes robbery, sexual assaults and assaults with force.[22] In industrialized countries men and women are at similar risk of assault, however risk for women is higher in Latin

America, Africa and Asia[23] and violence against women is also most prevalent in economically deprived, developing countries.

Citizen–police relations and police satisfaction are important issues for analysing crime trends. Crime statistics produced solely on the basis of crime reported to the police gives the least accurate picture of crime trends in the developing countries where relations between citizens and police are often marked by distrust. Within developing countries, reporting crime to police is lowest in Asian and Latin American countries, where only one in five serious cases of violence are brought to police attention. As stated earlier, victims' levels of satisfaction with the police are lowest in Latin America and Africa.[24]

Asia and the Pacific

Of all the world regions, developed and developing, Asia ranks lowest in almost all types of crime. While in Africa and Latin America up to two-thirds of the population living in cities with over 100,000 inhabitants or more are likely to be victims of crime once in five years, only in Asia is less than half of the population likely to be a victim during this same period of time.[25] Although many crimes are at lower rates in Asian countries, during the past ten years there have been increases in crimes against property, organized violent crime and drug trafficking.[26]

An exception to low rates of almost all types of crime in Asia is the prevalence of corruption, particularly bribery. UNICRI's ICVS found that the prevalence rate for bribery in Asia (16.6 per cent) was second only to that of Latin America (19.5 per cent) and surpassed that of Africa (15 per cent). Bribery in Asia is reported most often to be practised by government officials, followed by police officers.[27]

Transparency International's 2003 Corruption Perceptions Index (CPI) ranked 15 of the countries in the region. The highest with lowest corruption levels

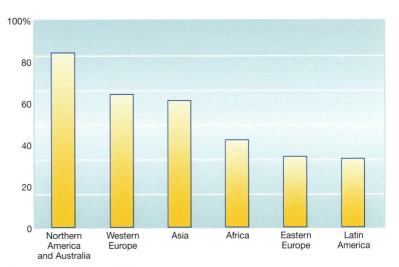

Source: Alvazzi del Frate, 2000.

FIGURE 6.3 **Percentage satisfied with police performance, by region, 1999**

were Malaysia and the Republic of Korea (37 and 50, respectively). Three countries were grouped together from 66 to 70; but the remaining eight countries were below this level. Half the world's population, or 95 per cent of the population of this region, live in countries in the bottom half of the Transparency International corruption index.

The real nature of the corrupt activities that ordinary persons meet in South Asia – and likely in most of the rest of the region – came through plainly in a 2002 Transparency International survey in urban and rural areas in India, Pakistan, Sri Lanka, Nepal, and Bangladesh.[28] The overall results are shown in Table 6.1.

TRANSNATIONAL CRIME Trafficking of women and children, especially for the purposes of commercial sexual exploitation, has been a serious problem in Asia and the Pacific for decades, with countries such as Thailand and the Philippines being primary sending countries.[29] While poor women and children may also

TABLE 6.1 **Corruption by sectors**

Country	Education	Health	Power	Land administration	Tax	Police	Judiciary
Bangladesh	40	58	32	73	19	84	75
India	34	15	30	47	15	100	100
Nepal	25	18	12	17	25	48	42
Pakistan	92	96	96	100	99	100	96
Sri Lanka	61	92	*	98	*	100	100

Note: Table shows percentage of respondents reporting corruption in interactions with the sectors. * Indicates sample too small.

Source: Transparency International, 2002

voluntarily become involved in prostitution as a way of surviving, they are more vulnerable to becoming victims of dishonest 'recruiters', being sold by their own families for small profit, or even being kidnapped. Traffickers frequently prey on women and children from Thailand, Viet Nam, China, the Philippines, Republic of Korea and Malaysia.[30]

Although the problem is worldwide, Southeast Asia could be referred to as the 'home' of the child sex tourism industry, where tours openly seek to cater to the child sex interests of wealthy adults. A 1999 study estimated that four-fifths of the foreign demand for child prostitution comes from the US, Germany, the UK, Australia, France and Japan.[31]

Part of the mission of organizations such as ECPAT (End Child Prostitution, Child Pornography and Trafficking of Children for Sexual Purposes) in Bangkok is monitoring governments' and countries' implementation of the Stockholm Agenda for Action adopted by 122 countries at the First World Congress against the Commercial Sexual Exploitation of Children, in Sweden in 1996. The Yokohama Global Commitment developed at the Second World Congress in Japan in 2001 reaffirmed the need to fight to end commercial sexual exploitation of children and was supported by 159 states and countries.[32]

Both of these declarations are guided by the United Nations 1949 Convention for the Suppression of Traffic in Persons and of the Exploitation of the Prostitution of Others, which has, however, not been widely ratified and did not involve the creation of a monitoring body to evaluate its implementation or effectiveness.[33] Two more recent protocols to the Convention Against Transnational Organized Crime, adopted by the United Nations General Assembly in 2000, focus on trafficking in persons, especially women and children, and the smuggling of migrants.

After a drastic decrease in 2001, illicit opium and heroin production recovered in 2002 due to resumption of large-scale opium poppy cultivation in Afghanistan. The rapid re-growth of opium production has fuelled the escalation of the heroin market in this region, as well as in the transition economies of Central Asia and Central and Eastern Europe.[34] In 2002, the main sources of opium were Afghanistan (76 per cent) and Myanmar (18 per cent). Lao People's Democratic Republic (2 per cent) and Colombia (1 per cent) were also smaller sources, followed by marginal production in Pakistan, Thailand and Viet Nam.[35]

Central Asian countries are facing a rapidly increasing drug problem, with a fourfold to sevenfold increase in the rate of new abusers during the past ten years. Opioids (heroin and opium) remain the main drugs of abuse in most of Asia, given that this is the primary area of their cultivation (Afghanistan, Pakistan, Myanmar and Lao PDR). This has serious implications in terms of the transmission of HIV, especially given that up to one third of heroin abusers inject the drug (with epidemic levels in northeast India, Myanmar, China's Yunnan Province and several cities in Viet Nam). However, the spread of methamphetamine abuse also continues to be a major concern in Southeast Asia and is beginning to have a serious impact on service provision, including drug treatment, psychiatric and other health services.[36]

Latin America and the Caribbean

Urban violence and firearms, youth gangs and violence, drugs and violence against women are issues of major concern in the region, as is illustrated by the case of Brazil (see Box 6.4). Latin America's cities and urban areas have, as Figure 6.4 shows, the highest gun ownership rates – 19.7 per cent.[37]

YOUTH CRIME Youth are central to the increasing violence in most countries in the region. Youth are often organized in gangs that use violence to meet their social and economic needs, further adding to already high levels of violence in their communities. About 29 per cent of homicides in Latin America are among youth 10 to 19 years of age – in fact, homicide is the second leading cause of death for this age group in 10 of the 21 countries with populations over 1 million in the region.[38] Youth homicide rates can be up to three times higher than national homicide rates. In Venezuela, 95 per cent of homicide victims were male, and 54 per cent of them were younger than 25.[39] In Brazil, homicides among youths increased by 77 per cent during the past ten years, mostly because of the use of firearms.[40]

BOX 6.4 Urban crime in Brazil

Crime rates have risen sharply in Brazil during recent years, largely due to increased organized crime and trafficking of drugs, firearms, human beings and endangered species involving local and international criminal organizations. While urban inhabitants are more vulnerable to crime than those in rural areas, residents of lower-income inner-city and informal settlements in urban areas are particularly at high risk. São Paulo, Rio de Janeiro, Espirito Santo and Pernambuco are the most violent states in Brazil. However, homicide rates vary greatly depending upon area and income. For example, tourist areas of Rio de Janeiro have a homicide rate of around 4 per 100,000 people, which is comparable to some of the safest cities in Europe. On the contrary, homicide rates can be as high as 150 per 100,000 people in *favelas*, slum areas only a few kilometres from these tourist areas.[i]

A large part of the almost 30,000 homicides registered annually in Brazil are linked to drug abuse and trafficking.[ii] The illegal drug trade often involves violent competition among gangs of producers and distributors for shares of the global drug market, given its immense profitability compared to other licit or illicit economic activities.

Along with mounting social exclusion of youth and linked to high availability of firearms, youth who resort to gangs

as a means of survival and as a feeling of belonging to 'substitute families' are also increasing. The drug trade provides lucrative work and traffickers have little difficulty in recruiting poorly educated youth in poorer countries who have few prospects for formal work. Street children are often recruited as drug couriers. Delivering drugs is estimated to create jobs for approximately 20,000 child and youth couriers, most of them between 10 and 16 years of age. A young courier's salary is often higher than that of their parents, earning them respect from their peers and a feeling of importance in the community.[iii]

Campaigns organized by the NGO Viva Rio in Rio de Janeiro are excellent examples of mobilizing women as agents of social change to reduce violence and arms proliferation. Diverse women gathered to launch the *Choose Gun-free! It's Your Weapon or Me* campaign on Mother's day in 2001. The campaign distributed white flowers and materials to help women disarm their loved ones, giving convincing arguments that a gun is much more likely to kill or injure than to protect loved ones. Another *Mother, Disarm your Son* campaign involved awareness-raising concerts by popular artists.[iv]

Notes: i Zvekic, 1998a. ii Zvekic, 1998a. iii Zvekic, 1998a. iv First International Seminar on Women's Safety, 2002.

VIOLENCE AGAINST WOMEN Latin America has the highest risk of all types of sexual victimization combined, with approximately 70 per cent of incidents described as rapes, attempted rapes or indecent assaults. Women in Latin America, particularly in Brazil and Argentina, were most frequently exposed to sexual victimization compared to other world regions.[41] The lowest average rates for reporting sexual incidents to authorities were in Bolivia, Brazil, Colombia and Costa Rica. Latin American cities have the highest rates of sexual assault (around 5 per cent compared to 2.4 per cent in African cities and 1.6 per cent in Asian cities).[42]

There are a series of factors contributing to the growth of violence against women. However, one of the strongest is a culture that emphasizes women's historical and socially constructed inferior status to men. Furthermore, public security policies have had little success in changing the conditions of women. For example, Brazilian legislation considers domestic aggression to be a minor crime comparable to a street fight and aggressors are often released quickly by police, only to return home to threaten the victim not to report him again. Thus, key challenges involve empowering women, promoting prevention and reducing women's social exclusion.[43]

In Costa Rica, women have mobilized through marches and seminars to lobby politicians to penalize murders and other types of aggression against women. Women in other Latin American countries have also organized peace campaigns, such as the Honduran *Visitación Padilla* that succeeded in changing forced military service to voluntary.

The lowest levels of citizens who are satisfied with the police in controlling local crime are in Latin

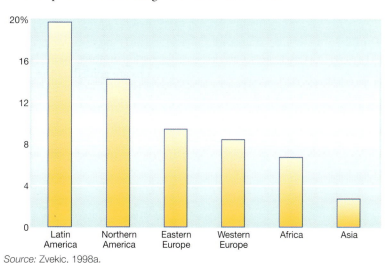

Source: Zvekic, 1998a.

FIGURE 6.4 **Overall gun ownership rates, 1996**

America (up to 70 per cent are unsatisfied, as measured by the International Crime Victim Survey). Of all public officials, police officers also appear to be most involved in bribery in Latin America.[44]

CORRUPTION AND TRANSPARENCY   With respect to corruption and transparency, Latin America and the Caribbean have experienced, with uneven progress, a general increase in democracy over the past 15 years. At the local level, this has meant increasing numbers of local governments with new responsibilities and new leaders. Rapid urbanization and the increasingly apparent urbanization of poverty have also meant an increasing incidence and higher levels of corruption. There has been internal pressure in a number of countries for increased transparency and greater accountability, supported by external donors and national civil societies. In spite of this gathering momentum for change, transparency and accountability remain generally elusive.

Trust in persons and institutions in Latin American countries hovers at very low levels.

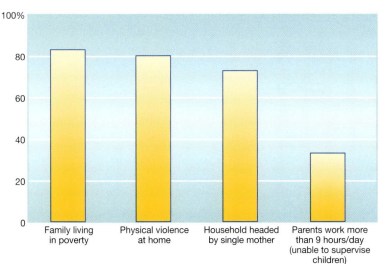

Source: Santa Cruz Giralt and Concha-Eastman, 2001.

FIGURE 6.5 **Characteristics of young gang members in El Salvador**

Furthermore, between 1996 and 2003, trust in public institutions has been gradually, but distinctly, declining. Because of Latin America's history of strong institutions, such as the Roman Catholic Church, the presidency and the military, this decline in trust is significant and has been directly related to people's perception of corruption.[45] Although leadership is an important factor in the fight against corruption, Latin America, as in other regions, has seen many instances of politicians espousing an anti-corruption platform, only to be exposed later as accomplices in corruption. This has contributed to a sense of disillusionment in some places.

Trust in most public institutions in the 17 countries in Latin America covered in a 2003 survey[46] has dropped appreciably during the life of the surveys. The police, the judiciary and municipalities generally score low; but government and political parties are graded even lower. These results have sparked considerable debate on the future of democracy in the region. The single most important factor affecting trust in public institutions is whether a person believes that she or he is being treated equitably. In turn, there appears to be a direct correlation between this desire for equal treatment and perceptions of corruption if treatment is not equal. Where there is progress in addressing corruption, there is also increased trust in the institution.

However, corruption clearly remains a major issue. The 2003 Transparency International CPI rated 23 countries in the region. Chile, Uruguay, Cuba, and Trinidad and Tobago came out with the lowest levels of corruption (at 20, 33 and 43, respectively).

TRANSNATIONAL CRIME   In the Latin America and Caribbean region, crime with an international dimension revolves mainly around drug trafficking. In terms of drug production, the majority of the world's cocaine is produced in Central and South America (primarily Bolivia, Colombia and Peru). The balloon effect, where crop reduction in one area has resulted in increase in other areas, has thus far prevented production at the global level from declining in absolute terms.[47]

Colombia's cocaine production increased roughly five times between 1993 and 1999, making the country the source of almost 75 per cent of the world's illicit supply of cocaine. More positively, after an eight-year increase, Colombia has managed to reduce its coca cultivation by 37 per cent between 2000 and 2002.[48] There are also some positive signs of progress in controlling cocaine supply and demand in Bolivia and Peru.

Although Brazil has traditionally been a country through which drugs were smuggled rather than

BOX 6.5 **MV Bill rapping from a Rio** *favela*

MV Bill is one of Brazil's most popular hip-hop artists. His name, MV (Mensageiro da Verdade, or Truth Messenger) depicts his mission. He uses his words and talents to paint a grim picture of the slums he grew up in and to demonstrate his strong opposition to racism, drugs and violence. He raps about promotion of positive things, of changing in a positive fashion. He has participated in a documentary that depicts life in a *favela*, including profiles of 16 young people who work in the drug chain. During the three years between 2000 and 2003, only one of the youngsters remained alive. MV Bill made the documentary to show the youth that death is real and to encourage them to look past their current situation. He also wanted to open up a dialogue between the people living in the *favelas* and the government.

Source: Habitat Debate, 2003.

primarily where they were produced or consumed, there is now a growing market for the consumption of illicit drugs in Brazil, as well.[49] After cannabis, cocaine appears to be the second most commonly abused drug and there is particular concern about the increase of its abuse in many other Central and South American countries. Slightly more than two-thirds of these countries reported an increase in cocaine abuse in 2001, while none reported a decrease. Use of amphetamine-type stimulants, especially ecstasy-type drugs, has also most noticeably increased across the Americas.[50]

Increased security and border controls following the 11 September 2001 terrorist attacks in the US

have had a very limited impact on the Caribbean's drug-trafficking activity, other than for marijuana.[51] It is estimated that about 30 to 40 per cent of the cocaine supply to the US and Canada and 50 to 80 per cent of Western Europe's cocaine supply transits through the Caribbean every year. The geography of the region makes it easy for smugglers to find routes and hiding places among the region's many islands, while making border control and customs enforcement more difficult and costly.[52] Limited trade barriers between many Caribbean countries and the relatively borderless European Union (EU) further facilitate trafficking to Europe, as cocaine is easily concealed within legitimate imports.[53]

Puerto Rico has been the largest cocaine hub since the early 1990s as it is the convergence point of several cocaine routes: cocaine flows directly north from South America, east from the Dominican

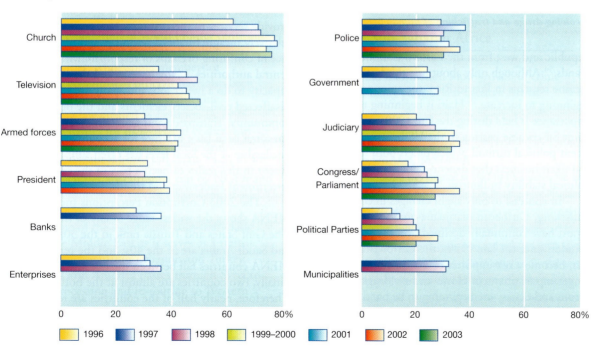

FIGURE 6.6 **Trust in institutions, Latin America, 2003**

BOX 6.7 Decline in frequency of bribery in Kenya's local authorities

Kenya is engaged in a campaign against corruption at all levels following the election of a new president and government in December 2002. Since then, measures taken include the suspension of over half the country's senior judges and magistrates and over 800 Forestry Department staff, among others. Enforcement of the anti-corruption law is under way, requiring declarations of wealth by high-ranking civil servants and the establishment of a new permanent secretary in the President's Office for Governance and Ethics. Land allocations are being investigated and police salaries have been raised. All of these measures have been accompanied by high-profile media exposure and it is fair to say that transparency in this country has increased as a result, and bribery is declining, as shown below.

Local authorities	Bribery frequency, 2002 (%)	Bribery frequency, 2003 (%)
Nairobi	33.8	22.6
Kisumu	29.6	24.0
Mombasa	29.2	22.6
Other local authorities	36.1	17.3

Source: Transparency International, 2004.

diamonds, endangered species, drugs and people and prevents the disarmament and demobilization of civilians and former combatants.[94]

Five hundred million small arms produced by 300 manufacturers in 74 countries are believed to be in circulation in the world either legally or outside of regulatory state controls. Despite this, international trade in small arms is currently highly unregulated. 40 per cent of the international flow of small arms is attributed to illicit trafficking, while the majority of illicit weapons originally come from licit international arms trade. This emphasizes the need for governments around the world to tighten arms regulation within their borders, as well as to accept stronger international standards for the legal transfer of arms between countries.[95]

90 per cent of conflict casualties are caused by small arms – they are, indeed, 'weapons of mass destruction'. Small arms are easily accessible and inexpensive – an AK-47 can be purchased for about the same price as a chicken or goat in many African countries. Africa has become a dumping ground of inexpensive surplus small arms that are not only causing escalation of local violence, but can also prolong or heighten interstate conflicts. If a conservative estimate that 200,000 firearms are illegal or unaccounted for in each country of Africa, at least 11 million illegal firearms can be estimated to be freely circulating or available on the continent.

However, this is still a conservative approximation, as it could be estimated that between 500,000 and 1 million weapons were imported into Mozambique alone during its civil war, while only about 190,000 were collected during the following United Nations peacekeeping operation in 1993–1995. It is also known that a majority of the remaining weapons were likely not destroyed, but were, instead, soon again on city streets, or being transferred to neighbouring states.[96] This already alarming estimate still does not consider firearms that are being used in the intrastate and international conflicts that are currently being waged across the continent.[97]

AK-47s are easy enough for a ten-year-old child to assemble and carry. The United Nations International Children's Fund (UNICEF) estimates that 250,000 to 300,000 children, some as young as eight years of age, are exploited as soldiers in armed conflicts in over 30 countries around the world.[98] Not only is child involvement in open hostilities dehumanizing and psychologically and emotionally traumatizing, but it also inculcates entire new generations of children, future adults and leaders of countries, into cultures of violence.

In 2000, ten countries in the Great Lakes and Horn of Africa sub-regions adopted the Nairobi Declaration and developed an action and implementation plan to guide efforts to address and reduce the proliferation of small arms and light weapons in East Africa. The United Nations first Conference on the Illicit Trade in Small Arms and Light Weapons in All its Aspects was held in 2001. Although the conference did not result in any firm commitments to develop legally binding international-level instruments to prevent or control illicit and unregulated transfers of small arms and light weapons, governments did at least agree on a programme of action to be monitored at biannual United Nations meetings. It was recommended that a second international conference be convened on the matter no later than 2006.

Two-thirds (67 per cent) of respondents to a city-wide victim survey in Nairobi in 2001 felt that the increase of firearms in the city was due to smuggling over porous borders. 51 per cent of respondents felt that illegal firearms came from neighbouring countries, particularly Somalia.[99]

Although there are exceptions, homicides are also generally higher where arms are widely and easily available, either legally or illegally.[100] Insecurity, whether real or perceived, is a key factor increasing citizens' demand for weapons, including firearms; however, their trafficking and wide availability at the same time fuel instability and conflict.

Another survey conducted in Nairobi in 2001 specifically on the prevalence of firearms found that

70 per cent of citizens believe that crime is increasing and 84 per cent believe that the number of firearms has increased in the city. 90 per cent of the business community surveyed in Nairobi thought that firearms were commonly used when committing crime.[101]

Transition economies

In Central and Eastern Europe, political and economic shifts from communist regimes towards market-driven pluralist democracies have brought new crime and safety concerns along with new-found freedom. The need to adapt quickly to drastic change has given rise to many challenges, exacerbated by economies and democratic institutions that are themselves still weak and adapting. Challenges have also arisen due to the related evolving relationship between citizens and the police.

On average, less than 25 per cent of the Central and Eastern Europe population surveyed by UNICRI's 1996 International Crime Victim Survey (ICVS) reported being satisfied with the police, while almost 50 per cent reported being dissatisfied.[102]

Perhaps surprisingly, rates of citizen satisfaction and reporting crime to the police did not improve between 1991 and 1996, when many of these countries' police forces began to reorganize and their role within society began to change in regimes that were establishing new relations between state and citizens. For example, victims of assault and threats complained that police were impolite and lacked respect for the needs of victims of violence.[103]

Far fewer crimes continue to be reported to police in Central and Eastern Europe than in industrialized regions. On average, reporting rates in urban centres that were already low in 1996 further decreased between 1996 and 2000 for all types of crime, except attempted burglary and robbery, which remained quite stable. When individual cities are compared, the greatest increases in reporting between 1997 and 2000 were for robbery, burglary and attempted burglary in Ljubljana (Slovenia), Minsk (Belarus), Sofia (Bulgaria), Warsaw (Poland) and Zagreb (Croatia). The greatest decreases were in Vilnius (Lithuania), Prague (Czech Republic) and Tirana (Albania).[104]

The Russian Federation's already high murder rate in 1990 (9.4 per 100,000 population) soared to 21.9 per 100,000 population by 2000. Furthermore, the Russian Federation, along with Hungary, reported the highest rate of youth sentencing (1.5 per cent of juveniles).[105]

Theft of personal property (22.2 per cent of all crimes) and theft from cars (20.7 per cent of all crimes) were the most common crimes in cities surveyed by the 2000 ICVS. Car vandalism (15.3 per

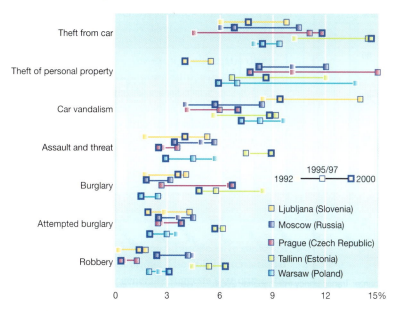

Source: Alvazzi del Frate and van Kesteren, forthcoming.

FIGURE 6.10 **Changes in prevalence rates (% of population victimized) of most common crimes in cities in countries in transition, 1992–2000**

cent) and assault and threat (10.3 per cent) were also relatively common. Burglary (7.5 per cent), attempted burglary (7.0 per cent) and robbery (6.2 per cent) made up another 20 per cent of all crimes in 2000. The proportion of all of these crimes changed very little between 1996 and 2000.[106]

On average, 9 of the 11 crimes measured by the ICVS decreased between 1996 and 2000, while the prevalence of robbery and theft of motorcycles or mopeds remained unchanged. The largest decreases were for theft of personal property (–1.5 per cent), car vandalism (–1.4 per cent) and assault and threat (–1.0 per cent).[107] Riga, Latvia (+0.8 per cent), had the largest increase in assaults with force between 1996 and 2000. However, the extent of decrease in assaults with force was more remarkable in cities such as Bucharest, Warsaw, Sofia, Prague and Zagreb.[108]

In 2000, assaults with force were most common in Tallinn, Estonia (experienced by 3.4 per cent of ICVS respondents), Riga, Latvia (1.9 per cent), and Vilnius, Lithuania (1.4 per cent), closely followed by Ljubljana, Slovenia, and Minsk, Belarus (1.3 per cent each).

The 1996 ICVS found that citizens in countries in transition felt least safe compared to citizens in all other world regions. More than half (53 per cent) said that they felt a little or very unsafe, while only 46 per cent said they felt safe and the lowest percentage (13 per cent) said they felt very safe in their city streets after dark. Citizens in Ukraine, Russia and Latvia felt least safe, while those

WOMEN: LOSERS IN THE BATTLE FOR THE HUMAN RIGHT TO ADEQUATE HOUSING
Miloon Kothari

The right to an adequate standard of living, including adequate food, clothing and housing, has been widely recognized as an important human right in the Universal Declaration of Human Rights and the International Covenant on Economic Social and Cultural Rights. These legal human rights instruments, including the Convention on the Elimination of All Forms of Discrimination against Women, also recognizes that women and men have equal rights to an adequate standard of living, which includes the right to adequate housing.

But inadequate and insecure housing and living conditions, such as overcrowding; indoor pollution; precarious housing; lack of water, sanitation and electricity; and inadequate building materials affect women more than men. Women living in extreme poverty face a much greater risk of becoming homeless or finding themselves in inadequate housing and health conditions. Women bear the brunt of forced evictions, especially when the evictions are violent. Some women, like the widows of HIV/AIDS victims, are especially at risk of eviction. The horrific lack of adequate housing, particularly for women, is a strong indicator of the extent to which governments across the world are literally failing to provide for the livelihood and dignity of people.

In Asia, loss in family income and diminishing sources of employment in rural areas, or forced evictions of families from indigenous and rural lands, as a result of large-scale development projects, globalization and armed conflict are resulting in large numbers of women and young girls migrating or being trafficked to urban areas or foreign countries to earn a living for their families. Many take employment as domestic workers. Often, they have to sleep on the kitchen floor or a corner of the bathroom. In one example, an Indonesian woman in Malaysia was kept locked in a cage without a toilet, and let out only for a couple of hours a day to do the cleaning. Often such women are raped by their employers.

When I visited Kenya on a mission in March 2004, the government had started the first large-scale planned eviction of people living under power lines, on land reserved for bypasses and along railway lines. These evictions were carried out, affecting primarily innocent women and children, in clear contravention of Kenya's international obligations. Advocacy from a remarkable coalition of national and international civil society organizations, church groups and United Nations human rights bodies has halted the evictions, at least temporarily, and compelled the government of Kenya to re-examine the premise and the process of evictions.

On a mission to Peru a year earlier to look at the housing crisis, I found that large numbers of people had been displaced in political violence, and that informal settlements have mushroomed, largely fuelled by poverty. They don't have title, lack utilities, particularly water and sanitation, their homes are built in dangerous places and they live in a polluted environment constantly facing the threat of eviction. The impact of these conditions, I witnessed and heard, is most severe on women. Successive governments have failed to tackle this immense problem, and the solutions, largely influenced by neo-liberal thinking of Hernando De Soto and the World Bank, advocating the provision of title as the main engine for pulling the poor out of poverty, have had a limited vision.

What is heartening in such situations is to see the positive efforts by civil society groups and local communities. A non-governmental organization (NGO) called Estrategia, trains community residents, both women and men, to build affordable homes. Conscious efforts are made to ensure participation of both men and women in the planning processes, training and execution of housing construction and local production of materials. Estrategia combines the technical assistance in housing construction with human rights awareness training, so that men and women become aware of their rights and can participate in meetings with local authorities.

I particularly wish to stress the frequent and widespread nature of violence, commonly experienced by women in situations where their right to adequate housing is also violated. Women experience a range of violence directly linked to inadequate housing conditions. The violation of

their right to adequate housing contributes to their vulnerability to gender violence. Additional problems that are faced by women in forced evictions include morbidity, loss of livelihood and income, increased workload, a lack of compensation, a lack of mobility and access to the public domain, community breakdowns, and sexual and gender-based violence. This is why I continue to stress the indivisibility of the human rights approach that calls for, in this context, equal respect for the economic, social and cultural rights (such as the right to adequate housing) of women, as well as their civil and political rights, such as the right to security of the home and person.

Within the home, violence can take the form of beatings, rape and harassment before, during and after forced evictions, or in situations of armed or ethnic conflict. Degrading housing and living conditions and the constant threat of rape makes women more vulnerable to HIV/AIDS and other sexually transmitted diseases.

Women refugees from Afghanistan, for example, face violence and can be deprived of their rights and property when they are repatriated. There is no security in the country and very little reconstruction. Most women returnees have no land or homes when returning, making them very vulnerable to violence. Women who own land are often denied access to it by traditional leaders and even the judicial system. Women have no legal recourse, and are forced to rely on male relatives. Women are culturally prohibited from living alone or living without men. In families headed by women, widows are forced to remarry or live with male relatives. Many women are unable to leave situations where they face violence from their husband or other family members. Women who escape are usually detained and prosecuted or risk being killed by their families. Women in detention or jails are often sexually abused.

The lack of implementation of laws and policies sustains ongoing gender-based discrimination that underlies such violations of women's human rights. The gap between the law and reality arises from the existence of gender-neutral laws, which do not always recognize the special circumstances of women. Gender-biased customs and traditions, as well as bias in the judiciary and public administration, results in the perpetration of male-dependent security of tenure. Even where legal remedies may be provided, many women cannot afford them. There is also increasing concern about the violence used by state and non-state actors against women who attempt to defend and secure their rights to adequate housing, particularly in situations of forced evictions.

These housing and land issues demonstrate the failure of governance on a wide scale. In my 2003 report, I outlined the need for identifying and designing suitable indicators that are contextually relevant for monitoring the targets of the Millennium Development Goals (MDGs) and their identified constituent aspects. These indicators reflect the human rights principles and concepts that underlie the development process – accountability, non-discrimination, the rule of law, gender equality, and progressive realization of economic, social and cultural rights. There remains a need to develop such mechanisms for monitoring that will contribute to greater measures being

taken by states to ensure human rights.

I have also consistently called for national housing policies to be implemented; but some of the richest countries in the world, like the US, Canada and Australia, continue to fail to implement these basic steps towards the realization of adequate housing. In the US, which upholds itself as a bearer of human rights and advocates good governance and democracy across the world, the human right of housing continues to be denied on a daily basis across the country. According to a new study, at least 840,000 people are homeless at any given time. Over the course of a year, 2.5 to 3.5 million are homeless. Among women who are homeless, domestic violence is a key factor.

While some countries are taking positive concrete steps, stronger measures both at the national and international level must be taken to prosecute housing rights violations, and to help the victims get recourse to justice.

I call on states to take concrete steps to secure the right of women to adequate housing and make serious attempts to implement existing laws and their international human rights

commitments. States are also urged to include anti-violence provisions in housing legislation and policies and to include provisions that protect women's right to housing in domestic violence, sex discrimination, and other related laws and policies. I also call on states to support and advance the work of the United Nations Commission on Human Rights' Open-Ended Working Group on the Optional Protocol to the International Covenant on Economic, Social and Cultural Rights to develop an adequate mechanism for individual and group complaints under this covenant.

Civil society has played an important role in mobilizing support for housing rights and monitoring developments. But I urge governments to recognize and respect the critical and constructive role of civil society and to adopt alternative solutions to securing housing rights for all.

MILOON KOTHARI IS SPECIAL RAPPORTEUR ON ADEQUATE HOUSING APPOINTED BY THE UNITED NATIONS COMMISSION ON HUMAN RIGHTS. INFORMATION AND DOCUMENTS ON THE RIGHT TO ADEQUATE HOUSING AND HIS MANDATE ARE AVAILABLE AT WWW.UNHCHR.CH/HOUSING.

---

in fewer arrests and lower police recording of crime.[125]

Domestic burglary fell by 15 per cent, on average, in EU countries between 1996 and 2000, although it soared by 33 per cent in Japan during this same period.[126] According to the 2000 ICVS, Australia (7 per cent), England and Wales (5 per cent), Canada, Denmark and Belgium (all 4 per cent) had the highest rates of burglary or attempted burglary.[127]

According to crimes recorded by the police, violent crime rose by 14 per cent in the EU and by 15 per cent in England and Wales between 1996 and 2000. The largest increases in violent crime were in Spain (38 per cent), France (36), The Netherlands (35), Portugal (28), Italy (20), Denmark (17) and England and Wales (15). Japan had an extremely high increase of 72 per cent in violent crime.[128]

The US ranks third in the incidence rate for 'very serious' crime among the 16 developed nations surveyed by the 1998 ICVS, behind England and Wales and Australia. The US is followed by Sweden, The Netherlands and Canada. The lowest incidences of very serious crime were in Portugal, Denmark, Japan and, finally, Finland.[129]

Contact crimes (robbery, assaults with force and sexual assaults) made up about one quarter of all crimes measured by the 2000 ICVS and the majority of these

contact crimes were assaults and threats. Contact crime was found to be highest in Australia, England and Wales, Canada, Scotland and Finland (over 3 per cent were victims in all of these countries). While Japan usually has low rates for almost all types of crime (40 per cent of all crime involved theft of bicycles, mopeds or motorbikes), Japan had an especially low rate of contact crime (0.4 per cent). Risk of assaults and threats was highest in Australia, Scotland, England and Wales (all about 6 per cent) and Canada (5 per cent). Risks were lowest in Catalonia (1.5 per cent), Japan and Portugal (less than 1 per cent each).[130]

According to the United Nations Economic Commission for Europe (UNECE) *2003 Statistical Yearbook*, England and Wales, Northern Ireland and the US (followed by Israel) had the highest rates of serious assaults reported to police in 2000 among the 55 UNECE member countries. Rates varied between 300 and 500 reported cases per 100,000 population.[131]

In considering violent crime and serious assaults, the US was one of the few countries where murder rate decreased between 1990 and 2000. However, despite the rate being less than in 1990, the US still had the highest number of rapes reported in 2000 (32 cases reported per 100,000 population) compared to the other UNECE member countries.[132]

The 11 September 2001 terrorist attacks have particularly had a recent effect on international marijuana trafficking. Local marijuana production in developed countries, especially in Northern America, has become a large industry as a result of increased security and border controls. Such countries have largely replaced their reliance on cannabis imported from Latin American countries with production at home.[150] It is now estimated that about half of marijuana demand in the US is met by local production,[151] while Canada has become a net exporter of the drug.[152]

While cannabis is the most commonly abused (75 per cent of current drug abusers), cocaine was the next most common, following illicit abuse of prescription psychotherapeutic drugs. There has been an increase in drug use in the US above rates of previous years; increases have been recorded for cannabis, cocaine and other illicit prescription drugs. About one in ten people (11.2 per cent) in the general US population report having ever abused cocaine.[153]

While European heroin addicts were reported to be an 'ageing, dwindling population', a new 'heroin chic' culture that prefers sniffing heroin rather than injecting it is apparently on the rise in the US. This regain in popularity of heroin comes after use of the drug had been decreasing in the US since the mid 1990s.[154]

Although drug abuse among the general population has increased, abuse among students in the US remained steady in 2001, except for an increase in ecstasy abuse that has risen drastically since 1998. The market for amphetamine-type stimulants, including ecstasy, has continued to expand; more laboratories than ever before were detected and dismantled over the last few years, especially in the US. However, Europe, especially The Netherlands and Belgium, continue to be the main locations of amphetamine production. Australia and New Zealand have also noted increases in ecstasy abuse.[155]

Is there a way forward?

The challenge to make cities safer cannot be overemphasized. Responsibilities for maintaining law, order and a sense of public security has traditionally been placed on the police and criminal justice system. Some governments have attempted to curb crime by strengthening their police forces and enacting zero-

---

BOX 6.8 **Urban planning for crime prevention**

Urban planning and resources of local governments, especially in developing countries, have not been able to keep up with the pressures of rapid urbanization, particularly rapid rural-to-urban migration, in addition to the influx of refugees from surrounding conflict-ridden countries. Uncoordinated, *ad hoc* urban planning has resulted in a few islands of well-organized, high-income suburbs within a vast sea of informal settlements with non-existent or, at best, seriously deteriorating basic services. However, it is in these informal settlements where the majority of urban citizens live, work and study, excluded from mainstream society and the possible economic and social benefits of globalization and urbanization.[i]

Poor areas and informal settlements tend to lack infrastructure or well-planned development, such as street lights, easily passable roads and well-maintained public space, which not only makes it more difficult for police and emergency vehicles to navigate these areas but also easier for criminals to hide or escape.[ii] A crime prevention study conducted in South Africa revealed that residents of such a township or informal settlement prioritized street lighting and bush clearing as important for their personal safety, while those in wealthier suburban areas prioritized burglar alarms and armed response services.[iii]

Urban planners often provide advice to local policy-makers and authorities on architecture and other urban design factors. They also frequently cross boundaries between multiple departments and professionals, such as city engineers, landscapers, public works and housing and transport departments, as well as with community residents themselves. Given these responsibilities and broad interactions, urban planners are therefore also well positioned to influence new developments and planning that is considerate of public safety concerns.

The role that urban planners can play in crime prevention and reduction extends beyond guiding the planning of social housing. Crime prevention through environmental design (CPTED) refers to the ways in which the environment (public spaces such as parks, walkways and transit stops) can be designed in order to reduce the opportunity for crime. As they often have a say in approving new development plans, urban planners can recommend that certain urban design criteria which reduce the opportunity for crime and make citizens feel safer should be incorporated within city landscaping and park design guides.

Likewise, urban planners can also recommend CPTED criteria when architectural design is being reviewed so that redesign and 'retrofitting' or adaptation of old designs consider new concerns, such as security and safety. CPTED expertise and how it relates to public security issues can and should also be shared with city-building, engineering and planning departments that are primarily responsible for modifying building codes and standards. In this way, the urban planner can also play a role in representing community interests and concerns to local authorities, helping to ensure that citizens' inputs are integrated within local authorities' planning and decision-making.[iv]

Notes: i UN-Habitat, 2002b. ii Louw and Shaw, 1997. iii Masuku and Louw, 2001. iv Rycus, 1995.

tolerance policies that have resulted in increased convictions, overpopulated prisons and children left without parents, despite decreased justification of the cost–benefit ratio of doing so.

The police and criminal justice systems certainly still have an important role to play in maintaining law and order. However, it has become clear that the police and criminal justice system alone cannot meet the increasing public demand for safety and security in many of the world's cities. Simply reacting to and punishing crime have been unsuccessful in deterring the escalation of crime, and countries and cities alike have begun to search for new solutions.

New approaches to policing, such as community or problem-oriented policing, require attitudinal and institutional change on the part of the police and citizens. This is particularly true in developing countries, where there are, often, mistrust and poor relations between citizens and police. There has been a move towards trying to address the root causes of crime in order to stop it before it starts. Rather than trying to tackle crime and insecurity through repression and punishment, many governments – national, provincial and local – are considering the potential of investing in prevention and risk management.

A conference entitled Sustainable Safety: Municipalities at the Crossroads, held in Durban, South Africa, in November 2003 and attended by over 300 participants representing local authorities, federal government officials, police, United Nations and other international agencies, NGOs, business circles and community organizations, highlighted this new policy direction in improving community safety. The conference declaration urged the tackling of root causes of problems rather than simply reacting to

It is clear that the police alone cannot meet the increasing public demand for safety in the world's cities

delinquency, violence and insecurity after the fact. In order to succeed, it was recommended that community safety needs to be addressed through partnerships that combine the expertise of all stakeholders who have influence over the diverse causes of crime and insecurity, such as employment, education and gender equality. Development dynamics, particularly, rural–urban dynamics also need to be considered to better address crime that is escalating along with rapid urbanization. The conference noted that improved urban planning techniques could work for crime prevention and urban development (see Box 6.8).

Notes

1 This chapter is based on a paper on safer cities prepared by Kathie Oginsky, a consultant on UN-Habitat's Safer Cities Programme, and a paper on transparency and urban governance prepared by Michaell J Lippe, an independent consultant, as well as urban adviser to Transparency International.
2 Interpol, 2004.
3 Hughes, 2001.
4 Hughes and Denisova, 2003.
5 Hughes and Denisova, 2003.
6 ILO, 2001.
7 ILO, 2001.
8 UNODC, 1999.
9 A broad view of the definition of corruption is taken here: 'Corruption means the *misuse of office for private gain*. The office is a position of trust, where one receives authority in order

to act on behalf of an institution, be it private, public or non-profit'.
10 UNODC, 1999.
11 UNODC, 1999.
12 UNICRI, 1995.
13 WHO, 1996.
14 van Kesteren et al, 2000.
15 WHO, 1996.
16 United Nations, 1995.
17 Zvekic, 1998a.
18 Zvekic, 1998a.
19 Zvekic, 1998a,
20 See www.Transparency.org.
21 For background information on governance indicators, see Kaufmann and Kraay, 2003, as well as extensive World Bank work on governance indicators to be found at www.worldbank.org/wbi/governance

22 UNICRI, 1998.
23 UNICRI, 1998.
24 UNODC, 1999.
25 UNICRI, 1995.
26 UNCHS (Habitat), 1996.
27 Zvekic, 1998a.
28 Transparency International, 2002.
29 Hughes and Denisova, 2003.
30 ILO, 2001.
31 ECPAT, 1999.
32 ECPAT, 1999.
33 Hughes, 2001.
34 UNODC, 2003a.
35 UNODC, 2003a.
36 United Nations Economic and Social Council, 2003.
37 Zvekic, 1998a.
38 Weaver and Maddalenno, 1999.

39 Waiselfisz, 1998.
40 UNODC, 2003b.
41 UNODC, 1999.
42 UNICRI, 1998.
43 First International Seminar on Women's Safety, 2002.
44 Zvekic, 1998a.
45 See www.latinobarometro.org, *Summary-Report, Democracy and Economy*, 2003, pp23–30.
46 See www.latinobarometro.org, 2003.
47 UNODC, 1999.
48 UNODC, 1999.
49 UNODC, 1999.
50 UNODC, 1999.
51 UNODC, 2003c.
52 UNODC, 2004b.
53 UNODC, 2003c.
54 UNODC, 2003c.
55 ONDCP, 2002.
56 UNODC, 2003c.
57 UNODC, 2003c.
58 United Nations Economic and Social Council, 2003.
59 UNODC, 1999.
60 UNODC, 2004b.
61 Masuku, 2002.
62 Interpol, 2004.
63 SAPS, 2002.
64 Robertshaw et al, 2001.
65 Robertshaw et al, 2001.
66 Robertshaw et al, 2001.
67 Stavrou, 2002.
68 OAU/UNICEF, 1992.
69 Kanji, 1996.
70 UN-Habitat, 2002c.
71 Andersson and Stavrou, 2000.
72 Andersson and Stavrou, 2000.
73 UN-Habitat, 2002c.
74 UNICRI, 1998.
75 South Africa, 1999.
76 SAPS, 2000.
77 Pretorius, 2000.
78 Hirschowitz, et al, 2000.

79 Hirschowitz, et al, 2000.
80 SAPS, 1999b.
81 Human Rights Watch, 1995.
82 Hirschowitz et al, 2000.
83 Porteus, 1999.
84 Robertshaw et al, 2001.
85 Robertshaw et al, 2001.
86 Robertshaw et al, 2001.
87 Robertshaw et al, 2001.
88 Robertshaw et al, 2001.
89 See, for example, Geschiere, 1995.
90 Press Release, Transparency International Corruption Perceptions Index, 2003, http://transparency.org.
91 Not all countries were counted as some countries did not receive sufficient numbers of ratings to be counted statistically.
92 See APNAC.org and www.tikenya.org for further information.
93 UNOSAA, 2003.
94 Reyneke, 2000.
95 Reyneke, 2000.
96 Gamba, 1999.
97 Reyneke, 2000.
98 Reyneke, 2000.
99 Stavrou, 2002.
100 Zvekic, 1998a.
101 Arms Management Programme, 2002.
102 Zvekic, 1998b.
103 Zvekic, 1998a.
104 Alvazzi del Frate and van Kesteren, forthcoming.
105 UNECE, 2003.
106 Alvazzi del Frate and van Kesteren, forthcoming.
107 Alvazzi del Frate and van Kesteren, forthcoming .
108 Alvazzi del Frate and van Kesteren, forthcoming .
109 Zvekic, 1998a.
110 Zvekic, 1998a.
111 World Bank, 2001a.
112 World Bank, 2001a, pxv.
113 Zvekic, 1998b.

114 UNDP, 2002.
115 Hughes and Denisova, 2003.
116 ILO, 2001.
117 IOM, 1998.
118 Hughes, 2001.
119 Paringaux, 1998.
120 Barclay and Tavares, 2002.
121 UNOSAA, 2003.
122 United Nations Economic and Social Council, 2003.
123 van Kesteren et al, 2000.
124 van Kesteren et al, 2000.
125 City of Vancouver, 2004.
126 Barclay and Tavares, 2002.
127 van Kesteren et al, 2000.
128 Barclay and Tavares, 2002.
129 Barclay and Tavares, 2002.
130 van Kesteren et al, 2000.
131 UNECE, 2003.
132 UNECE, 2003.
133 Barclay and Tavares, 2002.
134 van Kesteren et al, 2000.
135 NIJ, 1998.
136 UNECE, 2003.
137 WHO, 2002.
138 Tolan and Gorman-Smith, 1998.
139 Zvekic, 1998a.
140 Snyder and Sickmund, 1999.
141 Shaw, 2001.
142 Shaw, 2001.
143 Justice Canada, 1999.
144 O'Connor et al, 1998.
145 New Zealand, 2000.
146 Snyder and Sickmund, 1999.
147 Pfeiffer, 1998.
148 Shaw, 2001.
149 UNECE, 2003.
150 UNODC, 2003b.
151 United States Senate, 1998.
152 UNODC, 2003c.
153 United Nations Economic and Social Council, 2003.
154 Bruen et al, 2002.
155 Bruen et al, 2002.

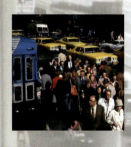

Chapter 7

Globalization and the Changing Culture of Planning[1]

Notable features of contemporary planning cultures   **160**

Planning cultures: a preliminary assessment   **172**

Principles of an emerging planning culture   **174**

Planning as an innovative practice   174

The expanded scope of planning   175

Expanded and multiple scales of planning   175

Planning for an endogenous development   176

Planning for cities of difference   177

The critical role of civil society   178

A strategic focus for planning   180

The governance of city planning   181

The future of spatial planning   **182**

The mantra of globalization poses two problems for a full understanding of its impact on cities. The first is its focus on economic relations to the exclusion of other possible perspectives – for example, social, cultural and political. The second is that it renders invisible the very real effects that global economic relations have on countries, regions and cities, including the daily lives of ordinary people. Not only do global economic relations – what has been dubbed the 'space of flows' [2] – ultimately have to come down to the ground into the 'space of places', but wherever they touch the ground, they will affect the everyday life of a city in numerous ways. For nearly 20 years now, research has been carried out to study these effects in major cities of the world, particularly in those that are closely linked to transnational networks.[3]

There is, at present, little agreement about which cities should be designated as world or global cities – that is, as important nodes in the dynamic global flows of finance, trade, migration and information that connect cities to each other.[4] Moreover, attempts at rank-ordering so-called world cities have shown that their relative position is by no means stable, and that new cities may join the roster from time to time, while other cities either drop out or lose their relative standing. The number of such cities is, in any event, quite small. One research approach, for example, suggests that there might be some 40 cross-border nodes, with heavy emphasis on the North Atlantic global subsystem, while another has identified 50 'world cities' and a further group of 67 showing 'some evidence' of world city formation.[5]

This chapter is about the changes in planning culture brought on by urban restructuring and it concentrates on the top echelon of cities, running from New York to São Paulo, from Tokyo to Singapore, from London to Johannesburg. Other cities, whether or not they are inserted into global circuits – and at the beginning of the 21st century, few cities, if any, are left out altogether – are, of course, also worthy of attention. But the focus here is on cities that dominate the global system of transactions because the restructuring that these cities are currently undergoing is challenging planners in unprecedented ways.

To start with, what does the term planning culture mean? The term was introduced some years ago, and, more recently, a series of national case studies of planning cultures has been carried out.[6] A firm definition of the term, however, has been elusive. For present purposes, *planning culture' refers to the ways, both formal and informal (community, city and regional, or spatial development), in which planning in a given country and/or city is conceived, institutionalized*

and enacted. Because planning in this sense continues to be primarily a responsibility of the state, even as it draws upon other societal actors, it is deeply embedded in the embracing political culture of the country or city and, as such, is historically grounded. Nevertheless, globalization is forcing major changes on the institutional structure, processes, influence and scope of planning. Some of these changes appear, so to speak, to be 'in the air', redefining what has traditionally been understood by 'planning'.

Before proceeding, however, it is necessary to dispel the widely held notion that as a scientifically grounded professional activity, planning practice is more or less the same regardless of where it is practised – in other words, that it is a profession like civil engineering, devoid of social, political or cultural content except for its own professional culture. If this were true, planners in Chongqing would talk the same professional talk and act in similar ways as planners do in Zurich or, for that matter, in Ankara or Beirut. In short, planners the world over would share the same professional *habitus* or disposition to act, giving rise to a uniform planning culture.[7] In fact, we know that, despite the growing volume of international communication within the profession, which is, indeed, drawing planners together into a globe-spanning, discursive community, major differences exist in the ways that planning is conceived, institutionalized and enacted.

In the next section, brief descriptions are given of planning as it is practised in a number of different countries and cities in different regions of the world, highlighting both similarities and differences in existing planning cultures. Some of these differences are then highlighted to illustrate the proposition that planning cultures worldwide can exist only in the plural, even as global restructuring is challenging them in similar ways. Finally, a number of trends, including normative principles, that appear to be emerging in response to globalization and the continuing restructuring of the world's cities and city regions (described in previous chapters) are described.

Notable features of contemporary planning cultures

It would be foolhardy to attempt a serious delineation of planning cultures for a number of countries or even multinational regions within the limited space devoted to it here. The intent is to do no more than point to some distinctive characteristics of how planning operates in different settings and for which documentation is readily available. There are, no doubt, numerous exceptions to any of the statements that appear below and, in any event, the specialized literature from which they are derived is already dated: significant changes, both positive and negative, may have occurred since the original research. The purpose of this exercise, then, is simply to highlight some differences in the way that planning is being done around the world. In most of the examples, the perspective will be national rather than local, even though the local is always the specific object of observation.

URBAN PLANNING UNDER RAPID ECONOMIC GROWTH: THE CASE OF CHINA [8]

China's current system of physical planning is, one might say, still 'under construction'. Underpinned by national legislation that went into effect in the 1970s and 1980s, it represents a significant departure from city planning during the 1960s, when, following the Soviet model, physical planning was narrowly focused. After a decade or so of rapid urban growth, the government decided to halt the flow of city-bound migrants and even attempted, though with only limited success, to reverse it. The development paths of every city are expected to conform to a long-term comprehensive physical plan. But under conditions of hyper-rapid economic growth, such planning tends to issue in plans whose capacity to guide development is undermined by the very speed of double-digit economic growth. Still, a formidable planning bureaucracy has come into existence that employs approximately 60,000 'planners' with varying degrees of competence to manage urban space for about 460 million people across the vast expanses of China's provinces. City planners work through their own institutions and are exclusively focused on the physical dimensions of planning. There is little coordination with economic and environmental planning bureaucracies, both of which work through their own organizational channels and are responsible to different ministries in Beijing.

Although local government officials in China, including the mayor, are centrally appointed, they enjoy a good deal of discretion, which becomes greater as one descends from city to district and especially to the 'street committees' that are responsible for a large variety of public services in their neighbourhoods. Street committees, along with other government organizations, have been called 'amphibious' because in order to fund the public work they do, they must engage in business activities for profit. In short, they are largely self-financing rather than dependent on central allocations. Amphibious organizations can, no doubt, accomplish a great deal, as is evidenced by the impressive physical appearance of major Chinese cities.

Globalization is challenging city planners in unprecedented ways

PLANNING IN THE CONTEXT OF A STRONG BUREAUCRACY AND A VIBRANT CIVIL SOCIETY: THE CASE OF INDIA [9]

Planning in India is a function of elite civil services at both federal and state levels that were designed to encourage separation between the political and administrative arms of the government. Admission and promotion within the civil services are considered to be based on merit, not patronage, and the administrator in Indian society is regarded as both an employee of the state and a servant of the public. To accommodate the diversity of Indian society within the civil service, an official policy is in place to attract women, ethnic and religious minorities, the disabled, individuals of certain castes and rural inhabitants.

At the federal level, economic planning through the creation of five-year plans has given the Indian civil service the primary role in development administration. Over the last half century, its strategy for stimulating development evolved from one of state-centred entrepreneurship through direct public-

BOX 7.2 Havana's 1998–2001 strategic plan

Mission: to raise the quality of life, the appearance of Havana and its international image by stimulating its economy in order to return the profits to urban recovery and its development, improving its environmental conditions and its socio-cultural values, with greater overall citizen participation.

Relevant projects given priority

1 Stimulate the economy of the city.
2 Upgrade discipline, modernize urban management and improve governance.
3 Encourage urban culture and citizens' education, reinforcing the role of neighbourhoods and communities in their social development.
4 Promote the national and international projection of Havana.
5 Improve hygienic, sanitary and environmental quality.
6 Raise satisfaction levels in commerce, gastronomy and domestic services.
7 Raise habitat quality and improve preservation of the built heritage.
8 Improve the transport system and ensure that the urban infrastructure functions properly.

Strategic areas

1 Historic inner city of 'World Heritage' status in Old Havana.
2 Malecon Rehabilitation Project (first stage).
3 Metropolitan park project.
4 Havana Port development: cruise terminal, container terminal and shipyard.
5 Tourism and real-estate development zone, Monte Barreto Business Centre.
6 Area of tourist development in Hemingway Marina.
7 Scientific pole, pharmaceutical industry, biotechnology development.
8 Freeport area, Wajay.
9 Freeport area, Berroa.
10 José Marti new international airport.
11 Tourism development in eastern Havana beaches.
12 Morro-Cabana park and tourist complex.
13 East Havana residential and real-estate development area.
14 China Town recovery project.
15 Political and administrative centre, Monumental Complex Revolution Square.
16 Malecon Protection Project.

focused on urban culture and citizens' education, as well as on environmental improvement and preservation of the city's built heritage. On the whole, strategic planning has changed Havana's planning culture in a way that is likely to last for a long time.

PLANNING RAPIDLY GROWING CITIES WITH SCARCE RESOURCES: CASES FROM AFRICAN COUNTRIES[16]

Given the stagnant and even negative rates of gross national product (GNP) growth over recent decades, many African countries can be said to be undergoing a process of *over-urbanization* – that is, a rate of urbanization out of proportion relative to actually existing jobs in the formal sector. The result is an accumulation of essentially rural poverty in the major cities of the continent and an implosion of an informal economy geared to physical survival.[17] None of the major cities in Africa are, in fact, financially capable of adequately servicing their population. One study, for example, asserts that 'the per capita levels of investment in infrastructure have declined to zero for most major cities'.[18] No governmental level currently has the resources to meet even the most minimal needs of African cities (let alone the needs of the rural population), and governments increasingly have had to rely upon the donations of foreign donors, which, for the most part, disperse contributions through national and foreign non-governmental organizations (NGOs). But these donations are equally inadequate to cope with a pattern of urban growth that leads to a doubling of population every 15 years or so.

Insufficient resources are only part of the problem, however. General plans exist for most major cities, but they are seriously in default of implementation (see Box 7.3). An action plan for Nairobi, adopted in 1993, was meant to address critical city issues; it also highlighted the need to restore and reinforce professionalism and ethics in the city hall. But 'there has been no follow-up in terms of implementation'.[19] This observation could be extended to other African cities:

…plans are developed with little or no local input or consultation. Further, even if these models were in themselves adequate as planning exercises, their implementation is generally beyond the resources and delivery capacity of the existing planning structures.

BOX 7.3 Urban planning in Abidjan, Côte d'Ivoire

Post-colonial urbanization in Côte d'Ivore was primarily a result of the expansion of agricultural exports, the concentration of public investments in newly established urban centres and the development of a bituminized road network. From 1960 to 1980, the average annual urban growth was 10 per cent. This has since reduced to around 5 per cent as a result of economic and political crises.

In order to tackle the intra-urban problems in Abidjan City, a series of master plans have been prepared to guide the city's development. The first was prepared in 1928, only two decades after the official start of construction of the city's first business establishments. The city's population stood at a mere 5000. The second was prepared by the Architect Badani in 1948 and the third plan (1960–1967) was prepared by a team whose mandate was, among other things, to transform the city from a colonial capital port to a modern capital.

The overall failure of the previous plans led to the preparation of a structure master plan in 1976, which was closely followed by the 1979–1980 master plan. This, in turn, has been succeeded by the Ten-Year Forecast Plan (1980–1990) and the Master Plan for Greater Abidjan (2000–2010). Detailed examination of the various plans and their implementation from the 1928 plan to the structure plans prepared resulting from the Ten-Year Forecast (1980–1990) reveals major gaps between objectives and outcomes. The gaps include population underestimation and adoption of stubbornly high planning standards. Other problems include institutional bottlenecks, such as the highly centralized urban planning and land administration systems. The Abidjan local authority is still not responsible for preparing and implementing the city development strategies and the related master plans. An additional problem is that the city development strategies and master plans so far prepared are not based on widely shared visions of the development of the Abidjan Metropolitan District.

Source: Ochieng'-Akatch, 1995, updated by Kofi Attahi (pers comm).

Governments' ability to enforce rules and regulations is generally very weak in Africa, particularly when they relate to unrealistic standards or activities that go against the grain of market forces. Plans are often not respected even by those government bureaucrats and politicians who approved them in the first place. In addition, projects are frequently abandoned before they are given a chance to mature. Much of the problem lies in the undemocratic nature of the state itself. This leads to favouritism, nepotism, biased allocation of resources, distorted priorities, and stifling of local initiative and innovation.[20]

In spite of this dismal assessment, planning degrees are now conferred in quite a number of leading universities, such as in Dakar, Nairobi, Ibadan, Cairo, Johannesburg, Durban and Cape Town, among other cities. Whether this new generation of planners will be able to turn things around in urban Africa remains to be seen.[21]

An exceptional story is the new planning regime in the Republic of South Africa. With the election of the first post-apartheid government in 1994, planning had to regain its legitimacy. The country's planning apparatus had been deeply compromised through its complicity with the apartheid system. After a decades-long struggle, the profession gained its statutory recognition through the Town and Regional Planners Act in 1984. Despite this, a small but energetic dissident movement of planners forged alliances with civic movements in South Africa's turbulent townships. Calling themselves Planact, the movement was primarily active in the Johannesburg region. As the profession tries to reinvent itself in the post-apartheid era, and fortified with new legislation, South Africa's planning culture has become more strategic, participatory, and integrated (see Box 7.4).

CHANGING PLANNING DOCTRINE: THE RECENT EXPERIENCE OF THE TRANSITIONAL COUNTRIES

With the transition from centrally planned to market economy systems, cities in the transition countries are now facing new challenges, including discontinuation of the centralized system of socio-economic planning; decentralization of decision-making authority on urban development issues; privatization of housing and real estate; and involvement of civil society and the private sector in local decision-making.

In the case of the then Union of Soviet Socialist Republics (USSR), the pre-transition Soviet doctrine of planning included long-term forecasting (over 30 years) of regional (*oblast*) development, city master planning (for 20 to 25 years), medium-term planning (for 10 to 15 years) and short-term development schemes (for 5 years), usually designed in conjunction with five-year economic and social development plans. The culmination of the Soviet planning pyramid was the General Scheme of the Residential Distribution on the Territory of the USSR, elaborated during 1972 to

BOX 7.4 Integrated Development Plans in South Africa

The clearest manifestation of the new culture of urban planning has been the adoption of statutory integrated development plans (IDPs) – the centrepiece of planning in post-apartheid South Africa – by every local authority in the country to provide strategic guidance to newly constructed municipalities. IDPs were introduced by legislation in 1996, and are currently being implemented through the 1998 White Paper on Local Government and the Municipal Systems Act of 2000. New municipal boundaries were delineated between 1998 and 2000, and in December 2000, local government elections were held.

IDPs share a striking similarity with international planning practices, including the reintroduction of regional planning policies by the new Labour government in the UK (1997); New Zealand's integrated planning performance monitoring; Switzerland's integrated regional policy; integrated area planning in the European Union (EU); and the multi-

sectoral investment planning promoted by the United Nations Development Programme (UNDP). But as one observer has noted: 'Progressive concerns over transformation and the role of the state in securing more equitable living environments are being meshed with neo-liberal concerns associated with efficiency and competitive cities.'

In June 2002, the IDP for the newly constituted metropolitan city of Johannesburg was launched. Its overarching vision promotes a 'world class city with service deliverables and efficiencies that meet world best practice. Its economy and labour force will specialize in the service sector and will be strongly outward orientated such that the city economy operates on a global scale.' How this is to be achieved when so many citizens are desperately poor, unskilled and without access to basic needs such as food and shelter, remains to be seen.

Sources: Winkler, 2002; Harrison, 2001a; Harrison, 2001b; Harrison and Kahn, 1999.

1975. This was a macro-scale planning exercise that aimed to identify spatial development perspectives and to channel urbanization trends in the socially desired directions through distribution and redistribution of productive forces, while improving environmental conditions. However, over-centralization of decision-making processes caused problems for further detailed elaboration and implementation of the scheme.

Until the beginnings of *perestroika* during the late 1980s, city planning was rigidly bureaucratized and 'enigmatic'. City general plans, and the process leading up to them, were classified documents. Physical planning was understood to be a problem of urban design and was handled by enormous planning institutes in Moscow, Leningrad, and the capital cities of union republics. And every city had to have such a plan: between 1945 and 1977, for example, central institutes in the Russian Soviet Federative Socialist Republic (RSFSR) completed 720 general plans. Typically, they projected a 30-year future for a city, though many of them were never strictly implemented.

The transition from a centrally planned to a market economy occurred more abruptly in Russia than in other transition economies, and, in light of the new challenges outlined earlier, Russia is now seeking forms of urban governance that allow market forces and smaller governmental units to assume more prominent roles. Its cities are also trying to find ways of redefining their positions within the new context of the international arena, as the example of Moscow presented in Box 7.5 shows.[22]

PROGRESSIVE EMPOWERMENT OF CITIES: TIGHT SPACE PLANNING IN JAPAN[23]

For most of the 20th century, planning was regarded as a function of the central state, which subordinated the variety of local conditions and concerns to the overriding interests of the nation: rapid industrialization, reconstruction from the devastations of the war, accelerated economic growth and efforts at economic revival since the early 1990s. The costs of achieving these goals – environmental pollution and its associated health costs, the rapid depopulation of rural areas, regional imbalances, crammed but expensive housing – were borne by a population who, by and large, concurred with these priorities. Japan's civil society has been described as extremely weak and, until very recently, has had little influence on local planning, while city governments have been subservient to the policy directives of central ministries and, more specifically, in the matter of planning, to the Ministry of Construction.

Major changes, however, took place during the last decade of the past century when financial stringencies at the centre led to the devolution of planning powers to local authorities. Most importantly, each municipality in Japan was mandated to develop a master plan as a guide for its future development. This plan and the policies that would give substance to the vision embodied in the plan were to be drawn up with the help of public consultation. For the first time in the country's history, a process of citizen participation in urban development was established. At the turn of the millennium, 608 local

BOX 7.5 **Urban planning in transition: the example of Moscow**

The 1935 Plan for the Reconstruction of Moscow (*Genplan*) was drawn up as the first attempt to restrict the growth of Moscow at a time when its population was 3.7 million. This master plan contained a forecast population estimate of 5 million to be attained by 1960. But, by 1960, the population had grown to over 6 million. Since the pro-urban versus anti-urban debate of the 1930s,[i] it has been official policy to restrain Moscow city's growth. The population of the city of Moscow has expanded by 1 million people in each of the last six decades. The 1971 General Plan for the Development of Moscow again sought to restrict the growth of the city, but this time within the context of the Moscow city region as a whole.[ii]

Broadly speaking, the city of Moscow, which is surrounded by a ring road, is the centre of a large agglomeration. It has an area of some 1200 square kilometres as of 1997, and a population of 8.7 million. Beyond the ring road is the remainder of the city region, which has a population of some 8 million.

The 1990s have seen a major change in Moscow's approach to its size and growth. The 1992 Moscow structure plan marked the end of restrictive growth policies for the city and identified the need to maintain and protect the city's existing size, given that its population had started to decline from 1991, after 60 years of continued and rapid growth. The 1996 review of the 1992 structure plan has confirmed and reinforced planning policies focused on regeneration and refurbishment, and the need for the city's economy to move away from an industrial base towards a service-sector oriented base. The current master plan (or *Genplan*) of Moscow addresses the city's development up to the year 2020. It aims to make the city more liveable,[iii] and opens up to market forces as a driver for the spatial development of the city.

Notes: i Kuzmin, 2002. ii Moscow, like London, attempted to contain its growth by using satellite cities to direct growth away from the centre. iii Kuzmin, 2002, p5.

governments had complied with this central directive and produced their first-ever master plans that reflected long-term visions for change and the policies to accommodate them.

Prior to this explosion of master planning activities, local planners' responsibilities had concentrated on zoning, the occasional preparation of district plans and land readjustment on the urban fringe. These activities were useful primarily for the improvement of small areas. Zoning, for instance, has always been the main planning tool in Japan, but it was relatively inflexible in application and was, in any case, a relatively 'porous' instrument.[24] In this context, the adoption of master plans by municipalities was regarded as a major innovation. For the first time, cities would be allowed to chart their own future without central guidance. Master plans, however, are in the nature of blueprints and, in practice, local governments have very limited powers to make them stick. Moreover, municipalities are not financially independent of the central government. And major projects in infrastructure and transportation are the responsibilities of other levels of government that are not required to match their decisions to the municipal plan.

The 1990s were also a decade during which civil society in Japan became particularly active around environmental issues. In planning, this new activism took the form of citizen participation in neighbourhood development, or *machizukuri*. The focus here was on the quality of urban life; the widening of narrow roads; providing parks, play areas and street trees; building community centres; and exercising development controls over urban sprawl. Municipalities could now pass *machizukuri* ordinances that would be binding; but for the most part, neighbourhood groups (called councils) could only lobby authorities and use moral suasion with property developers. Thus, what has been referred to as Japan's 'lost decade', in terms of reinvigorating the national economy, was anything but that in a city planning perspective, as cities and neighbourhoods became empowered to gain a measure of control over their own futures.

ENHANCING PARTNERSHIP IN PLANNING: THE CASE OF MEGA-PROJECT MANAGEMENT IN THE NETHERLANDS Having reclaimed much of their country from the sea, the Dutch, it is said, have a 'soft spot' in their heart for planning.[25] A dimension of planning that has become increasingly popular over the past two decades is the management of so-called mega-projects. As opposed to incremental zoning and the persisting attempts to chart the future of cities through a general plan that covers the entire territory of a municipality or region and embodies the restraining hand of government, mega-projects are undertaken in an entrepreneurial spirit to break through the routines of the everyday in order to build spectacular urban spaces that will, it is hoped, enhance a city's competitiveness in global capital markets. Because mega-projects often exceed the fiscal capacity of municipalities, the local state is obliged to seek out partners in the corporate (private) sector and central

Effectively managing the rapid growth of cities is a challenging task for urban planners

government. As a rule, a newly formed public–private partnership (PPP) of this sort will bypass routine planning procedures, creating their own organizational framework with varying degrees of autonomy, transparency and accountability. Frequently, it will also bring on board world-class architects who are expected to give memorable visual form to the undertaking.[26]

The Rotterdam Central Station project is one of these.[27] During the mid 1990s, it was identified as one of six 'strategic' projects that would give heightened international profile to this major port city. It was envisioned that a large area surrounding the central railway station would be given over to commercial developments, particularly in the service and leisure sectors, which would revitalize the city centre. The station itself would be converted into an inter-modal transport node. To get this project under way, a 'partnership' was formed among the City of Rotterdam, the Dutch rail company (NS) and two private property developers who had a long-term relationship with both the site and the city. A foreign

firm was selected to redesign the area.[28] The projected redevelopment period would extend for up to 18 years with three goals in mind:

1 the improvement and enlargement of the railway station;
2 an improvement of the interface between the station and the rest of the city; and
3 a property development programme covering an area of 650,000 square metres.

A plan was discussed to set up a joint land development corporation that would amalgamate all of the plans, buildings and rights in a common enterprise; but this idea was eventually abandoned. Instead, the original project was divided into two sub-projects, each with its own organization: the railway terminal and transport node (with the railway company NS in the driver's seat) and a profit-oriented real-estate venture guided by the council.

After four years of work, a master plan was published in April 2001. And then the sky fell in. In March 2002, a new political party, calling itself *Leefbaar Rotterdam* (Liveable Rotterdam),[29] received 30 per cent of the vote in municipal elections and fundamentally changed the coalition of forces that had supported the project. The Rotterdam Central Station project had been part of a strategy that was to turn Rotterdam into a 'world city'. The basic idea was to market the city to global capital, based on the argument that competitive economic growth was essential if the social needs of the city were to be met. But in 2002, the newly formed city council could not be convinced of this logic. A document published in September of that year shows a change in the privileged position of strategic projects and in the position of city marketing within the political domain. With more than half of the new budget devoted to it, the new emphasis was to be on safety in the streets. The exuberant 'champagne glass' design had to be scrapped. The old railway station was declared a heritage building, and a 'home-grown' architect would be enlisted for the project, replacing the 'foreign' firm. The project budget was downsized from 875 million to 410 million Euros.

In this dramatic instance, globalization did not eliminate the local; it strengthened it. The new council majority represented the interests of small businesspeople and petty bourgeois in the city who were feeling disoriented, their livelihood threatened by the forces of globalization. It was this majority that the formerly hegemonic social democrats, in their eagerness to put Rotterdam on the global map, had failed to perceive.

Waterfront redevelopment: popular among the mega-projects of globalization

BALANCING PLANNING POWERS: THE CASE OF THE UK[30]

Until the devolution reforms of the late 1990s, the UK possessed a strong bipolar system, with a weak local level and a strong central tier. The national government had the power to change territorial boundaries and to install or remove organizations engaged with regional matters. Above all, it retained the purse strings: 'the institutionalized government system is…strongly biased in favour of top-down, centralized regional governance, leaving much less scope for locally defined policy-making'.[31] Devolution seems to have worked particularly well in the case of Scotland, where a serious attempt was made to empower local communities. In England, on the other hand, the central government defined new development regions and set up regional development agencies (RDAs) that were centrally scripted and financed.

To give local legitimacy to RDAs, another innovation has been the establishment of regional chambers made up of local authority and business leaders. How well this new institutional structure will work remains to be seen. With the 2001 general election, enthusiasm for further regional devolution (the creation of regional assemblies, for example) seems to have waned and, on the whole, there appears to be a swing back to greater centralization. Draft economic strategies now have to be vetted by central government. The RDA specific functions (and a large slice of their budgets) include administering the government's urban renewal programmes. And instead of hoped-for interregional cooperation, competitive regional marketing has become a feature of the RDAs. Because of this, as well as difficulties in programme coordination, the regional oversight function of the Department of the Environment, Transport and the Regions has actually been shifted still further up the bureaucratic hierarchy to cabinet level.[32] It is not clear, however, that this will lead to greater overall coherence in the implementation of regional programmes. It has been observed that 'the central government has a deep-seated distrust of sub-national governments' ability to handle their own affairs effectively', though 'distrust' in this context may be no more than a rhetorical cover for what is more likely a continuing tug-of-war in the relations of power between centre, regions and local authorities.[33] Coordination and cooperation are not the same thing, however. The centre worries mainly about 'coordination', or its own ability to properly manage governmental actions on the ground. Cooperation, on the other hand, is a voluntary activity, less oriented towards vertical than horizontal relations in pursuit of common objectives. Too great insistence on coordination is likely not only to be resisted but to impede voluntary coordination of regional strategies. This dilemma has not yet been resolved in England.[34]

ENTREPRENEURS IN URBAN PLANNING: RECENT EXPERIENCE IN THE US [35]

In a formal, legalistic sense, city planning in the US is a local responsibility, which makes for a good deal of diversity across the country. There is another way of looking at planning, however, which expands the meaning of 'planning' to include all those actors who contribute to shaping the city, who may be called the city-builders. In addition to the local state and its particular institutions, they would include developers and other business interests, organized civil society and the legal system. How these several actors intersect in given circumstances is the story of planning in the US. Since the rise of neo-liberalist ideology, with its insistence that less government intervention is better than more, planning in this expanded sense has been market led, with planning by local government playing primarily a facilitating or passive role. City planning, with its former emphasis on land-use controls and its restraining hand on market forces, now has become more entrepreneurial as the fever of inter-city competition has spread across the land.

Over the past 20 or so years, during which many US cities rebuilt their core, attention was focused on large-scale building ensembles. Downtown malls, often combining offices, apartments, hotels, entertainment and other activities with retailing, and thus creating a virtual 'downtown' under one roof – a city-for-profit – were only part of the story. Major convention centres, huge stadiums for professional team sports (football, baseball), the so-called festival market place built as part of major waterfront regeneration projects, aquariums designed to attract millions of tourists, all preferably located in close proximity to each other and a sheltered tract of water, became a distinctively American contribution to urban regeneration planning.[36] Needless to say, these projects were planned and built by private enterprise with only marginal contributions from city planning departments.[37] The same might be said about the edge city phenomenon in suburban areas, the new 'downtowns' built out of town: 'Apart from fairly permissive zoning regimes, planning (and especially strategic planning) nowhere played much part in the growth of these places.'[38]

But could edge cities become real places, comparable to traditional downtowns? A response came from a group of private architect-planners who proposed subdivision developments, or even new towns, whose perceived virtues lay in their clear definition of space and compactness, in contrast with the low densities and open layouts of American suburbia. Places built according to this 'new urbanism', such as Seaside in Florida, created a sensation. The new urbanism spawned a formal organization, which called itself Congress for the New Urbanism, to propagate the idea. Some extrapolated the new urbanism into a model for sustainable metropolitan development, linking the classic garden city density of 12 houses per acre to the development of public transit.[39] At Redmond in suburban Seattle, for example, the approach was used to convey the feel of a traditional downtown, with open public spaces that avoided the typical enclosed mall.[40]

On the rising tide of concern over the 'sustainability' of US cities, a concern that was largely a product of the environmental movement, a new term came into wide circulation: 'smart growth'. In 1999:

> …the Federal Environmental Protection Agency sponsored the creation of the Smart Growth Network. An umbrella organization, this brought together a wide range of existing organizations, including the Congress for the New Urbanism, the Growth Management Leadership Alliance and many other professional and pressure groups in the field of conservation and environmental protection.[41]

The federal government had taken these ideas on board; but their origin was entirely within civil society and was linked to the profit motive: new urbanism and smart growth were workable concepts because developers and the architect-planners who worked for them could make good money out of them. Official city planners could do little more than to accommodate them and many have leaped on the bandwagon, embracing the concept of the city planning profession.

MACRO-REGIONAL PLANNING IN THE EUROPEAN UNION: THE EUROPEAN SPATIAL DEVELOPMENT PERSPECTIVE [42]

Meeting in Potsdam (Germany) in May 1999, the European Union's ministers responsible for spatial planning adopted a document that had been years in the making: the *European*

Spatial Development Perspective (ESDP) that aims towards a balanced and sustainable development of the territory of the European Union:

> *Spatial planning refers to the methods used largely by the public sector to influence the future distribution of activities in space. It is undertaken with the aims of creating a more rational territorial organization of land uses and the linkages between them to balance demands for development with the need to protect the environment, and to achieve social and economic objectives. Spatial planning embraces measures to coordinate the spatial impacts of other sector policies, to achieve a more even distribution of economic development between regions than would otherwise be created through market forces, and to regulate the conversion of land and property uses.*[43]

The ESDP proposes what would amount to a super-ordinate policy framework for Europe. As such, it is to be applied flexibly across the many regions of the continent. The competence for making spatial policy and planning decisions rests with the several states of the EU; but in making these policies and plans, the ESDP framework should be taken into account. Three major policy guidelines are proposed:

1 Development of a polycentric and balanced urban system and strengthening of the partnership between urban and rural areas. This involves overcoming the traditional dualism between city and countryside.
2 Promotion of integrated transport and communication concepts, which support the polycentric development of the EU territory and are an important pre-condition for enabling European cities and regions to pursue their integration into European Monetary Union (EMU). Parity of access to infrastructure and knowledge should be realized gradually. Regionally adapted solutions must be found for this.
3 Development and conservation of the natural and cultural heritage through wise management. This contributes to the preservation and deepening of identities and the maintenance of the natural and cultural diversity of the regions and cities of the EU in the age of globalization.[44]

The ESDP considerably broadens the focus of physical planning as traditionally conceived in Europe as a form of urban design. It advocates multi-sectoral spatial guidelines and forcefully pleads for a multi-

Growing tensions of contemporary urban life require the search for innovative planning solutions

scalar planning approach. Importantly, it argues for a 'partnership' between urban and rural areas, although the key role for this is assigned to cities as dynamic centres of economic growth. Its key terms are *balance*, *integration*, *sustainability*, *cooperation*, and *partnerships*. Networks, as in inter-city networks, are proposed as a means of implementing co-operative arrangements.[45] The document indicates a good deal of worry by the ministers about their lack of competence to impose this policy framework, invoking the mostly European *principle of subsidiarity* that the power to make binding decisions should be devolved to the lowest possible level capable of contributing to the achievement of overall EU policy objectives. There is also worry that the spatial development framework's Europe-wide vision could be seen as threatening cultural diversity and, thus, resisted.

EU member countries have committed themselves to begin applying the spatial development framework. The text of the Potsdam document is being translated into the official languages of all member countries and is widely disseminated. The European Commission will use the ESDP as a guide in allocating 'structural funds', amounting to hundreds of billions of Euros each year. Geography manuals will be prepared for use in secondary schools throughout Europe. And the spatial impacts of European Community policies will be monitored. Overall, the ESDP is beginning to filter down into academic discourse and will, undoubtedly, be discussed with growing frequency in regional planning circles.[46]

Planning cultures: a preliminary assessment

The foregoing thumbnail sketches of global planning cultures reveal an enormous variety of institutional and political settings. As a way of classifying emerging planning cultures, the following distinctions may be a bit crude; but these cultures do exert a substantial influence over both the substance of what planners do and how they do it. As a start, planning takes place in *unitary* states (such as Japan, China and the UK), in *federal* states (such as India, Russia and the US) and in states (some unitary, some federal) belonging to the EU, a *multi-national* entity that has no direct counterpart anywhere else. Superimposed on these constitutional structures, some countries are '*in transition*' from a command to a market economy and are still grappling with the institutional foundations through which a market economy can function effectively, while other countries, such as the US and the countries of the EU, are already *fully developed market societies*.

The achieved *level of economic development* is another criterion for differentiating societies in ways that influence planning cultures, ranging from impoverished nations and lower-income countries, to the high-income, post-industrial societies. In general, poorer countries are still *urbanizing rapidly* (some African countries may be already '*over-urbanized*' relative to their level of development), while other countries, such as The Netherlands and the UK with *mature urban systems*, are left with only a residual of rural areas and a dwindling agricultural population. Much of their urban growth is therefore the result of domestic inter-urban migration and immigration from abroad. In the case of mature systems, managing urban growth is less of an issue than it is in rapidly

urbanizing societies whose urban systems are still evolving. In both cases, however, social problems must be addressed as cities fill up with people of different cultural backgrounds and income inequalities become more pronounced.

Finally, there are marked differences in *political culture*, a broad term that includes the extent to which civil society is an active participant in public decisions, particularly at the local level: the degree to which the political process is dominated by a single party or subject to political competition; the degree of 'openness' in the political process and the role of the media; the application of principles of hierarchy and subsidiarity; the relative autonomy of local governments and of the judicial system; and so forth.

Within this conglomeration of differences, however, there is at least one constant: all existing planning systems (and cultures) are *in movement* in the sense that they are continually being revamped to adapt to perceived changes of both internal and external origin. Efforts at creating new institutions are particularly notable. The leading example, perhaps, is the Republic of South Africa. Between 1996 and 2000, integrated development plans (IDPs) were introduced, a new Municipal Systems Act passed, new municipal boundaries delineated and the first local government elections held (see Box 7.4). In other words, the entire local government system, including planning, was being restructured over a period of only four years! South Africa is reinventing itself and her planning culture will require a long period to adjust to the post-apartheid society that is coming into being.[47] Other countries are experiencing similar, if not quite so intensive, pressures to restructure the institutional setting for planning, including China, Russia and Japan.

Less dramatic but still important institutional innovations are the asymmetrical devolution under the UK's Labour government that was high on the list of national priorities during the late 1990s. Greater London elected its first-ever mayor in 2000. As mentioned earlier, Scotland and Wales elected local parliaments and Scotland added an executive branch as well, asserting its increased national autonomy. The see-saw struggle in the UK between central powers, local authorities and the regions continued throughout this period and remains without resolution. In The Netherlands, as indeed elsewhere, the national legislature authorized PPPs, facilitating large-scale infrastructure projects, such as the Rotterdam Central Station redevelopment, a PPP venture that was projected to last for nearly two decades. The insertion of the EU into local planning through its ESDP is yet another example. In all cases, the role of national governments in urban management is being weakened, while that of regional/local governments is being strengthened.

BEST PRACTICE
CITY MANAGEMENT IN TILBURG, THE NETHERLANDS: PAST, PRESENT AND FUTURE

The city of Tilburg has 165,000 inhabitants, making it the seventh largest city in The Netherlands. Tilburg presents itself as a 'modern industrial city' with a strategic vision for the future that is key to the city's development in many policy areas. As a result, the city is administered and managed like a business venture. The municipality is split into divisions, which operate like profit centres that produce clearly defined products. The basis for the new city management was set in the first city management plan in 1989 and, from then on, city planning and programming in Tilburg has been carried out in an organized process with the participation of the residents in decision-making. 1 per cent of the city's budget is reserved for initiatives by citizens to improve their neighbourhoods.

Source: www.bestpractices.org.

Culture-driven city planning

Overall, there is a trend away from planning conceived as a *restraint* on market forces (for example, through zoning legislation) to a kind of *entrepreneurial planning* that seeks to facilitate economic development through the market. The extreme case of this is, perhaps, the US. Here, both suburban and inner-city mega-malls have created virtual cities-for-profit; suburban edge cities across the continent have sprung up without significant inputs from public planning (but with a great deal of *ad hoc* private planning); and the privately promoted and popular new urbanism (which has been taken on board by the federal government) has offered to tackle the problems of metropolitan regions primarily through neo-classical urban design.

The *differential role of civil society* in city and regional planning is yet another dimension that differentiates emerging planning cultures. If civil society refers to a range of social organizations that lie beyond the direct control of the state and, more specifically, to social organizations that participate in the debates over public issues, then countries such as China can be said to have hardly any civil society. By contrast, other countries – Japan being the prime example – have a weak civil-society sector relative to centrally wielded power. However, a new era may be dawning in Japan, as shown earlier: social movements around environmental issues, as well as the

machizukuri movement, focused on small, neighbourhood-level projects are gaining ground. It is true that Japanese municipalities can now pass *machizukuri* ordinances; but not being a part of the traditional hierarchy of government, empowered neighbourhood groups (called councils), are principally engaged in lobbying local authorities or using moral suasion with property developers. In The Netherlands, by contrast, local civil society is playing a significant oppositional role. In municipal elections, movement coalitions, such as Liveable Rotterdam, can present themselves as political parties and be elected to local councils in order to further their agendas. But it is again the US which has by far the greatest role for civil society in local affairs. A side-effect of this is the weakening of city government relative to both business interests and a civil society that often avails itself of the legal system to countermand public decisions. A well-known example is that of a coalition of the Labour Community Strategy Centre (LCSC), the National Association for the Advancement of Coloured People (NAACP) and the Bus Riders Union (BRU) who successfully fought the Metropolitan Transportation Authority (MTA) in the city's federal court over an increase in bus fares, but with the wider objective of creating a more equitable public transit system.[48] The case illustrates the options that are open to an engaged, activist civil society in the US, as well as the critical role of the judicial system in mediating conflicts over urban policy issues.

Given the great diversity in planning cultures, what lessons can be drawn from this brief, stylized account for the emerging features of planning? Is it possible to delineate some general planning principles underlying emerging planning practice in the interdependent world of the early 21st century? The rest of this chapter attempts to cut across national and local differences by suggesting a number of emerging planning principles – a new culture of planning, as it were.

In doing this, a broader view of planning that goes beyond narrow professionalism and public institutions is taken. Planning in this more inclusive sense can be seen as contributing to, though not necessarily guiding, the complex processes of city-building. It involves multiple actors from both the private sector and civil society, each of whom brings relevant knowledge to the table. Viewed in this light, planning is not only about getting a comprehensive perspective on the city, as in master planning or its equivalent; nor is it just about the hierarchical coordination of diverse elements. It is not only, as theory has often narrowly claimed, a more 'rational' way of making decisions or of laying out courses of action in advance, or even of charting the long-term future – a normative vision – of the city. Nor is planning, in this context, a purely professional practice, dissociated from politics. It may be all of these, but it is also more. *In contributing to city-building, planning can be described as a set of interdependent processes that, acting together, seek to create more liveable, life-enhancing cities and regions.* Such a practice is oriented to action more than to documents, though documents may underlie the action. Planning is increasingly conforming to certain principles – a new habitus, a certain disposition to act – that ensure positive results in today's world. Liveability, a term popularized recently,[49] draws attention to the sustainability of human settlements. It refers not only to the proper stewardship of the enveloping natural processes that sustain human life, but equally to the social dimensions of cities, to social equity and justice and community, and to the aesthetic and spiritual qualities of the built environment.

Principles of an emerging planning culture

The principles set out below suggest the way that this new planning culture feels and looks. They are presented here in a generalized way; but local variances do, of course, bring these principles into accord with local conditions, including the prevailing political culture.

Planning as an innovative practice

The tradition of modern city planning took it to be axiomatic that government planning seeks to restrain market forces in city-building processes with the intent of furthering public well-being, or the public good. Zoning and building ordinances are still among the primary tools of such planning. In addition, master plans (or general plans, as they are sometimes called) seek to lay out a physical pattern of land uses and transportation routes for the city, as a whole (usually a local council area, but occasionally also the entire metropolitan area), as a guide for public agencies that are expected to conform their sectoral programming to the plan while hoping to constrain private investments in much the same manner. Master plans are typically drawn up for periods of up to 15 years; they are not meant to serve as 'daily blueprints'. Occasionally, they are revised; but more often than not, they are left without substantial change for long periods of time, long after they have lost their relevance in the face of rapid, even hyper-rapid, changes on the ground.[50]

But today, cities everywhere are in movement. Planning, in an attempt to be relevant, is in movement too. In country after country, deep-reaching institutional changes are creating new settings for local planning. Physical and institutional boundaries are being redrawn. Newcomers to the city create demands for new infrastructure and services that usually exceed the city's fiscal capacity. New spatial configurations emerge that push the urban frontier further and further out into the suburbs and beyond. Inequalities in income and life chances widen. Unemployment is everywhere on the rise, even as indicators of total production keep pointing upwards. And where the economy is stagnant, the problem is not so much growth as it is urban decline, with local economies overwhelmed by informality and illegal practices of many kinds.

In response, planning is becoming more innovative in finding new solutions and discovering new institutional arrangements through which change can be effected, rather than serving mainly as a restraint on market forces in the physical development of cities and regions. To be innovative does not, of course, imply abandoning traditional planning approaches, including master planning. Being innovative means building on the strengths of existing planning systems while discarding their weaknesses. In the final analysis, to be innovative does not ensure success simply because something new is being tried: every innovation needs to be treated as an *experiment* that allows planners to learn from their mistakes. Planning for structural change is therefore increasingly construed as a *social learning process* that requires continuous monitoring and critical reflection on the part of planners and relevant publics.[51] How such planning is to be institutionalized is itself one of the greatest challenges that has now to be faced.

The expanded scope of planning

In most parts of the world, city planning has its roots in architecture and engineering.[52] Especially in Europe, professional planners are trained primarily in urban design and land-use planning, while other professions – civil engineering, social work, public health and development economics – concern themselves with the environmental, social and economic issues at the urban scale, but rarely use a spatial template for their work. This European approach has been transferred to Asia and Africa and is now widely apparent in planning organizations throughout the world. In China, for example, city planning is responsible only for certain physical aspects of city-building, while separate administrative entities, accountable to different central ministries in Beijing, are in charge of infrastructural, economic and environmental planning. Social planning scarcely exists either as a practice or as a professional field. Because of their hierarchical structure, these different municipal agencies rarely touch base with each other.

In contrast, some North American and (now also) UK planners, especially graduates of major planning schools, are trained to work across all four dimensions of urban development – spatial, environmental, socio-cultural and economic – and are thus able to communicate effectively with specialists both inside and outside the public domain. In Canada, for example, a major thrust has recently been made towards giving a great deal more emphasis to urban sustainability, with its three-pronged model of economics, the natural environment and social concerns. This broader horizon has allowed Canadian planners to refer to their work as planning for communities, a term that focuses attention on social relations, the human scale, the historical continuity of human settlements and social participation in public decisions. In actual practice, these elements are frequently joined up, even though different cities, at different times, will give priority to one or another of these elements.

There is little question that something like the three-pronged model of sustainability is needed to make cities more liveable. The problem is not whether to promote planning for sustainability in this sense, but how to do it effectively. All sorts of boundaries are beginning to break down: in trade between cities; in transboundary migrations; in the global 'space of flows' of finance capital; in political coalitions; in the separation of public and private sectors; in male and female social domains; in the fusions and hybrid creations of culture; and so forth. This blurring of boundaries is sometimes seen as part of the post-modern condition. Whatever the name, something very important is clearly happening. For planners, it specifically means that the traditional concern with land use is being brought into relation with *sustainable economic growth*, *social diversity and justice and spatial equity*. This is not something that is happening or will happen quickly; ultimately, it will require both a changed approach to planning education[53] and to official planning practice.

Expanded and multiple scales of planning

The scale of today's global corporations and their interdependencies on the ground, particularly in the matter of production and distribution, has reached gigantic dimensions, confronting 'local' governments with unprecedented problems of governance and planning. Scholars have discussed this new scale of planning under the broad heading of city regions[54] or, as others prefer to call them, multi-centred metropolitan regions (see Chapter 3).[55] These urban giants are now found on every continent: in Europe (for example, southeast England and the Paris region), in North America (for example, the New York metropolitan region and the Los Angeles conurbation), in Asia (for instance, Tokyo, Seoul, Beijing-Tianjin, Shanghai, the Pearl River Delta, the Jakarta region called Jabotapek, Calcutta and Mumbai), in Africa (for example, Lagos, Johannesburg and Cairo), in Latin America (for instance, Mexico City and São Paulo) and so on. In population size, they range from 5 or 6 million up to 35 million, as does the newly designated provincial-level municipality of Chungqing.

In China, large cities have been designated 'leading' cities for a set of more or less rural counties under their sway. But to be a 'leading' city does not, by itself, ensure the smooth coordination of actions. District-level governments accountable to their leading municipality may have their own views about the direction of urban development within their smaller but still sizeable administrative domain, while still further down the hierarchy, so-called street offices at neighbourhood levels are charged with significant responsibilities affecting people in their day-to-day lives.[56] Street offices (SOs) in Shanghai:

> *...are expected to manage service for communities. In Shanghai, the SOs' official functions have increased from 3 to 8, and the*

areas in which SOs are involved have increased from 3 to 15... The SOs' new responsibilities include local justice, community security, traffic control, fire protection, sanitation, streetscaping, maintenance of open spaces, environmental protection, family planning, employment and labour force administration, day-care service, disaster protection, collective-owned businesses, community services and farmers' markets. These changes demonstrate a shift of the SO from a low-level administrative body obeying higher government's decisions to a more independent entity representing local interests.[57]

At the bottom of this hierarchy, SOs meet up with residents' committees, which undertake a variety of tasks that are assigned to them by the municipality, such as the maintenance of public order, basic welfare provision and mobilizing people when political movements are called into action. Typically, a residents' committee is in charge of 100 to 600 households and is staffed by 7 to 17 people, some of whom are volunteers.[58]

Here is a system of multilevel planning, but where the different levels – municipality, district government, street office, residents' committee – are only loosely coordinated. In the other direction, beyond the level of the leading city, there are still higher-order planning regions. In Guandong Province, for instance, the Pearl River Delta (PRD) has been identified as such a region, which includes a number of other municipalities besides the provincial capital of Guangzhou (notably Shenzhen) and the Special Administrative Region of Hong Kong. A region of this size, with so many centres of independent power, cannot be effectively coordinated according to a single vision even when the different parts of the region are closely articulated with each other – economically, socially, culturally and even politically. Officials from representative cities meet from time to time to discuss common problems and intentions; but, for the most part, each urban centre and each separate city region are on their own and in competition with the rest.

This does not, however, mean that the hyper-urban/regional scale is unimportant, because the future of each region hinges on the nature of its links with all of the others and on the performance of the entire set of urban regions within the PRD. The hyper-region thus constitutes the operative framework for more detailed planning in any of the city regions that comprise it. In addition, however, inter-city collaboration is necessary for dealing with problems of environmental pollution (especially water and air) and in network planning for highways, airports, electric power, river ports and major industrial locations.

Planning for an endogenous development

The global economy has set cities against each other in a desperate race for a share of footloose capital and trade. An entire new consulting industry has come into being to advise local governments on city marketing. What marketing gurus overlook, however, is that genuine urban development is not a question of 'seducing' investors to put their money into 'your' rather than your competitor's city, but to develop the city 'from within' by *caring for and improving its asset base*. This development from within can be called a form of *endogenous* development.

In the perspective of city marketing, cities are expected to sell themselves to global capital or to 'offer real value...to capture the investor's imagination'.[59] 'Real value' is often defined as gifts of land and infrastructure and tax holidays, as well as the construction of urban enclaves that cater to the tastes of global investors, from luxury housing to upscale shopping districts and similar enticements. This is the strategy that many cities have adopted. According to this logic, a developing country city will try to promote itself as a venue for major sporting events, world cultural exhibitions, millennium domes, and similar extravaganzas, as shown in Chapter 2. It will also try to hide its poverty from the foreigner's gaze, building up entire urban districts to foreign tastes that can compare with the best of what Europe or the US has to offer.

Policies that are focused on the needs and desires of global capital need to be balanced with policies based on the needs of the region's own inhabitants. Otherwise household- and community-centred efforts at 'poverty alleviation' will be left as meaningless gestures that provide little more than temporary relief. The continued disempowerment of large portions of the urban population has led, ultimately, to polarized cities, leaving the gap between rich and poor to grow larger and larger (see Box 7.6).

An endogenous development aims for a liveable, more egalitarian city. Decades ago, at a time when dependency theory was popular, it used to mean erecting tariff barriers to protect a country's infant industries and other economic sectors from foreign competition. But now, in the age of globalization, it refers, instead, to policies at the meso-level of the city region that will *direct local investments towards the development of the multiple resource assets that a city- or multi-centred metropolitan region possesses*. Endogenous development seeks to strengthen a region's relative autonomy through public investment in seven interrelated resource complexes that are essential for sustaining its long-term capacity to compete globally. These complexes include:

1 *human assets*, or all the things that nurture the ability of people to grow into healthy and productive human beings: good nutrition, housing and viable neighbourhoods, healthcare, and education for both boys and girls;

2 *social assets*, which entails a robust, self-organizing civil society deeply engaged with the everyday life of its communities;

3 *cultural assets*, or a region's physical heritage and the distinctiveness and vibrancy of its cultural life;

4 *intellectual assets*, or the quality of regional universities and research institutions and what the Japanese would call the region's 'living human treasures': its leading artists, intellectuals and scientists who embody the city's creative powers;

5 *environmental assets*, which include those qualities of the physical environment that are essential for sustaining life itself, such as air, water and the capacity of the land to sustain permanent human settlement;

6 *natural assets*, or the region's natural resource endowment, such as land, landscapes, beaches, forests, fisheries, and mineral deposits, whose use is for production and enjoyment;

7 *urban assets*, commonly referred to as urban infrastructure, which includes facilities and equipment for transportation, energy, water supply, sewage treatment and solid waste disposal or, in a more general sense, the built environment.

These seven tightly interwoven resource complexes constitute a city region's major productive assets. The benefits of investing in them are calculated over a long period of time in social rather than purely economic terms – that is, they are measured against broad societal goals and values. Nurturing them is the *sine qua non* for a development that puts human life and livelihood ahead of short-term market calculations.

Cities developing themselves in this way discover that they can attract foreign capital, as well. It is not a question of '*either/or*' but of '*both/and*'. A city that aspires to be liveable forms new partnerships, or enters into social contracts, with its civil society. It promotes the participation of local capital. It invests in people, not only in hardware. It promotes a form of social mobilization that gathers public support because the results benefit the many, not merely a few.

Those who argue that cities lack the financial means of carrying out a vigorous development based on the principle of acting endogenously may want to consider the case of Cairo, Egypt. In that Mediterranean capital of approximately 14 million

BOX 7.6 Mumbai: the polarizing impact of international investment

One recent study has amassed evidence from around the world of the results of lopsided kow-towing to finance capital.

Mumbai, long a symbol of India's hoped-for progress towards emancipation, has, in effect, become deeply polarized. All aspects of consensus between rich and poor, and their political groups, have broken down. Carefully networked high-rise structures provide a three-dimensional landscape of exclusion and polarization. They create 'localities of the ultra-wealthy and the upper middle class', groups who have benefited enormously from the liberalization of India's economy and Mumbai's key role in articulating that economy with the rest of the world.

Building works and public subsidy have gone overwhelmingly to serve the living, working, leisure and transport needs, and desires of these groups. Shanty residents, meanwhile, have to make do with highly inadequate standpipes or, worse still, private water vendors who charge exorbitant rates.

Source: Graham and Marvin, 2001.

inhabitants, more than half of whom are poor and 'ultra-poor', a hyper-active civil society has created what amounts to an alternative government over many of Cairo's popular quarters and shantytowns, providing essential services in housing, health and education for the local population. Religious organizations have gained people's trust and their willing collaboration. They have been able to exact a traditional tithing (*zakat*) of 10 per cent from small businesses that is channelled through the thousands of independent mosques scattered throughout the neighbourhoods, as well as draw on the substantial capital resources of Islamic banks. Foreign assistance from the Saudis and the Gulf states has also been an important contributor.[60]

Planning for cities of difference

Liveable cities are, and always have been, socially diverse cities. Indeed, diversity (along with mobility) is one of the hallmarks of city life; it is what gives cities their vitality and creative energy. Diversity exists along numerous dimensions, such as cultural identity, race, age, gender, occupation, wealth, length of residence in the city, physical disabilities, language and religion. These differences sort themselves out spatially, with housing markets and the state providing institutional frameworks that constrain city residents as they make choices that are more or less forced about where to make their homes. At the same time, multiple diversities come together in the city's public spaces: its streets, squares and parks; its churches, synagogues, temples and mosques; and its transit modes. Diversity, especially a spatially constrained diversity that leads to ghettos and 'ethnic' enclaves, the walled compounds of the super rich, and an unjust distribution of public facilities that benefits some groups while depriving others, will contribute to social tensions and outbreaks of violence unless countered by appropriate social planning, as shown in Chapter 1.[61]

From a planning perspective, the central problem is one of access to housing, water, sanitation, health facilities, markets, physical security, affordable transportation, recreation, places of worship, public services, and the possibility of good neighbourliness. Left to themselves, the spatial outcomes of residential choices, private capital investments and insensitive or inattentive public actions lead to uneven – often grossly uneven – access to basic human needs. Uneven access is not only a matter of social justice, however. It empowers the already privileged sectors of the population while disempowering the less fortunate, not only impeding the latter as they struggle to work their way out of poverty, but facilitating the further aggrandizement of the rich, thus setting in motion the dangerous and, ultimately, unsustainable dynamic of social polarization.

Equalizing access to the means for satisfying basic human needs and removing artificial barriers to neighbourliness, such as walled enclaves,[62] are increasingly considered as fundamental to good planning. But this is only part of the story. For one thing, priorities may differ according to the condition of each diversity group: people with physical disabilities have special needs with regard to moving about the city, and what these needs are must be determined, preferably through direct contact with the affected groups.[63] The universal need of women for security in public spaces is generally familiar, but rarely meets with a serious planning response. There are also age-specific needs: young people need access to playing fields for soccer, basket ball courts, etc;

older folks need community centres; young mothers need access to baby clinics and convenient shopping. People adhering to different religious faiths need to have convenient access to places of worship and social conviviality with co-religionists. Preferred forms of public recreation also vary a good deal across urban demographics. These and other group needs and their relative priorities have to be determined, with results worked into spatial plans that can be applied equitably across all groups.

Planners are not the only actors concerned with 'planning for difference'. In some countries, the judicial system is playing an increasingly important role in enforcing legislation whose aim is to guarantee citizens' rights to the city. Inevitable inter-group conflicts need to be acknowledged and negotiated before they turn into violent confrontations. These are matters that, in the present context, can only be described briefly, but are becoming essential to the building and management of liveable cities.[64]

The critical role of civil society

The liveability of cities is especially problematic for the poorest, most disempowered sectors of the population. In light of this, civil society has assumed a critical role in planning.[65] Over the past 30 or more years, the term civil society has come into widespread use. However, insofar as meaning depends upon context, what constitutes civil society is subject to different interpretations. In the broadest sense, the term refers to organizations, both formal and informal, that do not belong to the state or to the corporate sector and enjoy substantial autonomy of action.[66] Civil society organizations (CSOs) can be specified further by distinguishing between those that work primarily for civil society itself (that are inward directed) and those that, being outward directed, operate in the political (or public) domain. Examples of the former are organizations that largely work independently of the state to improve the living conditions of target populations, such as the Immigration Services Society of British Columbia, Canada, or the similarly focused Chinese immigrant society in Vancouver, Canada, called SUCCESS. The Islamic religious organizations mentioned earlier that are working in the popular sectors of Cairo are another example of an inward-looking civil society, even though they are very differently oriented from those in Vancouver and, ultimately, have political objectives.[67]

Outward-directed CSOs include social movements that become public advocates of citizen rights, as well as of broader societal interests that are insufficiently acknowledged by the state, such as the

BOX 7.7 **Participatory budgeting in Porto Alegre, Brazil**

One of the best-known examples of civil society–state collaboration is the participatory municipal budgeting process that was initiated in 1989 by the Workers Party (PT) government in Porto Alegre, capital of the Brazilian state of Rio Grande do Sul, and has since spread throughout major Brazilian cities. The story begins during the early 1980s, when groups of neighbourhood leaders began forming a 'regional' organization linking adjacent neighbourhood associations. This effort culminated in the formation of the Union of Neighbourhood Associations of Porto Alegre (UAMPA). With support from the union, the PT was elected to head the local government and initiated a participatory process that called for open assemblies in 16 'regions' of the city where citizens would present their demands for investment.

In many ways, the participatory budget is a small policy with small objectives – bringing ordinary people into the discussion of how to distribute basic investments among their neighbourhoods. Yet the policy has gone far beyond most efforts of government reform that make efficiency and cost reduction their main objectives. The result is more than an isolated 'successful' government effort. Significant transformations in the way that civil society functions in Porto Alegre have taken place on a level that it is difficult to believe would simply disappear should the PT be voted out of office and the policy eliminated. Even where movement corporatism and self-interested action are the rule, the practice of participation involves a learning process through which some of the contradictions of democratization can be overcome and through which organized civil society can expand. Or, as democratic theorists have proposed, participation is developmental: its practice can have a 'cascade' effect, which both improves the participatory process itself and transforms public life more generally.

Source: Abers, 1998, p63.

women's and environmental movements. Some urban movements have been formed in the process of offering resistance to specific initiatives of local governments, such as squatter removal projects or the proposed construction of highways through densely populated neighbourhoods.[68] *Leefbaar Rotterdam* (Liveable Rotterdam), the citizen movement discussed earlier in this chapter, is one such CSO that presented its platform to the voters of their city as a local political party. Finally, there are CSOs that, in various ways, collaborate with the local state (see Box 7.7). Some of these may be wholly or in part funded by the municipality, or they may receive funds from overseas charities and religious organizations. Other CBOs mobilize contributions in the form of 'sweat equity' from local communities in jointly agreed projects, as is demonstrated by the well-known *kampung* improvement programmes of Indonesia.

Whether or not CSOs exist at all or are suppressed by the state, and their relative strengths or weaknesses, vary considerably from country to country. Authoritarian governments, fearful of challenges to their power, often suppress civil society organizations or else try to co-opt them. Political traditions shape the extent to which CSOs become outward oriented or remain active largely for themselves. CSOs are politically very active in Canada and the US, weaker in the UK, and quite limited in their aspirations in Japan. In countries such as Egypt, on the other hand, where CSOs are religiously based, they are vigorous in the delivery of services and in promoting the regeneration of popular

neighbourhoods. Regardless of these differences, it is clear that the presence of civil society today is a fact that planners cannot afford to ignore. Planners are increasingly engaging representative CSOs in dialogue, listening to their concerns, grievances and demands, and enlisting them in the larger project for a liveable city.

It has become popular internationally to assign the task of poverty alleviation programmes to NGOs, thus freeing the hand of government to concentrate on 'developmental' issues, and particularly on those that support the inflow of private capital from abroad. This strategy has not been outstandingly successful, however. Recent research on the performance of NGOs in service delivery[69] has revealed widespread failure to meet popular expectations. The following conclusions have emerged from the research:

- *Reaching the poorest*: though most NGOs serve the poor, they do not necessarily reach the poorest.
- *Poverty reduction*: NGO projects in health, education and water supply alleviate poverty in the communities where they operate; but, generally, they fail significantly to reduce it.
- *Coverage*: the scale of their operations is limited and the coverage patchy. Moreover, NGOs are not very good at coordinating with each other or with the state.
- *Quality*: there is little evidence that NGOs provide better-quality services than does the state. What seems to matter more is which of the two has more money.

- *Technical capacity*: NGOs perform better in sectors where they have built up expertise. They have considerable capacity for innovation, experimentation and flexible adaptation of projects to suit local needs and conditions. But they are less successful at more complex interventions.
- *Cost-effectiveness*: there is little evidence that NGOs are inherently more cost-effective than the state.
- *Policy direction*: one of the major concerns about relying upon NGOs for service provision is that they cannot provide a broader framework for action. Only a government can develop clear policy guidelines and regulations in such fields as health and education.[70]

The most significant problems emerging from these conclusions concerning the role of NGOs in poverty alleviation programmes are inadequate resources, policy direction and fragmentation. Only government can overcome these obstacles to an urban development inclusive of the popular sectors. As the example of Porto Alegre shows, it is possible to engage CSOs in a partnership with local government. Such a partnership is not without conflicts and political tensions, and it requires a civil society that is reasonably united and can speak with a strong voice. The Brazilian example grew out of a particular conjunction of forces and a specific context, and cannot be copied directly. Even so, it remains an inspiring example and has set a direction that many cities are trying to follow.

A strategic focus for planning

In many countries, urban planning is increasingly becoming more strategic. The adjective 'strategic' can have several meanings in planning discourse. It can refer to a strategy for implementing a plan or part of a plan. It could also be said that such a strategy involves decisions about priorities, the identification of partners, the degree of confidentiality and financial strategies. Important though it is, this usage will not be further explored here.

A quite different meaning is found in the context of so-called 'strategic planning'. This is a fairly recent coinage, at least in spatial development planning, and it generally refers to comprehensive spatial plans with a planning horizon of 20 or more years.[71] An example is the current strategic plan for Hong Kong called *Hong Kong 2030: Planning Vision and Strategy*.[72] Other examples include the 2050 programmes in Buenos Aires, Barcelona and New York mentioned in Chapter 1. This is still a controversial form of planning that may be undertaken for a variety of reasons (which are not always articulated).[73] Some see strategic planning as a way of setting out an ideal vision of the future; others see it as a vehicle for generating technical studies that would otherwise not be undertaken; still others see it as a way of substituting technical for political rationality or, alternatively, of undergirding and, thus, strengthening political reason with technical studies. A fourth reason is to create a broad conceptual framework for wider public discussion and/or collaborative planning. All of these justifications of strategic planning have some validity; but there are also serious drawbacks, not the least of which are the large imponderables concerning the long-term future. Moreover, few local governments have the political continuity that is always implicit in long-range planning. Finally, major decisions on, for example, infrastructure planning are almost always highly contested, and in lively democracies such as The Netherlands may be decided by elections rather than technical fiat.

A third meaning, completely different from the other two, is expressed by the phrase 'strategic focus'. Briefly, this refers to a focus on high-priority projects of some magnitude whose implementation requires active collaboration from stakeholders, as evidenced by the experiences of several Latin American and Caribbean cities described earlier in this chapter. It is often proposed as a substitute for master planning (or its equivalent) and is in contrast to the perceived static document-orientation of the latter. It may thus be called a form of *dynamic action planning*. Action planning is a multidimensional and ongoing process that takes place in real time. Documents – plans, memoranda and research reports – underlie it; but the process itself is collaborative. Action planning is focused on outcomes that cannot be completely known in advance of their realization. With large-scale renewal projects, such as the Central Station in Rotterdam (discussed earlier) or waterfront projects, such as Melbourne's River Revitalization[74] or the better-known London Docklands, whose execution stretches out over many years and may take decades to fully bring to completion, planning is often conducted outside of the regular planning system, and project designs may undergo major changes in the course of implementation.[75] They may also lead to detailed studies that explore their impact on the environment, related urban subsystems (such as transportation), potential social consequences and political implications. In the course of these studies, a new range of stakeholders is often identified (for example, opposition groups to the project by affected neighbourhoods) who, in turn, may modify project design.

Because action planning takes place in 'real time', it brings together all relevant actors in a 'transactive' (interactive) process that is fundamentally face to face even as it is mediated through the internet, the telephone or fax machines. It is this face-to-face quality that makes action planning a dynamic process.[76] Collaborations centred on the project in question may be formalized as 'partnerships'; but a partnership is merely the form, not the substance of the undertaking. The substance is found in the constant give and take, where the search is for agreement rather than for 'winning' against adversaries because, as it evolves, the project enforces its own discipline on stakeholders who want to stay in the game.

Master plans, and even strategic plans, that do what they are supposed to do, which is to guide spatial development, can work quite well under conditions of slow and incremental change. But they belong to an era that was somehow calmer than the present, and additional tools are needed. As globalization obliges cities to re-imagine themselves, today's world is seemingly in turmoil. Most infrastructure projects are on a scale so monumental that they 'drive' urban development more than they are a result of other developments. For better or worse, the very 'grain' of the city is turning coarser, becoming less 'homey' and less neighbourly. Major interventions give the city a new face and traditional forms of planning need to be revised in order to incorporate newer and more flexible approaches.

The governance of city planning

Planning for city regions is becoming increasingly more important during the 21st century. It is an inherently collaborative practice.[77] This follows from its multi-scalar setting, the intertwined economic, environmental, social, political and aesthetic objectives of spatial development, the growing focus on special projects that fall outside of planning's regulatory environment, and the exigencies of action planning. It is likely that planners will have to relinquish their traditional desire for the close coordination of spatial development, where all aspects of development are

Planning culture, like overall urban culture, is inherited and developed by generation of ideas and resources

carefully articulated in a plan designed to serve as a beacon light for all actors.

On the other hand, if all actors proceeded on their own without regard for what is happening in the city, sectoral plans would soon be at loggerheads with each other, resulting in needless conflicts. In the absence of public planning, markets would remain the most important force in shaping the spatial order (or disorder) of the city. But leaving it to the market alone is not likely to lead to a liveable and inclusive city in which life can flourish.

Nevertheless, it is now clear that a great deal of coordination occurs spontaneously through informal ways of networking, coalition-building and mutual adjustment.[78] Across the divides of status and power, voluntary cooperation occurs most readily among actors when shared interests are at stake. This is the basis for a form of collaborative action planning that brings together potential actors from the local state, the corporate sector and organized civil society around the design and implementation of major projects. For those taking part in this process of action planning, the experience is one of learning in order to view the project from different perspectives.

Each collective actor brings special information and knowledge to the table, expresses views that derive from different value perspectives, and has different interests at stake that, nevertheless, may overlap to some extent with those of others. It is these overlapping interests that form the basis of collaborative action. As trust among actors is gradually established, and each of the participants becomes aware of the different 'rationalities' that are activated during ongoing negotiations, the stage is set for social learning. At some point, formal 'partnerships' that take a contractual form are often established. But such arrangements grow out of the process; they are not its starting point.[79]

All action planning, of course, faces uncertainties and poses risks. In the end, it must be held accountable – to citizens, the corporate stockholders of participating business interests and the base organizations of civil society. And because it takes place in the public domain, it must be designed as a transparent process that is open to public inspection. Action planning for a sustainable city is a daunting task that calls for the highest qualities of visionary leadership. But it is not impossible and is becoming an important characteristic of some planning cultures.

The future of spatial planning

The future of cities is likely to be influenced by three important trends: the continued expansion and consolidation of global capital; the completion of the urban transition over the next several decades; and the strengthening of city-mediated and increasingly transnational relations.[80] The urban transition here simply means that the proportion of the population living in 'cities', however defined, will continue to increase, especially in countries such as India and China that are still predominantly rural, reaching, perhaps, 70 per cent of a vastly larger world population than today's. But in addition to 'citification', urban transition refers to the socio-economic and cultural transformation of much of the countryside as rural people in even remote parts of the globe adopt urban lifestyles and modes of production that are increasingly oriented towards capital accumulation. The 21st century will be the century when the world, as a whole, will for the first time turn predominantly urban in the sense that this term is understood today.

This does not mean that urbanization will necessarily lead to cultural uniformity. National cultures survive and thrive under urbanization in even the most economically advanced countries. No one, for example, would seriously argue that France and the UK are culturally assimilated to each other. Despite European colonial influences, variety continues to characterize national cultures of planning all over the world. It could be argued that the current era of globalization and the insertion of cities into the 'space of flows' of global finance, information and cultural exchanges will eventually lead to a greater homogenization of practices, and that the profession of city and regional, or spatial, planning will exhibit more and more common characteristics. But even if this were the case on the technical side, actual planning practices must still respond to the particular conditions under which they operate; conform to the prevailing political culture; accommodate its institutional settings; adapt to the limitations of resources for local development; battle with entrenched interests and traditions; and gradually evolve their own national and even local style.

Notes

1 This chapter is based on a draft prepared by John Friedmann, University of British Columbia, Canada.

2 Introduced by Manuel Castells.

3 Friedmann and Wolff, 1982; Friedmann, 1986; Taylor, 2002; Sassen, 2001, 2002.

4 Taylor et al, 2002, p99.

5 Sassen, 2002; Taylor et al, 2002, p100.

6 When three European planners undertook what they described as a 'journey into the planning cultures of four countries': Switzerland, Germany, Italy and France. Keller et al, 1996; see also Sanyal, 2004.

7 Bourdieu, 2002; Friedmann, 2002b.

8 Based on Friedmann, forthcoming.

9 This section on India was contributed by Mattie Siemiatycki and is based on Mishra, 1997.

10 Gopalakrishnan, 2003.

11 Tiwari (undated);, see also Mohanty, 1996.

12 Verma, 2002.

13 Steinberg, forthcoming; Fernandez Guell, 1997.

14 Steinberg, forthcoming.

15 Steinberg, forthcoming.

16 Based on Rakodi, 1997.

17 Some observers estimate that across Africa, 75 per cent of the labour force is engaged in so-called informal activities, and that 'many formal institutions now exist simply as a context in which a wide range of informal business and activity can be pursued' (Simone, 2001, p103).

18 Wekwete, 1997, p534.

19 Wekwete, 1997, p549.

20 El-Shakhs, 1997, pp505–506.

21 Four hundred delegates from many African countries, as well as from the UK, took part in a pan-African planning conference that was held in Durban, South Africa, from 17–20 September 2002. But what strikes one from a perusal of the papers is how much they sound as though the conference might have been held in Europe or North America, despite the five themes on which the plenary and parallel sessions were based. There was no sense of imminent crisis. The topics chosen are conveniently fashionable in professional circles, such as transnational planning, identity formation, the integration of planning with development, sustainability, what to do about peripheral settlements, and so forth. One did not get a sense from these papers that African cities could be 'saved' only through extraordinary, unorthodox means. The conference was very much in tune with 'business as usual'. See www.saplanners.org.za/SAPC/pa-sum.htm.

22 National Research Council, 2003.

23 Based on Sorensen, 2002. For a specific case study, see Burayidi, 2000.

24 Sorensen, 2002, 303.

25 Faludi and van der Valk, 1994.

26 Well-known mega-projects of recent memory include East Shanghai (Pudong) – see Olds, 2001 – the Potsdamer Platz in Berlin – see Lehrer, 2004 – and a series of infrastructure projects with Frank Gehry's Guggenheim Museum at its centre, designed to reinvent the old rust-belt city of Bilbao, Spain – see Siemiatycki, 2003.

27 The following account is based on Kooijman and Wigmans, 2003.

28 The UK urban design firm, Alsop Architects.

29 Led by the charismatic Pim Fortuyn who was tragically murdered two months later.

30 Based on Herrschel and Newman, 2002.

31 Herrschel and Newman, 2002, p118.

32 Herrschel and Newman, 2002, p124. Herrschel and Newman comment: 'only two years into the RDA experiment, the two forces of devolution and centralization continue to pull in different directions, and traditional tensions in the structure of British government have reasserted themselves.'

33 Herrschel and Newman, 2002, p145.

34 Marvin and May (2003) suggest that the main challenge is what they term the 'implementation gap', which is a conflict between central control and local autonomy.

35 Based on Ward, 2002, p341–354.

36 Ward, 2002, 346.

37 As Stephen Ward observes: 'National policies which cut federal spending programmes and relied on market solutions encouraged a pragmatic and often reckless entrepreneurialism at city level' (Ward, 2002).

38 Ward, 2002, p347.

39 Calthorp, 1993.

40 Ward, 2002, pp348–349.

41 Ward, 2002, p350.

42 Based on Faludi and Waterhout, 2002, and Commission of the European Communities (CEC), 1999.

43 Faludi and Waterhout, 2002.

44 Commission of the European Communities, 1999, pp19–20.

45 For an example of the potential role of inter-city networks in regional development, see Friedmann, 2000.

46 See, for example, Harris and Hooper, forthcoming.

47 Another constant is corrupt and illegal practices that arise in the context of entrepreneurial planning and are found in all countries, though in varying degree.

48 Grengs, 2002.

49 UNCHS (Habitat), 2001a; Evans, 2002.

50 Master planning has long been criticized for these and other reasons. See, for example, UNESCAP, 1994. Nevertheless it continues to be practised in countries such as Japan and China.

51 See Schön, 1971; Argyris and Schön, 1974; Schön, 1983; Friedmann, 1987, Chapter 5.

52 Friedmann, 1987.

53 Sandercock, 1998b.

54 Scott, 2001.

55 Gottdiener, 2000.

56 Friedmann, forthcoming, Chapter 6.

57 Zhang, 2002, pp312–313.

58 Wu, 2002, p1084.

59 Ohmae, 2001, p34

60 Lubeck and Britts, 2002.

61 Leonie Sandercock formulates the central question: 'How can "we" (all of us), in all of our differences, be "at home" in the multicultural and multiethnic cities of the 21st century' (Sandercock, 2003, p 1).

62 Caldeira, 1999.

63 Gleeson, 1998.

64 See Sandercock, 1998b, and Sandercock, 2003, for the best overall discussion of these issues from a planning/policy perspective.

65 Douglass and Friedmann, 1998.

66 UNRISD, 2003.

67 Lubeck and Britts, 2002.

68 Pezzoli, 1998.

69 Conducted by the United Nations Research Institute for Social Development.

70 UNRISD, 2003, p85.

71 Salet and Faludi, 2000; Albrechts et al, 2003.

72 See www.info.gov.hk/planning.

73 Friedmann, 2004.

74 Sandercock and Dovey, 2002.

75 In Sydney, Australia, state interventions in major urban developments led to the creation of 'authorities' to carry out the projects outside the normal routines of the state planning department. See McGuirk, 2003.

76 A model of 'transactive' planning was first proposed by Friedmann, 1973.

77 Healey, 1997.

78 Lindblom, 1959; Lindblom, 1979.

79 For case studies of action planning (most of them from the US), see Susskind et al, 1999.

80 Friedmann, 2002b, p3.

References

Abel, C and C M Lewis (eds) (2002) *Exclusion and Engagement: Social Policy in Latin America*. Institute of Latin American Studies, University of London, London

Abers, R (1998) 'Learning democratic practice: distributing government resources through popular participation in Porto Alegre, Brazil' in M Douglass and J Friedmann (eds) *Cities for Citizens: Planning and the Rise of Civil Society in a Global Age*. John Wiley and Sons, Chichester, pp39–66

Abrahamson, M (2004) *Global Cities*. Oxford University Press, New York

Acharya, S (2003) 'Migration patterns in Cambodia. Causes and consequences' paper prepared for the Expert Group Meeting on Migration and Development 27-29 August, United Nations Economic and Social Commission for Asia and the Pacific, Bangkok

Adams, R and J Page (2001) *Holding the Line: Poverty Reduction in the Middle East and North Africa, 1970–2000*. World Bank Paper, Washington, DC

ADB (Asian Development Bank) (1999) *Fighting Poverty in Asia and the Pacific: The Poverty Reduction Strategy*. ADB Policy Paper, November 1999, www.adb.org/Documents/Policies/Poverty_Reduction/Poverty_Policy.pdf

ADB (2002) *Beyond Boundaries: Extending Services to the Urban Poor*, http://beyondboundaries.adb.org/ch1/index.htm

Afsah S (1998) 'Impact of financial crisis on industrial growth and environmental performance in Indonesia', www.worldbank.org/nipr/work_paper/shakeb/index.htm

Afshar, F (2001) 'Preparing planners for a globalizing world: the planning school at the University of Guelph' *Journal of Planning Education and Research* 20(3): 339–352. AgaKhan Development Network, www.akdn.org

Albrechts, L, P Healey and K Kunzmann (2003) 'Strategic Spatial Planning and Regional Governance in Europe' *Journal of the American Planning Association* 69(2): 113–129

Alden, J, Y Beigulenko and S Crow (1998) 'Moscow: planning for a world capital city towards 2000' *Cities* 15(5): 361–374

Alvazzi del Frate, A (1998) *Victims of Crime in the Developing Countries*. UNICRI, Publication No 57, Rome

Alvazzi del Frate, A (2000) *International Crime Victim Survey*. UNODC, Rome

Alvazzi del Frate, A and J van Kesteren (forthcoming) *Criminal Victimization in Urban Europe*, UNICRI, Turin www.unicri.it/icvs/statistics/files/Table ECE.PDF

Anas, A, R Arnott and K Small (1998) 'Urban spatial structure' *Journal of Economic Literature* 36(3): 1426–1464

Anderson, K (1991) *Vancouver's Chinatown: Racial Discourse in Canada, 1875–1980*. McGill Queens University Press, Toronto

Andersson, C and A Stavrou (2000) *Youth and Delinquency and the Criminal Justice System in Dar es Salaam, Tanzania*. UN-Habitat Safer Cities Programme, Nairobi

APHRC (African Population and Health Research Centre) (2002) *Population and Health Dynamics in Nairobi's Informal Settlements*. APHRC, Nairobi

Appadurai, A (2001) 'Deep democracy: urban governmentality and the horizon of politics' *Environment and Urbanization*, 13(2): 23–43

Applbaum, K (2003) *Marketing Observed: From Professional Practice to Global Provisioning*. Routledge, New York

Argyris, C and D A Schön (1974) *Theory in Practice: Increasing Professional Effectiveness*. Jossey-Bass, San Francisco

Arms Management Programme (2002) 'Attitudes to firearms and crime in Nairobi: results of a city survey' Institute for Security Studies (ISS) Occasional Paper No. 59, ISS, Pretoria

Asian Migration Centre (2002) *Migration. Neeeds, Issues and Response in the Greater Mekong Subregion. A Resource Book*. Mekong Migration Network with the support of The Rockefeller Foundation, Hong Kong

Avramov, D (1998) 'Youth homelessness as a social construction' in *Youth Homelessness in the European Union*. FEANTSA, Brussels

Bahl R W and J Linn (1992) *Urban Public Finance in Developing Countries*. Oxford University Press, New York

Bairoch, P (1985) *De Jericho à Mexico Villes et Economie dans l'Histoire*. Editions Gallimard, Paris

Barclay, G and C Tavares (2002) *International Comparisons of Criminal Justice Statistics 2000*, Issue 05/02, July, The Home Office Research Development and Statistics Directorate (RDS), London

Bayoumi, M (2002) 'Letter to a G-Man' in M Sorkin and S Zukin (eds) *After the World Trade Center: Rethinking New York City*. Routledge, New York, pp131–142

Beall, J (2002) 'Globalization and social exclusion in cities: framing the debate with lessons from Africa and Asia' *Environment and Urbanization* 14(1): 41–51

Beatty, C, S Fothergilland and A Green (2002) *The Real Level of Unemployment 2002*. CRES, Sheffield Hallam University, Sheffield

Bender, T (2001) 'The new metropolitanism and a pluralized public' *Harvard Design Magazine* 13, www.gsd.harvard.edu/research/publications/hdm/back/13boym.html

Benna, U (2002) 'From planning for to planning with MENA children', Background paper for Children and the City Conference. Amman, December 2002

Berengo, M (1965) *Nobili a Mercanti nella Lucca del '500*. Einaudi, Turin

Berke, P R, N Ericksen, J Crawford and J Dixon (2002) 'Planning and indigenous people: human rights and environmental protection in New Zealand' *Journal of Planning Education and Research* 22: 115–134

Berman, M (1982) *All That is Solid Melts into Air*. Simon and Schuster, New York

Berry, B (ed) (1986) *Urbanization and Counter-urbanization* (*Urban Affairs Annual Review, 11*). Sage, Beverly Hills

Bianchini, F and M Parkinson (eds) (1993) *Cultural Policy and Urban Regeneration: The West European Experience*. Manchester University Press, Manchester

Bielby, W T and D Bielby (1998) *The 1998 Hollywood Writers' Report: Telling All Our Stories*. Writers Guild of America West, Los Angeles

Bird, R and E Slack (2003) *Fiscal Aspects of Metropolitan Governance*. Inter-American Development Bank, Washington, DC

Birdsall, N (2001) 'Why inequality matters' *Ethics and International Affairs* 15(2): 3–28

Black, D and V Henderson (1999) 'A theory of urban growth' *The Journal of Political Economy* 107(2): 252–284

Blokland, T (2001) 'Bricks, mortar, memories: neighbourhood and networks in collective acts of remembering' *International Journal of Urban and Regional Research* 25(2): 268–283

Bonazzi, G (1996) *Lettera da Singapore Ovvero it Terzo Capitalismo*. Il Mulino, Bologna

Boonchuen, P (2002) 'Globalisation and urban design: transformations of civic space in Bangkok' *International Development Planning Review* 24: 401–417

Borja, J and Z Muxi (2003) *El Espacio Publico: Cuidad y Ciudadania*. Electa, Barcelona

Boubakri, H (2001) *Le Maghreb et les Nouvelles Configurations Migratoires Internationales: Mobilité et Réseaux*. Correspondances n°68 octobre-novembre-décembre, Université de Poitiers

Boulding, E (1999) 'Peace culture: living with difference', Keynote address, 5 February, Boston Research Center

Bourdieu, P (1984) *Distinction: A Social Critique of the Judgment of Taste*, translated by R Nice. Harvard University Press, Cambridge MA

Bourdieu, P (2002) 'Habitus' in J Hillier and E Rooks (eds) *Habitus: A Sense of Place*. Ashgate, Aldershot, pp27–34

Boye, O (2002) *Migration, one of globalization's few exclusions*, International Migrations in Latin America and the Caribbean, edition no 65

Bradbury, B, S Jenkins and J Micklewright (eds) (2002) *The Dynamics of Child Poverty in Industrialised Countries*. Cambridge University Press, Cambridge

Braithwaite, J (1995) *The Old and New Poor in Russia: Trends in Poverty*. Background paper for Russian Poverty Assessment. Education and Social Policy Department Working Paper. World Bank, Washington, DC

Brecher, J and T Costello (1994) *Global Village or Global Pillage*. South End Press, Cambridge

Brettell, C and R V Kemper (2002) 'Migration to cities' in *Encyclopedia of Urban Cultures*. Scholastic/Grolier, Bethel

Brockerhoff, M (1999) 'Urban growth in developing countries: a review of projections and predictions' *Population and Development Review* **24**(4): 757–778

Bromley, R D F (2000) 'Planning for tourism and urban conservation: evidence from Cartagena, Colombia' *Third World Planning Review* **22**: 23–43

Bruen, A-M et al (2002) *The Estimation of Heroin Availability: 1996-2000*. Office of National Drug Control Policy, Washington DC

Burayidi, M A (ed) (2000) *Urban Planning in a Multicultural Society*. Praeger, Westport, Conn

Burrows, E G and M Wallace (1999) *Gotham: A History of New York City to 1898*. Oxford University Press, New York

Burt, M R (2001) 'What will it take to end homelessness?', 1 October 2001, www.urban.org/url.cfm?ID=310305

Caldeira, T (1999) 'Fortified enclaves: the new urban segregation' in J Holston (ed) *Cities and Citizenship*. Duke University Press, Durham

Caldeira, T (2001) *City of Walls: Crime, Segregation, and Citizenship in São Paolo*. University of California Press, Berkeley and Los Angeles

Calthorp, P (1993) *The Next American Metropolis: Community and the American Dream*. Princeton Architectural Press, Princeton

Carmona, M (2000) 'Globalization and spatial restructuring' in M Carmona and M Schoonraad (eds) *Globalization, Urban Form and Governance*, Delft University Press (DUP), Delft

Castells, M (1996) *The Information Age: Economy, Society, and Culture*. Blackwell, Oxford

Catenazzi, A (1999) *Jornadas sobre Gestion del Territorio*. Facultad del Arquitectura, Diseno, y Urbanismo, Buenos Aires

Cattaneo, C (1972) *La Cittá Come Principio*. Marsilio, Venice

Cecchini, D and J Zicolillo (2002) *Los Nuevos Conquistadores*. Foca, Madrid

Chang, T C (2000) 'Renaissance revisited: Singapore as a "global city for the arts"' *International Journal of Urban and Regional Research* **24**(4): 818–831

Cheng, M M (2004) 'Mexico, India dominate new immigration'. *New York City – Manhattan news*, http://www.nynewsday.com/news/local/manhattan/ny-census-diversity,0,6709391.story

Chervyakov, V V, V M Shkolnikov, W A Pridemore and M McKee (2002) 'The changing nature of murder in Russia' *Social Science and Medicine* **55**(10): 1713–1724

Chia Siow Yue (2003) 'Economic globalization and equity in East Asia', Global Development Network Forum, 19–21 January 2003, Cairo

Chua, B H (1998) 'World cities, globalization, and the spread of consumerism: a view of Singapore' *Urban Studies* **35**: 981–1000

Citizens' Committee for Children of New York (2002) *Keeping Track of New York City's Children*. Committee for Children, New York

City of New York (2001) *The Impact of the September 11 WTC Attack on NYC's Economy and Revenues*. Office of the Comptroller, 4 October

City of Vancouver (2004) *City Plan Arbutus Ridge/Kerrisdale/Shaughnessy (ARKS) Crime Rates*, Fact Sheet 1.3.6, City of Vancouver, www.city.vancouver.bc.ca/commsvcs/planning/cityplan/Visions/arks/factsheets/1.3.6CrimeARKS.pdf

Coe, N M (2000) 'On location: American capital and the local labour market in the Vancouver film industry' *International Journal of Urban and Regional Research* **24**(1): 79–94

Cohen, M (1997) 'From the virtual city to the city of virtue, from stock/flow to heritage and values' *Traditional Dwellings and Settlements Review* **IX**(1): 51–54

Cohen, M (1998) 'Stock and flow: making better use of metropolitan resources' *Brookings Review* **16**(4): 37–38

Cohen, M A and D Debowicz (2001) 'Los cinco ciudades de Buenos Aires: pobreza y desigualdad' *Medio Ambiente y Urbanización* **56**, July: 3–20

COHRE (Centre on Housing Rights and Eviction)(2003) *Global Survey of Forced Evictions. Violation of Human Rights.* COHRE, Geneva

Commission of the European Communities (CEC) (1999) *European Spatial Development Perspective: Towards Balanced and Sustainable Development of the Territory of the EU*. Office for Official Publications of the European Communities, Luxembourg

Commission on Narcotic Drugs (2003) *World Situation with Regard to Drug Abuse*. Report of the Secretariat, 46th session, 8–17 April 2003, Vienna

Contreras, J and S Johnson (2004) 'The migration economy' *Newsweek International*, January, Issue 19 http://msnbc.msn.com/id/3927843/site/newsweek/

Cordesman, A (1999) 'Transitions in the Middle East' Address to the 8th Middle East Policy-makers Conference, 9 September 1999

Cowen, T (2002) *Creative Destruction: How Globalization is Changing the World's Cultures*. Princeton University Press, Princeton

Crawford, M (1992) 'The world in a shopping mall' in M Sorkin (ed) *Variations on a Theme Park: The New American City and the End of Public Space*. Noonday, New York, pp3–30

Curry, J (2000) 'Homelessness and HIV, ACRIA update' **9**(3), Summer, AIDS Community Research Initiative of America, p7-8

Davis, M (2000) *Magical Urbanism: Latinos Reinvent the US Big City*. Verso, New York and London

Day, K (1999) 'Embassies and sanctuaries: women's experiences of race and fear in public space' *Environment and Planning D: Society and Space* **17**: 307–328

Day, K (2003) 'New urbanism and the challenges of designing for diversity' *Journal of Planning Education and Research* **23**: 83–95

de Ferranti, D et al (2004) *Inequality in Latin America and the Caribbean: Breaking with History?* World Bank, Washington, DC

De Varennes, F (2003) *Strangers in Foreign Lands. Diversity, Vulnerability and the Rights of Migrant*. UNESCO, Paris.

Devereux, M, B Lockwood and M Redoano (2003) 'Is there a "race to the bottom" in corporate taxes? An overview of recent research', Centre for the Study of Globalization and Regionalization (CSGR) at the University of Warwick, Warwick, UK, October

Dixon, A and K Mason (2000) 'Women hard hit by transition' *International Herald Tribune*, 1 March http://lnweb18.worldbank.org/eca/eca.nsf/0/3A20414A4BD3F21585256C130050F5DD?OpenDocument

Douglass, M (1995) 'Global interdependence and urbanization' in McGee, T and I Robinson (eds) *The Mega-urban Regions of Southeast Asia*. UBC, Vancouver

Douglass, M (2000) 'Mega-urban regions and world city formation' *Urban Studies* **37**(12):2315–35

Douglass, M and J Friedmann (eds) (1998) *Cities for Citizens: Planning and the Rise of Civil Society in a Global Age*. John Wiley and Sons, Chichester

Downs, A (1994) *New Visions for Metropolitan America*. Brookings Institution, Washington, DC

Drennan, V et al (1986) 'Health visitors and homeless families' *Journal of Environmental Health Research* **59**(11): 340–342

Dupont, V (2004) 'Socio-spatial differentiation and residential segregation in Delhi: a question of scale?' *Geoforum* **35**(2): 157–175

Durand-Lasserve, A (2004) 'Land for housing the poor in African cities' in N Hamdi (ed) *Urban Futures: Economic Growth and Poverty Reduction*. ITDG Publishing, London

ECLAC (2002) *Meeting the Millennium Poverty Reduction Targets in Latin America and the Caribbean*. ECLAC, Santiago

ECPAT International (End Child Prostitution, Child Pornography and Trafficking of Children for Sexual Purposes) (1999) *A Step Forward: The third report on the implementation of the Agenda for Action adopted at the World Congress against Commercial Sexual Exploitation of Children*, ECPAT, Bangkok

ECPAT International (2004) 'Programmes', ECPAT web site, Bangkok www.ecpat.net

Edgar, B, J Doherty and H Meert (2002) 'Review of statistics on homelessness in Europe' *European Observatory on Homelessness*, November, p5

Edgington, D W and T A Hutton (2000) 'Multiculturalism and local government in Vancouver' *Western Geography* **10/11**(1): 1–29

Ellin, N (ed) (1997) *Architecture of Fear*. Princeton Architectural Press, New York

El-Shakhs, S (1997) 'Towards appropriate urban development policy in emerging megacities in Africa' in C Rakodi (ed) *The Urban Challenge in Africa*. UNU, Tokyo, pp497–526

Environment and Health Project Brief (2003) 'Urban poor child health in Asia and the Near East', **14**, April

Erendil, A T and Z Ulusoy (2002) 'Reinvention of tradition as an urban image: the case of Ankara Citadel' *Environment and Planning B – Planning and Design* **29**: 655–672

Eurostat (1996) *European Community Household Panel*, Eurostat

Evans, B (1999) *The Plight of Foreign Workers in Saudi Arabi.*, Center for Middle Eastern Studies at the University of Texas, Austin

Evans, G (2003) 'Hard-branding the cultural city: from Prado to Prada' *International Journal of Urban and Regional Research* **27**(2): 417–40

Evans, P (ed) (2002) *Livable Cities? Urban Struggles for Livelihood and Sustainability*. University of California Press, Berkeley

Faludi, A and A J van der Valk (1994) *Rule and Order: Dutch Planning Doctrine in the Twentieth Century*. Kluwer Academic Publishers, Dordrecht

Faludi, A and B Waterhout (2002) *The Making of the European Spatial Development Perspective: No Masterplan*. Routledge, London

FEANTSA (2002) *Immigration and Homelessness in the European Union. Analysis and Overview of the Impact of Immigration on Homeless Services in the European Union*. FEANTSA, Brussels

Fejos, Z (2001) 'Old and new in urban culture: dilemmas in interpreting recent urban transformation in Budapest' in R Kiss and A Paladi-Kovacs (eds) *Times, Places, Passages: Ethnological Approaches in the New Millenium; Plenary Papers of the 7th SIEF Conference*, Budapest, pp79–108

Fernandez Guell, J M (1997) *Planificacion estrategia de cuidades*, Gustavo Gili, Barcelona

Ferreira, D and K Khatami (1996) 'Financing private infrastructure in developing countries' World Bank Discussion Paper No 343, Washington, DC

First International Seminar on Women's Safety: Making the Links (2002) *Femmes et Villes*. Conference proceedings May 2002, Montreal, www.femmesetvilles.org

Fischer, C (1984) *The Urban Experience* (2nd revised ed). Harcourt Brace Jovanovich, San Diego

Fischer, C S (1994) *America Calling: A Social History of the Telephone to 1940*. University of California Press, Berkeley

Fitch, R (1977) 'Planning New York' in R E Alcaly and D Mermelstein (eds) *The Fiscal Crisis of American Cities*. Vintage, New York, Chapter 16

Florida, R L (2002) *The Rise of the Creative Class: and how It's Transforming Work, Leisure, Community and Everyday Life*. Basic Books, New York

Flyvbjerg, B, N Bruzelius and W Rothengatter (2003) *Megaprojects and Risk; an Anatomy of Ambition*. Cambridge University Press, Cambridge

Forrest, J, M Poulsen and R Johnston (2003) 'Everywhere different? Globalisation and the impact of international migration on Sydney and Melbourne' *Geoforum* **34**(4): 499–510

Freire M and M Polese (2003) *Connecting Cities with Macro-economic Concerns: The Missing Link*. The World Bank and the Institut National de la Recherche Scientifique, Universite de Quebec, Washington, DC

French Federation of Town Planning Agencies (2001) *Report to the 25th Special Session of the General Assembly of the United Nations*, June 2001, New York

Friedmann, J (1973) *Retracking America: A Theory of Transactive Planning*. Anchor/Doubleday, Garden City

Friedmann, J (1986) 'The world city hypothesis' *Development and Change* **17**(1): 69–83

Friedmann, J (1987) *Planning in the Public Domain: From Knowledge to Action*. Princeton University Press, Princeton

Friedmann, J (1995a) 'Where we stand: a decade of world city research' in P L Knox and P J Taylor (eds) *World Cities in a World System*. Cambridge University Press, Cambridge, pp21–47

Friedmann, J (1995b) 'The world city hypothesis' in P L Knox and P J Taylor (eds) *World Cities in a World System*. Cambridge University Press, Cambridge, Appendix

Friedmann, J (2000) 'The good city: in defense of utopian thinking' *International Journal of Urban and Regional Research* **24**: 460–72

Friedmann, J (2001) 'Intercity networks in a globalizing era' in A J Scott, (ed) *Global City-regions: Trends, Theory, Policy*. Oxford University Press, Oxford, pp119–138

Friedmann, J (2002a) 'City of fear or open city?' *Journal of the American Planning Association* **68**:237–243

Friedmann, J (2002b) *The Prospect of Cities*. University of Minnesota Press, Minneapolis

Friedmann, J (2004) 'Hong Kong, Vancouver and beyond: strategic spatial planning and the longer range' *Planning Theory and Practice* **5**: 1

Friedmann, J (forthcoming) *China's Urban Transition: An Interpretation*

Friedmann, J and G Wolff (1982) 'World city formation: an agenda for research and action' *International Journal of Urban and Regional Research* **6**(3): 309–344

Fry, S, B Cousins and K Olivola (2002) *Health of Children Living in Urban Slums in Asia and the Near East: Review of Existing Literature and Data*. Environmental Health Project, USAID, Washington, DC

Fuccaro, N (2001) 'Visions of the city urban studies on the gulf' *Middle East Studies Association Bulletin* **35**(2): 175–187

Galster, G (1998) *An Econometric Model of the Urban Opportunity Structure: Cumulative Causation among City Markets, Social Problems, and Underserved Areas*. Fannie Mae Foundation, Washington, DC

Gamba, V (1999) *Small arms in Southern Africa: Reflections on the Extent of the Problem and its Management Potential*, ISS

Monograph Series No. 42, Institute for Security Studies (ISS), Pretoria

Garcia Canclini, N (2001) *Consumers and Citizens*, translated by G Yudice. University of Minnesota Press, Minneapolis

Garreau, J (1991) *Edge Cities: Life on the New Frontier*. Doubleday, New York

Geschiere, P (1995) 'University of Leiden, Culture: Pandora's Box?' Paper presented at the Good Governance for Africa: Whose Governance Conference, University of Limburg and ECDPM, Maastricht, 23–24 November 1995

Ghosh, A (2003) 'Down and out in Europe' *Time Magazine*, 10 February www.time.com/time/europe/magazine/2003/0210/homeless/story.html

Gibson, W (2003) *Pattern Recognition*. Putnam's Sons, New York

Giddens, A (1990) *The Consequences of Modernity*. Stanford University Press, Stanford

Glass, R (1964) *London: Aspects of Change*. Centre for Urban Studies and MacGibbon and Kee, London

Gleeson, B (1998) 'Justice and the disabling city' in R Fincher and J Jacobs (eds) *Cities of Difference*. Guilford, London

Global Development Research Centre (1999) *Prioritizing Cultural Heritage in the Asia-Pacific Region: Role of City Governments*, www.gdrc.org/heritage/heritage-priority.html

Gomez, M V (1998) 'Reflective images: the case of urban regeneration in Glasgow and Bilbao' *International Journal of Urban and Regional Research* **22**(1): 106–21

González, G (2002) 'Latin America: more poverty, fewer social services', www.ipsnews.net/FSM2003/eng/note1.shtml

Gopalakrishnan, A (2003) 'A house in disorder' *Frontline* **10**: 20, www.frontlineonnet.com

Gottdiener, M (2000) *The New Urban Sociology* (2nd ed). McGraw Hill, Boston

Gottdiener, M (2001) *The Theming of America: American Dreams, Media Fantasies, and Themed Environments*. Westview, Boulder

Gottmann, J (1961) *Megalopolis*. MIT Press, Cambridge

Graham, S and S Marvin (2001) *Splintering Urbanism: Networked Infrastructures, Technological Mobilities, and the Urban Condition*. Routledge, London and New York

Gramberg, A (2003) 'Macro-economy of the Russian regions', Paper presented at the 34th Congress of the European Regional Science Association, October 2003, Jyväskylä

Gras, A (2003) *Fragilité de la Puissance*. Fayard, Paris

Gras, N S B (1922) *An Introduction to Economic History*. Harper, New York

Grengs, J (2002) 'Community-based planning as a source of political change: the transit equity movement of Los Angeles' Bus Riders Union' *Journal of the American Planning Association* **68**(2): 165–178

Griffiths, R (1995) 'Cultural strategies and new modes of urban intervention' *Cities* **12**(4): 253–265

Grootaert, C and J Braithwaite (1998) *Poverty Correlates and Indicator-based Targeting in Eastern Europe and the Former Soviet Union*. Poverty Reduction and Economic Management Network, World Bank, Washington, DC

Guilbaut, S (1983) *How New York Stole the Idea of Modern Art*, translated by A Goldhammer. University of Chicago Press, Chicago

Habitat Debate (2003) **9**(2) June www.un-habitat.org

Hall, E T (1969) *The Hidden Dimension*. Double Day, Garden City, New York

Hall, P (1998) *Cities in Civilization*. Pantheon Books, New York

Hall, P and U Pfeiffer (2000a) *Urban Future 21: A Global Agenda for 21st Century Cities*. E&FN Spon, London

Hall, P and U Pfeiffer (2000b) *Urban 21: The Report of the Global Commission on the Urban Future*. E&FN Spon, London

Hancock, M (2002) 'Subjects of heritage in urban Southern India' *Environment and Planning D: Society and Space* **20**: 693–717

Hannigan, J (1998) *Fantasy City: Pleasure and Profit in the Postmodern Metropolis*. Routledge, London

Harris, J and M Todaro (1960) 'Migration, unemployment, and development: a two sector analysis' *American Economic Review* **60**(3): 126–142

Harris, N and A Hooper (forthcoming) 'Rediscovering the "spatial" in public policy and planning: an examination of the spatial content of sectoral policy documents' *Planning Theory and Practice*

Harrison, P (2001a) 'Romance and tragedy in (post)modern planning: a pragmatist's perspective' *International Planning Studies* **6**(1): 69–88

Harrison, P (2001b) 'The genealogy of South Africa's integrated development plan' *Third World Planning Review* **23**(2): 175–193

Harrison, P and M Kahn (1999) 'Ambiguities of change: the case of the planning profession in the Province of Kwa-Zulu, Natal, South Africa' *Planning Africa 2002: Regenerating Africa Through Planning*, http://saplanners.org.za/SAPC/pasum.htm

Harvey, D (1989) *The Condition of Postmodernity*. Blackwell, Oxford

Harvey, D (2003) 'The right to the city' *International Journal of Urban and Regional Research* **27**: 939–941

Hasan, A (2002) 'The changing nature of the informal sector in Karachi as a result of global restructuring and liberalization' *Environment and Urbanization* **14**(1): 69–78

Hayden D (1995) *The Power of Place*. MIT Press, Cambridge MA

Healey, P (1997) *Collaborative Planning: Shaping Places in Fragmented Societies*. Macmillan, London

Healey, P (2004) 'The treatment of space and place in the new strategic spatial planning of Europe' *International Journal of Urban and Regional Research* **28**: 45–67

Hensli, J M (2004) *Essentials of Sociology: A Down to Earth Approach* (5th ed). Allyn and Bacon, Boston

Herrschel, T and P Newman (2002) *Governance of Europe's City Regions: Planning Policy and Politics*. Routledge, London

Hicks, U (1974) *The Large City: A World Problem*. Macmillan, London

Hirschowitz, R, S Worku and M Orkin (2000) *Quantitative Research Findings on Rape in South Africa*. Statistics South Africa, Pretoria

Horton, J (1995) *The Politics of Diversity: Immigration, Resistance, and Change in Monterey Park, California*. Temple University Press, Philadelphia

Hu, H (2003) 'Globalization and huge urban projects: the case of Shanghai' in Delft University *Globalization and Large Urban Projects*. Delft University Press, Delft

Hughes, D (2001) *The "Natasha" Trade: Transnational Sex Trafficking*. International Center of the United States National Institute of Justice (NIJ), Washington DC

Hughes, D and T Denisova (2003) *Trafficking in Women from Ukraine*. International Center of the United States National Institute of Justice (NIJ), Washington DC

Hugo, G (2003) *Migrants and their Integration: Contemporary Issues and Implications*. National Centre for Social Applications of GIS, University of Adelaide

Human Rights Watch (1995) *Violence Against Women in South Africa: State Response to Domestic Violence and Rape.* Human Rights Watch, New York

Hutton, T A (2004) 'Service industries, globalization, and urban restructuring within the Asia-Pacific: new development trajectories and planning responses' *Progress in Planning* **61**: 1–74

Iglicka, K (2001) 'Poland: between geopolitical shifts and emerging migratory patterns' Migration working paper n°42. Institute for Social Studies, University of Warsaw.

ILO (International Labour Organization) (2001) 'Child labour in developed economies', ILO Working Paper, ILO, Geneva

ILO (2004) *Global Employment Trends 2004.* ILO, Geneva

IMF (International Monetary Fund) (2003) *Balance of Payments Statistics Yearbook.* IMF, Washington DC

Indergaard, M (2004) *Silicon Alley: The Rise and Fall of a New Media District.* Routledge, New York

Indonesia Crisis Bulletin (1999) 'High prevalence of acute malnutrition in urban slums', Hellen Keller International, **1**(7), November, http://hkiasiapacific.org/index.html

Ingram, G K (1997) 'Patterns of metropolitan development: what have we learned' *Policy Research Working Paper* 1841. World Bank, Washington, DC

Ingram, G K and A Carroll (1978) *The Spatial Structure of Latin American Cities.* World Bank, Urban and Regional Report No 79–9, Washington, DC

Interpol (2004) *International Crime Statistics.* Interpol, Lyons, www.interpol.int

IOM (International Organization for Migration) (1998) *Information Campaign Against Trafficking in Women from Ukraine* Research Report, IOM, Geneva

IOM (2003) *World Migration 2003. Managing Migration Challenges and Responses for People on the Move.* Volume 2, IOM, Geneva

Jacobs, J (1961) *The Death and Life of Great American Cities.* Random House, New York

Jauch, H (2002) 'Export processing zones and the quest for sustainable development: a Southern African perspective' *Environment and Urbanization* **14**(1): 101–113

Jayasuriya, S (2002) 'Globalization, equity and poverty: the South Asian experience', Paper prepared for the 4th Annual Global Development Conference of the Global Development Network on Globalization and Equity, Cairo, 19–21 January

Jones, A et al (2002) *Shelter Homeless to Home: An Evaluation.* www.homeless.org

Jones, G (2001) 'Studying extended metropolitan regions in Southeast Asia', Paper presented at the 24th Conference of the IUSSP, Salvador, Brazil

Jones, G A and A Varley (1999) 'The reconquest of the historic centre: urban conservation and gentrification in Puebla, Mexico' *Environment and Planning A* **31**: 1547–1566

Judd, D R and D Simpson (2003) 'Reconstructing the local state: the role of external constituencies in building urban tourism' *American Behavioral Scientist* **46**: 1056–1069

Justice Canada (1999) 'Canada's Youth Justice Renewal Initiative', Youth Justice Information Network Bulletin No. 2, Justice Canada, Ottawa

Kanji, N (1996) *Review of Urbanization Issues Affecting Children and Women in Eastern and Southern African Region.* UNICEF Eastern and Southern African Region, Nairobi

Kaufmann, D and A Kraay (2003) *Governance and Growth in the Very Long Run: Updated Indicators, New Results.* Global Corruption Report, Transparency International, www.worldbank.org/wbi/governance/pdf/kaufmann_papers.pdf

Kearns, G and C Philo (eds) (1995) *Selling Places.* Pergamon, Oxford

Keivani, R, A Parsa and S McGreal (2001) 'Globalisation, institutional structures and real estate markets in central European cities' *Urban Studies* **38**(13): 2457–2476

Keivani, R, A Parsa and S McGreal (2002) 'Institutions and urban change in a globalising world: the case of Warsaw' *Cities* **19**(3): 183–193.

Keller, D A, M Koch and K Selle (1996) '"Either/or" and "and": first impressions of a journey into the planning cultures of four countries' *Planning Perspectives* **11**: 41–54

Kemmis, D (1995) *The Good City and the Good Life* Houghton Mifflin Company, Boston

Kharoufi, M (1996) 'Urbanization and urban research in the Arab world' UNESCO, MOST Discussion Paper Series, No 11

Kloosterman, R and J Rath (2001) 'Immigrant entrepreneurs in advanced economies: mixed embeddedness further explored' Special Issue on Immigrant Entrepreneurship, *Journal of Ethnic and Migration Studies* **27**(2): 189–202

Kloosterman, R and S Musterd (2001) 'The polycentric urban region: towards a research agenda' Urban Studies **38**(4): 623–633

Knox, P and P J Taylor (1986) *World Cities in a World System.* Cambridge University Press, Cambridge

Kohler, B and M Wissen (2003) 'Globalizing protest: urban conflicts and global social movements' *International Journal of Urban and Regional Research* **27**: 942–951

Kooijman, D and G Wigmans (2003) 'Managing the city: flows and places at Rotterdam central station' *City* 7(3): 301–326

Kusno, A (2000) *Beyond the Postcolonial: Architecture, Urban Space, and Political Cultures in Indonesia* Routledge, New York

Kuzmin, A (2002) 'General'nyi plan razvitija Moskvy do 2020 goda: traditsii i novatorvstvo' *Arkhitektura i Stroitel'stvo Moskvy* **5–6**: 5

Kyem, P A K (2000) 'Embedding GIS applications into resource management and planning activities of local and indigenous communities: a desirable innovation or a destabilizing enterprise?' *Journal of Planning Education And Research* **20** (2): 176–186

Kyu Sik Lee (1989) *The Location of Jobs in a Developing Metropolis.* Oxford University Press, New York

Kyu Sik Lee, A Anas and Gi-Taik Oh (1999) 'Costs of infrastructure deficiencies for manufacturing in Nigerian, Indonesian, and Thai cities' *Urban Studies* **36**(12): 2135–2149

Ladanyi, J (2000) 'The Hungarian neoliberal state, ethnic classification, and the creation of a Roma underclass' in I Szelenyi and R Emigh (eds) *Poverty, Ethnicity, and Gender in Eastern Europe.* Praeger, Westport

Laguerre, M (2004) *Urban Multiculturalism and Globalization.* Palgrave Macmillan, London

Landry, C and F Bianchini (1995) *The Creative City.* Demos, London

Laquian, A (1995) 'The governance of mega-urban regions' in McGee, T and I Robinson (eds) *The Mega-urban Regions of Southeast Asia.* University of British Columbia, Vancouver

Lazzaretti, L (2003) 'City of art as a high culture local system and cultural districtualization processes: the cluster of art restoration in Florence' *International Journal of Urban and Regional Research* **27**(3): 635–48

Leckie, S (ed) (2003) *National Perspectives on Housing Rights'.* Nijhoff, New York

Lehrer, U (2004) 'Reality or image? Place selling at Potsdamer Platz, Berlin' in INURA (International Network for Urban Research and Action) (ed) *The Contested Metropolis: Seven Cities at the Beginning of the Twenty-first Century.* Birkhäuser, Berlin, pp45–52

Lindblom, C E (1959) 'The science of muddling through' *Public Administration Review* **19**(2): 79–99

Lindblom, C E (1979) 'Still muddling, not yet through' *Public Administration Review*, **39**(6): 517–26

Lloyd, M G and J McCarthy (2002) 'Asymmetrical devolution, institutional capacity and spatial planning innovation' in Y Rydin and A Thornley (eds) *Planning in the UK: Agendas for the New Millennium.* Ashgate, Aldershot

Logan, J R and H Molotch (1987) *Urban Fortunes.* University of California Press, Berkeley

Long, C (2002) 'A history of urban planning policy and heritage protection in Vientiane, Laos' *International Development Planning Review* **24**(2): 127–144

Longo, G (1996) *A Guide to Great American Places.* Urban Initiatives, New York

Louw, A and M Shaw (1997) *Stolen opportunities: the impact of crime on South Africa's poor,* Institute for Security Studies (ISS) Monograph Series, No. 14, Institute for Security Studies, Pretoria

Lubeck, P M and B Britts (2002) 'Muslim civil society in urban public spaces; globalization, discursive shifts, and social movements' in J Eade and C Mele (eds) *Understanding the City: Contemporary and Future Perspectives.* Blackwell, Oxford pp305–336

Magalong, M D (2003) 'The search for P-town: Filipino American place(s) in Los Angeles' *Critical Planning* **10**, Summer:13–28

Mahler, S J (2000) 'Migration and transnational issues. Recent trends and prospects for 2020' Working Paper no 4, Intitut für Iberoamerika-Kunde 2000, Hamburg

Malmberg, A, O Solvell and I Zander (1996) 'Spatial clustering, local accumulation of knowledge, and firm competitiveness' *Geografiska Annaler*, Series B, Human Geography **78**(2): 85–97

Markusen, A, G Schrock, and M Cameron (2004) *The Artistic Dividend Revisited.* Project on Regional and Industrial Economics, Humphrey Institute of Public Affairs, University of Minnesota, Minneapolis

Martinotti, G (1996) 'Four populations: human settlements and social morphology in contemporary metropolis' *European Review* **4**(1): 3–23

Martinotti, G (1997) *Metropoli: La Nuova Morfologia Dociale della Città.* 11 Mulino, Bologna

Martinotti, G (with C Pozzi) (2004) 'From Seattle to Salonicco (and beyond). Political tourism in the Second generation Metropolis' *Urban Economics Review* **1**: 37–61

Marvin, S and T May (2003) 'City futures: views from the centre' *City* 7(2): 213–26

Masser, I, O Svidén and M Wegener (1992) *The Geography of Europe's Futures.* Belhaven, London

Massey, D and N C Denton (1993) *American Apartheid.* Harvard University Press, Cambridge

Masuku, S (2002) 'Prevention is better than cure – addressing violent crime in South Africa' *South Africa Crime Quarterly* 2, November, Institute for Security Studies, Pretoria

Masuku, S and A Louw (2001) *Towards a Crime Reduction Strategy in Highveld East Municipality,* Institute for Security Studies (ISS) (Unpublished report), Pretoria

May, A (2003) 'Maasai migrations: implications for HIV/AIDS and social change in Tanzania', University of Colorado, Colorado

McCormick, B and J Wahba (2002) *Return International Migration and Geographical Inequality: the Case of Egypt.* Department of Economics, University of Southampton

McEvedy, C (1972) *The Penguin Atlas of Modern History (to 1815).* Penguin Books, London

McGee, T (1995) 'Metrofitting the emerging mega-urban regions of ASEAN' in T McGee and I Robinson (eds) *The Mega-urban Regions of Southeast Asia*. University of British Columbia, Vancouver

McGee, T G and I M Robinson (eds) (1995) *The Mega-urban Regions of Southeast Asia*. University of British Columbia Press, Vancouver

McGuire, S (2003) 'Ireland's New Face' *Newsweek International Edition*, 15 December, http://msnbc.msn.com/id/3660204/ Accessed March 28, 2004

McGuirk, P (2003) 'Producing the capacity to govern in global Sydney: a multiscaled account' *Journal of Urban Affair* **25**(2): 201–33

Middleton, A (2003) 'Informal traders and planners in the regeneration of historic city centres: the case of Quito, Ecuador' *Progress in Planning* **59**: 71–123

Miller, T, N Govil, J McMurria, and R Maxwell (2001) *Global Hollywood*. British Film Institute, London

Mishra, R K (1997) 'National civil service system in India: a critical view', Paper presented at the Civil Service Systems in Comparative Perspective Conference, School of Public and Environmental Affairs, Indiana University, Bloomington, 5–8 April

Mitchell, W J (2000) *E-topia. Urban-Life, Jim – But Not as We Know It*. MIT Press, Cambridge

Mohanty, P K (1996) 'Urban development planning in India' in J Stubbs and G Clarke (eds) *Megacity Management in the Asian and Pacific Region*. ADB, Manila pp286–97

Mollard, C (1977) *L'enjeu du Centre Georges Pompidou*. Union General d'Editions, Paris

Molotch, H (1996) 'LA as design product: how art works in a regional economy' in A J Scott and E W Soja (eds) *The City: Los Angeles and Urban Theory at the End of the Twentieth Century*. University of California Press, Berkeley and Los Angeles

Molotch, H (2003) *Where Stuff Comes From*. Routledge, New York

Montaner, J M (2002) *Las Formas del Siglo XX*. Editorial Gustavo Gili, SA, Barcelona

Moomaw, R and A M Shatter (1996) 'Urbanization and economic development: a bias towards large cities' *Journal of Urban Economics* **40** (July): 13–37

Morales, G A (2002) 'Situación de los trabajadores migrantes en América Central', Programa de Migraciones Internacionales, Oficina Internacional del Trabajo (ILO), Ginebra

Moser, C (1996) *Confronting Crisis: A Summary of Household Responses to Poverty and Vulnerability in Four Poor Urban Communities*. Environmentally Sustainable Development Studies and Monographs Series 7, World Bank, Washington, DC

Mulenga, M (2000) 'SADC migration policies not harmonised' *Africa News Online*, 8 March.

Murphy, B (2000) *On The Street: How We Created Homelessness*. J Gordon, Shillingford

National Coalition for the Homeless (1999), April, www.nationalhomeless.org/hivaids.html

National Research Council (2003) *Cities Transformed: Demographic Change and its Implications in the Developing World*. Panel on Urban Population Dynamics, National Academies Press, Washington, DC

Nayak, A (2003) *Race, Place and Globalization: Youth Cultures in a Changing World*. Berg, New York

Nevarez, L (2003) *New Money, Nice Town: How Capital Works in the New Urban Economy*. Routledge, New York

Newman, G (ed) (1999) *Global Report on Crime and Justice*. Oxford University Press/United Nations, New York

Newman, H K (2002) 'Race and the tourist bubble in downtown Atlanta' *Urban Affairs Review* **37**: 301–321

Newman, O (1980) *Community of Interest*. Doubleday, New York

New Zealand (2000) *Police Youth at Risk Programmes – Executive Summary of Evaluation Reports Covering the Period 1 July 1997 to 30 June 1999*. New Zealand Police, Wellington

NIJ (National Institute of Justice) (1998) 'Trends in juvenile violence in European Countries', NIJ Research Preview based on a presentation by Christian Pfeiffer, Kriminologisches Forschungsinstitut Niedersachsen, Hanover, Germany/US Department of Justice, Washington, DC

Nuvolati, G (2002) *Popolazioni in Movimento, Città in Trasformazione*. Il Mulino, Bologna

OAU (Organisation of African Unity)/UNICEF (1992) *Africa's Children, Africa's Future*, Background Sectoral Papers, Dakar, Senegal

O'Brien, K J and Lianjiang Li (2004) 'Suing the local state: administrative litigation in rural China' *The China Journal* **51**: 75–95

Obudho, R A (1997) 'Nairobi: national capital and regional hub' in C Rakodi (ed) *The Urban Challenge in Africa*. United Nations University, Tokyo, pp292–336

Ochieng'-Akatch, S (1995) Evaluative review of urban planning practice and experiences in the Africa region' in UNCHS (Habitat) *A Reappraisal of the Urban Planning Process*. UNCHS (Habitat), Nairobi, pp39–56

Ockman, J and A Vidler (2001) 'Wrap Session' *Artforum International* **39**(10): 141–51

O'Connor, P, K Daly and L Hinds (1998) 'An international perspective on problems and solutions' Presentation on Australia to Youth Justice System Conference, Canadian Research Institute for Law and the Family, Calgary

OECD (Organisation for Economic Co-operation and Development) (2002) *Poverty Dynamics in Six OECD Countries*. OECD, Paris

OECD (2003) *Trends in International Migration*. OECD, Paris

Ohmae, K (2001) 'How to invite prosperity from the global economy into a region' in A J Scott (ed) *Global City-regions: Trends, Theory, Policy*. Oxford University Press, Oxford pp33–43

Olds, K (2001) *Globalization and Urban Change: Capital, Culture, and Pacific Rim Megaprojects*. Oxford University Press, Oxford

ONDCP (Office of National Drug Control Policy) (2002) *Estimation of Cocaine Availability 1996–2000*, ONDCP, Washington DC

Orfield, M (1997) *Chicago Metropolitics: A Regional Agenda for Community Stability*. Brookings Institution, Washington, DC

Oucho, O J and S Peberdy (2001) *Migration and Poverty in Southern Africa*. Southern African Migration Project, Cape Town

Pangestu, M (2000) *The Social Impact of Globalization in Southest Asia*. OECD Development Centre, Technical Paper No 187, Paris

Papper, R A, M E Holmes, and M N Popovich (2004) 'Middletown media studies: media multitasking…and how much people really use the media' *International Digital Media and Arts Association Journal* **1**(1), www.bsu.edu/web/icommunication/news/idmaajournal.pdf, accessed 25 March 2004

Paringaux, R P (1998) 'Prostitution takes a turn for the West' *Le Monde*, 24 May 1998

Parrott, J (1999) 'Bolstering and diversifying the New York City economy', Paper delivered at CUNY Graduate Center, 2 December, New York

Peden, M, R Scurfield, D Sleet, D Mohan, A A Hyder, E Jarawan and C Mathers (2004) *World Report on Road Traffic Injury Prevention*. WHO, Geneva

Pellegrino, A (2000) *Trends in International Migration in Latin America and the Caribbean* UNESCO, Paris

Pendakur, V (1995) 'Gridlock in the Slopopolis' in T McGee and I Robinson (eds) *The Mega-urban Regions of Southeast Asia*. University of British Columbia, Vancouver

Pérouse, J-F (1998) 'Istanbul, an Eurasian metropolitan area in progress', Working paper for the MESA 32nd Annual Meeting, Chicago

Pezzoli, K (1998) *Human Settlements and Planning for Ecological Sustainability: The Case of Mexico City*. MIT Press, Cambridge

Pfeiffer, C (1998) 'Juvenile crime and violence in Europe' in M Tonry (ed) *Crime and Justice. A Review of Research*, University of Chicago Press, Chicago

Pichler-Milanovich, N (2000) 'Urban housing markets in Central and Eastern Europe: convergence, divergence and policy collapse', Paper presented at the ENHR Conference on Housing in the 21st Century: Fragmentation and Reorientation, June, Gavle, Sweden

Piermay, J (1997) 'Kinshasa: a reprieved megacity?' in C Rakodi (ed) *The Urban Challenge in Africa*. United Nations University, Tokyo

Pirenne, H (1980) *Le città del Medioevo*. Laterza, Bari

Plaza, B (2000) 'Evaluating the influence of a large cultural artifact in the attraction of tourism: the Guggenheim Museum Bilbao case' *Urban Affairs Review* **36**(2): 264–274

Pohl, R (2001) *Homeless in Canada*. Ottawa Innercity Ministries, Ottawa

Polese, M and R Stren (eds) (2000) *The Social Sustainability of Cities: Diversity and Their Management of Change*. University of Toronto Press, Toronto

Pollard, J and M Storper (1996) 'A tale of twelve cities: metropolitan employment change in dynamic industries in the 1980s' *Economic Geography* **72**(1): 1–22

Portes, A and A Stepick (1993) *City on the Edge: The Transformation of Miami*. University of California Press, Berkeley and Los Angeles

Porteus, K (1999) *Tirisano: Towards an Intervention Strategy to Address Youth Violence in Schools Working Document*. South Africa Secretariat for Safety and Security, Department for Education and the National Youth Commission, Pretoria

Poulsen, M, Johnston, R and Forrest, J (2002) 'Plural cities and ethnic enclaves: introducing a measurement procedure for comparative study' *International Journal of Urban and Regional Research* **26**(2): 229ff

Pratt A (in press) 'Mapping the cultural industries: regionalisation; the example of Southeast England' in A J Scott (ed) *The Cultural Industries and the Production of Culture*. Routledge, London

Pretorius, A (2000) 'One in four men say they are rapists', *Johannesburg Sunday Times*, June 25, 2000

Public Employees for Environmental Responsibility (2004) *Can You Hear Me Now? Cell Towers Spreading throughout National Park Systems*. Public Employees for Environmental Responsibility, Thursday, 8 April 2004, Washington, DC

Purcell, M (2003) 'Citizenship and the right to the global city: reimagining the capitalist world order' *International Journal of Urban and Regional Research* **27**: 564–90

Qadeer, M A (1997) 'Pluralistic planning for multicultural cities: the Canadian practice' *Journal of the American Planning Association* **63**: 481–494

Rakodi, C (ed) (1997) *The Urban Challenge in Africa: Growth and Management of its Large Cities*. UNU, Tokyo

Rantisi, N M (2004) 'The ascendance of New York fashion' *International Journal of Urban and Regional Research* **28**(1): 86–106

Rath, J, R Kloosterman, and E Razin (eds) (2002) 'The economic context, embeddedness and immigrant entrepreneurs' *Special Issue. International Journal of Entrepreneurial Behavior and Research* **8**(1–2)

Rauen, M (2001) 'Reflections on the space of flows: the Guggenheim Museum Bilbao' *Journal of Arts Management, Law and Society* **30**(4): 283–301

Revenga, A, D Ringold and W M Tracy (2002) *Poverty and Ethnicity: A Cross-country Study of Roma Poverty in Central Europe*. World Bank Technical Paper No 531, World Bank, Washington, DC

Reyneke, E (2000) *Small Arms and Light Weapons in Africa: Illicit Proliferation, Circulation and Trafficking*. Institute for Security Studies (ISS), Pretoria

Reyniers, A (2000) 'Gypsies: trapped on the fringes of Europe' *UNESCO Courier*, June www.unesco.org/courier/2000_06/uk/

Rifé (undated) 'Does the design of the US and EU urban policy differ substantially?', www.ub.es/graap/WP0900_Termes.PDF

Rimmer, P (1995) 'Moving goods, people and information: putting the ASEAN mega-urban regions in context' in T McGee and I Robinson (eds) *The Mega-urban Regions of Southeast Asia*. University of British Columbia, Vancouver

Ringold, D, M A Orenstein and E Wilkens (2003) *Roma in an Expanding Europe: Breaking the Poverty Cycle*. World Bank, Washington, DC

Robertshaw, R, A Louw and A Mtani (2001) *Crime in Dar es Salaam – Results of a City Victim Survey*. Institute for Security Studies (ISS), Pretoria

Rodgers, J (2003) 'Iraq freedom and poverty tug-of-war', BBC News, 18 December

Rodrik, D with F Rodríguez (2001) 'Trade policy and economic growth: a skeptic's guide to the cross-national evidence' in B Bernanke and K S Rogoff (eds) *Macroeconomics Annual 2000*. MIT Press for National Bureau of Economic Research, Cambridge

Romano, M (1993) *L'estetica della Citta Europea: Forme a Immagini*. Einaudi, Turin

Ruble, B A (1995) *Money Sings: The Changing Politics of Urban Space in Post-Soviet Yaroslavl*. Cambridge University Press, Cambridge

Ruble, B A (1990) *Leningrad: Shaping of a Soviet City*. University of California Press, Berkeley

Ruble, B, R Stren and J Tulchin (eds) (2000) *Urban Governance Around the World*. Woodrow Wilson International Center for Scholars, Comparative Urban Studies Project, Washington, DC

Rumford, C (2004) 'The organization of European space: regions, networks, and places' *International Journal of Urban and Regional Research* **28**: 225–233

Rycus, M (1995) 'The role of urban planning in crime reduction' *City Planning and Management News* Winter 1995–1996 Issue, American Planning Association

Saikia, U (2002) *Adjustment Process of Immigrants in the Midst of Ethnic Conflict: a Case of Bangladeshi Immigrants in India*. Development & Research Services, New Delhi

Salet, W and A Faludi (eds) (2000) *The Revival of Spatial Strategic Planning*. Royal Netherlands Academy of Arts and Sciences, Amsterdam

Salmon, F P (1999) *Globalizacion, Gobernabilidad y Metropolizacion: El caso de Santa Cruz*. Foro Internacional sobre Metropolizacion, Santa Cruz, Bolivia

Sanagata, W (2002) 'Cultural districts, property rights and sustainable economic growth' *International Journal of Urban and Regional Research* **26**(1): 9–23

Sandercock, L (1998a) *Making the Invisible Visible: A Multicultural Planning History*. University of California Press, Berkeley, CA

Sandercock, L (1998b) *Towards Cosmopolis: Planning for Multicultural Cities*. John Wiley and Sons, Chichester

Sandercock, L (2003) *Cosmopolis II: Mongrel Cities of the 21st Century*. Continuum, London

Sandercock, L and K Dovey (2002) 'Pleasure, politics, and the "public interest": Melbourne's riverscape revitalization' *Journal of the American Planning Association* **68**(2): 151–64

Santa Cruz Giralt, M and A Concha-Eastman (2001) *Barrio Adentro: La Solaridad Violenta de las Pandillas*, Instituto Univeritario de Opinion Publica, Universidad Centroamericana 'Jose Simeon Canas', San Salvador

Sanyal, B (ed) (2004) *Hybrid Planning Cultures*. Unpublished manuscript

SAPS (South African Police Services) (1999a) 'Semester Report 1/1999, Annexure E: International crime ratios according to the 1996 Interpol Report' in *The Incidence of Serious Crime in South Africa Between January and December 1998*, SAPS Crime Information Analysis Centre, Crime Intelligence, Pretoria

SAPS (1999b) 'Statistical analysis of reported rape cases' in *The Incidence of Serious Crime in South Africa Between January and December 1999*, SAPS, Pretoria

SAPS (2000) 'Semester Report 1/2000, Annexure A: National and provincial crime statistics: January–December 1994-1999' in *The Incidence of Serious Crime in South Africa Between January and December 1999*, SAPS Crime Information Analysis Centre, Crime Intelligence, Pretoria

SAPS (2002) *Annual Report of the National Commissioner of South African Police Service, 1 April 2001 to 31 March 2002*, SAPS, Pretoria

Sasaki, M (2001) 'Tokyo and Kanazawa: culture and economy of contemporary Japanese cities' in W B Kim (ed) *The Culture and Economy of Cities in Pacific Asia*. Korea Research Institute for Human Settlements, Seoul

Sassen, S (1991) *The Global City: New York, London, Tokyo*. Princeton University Press, Princeton

Sassen, S (1994) *Cities in a World Economy*. Pine Forge Press, Thousand Oaks

Sassen, S (2001) *The Global City: New York, London, Tokyo* (2nd ed). Princeton University Press, Princeton

Sassen, S (ed) (2002) *Global Networks, Linked Cities*. Routledge, New York

Satterthwaite, D (2002) *Reducing Urban Poverty: Some Lessons from Experience*. International Institute for Environment and Development, London

Saul, J R (2004) 'The collapse of globalism' *Harper's Magazine*. March: 33–43 www.harpers.org/Newsstand2004-03.html

Savitch, H V (2002) 'What is new about globalization and what does it portend for cities?' *International Social Science Journal* **54**(2): 179ff

Savitch, H V (2003) 'Does 9-11 portend a new paradigm for cities?' *Urban Affairs Review* **39**: 103–127

Savitch, H V and G Ardashev (2001) 'Does terror have an urban future?' *Urban Studies* **38**: 2515–2533

Savitch, H V and P Kantor (2003) 'Urban strategies for a global area; a crossnational comparison' *American Behavioral Scientist* **46**: 1002–1033

Saxenian, A L (1994) *Regional Advantage: Culture and Competition in Silicon Valley and Route 128*. Harvard University Press, Cambridge

Scarpaci, J L (2000) 'Reshaping Habana vieja: revitalization, historic preservation, and restructuring in the socialist city' *Urban Geography* **21**: 724–744

Schön, D A (1971) *Beyond the Stable State*. WW Norton, New York

Schön, D A (1983) *The Reflective Practitioner*. Basic Books, New York

Scott, A J (2000) *The Cultural Economy of Cities*. Sage, London

Scott, A J (ed) (2001) *Global City-regions: Trends, Theory, Policy*. Oxford University Press, Oxford

Sennett, R (1990) *The Conscience of the Eye. The Design and Social Life of Cities*. Alfred Knopf, New York

Seong-Kyu Ha (2002) *Redevelopment of Substandard Settlements and Evictions in Seoul*. Chung-Hang University, Chung-Hang

Seyfang, G (2003) 'Growing cohesive communities one favour at a time: social exclusion, active citizenship and time banks' *International Journal of Urban and Regional Research* **27**: 699–706

Sharma, K (2001a) *Rediscovering Dharavi, Stories From Asia's Largest Slum*. Penguin India

Sharma, K (2001b) 'Housing Mumbai's Millions' *The Hindu*, 1 February [Mumbai]

Shaw, M (2001) *Investing in Youth: International Approaches to Preventing Crime and Victimization*, International Centre for the Prevention of Crime, Montreal

Shelter NCVCCO (1995) 'No fault of their own, the plight of homeless children and young people' www.shelter.org.uk

Shelter Partnership, Inc (1999) *A Report on Housing for Persons Living with HIV/AIDS in the City and the County of Los Angeles*. www.shelter.org.uk

Shelter Partnership, Inc (2002a) 'Child poverty, housing and homelessness', Briefing Paper. www.shelter.org.uk

Shelter Partnership, Inc (2002b) 'Growing up homeless' www.shelter.org.uk

Shevky, E and W Bell (1955) *Social Area Analysis: Theory, Illustrative Application and Computational Procedures*. Auflage, Stanford, California

Shields, R (1992) 'A truant proximity: presence and absence in the space of modernity' *Environment and Planning D: Society and Space* **10**: 181–98

Shkolnikov, V M and G A Cornia (2000) 'Population crisis and rising mortality in transitional Russia' in *The Mortality Crisis in Transitional Economies*. Oxford University Press, Oxford, pp253–279

Sieber, R E (2003) 'Public participation geographic information systems across borders' *Canadian Geographer-Geographe Canadien* **47**(1): 50–61

Siemiatycki, M (2003) *Beyond Moving People: Excavating the Motivations for Investing in Urban Public Transit Infrastructure in Bilbao, Spain*. Unpublished MSc thesis, Oxford University, Oxford

Simmel, G (1950) 'The metropolis and mental life' in K H Wolff (ed) *The Sociology of Georg Simmel*. Free Press, New York, pp409–424

Simone, A M (2001) 'Straddling the divides: remaking associational life in the informal African city' *International Journal of Urban and Regional Research* **25**(1): 102–117

Simpson, D, O Adeoye, R Feliciano and R Howard (2001) 'Chicago's uncertain future since September 11, 2001' *Urban Affairs Review* **38**: 128–134

Simpson, L (2004) 'Statistics of racial segregation: measures, evidence and policy' *Urban Studies* **41**(3): 661–681

Siravo, F (undated) *Zanzibar Stone Town Projects: A Plan for the Historic Town*. AgaKhan Development Network, www.akdn.org/aktc/hcsp_zanzibar5.html

Sivaramakrishnan, K C and L Green (1986) *Metropolitan Management: the Asian Experience*. Oxford University Press, New York

Smart, A and J Smart (2003) 'Urbanization and the global perspective' *Annual Review of Anthropology* **32**: 263–285

Smith, D and M Timberlake (2002) *Global Cities and Globalization in East Asia: Empirical Realities and Conceptual Questions.* Center for Study and Democracy, University of California, Irvine

Smith, N and P Williams (eds) (1986) *Gentrification of the City.* Allen and Unwin, Boston

Smolka, M (2002) 'Access to serviced land by the urban poor', Paper presented at the Workshop on Spatial Segregation and Urban Inequality in Latin America. Austin, 15–16 November

Snyder, H N and M Sickmund (1999) *Juvenile Offenders and Victims: 1999 National Report*, United States Department of Justice Office of Juvenile Justice and Delinquency Prevention (OJJDP), Washington DC

Soja, E (2000) *Postmetropolis: Critical Studies of Cities and Regions.* Blackwell, Oxford

Sorensen, André, 2002, *The Making of Urban Japan: Cities and Planning from Edo to the Twenty-first Century.* Routledge, London

Sorkin, M (ed) (1994) *Variations on a Theme Park.* Noonday, New York

Sorkin, M and S Zukin (eds) (2002) *After the World Trade Center: Rethinking New York City.* Routledge, New York

South Africa (1999) *Towards an Intervention Strategy Addressing Youth Violence in Schools*, Joint Framework Document, South Africa Secretariat for Safety and Security, Department of Education, National Youth Commission, Pretoria

Spiller, K (2001) '"Little Africa," Parnell Street, Food and Afro-Irish Identity', www.ucc.ie/ucc/depts/geography/stafhome/denis/spiller.htm, accessed 28 March 2004

Spirou, C S and L Bennett (2002) 'Revamped stadium...new neighborhood?' *Urban Affairs Review* **37**: 675–702

Stahre, U (2004) 'City in change: globalization, local politics and urban movements in contemporary Stockholm' *International Journal of Urban and Regional Research* **28**: 68–85

Stavrou, A (2002) *Crime in Nairobi: Results of a Citywide Victim Survey.* UN-Habitat Safer Cities Programme, Nairobi

Steinberg, F (forthcoming) 'Strategic planning in Latin America: experiences of building and managing the future', *Habitat International*, in press

Stiglitz, J (1999) 'Whither reform? Ten years of the transition', Keynote address to the World Bank's Annual Bank Conference on Development Economics, Washington DC

Stiglitz, J (2002) *Globalization and Discontent.* W W Norton and Company, New York

Sudjic, D (1993) *The 100 Mile City.* Flamingo, London

Susskind, L, S McKearnan and J Thomas-Learner (eds) (1999) *The Consensus-building Handbook: A Comprehensive Guide to Reaching Agreement.* Sage, Thousand Oaks

Swanstrom, T (2002) 'Are fear and urbanism at war?' *Urban Affairs Review* **38**: 135–140

Talwar, J P (2002) *Fast Food, Fast Track: Immigrants, Big Business, and the American Dream.* Westview, Boulder

Taylor, P J, D R F Walker and J V Beaverstock (2002) 'Firms and their global service networks' in S Sassen (ed) *Global Networks, Linked Cities.* Princeton University Press, Princeton

Tchen, J K W (1999) *New York Before Chinatown.* Johns Hopkins University Press, Baltimore

Teo, P (2003) 'Limits of engineering: a case study of Penang' *International Journal of Urban and Regional Research* **27**: 545–557

Thomas, T (2003) 'Feeling the heat: globalization and the Latin American-Caribbean region' *Stabroek News*, 19 January

Thompson, E P (1967) 'Time, work-discipline, and industrial capitalism' *Past and Present* **38**: 56–97

Thorp, R (1998) *Progress, Poverty, and Exclusion: An Economic History of Latin America in the 20th Century.* The Inter-American Development Bank, Washington, DC

Timms, D W G (1971) *The Urban Mosaic: Towards a Theory of Residential Differentiation.* Cambridge University Press, Cambridge

Tiwari, D P (undated) 'Challenges in urban planning for local bodies in India', http://grisdevelopment,net/application/urban/overview/urbano0037.htm

Tolan, P H and D Gorman-Smith (1998) 'Development of serious and violent offending careers' in R Loeber and D P Farrington (eds) *Serious and Violent Juvenile Offenders.* Sage Publications, Thousand Oaks

Transparency International (2002) *Corruption in South Asia: Insights & Benchmarks from Citizen Feedback Surveys in Five Countries.* www.transparency.org/pressreleases_archive/2002/dnld/south_asia_report.pdf

Transparency International (2004) *Global Corruption Report.* www.globalcorruptionreport.org

Trebay, G (2001) 'Paris diary: American style from the 60s captures new imaginations' *New York Times*, 17 July

Uitermark, J (2003) '"Social mixing" and the management of disadvantaged neighbourhoods: the Dutch policy of urban restructuring revisited' *Urban Studies* **40**: 531–549

Umemoto, K (2001) 'Walking in another's shoes: epistemological challenges in participatory planning' *Journal of Planning Education and Research* **21**: 17–31

UNAIDS and World Bank (2001) *AIDS, Poverty Reduction and Debt Relief: Implications for Poverty Reduction.* UNAIDS and World Bank

UNCHS (Habitat) (United Nations Centre for Human Settlements (Habitat)) (1996) *An Urbanizing World: Global Report on Human Settlements 1996.* Oxford University Press/UNCHS (Habitat), Oxford

UNCHS (Habitat) (2001a) *Cities in a Globalizing World: Global Report on Human Settlements 2001.* Earthscan/UNCHS (Habitat), London

UNCHS (Habitat) (2001b) *The State of the World's Cities 2001.* UNCHS (Habitat), Nairobi

UNCHS (Habitat) (2001c) *Urban Violence Statistical Report.* UNCHS (Habitat), Nairobi

UNCTAD (United Nations Conference on Trade and Development) (2002) *Economic Development in Africa. From Adjustment to Poverty Reduction: What's New?* UNCTAD/GDS/AFRICA/2

UNCTAD (2003) *Trade and Development Report.* United Nations, New York and Geneva

UNDP (United Nations Development Programme) (2002) *Human Development Report.* UNDP/Oxford University Press, New York

UNDP (2003) *Arab Human Development Report.* UNDP, New York

UNECE (United Nations Economic Commission for Europe) (2003) *Statistical Yearbook of the Economic Commission for Europe 2003.* UNECE, Geneva, www.unece.org/stats/trend/ch13.htm

UNECLAC (United Nations Economic Commission for Latin America and the Caribbean) (1998) *Sustainable Development of Human Settlements. Serie Medio Ambiente y Dessarollo* No 7, ECLAC, Santiago

UNECLAC (2000) *From Rapid Urbanization to the Consolidation of Human Settlements in Latin America and the Caribbean.* ECLAC, Santiago

UNECLAC (2003) *Social Panorama of Latin America 2002–2003.* ECLAC, Santiago

UNESCAP (United Nations Economic and Social Commission for Asia and the Pacific) (1994) *Guidelines: Subnational Area Planning and Sustainable Development of Secondary Cities in Countries of Asia and the Pacific—A Methodological Approach.* United Nations, Manila

UNESCAP (2003) *Promoting the Millennium Development Goals in Asia and the Pacific.* United Nations, Bangkok

UNESCO (United Nations Educational, Scientific and Cultural Organization) (undated) *Cultural Activities*, www.unesco.org

UNFPA (United Nations Population Fund) (2002) *Eastern Europe and Central Asia: Demographic Issues.* UNFPA, New York

UNFPA (2003) *Country Profiles for Population and Reproductive Health: Policy Developments and Indicators.* UNFPA, New York

UN-Habitat (United Nations Human Settlements Programme) (2002a) *Global Urban Indicators Database: Version 2.* UN-Habitat, Nairobi

UN-Habitat (2002b) *Expert Group Meeting on Urban Indicators*, 28–30 October 2002

UN-Habitat (2002c) *Youth and Crime in Nairobi.* UN-Habitat, Nairobi

UN-Habitat (2003a) *The Challenge of Slums: Global Report on Human Settlements 2003.* Earthscan/UN-Habitat, London

UN-Habitat (2003b) *Slums of the World: The Face of Urban Poverty in the New Millennium.* UN-Habitat, Nairobi

UNHCR (United Nations High Commissioner for Refugees) (2000) *The State of the World's Refugees.* UNHCR, Geneva

UNICRI (United Nations Interregional Crime and Justice Research Institute) (1995) *Criminal Victimisation in the Developing World*, Publication No 55. UNICRI, Rome

UNICRI (1998) *Victims of Crime in the Developing World*, Publication No 57. UNICRI, Rome

United Nations (1995) *The World's Women 1995: Trends and Statistics.* United Nations, New York

United Nations Economic and Social Council (2003) *World Situation with Regard to Drug Abuse.* Report of the Secretariat, Commission on Narcotic Drugs, forty-sixth session, 8-17 April 2003, Vienna

United Nations Population Division (2002a) *World Urbanization Prospects: The 2001 Revision.* United Nations, New York

United Nations Population Division (2002b) *International Migration Report 2002.* United Nations, New York

United Nations Population Division (2003) *World Urbanization Prospects: The 2003 Revision.* www.unpopulation.org

United Republic of Tanzania, Ministry of Lands and Human Settlements Development (2001) 'Environmental Planning and Management in Dar-Es-Salaam, Tanzania', Paper presented to the Thematic Committee, Istanbul + 5, New York

UNODC (United Nations Office on Drugs and Crime) (1999) *Global Report on Crime and Justice.* UNODC, Vienna, www.unodc.org/unodc/en/publications/publications.html

UNODC (2003a) *Brazil Country Profile.* UNODC Regional Office Brazil, Brasilia

UNODC (2003b) *Global Illicit Drug Trends.* UNODC, Vienna

UNODC (2003c) *Caribbean Drug Trends 2001–2002*, UNODC, Bridgetown, Barbados www.unodc.org/pdf/barbados/caribbean_drug_trends_2001-2002.pdf

UNODC (2004a) *Law Enforcement: Latin America and the Caribbean*, UNODC web site www.unodc.org/unodc/en/law_enforcement_southamerica.html

UNODC (2004b) *Barbados Sub-Regional Strategy*, UNODC, Bridgetown, Barbados www.odccp.org/barbados/subreg.html

UNOSAA (United Nations Office of the Special Adviser on Africa) (2003) 'Organized crime spreading, using modern technology, UN panel told' Press release, 10 October 2003, OSAA, www.un.org/esa/africa/UNNews_Africa/modern.htm

UNRISD (United Nations Research Institute for Social Development (2003) *Research for Social Development (UNRISD Fortieth Anniversary Report)*. UNRISD, Geneva

Urban Institute (2000) 'A new look at homelessness in America', www.urban.org/url.cfm?ID=900302

US Department of Commerce (1997) *Report of Bureau of Economic Analysis*. US Department of Commerce, Washington, DC

US National Academy of Sciences (1993) *In Our Own Backyard: Principles for Effective Improvement of the Nation's Infrastructure*. National Academies Press, Washington, DC

United States Senate (1998) *U.S. and Mexican Counterdrug Efforts Since Certification*. Joint hearing before the Senate Caucus of International Narcotics Control and the Committee on Foreign Relations, Government Printing Office, Washington, DC

van den Berg, L et al (1990) *Marketing Metropolitan Regions*. Erasmus University, Rotterdam

van Kesteren, J N, P Mayhew and P Nieuwbeerta (2000) *Criminal Victimisation in Seventeen Industrialised Countries: Key findings from the 2000 International Crime Victims Survey*. WODC Ministry of Justice, The Hague

Verma, G D (2002) *Slumming India: A Chronicle of Slums and their Saviours*. Penguin, New Delhi

Vernez, G and K F McCarthy (1995) *The Costs of Immigration to Tax Payers: Analytical and Policy Issues*. Rand Corporation, London

Vicario, L and P M M Monje (2003) 'Another "Guggenheim effect?" The generation of a potentially gentrifiable neighbourhood in Bilbao' *Urban Studies* **40**: 2383–2400

Vostanis, P et al (1999) *Homeless Children: Problems and Needs*. www.homeless.org

Waiselfisz, J (1998) *Mapa da Violencia: Os Jovenes do Brasil*. UNESCO, Rio de Janeiro

Ward, P (1996) 'Contemporary issues in the government and administration of Latin American mega-cities' in A Gilbert (ed) *The Mega-city in Latin America*. UNU Press, Tokyo

Ward, S V (2002) *Planning the Twentieth Century City: The Advanced Capitalist World*. John Wiley and Sons, Chichester

Weaver, K and M Maddalenno (1999) 'Youth violence in Latin America: current situation and violence prevention strategies' *Pan American Journal of Public Health* **5** abril: 338-343

Webber, M M (1964) 'The urban place and the non-place urban realm' in M Webber (ed) *Explorations in Urban Structures*. University of Pennsylvania Press, Philadelphia, pp79–153

Webster, D (1995) 'Mega urbanization in ASEAN' in T McGee and I Robinson (eds) *The Mega-urban Regions of Southeast Asia*. University of British Columbia, Vancouver

Wegelin, E A (2003) 'Refugee-related housing issues in selected South-Eastern European countries', Paper presented to High-Level Conference on Housing Reforms in South-Eastern Europe, Geneva

Wekwete, K H (1997) 'Urban management: the recent experience' in Carol Rakodi (ed) *The Urban Challenge in Africa*. UNU, Tokyo pp527–54

WHO (World Health Organization) (1996) *Consultation on Violence Against Women*, 5–7 February 1996. WHO, Geneva

WHO (2002) *World Report on Violence and Health*. WHO, Geneva

Williams, P (1999) 'Emerging issues: transnational crime and its control' in G Newman (ed) *Global Report on Crime and Justice*. Oxford University Press/United Nations, New York

Wilson, M G and E Whitmore (1998) 'The transnationalization of popular movements: social policy making from below' *Canadian Journal of Development Studies* **XIX**: 7–36

Winkler, T (2002) *South Africa's Complex Planning Culture*. Unpublished manuscript

Wo-Lap Lam, W (2002) 'Race to become China's economic powerhouse', CNN, 11 June 2002

Wood, R (1959) *New York's 1400 Governments*. Public Records, Boston

World Bank (1991) *Urban Policy and Economic Development: An Agenda for the 1990s*. World Bank, Washington, DC

World Bank (1994) *World Development Report 1994: Infrastructure for Development*. World Bank, Washington, DC

World Bank (2000a) *Cities in Transition*. World Bank, Washington, DC

World Bank (2000b) *Feminization of Poverty in Russia*. World Bank, Izdatelstvo Ves Mir, Moscow.

World Bank (2001a) *World Development Report*. Oxford University Press, New York

World Bank (2001b) *Global Development Finance*. World Bank, Washington, DC

World Bank (2002a) *World Development Report 2002*. World Bank, Washington, DC

World Bank (2002b) *Global Development Finance*. World Bank, Washington, DC

World Bank (2002c) *Global Economic Prospects and the Developing Countries: Making Trade Work for the World's Poor*. World Bank, Washington, DC

World Bank (2003a) *Global Development Finance*. World Bank, Washington, DC

World Bank (2003b) *Inequality in Latin America and the Caribbean: Breaking with History?* World Bank, Washington, DC

World Bank (2003c) *World Development Indicators 2003*. World Bank, Washington, DC

World Bank (2003d) *World Development Report 2003*. World Bank, Washington, DC

World Bank (2003e) *Better Governance for Development in the Middle East and North Africa*. World Bank, Washington, DC

World Bank (2003f) 'Press Release', 9 September 2003, www.worldbank.org.cn/English/Content/267u61215996.shtm

World Resources Institute (1996) *World Resources 1996-97*. Oxford University Press, New York

World Security Services (2004) *Industry Study with Forecasts to 2006 & 2011*, www.the-infoshop.com/study/fd13043_wsecurity.html

Wu, Fulong (2002) 'China's changing urban governance in the transition towards a more market-oriented economy' *Urban Studies* **39**(7): 1071–1093

Yan, Y X (2000) 'Of hamburger and social space: consuming McDonald's in Beijing' in D S Davis (ed) *The Consumer Revolution in Urban China*. University of California Press, Berkeley and Los Angeles, pp201–225

Yeoh, B S A and S Huang (1996) 'The conservation-redevelopment dilemma in Singapore: the case of the Kampong Glam historic district' *Cities* **13**: 411–422

Yeung, Y M and D Chu (eds) (2000) *Fujian: A Coastal Province in Transition and Transformation*. The Chinese University Press, Hong Kong

Yudice, G (2003) *The Expediency of Culture: Uses of Culture in the Global Era*. Duke University Press, Durham

Zhang, Tingwei (2002) 'Decentralization, localization, and the emergence of a quasi-participatory decision-making structure in urban development in Shanghai' *International Planning Studies* **7**(4): 303–23

Zohry, A (2002) *Unskilled Temporary Labour Migration from Upper Egypt to Cairo*. Centre d'Etudes et de Documentation Economiques, Juridiques et Sociales, Cairo

Zukin, S (1989) *Loft Living: Culture and Capital in Urban Change* (2nd ed). Rutgers University Press, New Brunswick

Zukin, S (1995) *The Cultures of Cities*. Blackwell, Oxford and Cambridge

Zukin, S (2004) *Point of Purchase: How Shopping Changed American Culture*. Routledge, New York

Zulu, E M, F N-A Dodoo and A Chika-Ezeh (2002) 'Sexual risk-taking in the slums of Nairobi, Kenya' *Population Studies* **56**: 311–323

Zvekic, U (1998a) *Criminal Victimization in Countries in Transition*. UNICRI, Publication No 61, Rome

Zvekic, U (1998b) *Citizens, Crime and Criminal Justice in Central and Eastern Europe*. Konrad Adenauer Foundation website: www.kas.org.za/publications/seminarreports/crimeandpolicingintransitionalsocieties/zvekic.pdf

Zvekic, U (2000) *International Crime Victim Survey*. UNODC, Geneva

Photo credits

Overview

Topfoto/The Image Works, p1

Chapter 1

Justo Casal, p9 (background)
Topfoto/The Image Works, pp9 (inset), 11, 21, 25
Topfoto, pp9 (inset), 12, 29
Topfoto/UPPA, pp9 (inset), 13
UNEP/Chris Wormald/Topfoto, p20

Chapter 2

Topfoto, pp31 (background and inset), 35, 36, 38, 46, 47
Topfoto/The Image Works, pp31 (inset), 32, 39
AAAC/Topfoto, pp31 (inset), 33

Chapter 3

Topfoto/The Image Works, pp49 (background and inset), 51, 63
Topfoto, pp49 (inset), 55, 65, 68, 70, 72
UNEP/Teddy A Suyasa/Topfoto, p60
Topfoto/UPPA, pp61, 74

Chapter 4

Topfoto/The Image Works, pp76 (background and inset), 78, 84, 89, 92, 95, 97

Chapter 5

Topfoto/The Image Works, pp101 (background and inset), 109, 129
Topfoto, pp101 (inset), 105
Topfoto/Novosti, p125
Topfoto/UPPA, pp101 (inset), 128

Chapter 6

Topfoto/The Image Works, p131 (background)
Topfoto/PressNet, pp135, 155
Topfoto, pp131 (inset), 142, 157
Topfoto/UPPA, pp131 (inset), 146

Chapter 7

Topfoto/The Image Works, pp159 (background and inset), 161, 168, 173, 181
Topfoto, pp159 (inset), 169, 171

Index

Page numbers in *italics* refer to maps, figures, tables and boxes. Those followed by 'n' refer to notes

Abidjan, Côte d'Ivoire *16*, *71*, 79, *82*, 91, *93*, 120, *165*
Addis Ababa, Ethiopia 92
advanced economies
    corruption in government 136, 155
    crime 136, 151, 152–6
    cultural heritage preservation 36
    drug abuse *128*, 155, 156
    drug trafficking 141–2, 155–6
    employment issues 2, 17, 126
    ethnic spaces 82, 97, *117*, 122
    governance issues 74, 155
    homelessness 124–9, 130n
    immigrants 3, 77–8, *82*, 94, 96–9
    metropolitanization 73–4
    migration policies 97, *98*
    people trafficking 138, 151
    police satisfaction 135
    population growth 77–8
    relocation of industry 4–5, 17, *19*, *21*, 35, 39, 52, 126
    slums 104, 105, *107*
    social segregation 59, 82, 99
    urban planning 166–71
    urban poverty *102*, 103–25, 130n
    violence against women *151*, *154*
    youth crime 154
    see also individual cities, countries and regions
Afghanistan 83, 95, 138, *152*
Albania 79
Alexandria, Egypt 68
Algeria *11*, 68, 90, *114*, 115
Almaty, Kazakhstan *40*
Amman, Jordan 82, 90
Amsterdam, Netherlands 74, 96, 153–4
Andean Community 83, 88
Angola *121*
apartheid 75n, 79, 92, 146
Argentina 17, 50, 86, *87*, 88, 111, 139
Armenia 95, 96
Asia and the Pacific
    arts and crafts *111*
    corruption in government 137
    crime 134, 136, 137–8, 143
    culture *18–19*
    drug trafficking and abuse 138, 143
    governance issues 63–4
    housing issues *152*
    immigrants 83, 84–6
    industrialization 62, 84
    mega-urban regions (MURs) 23, 62, 63
    metropolitanization 55, 58, 62–4, 175
    migration 77, 78, 83–4, 95, 96, 99
        migration policies 83, 84, 85
        rural–urban 63, 108
    people trafficking 133, 137–8, 151
    police satisfaction 137
    population growth 62
    slums 107, 108–9
    urban poverty 84, *102*, 106–11, 130n

    urbanization *18–19*, 62, 63, 108
    violence against women 136
    water supply 108
    see also individual cities, countries and regions
Asmara, Eritrea *44–5*
Assam, India 84
Association of East Asian States (ASEAN) 63
Australia 96, 99, *126*, *129*, 153, 154–5, 156
Austria *126*
Azerbaijan *40*, 95

Baghdad, Iraq 113
Bahamas 87, 88
Bahrain 67, 90, *115*
Baku, Azerbaijan *94*
Bangkok, Thailand *16*, 51, 62, *64*, 82, 85, 86
Bangladesh 83, 84, *98*, 108, *109*, 137
Barbados 87
Barcelona, Spain 27, *34*, 47, 96
Basrah, Iraq 113
Beijing, China 29, 47, 107
Beirut, Lebanon 90, *114*, 115
Belarus 94, 151
Belgium *126*, 155, 156
Belize 86
Berlin, Germany 12, 43, 46, 59, *82*, 98
Bilbao, Spain 5, 34, *35*
Birmingham, UK 97, *129*
Bishkek, Kyrgyzstan *40*, 123
Bogotá, Colombia 52, 64, 66, *98*, *140*
Bolivia 88, *107*, 112, 139, 140
Bosnia and Herzegovina 79, 124
Brazil 66, 88, 112, *139*, 140, 151
Brussels, Belgium 96, 153–4
Bucharest, Romania 72, 149
Budapest, Hungary 12, 14, 20, 95, 96, 124
Buenos Aires, Argentina
    economic issues *16*, 17, 23, 27
    governance issues 66
    immigrants *87*, 88
    metropolitanization 58, 64, 65
    planning for the future 180
    population *16*, 58, 112
Bulgaria *122*, 123, 124, *125*, 150
Burkina Faso 92, *119*
Burundi *120*

Cairo, Egypt 90, 115, 177
Calcutta, India *see* Kolkata
Cambodia 14, 84, *85*, *107*
Cameroon 92, *107*
Canada
    anti-violence initiatives *151*
    civil society 179
    crime 141, 151, 153, 154, 156
    drug trafficking 141, 156
    homelessness 124, *126*
    immigrants 96, 97

    unemployment 126
    urban planning 175
    youth crime 154
Cape Town, South Africa 12, 94
Caracas, Venezuela 66–7, 88
Casablanca, Morocco *16*, 90
Central African Republic *90*, *107*, *120*, 119
Central America 64, 79, 86, 112, 140
Central Asia *40*, *41*, *77*, 121, 124, 138
Chennai, India 36–7, *42*
Chicago, US 47, 58, 59
children
    homelessness *126*, 129
    mortality rates 56, 104, *114*, 116, 118, *122*
    in slum areas 107–8, 110
    traffick in 133, 137–8
    urban poverty affects 59, 107–8, 125, 130n
    in wars 148
Chile 88, 140, 163
China
    civil society 173
    drug trafficking 151
    economic growth 161
    governance issues 161, 175
    HIV/AIDS 138
    metropolitanization 23
    migration 12, 14, *15*, 82, 95, 96, 97, 99
    people trafficking 138
    slums 109
    urban planning 161, 172, 175–6
    urban poverty 106, 108, *109*
    welfare reforms 110
cities
    central business districts (CBDs) *18*, *19*, 51–2, 53
    'cities of culture' competitions vii, 5, 34
    city-branding 5, *34*, *36*, 38–9
    cultural consumption spaces 32, 42–7
    cultural districts 34–5, 41–2, 43, 45–7
    cultural identities 5–6, 11, 13, 32, 171, 177
    'edge cities' 52, 61, 170, 173
    ethnic spaces *12*, 13–15, 25–6, 82, 97, *122*
    gentrification 34, 36, 37–8
    ghettos 13, *14*, *122*
    inclusive 2, 6–7, 25–6, 47, 174, 177–8
    inner-city areas 33–5, 36, 37–8, 99
    multicultural *see* multiculturalism
    polycentric 3, 52, 61, 65, 73, 74, 171
    population growth *23*, 24–5, 50
    see also metropolitanization
city governments *see* municipal governments
city regions 74, 175
civil service 102, 161, 162
civil society
    defined 178
    governance role 133, 150, 155, 172, 173, 177
    government relationships 6, *18*, 173–4, 179, 180
    growth of 6, *18*, 178
    housing initiatives *152*, *153*

in urban planning 6–7, 162, 166, 167, 170, 173–4, 178–80, 181–2
Colombia 58, 88, 138, 139, 140, 142
communities
    crime prevention initiatives 6, 139, *143*, *151*, 155, 157
    cultural heritage preservation 36, *109*, *111*
    networks 5, 81–2, 88, 95, *122*, 120
    in urban planning 7, 175–6
conflicts *see* wars
corporations
    cultural strategies to attract 33–4, *35*, *36*, 38, 42
    government relationships 20, 33–4, *37*, 42, 46, 167–8, 172
    in public–private partnerships 167–8, 172
    in urban planning 167–8, 170, 172, 173, 181–2
Costa Rica 86–7, 88, 139
Côte d'Ivoire 71, 79, 92, *120*, *165*
crime
    assaults 4, 134, 135, 136, 149, 153
    burglary/theft *132*, *134*, 144–5, 149
    crime prevention initiatives 6, 139, *143*, 151, *154*, 155, *156*, 157
    drug abuse 138, *139*, 140–1, 142, 143
    drug trafficking vii, 4, 132, 138, *139*, 140–2, 143, 151
    fear of *132*, 144, *145*, 148–9, 149–50
    globalization relationship vii, 4, 61, 132
    government policies 155, 156–7
    gun smuggling vii, 132, 133, *142*, 147–9
    homicide 4, 133, 138, *139*, 144, 148, 153–4
    housing relationship 135
    by immigrants 3, 95, 99, 143, 154
    organized *see* transnational crime below
    people trafficking vii, 4, *81*, 132–3, 137–8, 151
    police satisfaction 135–6, 137, 139, 149, 150, 157
    transnational 4, 132, 137–8, 140–2, 147–9
    urban poverty relationship vii, 134, 135
    youth crime 135, 138, *139*, *140*, 145, 154–5
    see also violence
Croatia 124, 150
Cuba 88, 99, 140
Curitiba, Brazil 29
Czech Republic 124, 150, 151

Damascus, Syria 90
Dar es Salaam, Tanzania 91, 94, *143*, 144, 145, 146
Davao, Philippines 59
Delhi, India 62, 84
Democratic Republic of Congo 90, 92, *120*, *121*
Denmark *126*, 153, 155
developing economies
    corruption in government 136
    crime 132, 134
    cultural heritage preservation 36, *38*, *39*
    governance issues 114, 116
    migration 50, *77*, 83–94
    police satisfaction 137, 157
    population growth 3, 15, *16*, 50, 78, *108*
    relocation of industry 4–5, *19*, 51–2, 126
    slums 4, 104, 105, *107*, 109
    social segregation 59, 82
    urban poverty 103, 106–21
    urbanization 15, 105
    violence against women 136
    see also individual countries and regions
Dhaka, Bangladesh 62
disease 24, *56*, 113, *121*, *122*
    see also HIV/AIDS
Djibouti 92
Dominican Republic 79, 86, 87–8, 141
Dubai, United Arab Emirates 67
Dublin, Ireland 14, *15*
Durban, South Africa 91, 94, 144

East Asia 2, 17, 63, 84, 107
Eastern Europe
    crime 138, 143, 147, 149, 151
    drug trafficking 138, 143, 151
    housing issues 123
    immigrants 94
    migration 3, 14, 77, 78, 89, 95, 96
    police satisfaction 149
    slums 124
    unemployment 121, *122*
    urban poverty 20, 121, *122*
economic growth
    culture relationship vii, 4–5, *18–19*, 32, 35
    inequality affects 2, 17, 20, 66, 108
    migration relationship 3, 79, 81, 99
    urban planning affected 161, 172, 174
    urban poverty relationship 59, 108, 111, 118–19
    urbanization relationship 15–16, 50, 71
economic issues
    of differentiation 2, 3, 5, 19–20
    economies of agglomeration 3, 50, 73
    of globalization 2, 15–19, 107, 160
    of industry 2–3, 17, 19
    informalized economy 2, 17, 19, 102
    of metropolitanization 3, 50, 57–8, 60, 61, 63
    symbolic economy 32, 41, 43
    see also economic growth
economies in transition *see* transition economies
Ecuador 79
education 17, 20, 24, *56*, 59, 91, 114, *129*
Egypt 67, 68, 90, 113, *114*, 115, 142–3, 179
El Salvador 79, *140*
employment
    globalization affects 2, 12, 13–14, 15, 17–19, 20, 52, 61
    of immigrants 13–15, 81, 83–4, 85–93, 96, 97
    in metropolitan areas 52, 57–8, 61, *66*
    of women 2, 17, 58, 84, *90*, *98*, *116*, *152*
England *128*, 151, 153, 154, 155, 169–70
Equatorial Guinea 92
Eritrea *44–5*, 92, *120*
Estonia 94, *123*, 150
Ethiopia 92, *120*
Europe
    crime 141, 143, 151, 153–4, 156
    cultural heritage preservation 33, 36
    drug trafficking and abuse 141, 143, 151, 156
    gentrification 38
    governance issues 74
    homelessness 124–9
    homicide rates 153–4
    immigrants 14, 78, *80–1*, 90–9
    metropolitanization 73, 74, 175
    police satisfaction 135
    Roma (gypsy) communities *122*, 124, *125*
    rural to urban migration 50
    unemployment *117*, 126
    urban planning 171, 175
    urban poverty 103, 121–6
European Union (EU)
    crime 153, 154
    cultural strategies 5, 34
    governance issues 74
    homelessness 128–9
    immigrants 96–9
    migration policies 83
    unemployment 126
    urban planning *166*, 170–1, 172
    urban poverty 126
    youth crime 154
financial markets 2, 16–17, *18*, 21
Finland *126*, 151, 153, 154, 155
Florence, Italy 5
France 74, 78, 82, 96, 97, *126*, 153, 155

Gabon 79, 91, 92
Gambia *90*, *122*
Gauteng, South Africa 70
gender issues *see* women
Georgia 150
Germany 78, 95, 96, 126
Ghana *90*, 92, *107*, *119*
Glasgow, Scotland *34*
globalization
    as agent of change 2–4, 6, 10–29
    crime relationship vii, 4, 61, 132
    cultural dimension 4, 10–15, *18–19*
    demographic dimension 3, *23*, 24–5, 50
    economic dimension 2, 15–19, 107, 160
    employment issues 2, 12, 13–14, 15, 17–19, 20, 52, 61
    governance influenced vii, 132, 133–4
    industry affected 13, 17, *18*, 39, 102
    inequality as a result 2, 4, 17, 19, 102, 112
    metropolitanization relationship 58, 60–2
    migration as a result 3, 77
    multiculturalism as a result 5, 10–15, 182
    political dimension vii, 2, 20–1
    social dimension 19–20, 124–5
    spatial dimension vii, 2–3, *18*, 21–3, 32, 52, 61
    standardization as a result 11, 12–13, *19*, *40*, *41*
    urban development affected *18–19*
    urban poverty relationship vii, 19, 102, 112, 126
governance
    accountability issues 4, 28, 67, 133, 142, 150
    civil society's role 133, 150, 155, 172, 173–4, 177
    corruption affects 4, 113, 132, 133, 136, 150, 155
    decentralization 3, 6, 22, *64*, 69, 70, 71
    in developing economies 114, 118
    globalization influences vii, 132, 133–4
    in metropolitan areas 3, 50–1, 54–5, 72, 73
    norms standardization *133*, 134, 147
    state capture 150
    transparency issues 4, 29, 67, 132, 133, 134, 136, 150 *see also* corruption above
    urban planning relationship 6, 163, 165–7, 169–70, 172, 181–2
    see also individual cities, countries and regions
government issues
    anti-crime policies 155, 156–7
    civil society relationship 6, *18*, 173, 179
    corporations relationship 33, 42, 46, 167–8, 172
    cultural strategies 5, 33, 42
    financial policies 26, 28, 46
    housing policies 37, *153*
    infrastructure responsibility 20, 21–3, 28
    local government relationships 74
    managing change 3, 26–9
    metropolitan government relationship 55, *57*, *71*
    migration policies 82–3, 84, 85–6, 88, 89, 91, 94, 96, 97
    planning for the future 27–8
    in public–private partnerships 167–8, 172
    slum policies *114*, *115*
    sustainability policies 29, 170
    urban planning responsibility 6, 160, 161, 166, 167–8, 169–70, 172
    urban poverty strategies 102
Greenland 11
Guatemala 86, *107*, 112
Guayaquil, Ecuador *16*, 20
Guinea-Bissau 92, 118
Guinea-Conakry 92
Gulf States *see* Middle East and North Africa
guns
    gun ownership 138, *139*, 148, 150, 154
    opposition groups *139*
    smuggling vii, 132, 133, *142*, 147–9
    in violent crime 133, 134, 138, 147

The Hague, Netherlands 97
Haiti 87–8, 112, 141
Havana, Cuba 163–4
health issues
    of immigrants 3, 85, 93
    of public service provision 23, 24, 110
    in slum areas 103, 107–8, 109–10
    of urban poverty 20, 24, 103, 107–8
    see also disease; HIV/AIDS
Helsinki, Finland 34, 74
HIV/AIDS
    in advanced economies 129
    in developing economies 11, 105, 116–20, 138, 147
    drug abuse relationship 123, 151
    in slum areas 103, 105, 118, 119, 120
    urban poverty relationship 118, 119–20, 123
    women at risk 118, 119, 152
    young people at risk 129
homelessness 66, 105, 124–9, 135
Honduras 79, 107, 139, 151
Hong Kong, China SAR 106, 180
housing
    crime relationship 135
    durability 66, 103, 106
    gated 12, 61, 129
    government policies 37, 71, 153
    housing estates 72, 114
    immigrants' problems 87, 88, 93–4, 128–9
    inequality issues 2, 23, 128
    loft living 5, 36, 37
    overcrowding 103, 104, 106, 118, 130n
    privatization 124, 165
    public housing 72, 123–4
    women affected 126, 128, 152–3
    see also homelessness; slums
Hungary 123, 124, 125, 149, 150, 151

immigrants
    asylum seekers 3, 80, 93, 94, 117
    community networks 5, 81–2, 88, 95, 119–20, 122
    as criminals 3, 95, 99, 143, 154
    cultural contribution 11–13, 14, 26, 42
    cultural identities 13, 87
    economic contribution 3, 79, 81, 99
    employment 13–15, 81, 83–4, 85–93, 96, 97
    ethnic spaces 12, 13–15, 25–6, 82, 97, 117
    feared 11, 12, 13, 15, 26, 82, 84
    female 84, 90, 98
    health issues 3, 85, 93
    housing problems 87, 88, 93–4, 128–9
    illegal 81, 84, 85, 89, 95–6, 99, 117, 132
    municipal committees to deal with 26
    racism issues 3, 10, 11, 57, 84
    religious issues 12, 13, 84, 97, 120–1, 129
    remittances 3, 79, 91, 98, 100n
    in slums 82, 85, 93, 114
    social segregation 59, 66, 71, 81–2, 93, 99
    sponsorship system 89
    urban poverty affects vii, 88, 102
    xenophobia issues 3, 81, 82, 84, 92, 93
    see also migration; refugees
India
    arts and crafts 111
    civil service 161, 162
    corruption in government 137
    cultural heritage preservation 36–7, 42, 109
    economic issues 16, 50
    HIV/AIDS 138
    immigrants 83
    inequality 107
    migration 3, 78, 81, 84, 92, 95
    relocation of industry 19, 126
    remittances received 3, 81
    slums 107, 109, 110

urban planning 161–2
urban poverty 108, 109
Indonesia 84, 106, 107–8, 109
industry
    cultural industries 32, 38–9, 41–2
    dot.com industries 41, 43
    economic dimension 2–3, 17, 19
    financial 17, 18
    garment industry 41, 43
    globalization affects 13, 17, 18, 39, 102
    oil industry 67
    relocation 4–5, 17, 19, 21, 22, 35, 39, 51–2
    urban poverty relationship 102, 123, 126
inequality
    economic growth affected 2, 17, 20, 66, 108
    globalization causes 2, 4, 17, 19, 102, 112
    in housing provision 2, 23, 128
    of infrastructure provision 3, 4, 23, 59
    in metropolitan areas 50, 58, 59, 61, 66
    of service provision 17, 19, 23, 24, 58–9, 85, 103–4, 111
    slums relationship 102, 104, 107, 109, 117–118
    in urban development 50, 157, 176–7
    urban planning relationship 5, 29, 177–8
    urban poverty relationship 2, 19, 102, 108, 111, 116, 123–4
    violence relationship 61, 134, 146
information technology 2, 6, 16, 53–4, 126
infrastructure
    government responsibility 20, 21–3, 28, 35
    inequality in provision 3, 4, 23, 59
    in urban planning 163
Iran 95
Iraq 95, 113, 114, 116, 130n
Ireland 126
Israel 67, 89, 143, 153
Istanbul, Turkey 59, 89–90
Italy 80–1, 82, 97, 126, 153

Jakarta, Indonesia 107
Jamaica 79
Japan 73, 99, 153, 154, 166–7, 172, 173, 179
Jeddah, Saudi Arabia 67, 68
Johannesburg, South Africa
    crime 144, 145
    immigrants 91, 93–4
    metropolitanization 51, 69, 70, 82
    urban planning 165, 166
Jordan 79, 89, 113, 114, 115, 130n, 142, 143

Kampala, Uganda 147
Karachi, Pakistan 16, 85
Kathmandu, Nepal 39
Katowice, Poland 72, 73
Kazakhstan 40, 94, 121, 124
Kenya 16, 92, 107, 117–118, 147, 148, 152
Khartoum, Sudan 115
Kiev, Ukraine 72
Kinshasa, Democratic Republic of Congo 70, 91
Kolkata, India 55, 59
Korea, Republic of 50, 57, 95, 106, 107, 109, 137, 138
Krakow, Poland 34
Kuwait 67, 89, 114
Kyrgyzstan 40, 121, 123, 124

Lagos, Nigeria 56–7, 70, 91, 120–1
language in multicultural cities 5, 6, 13, 14, 15, 26
Lao PDR 84, 107, 138
Latin America and the Caribbean
    arts and crafts 111
    corruption in government 140
    crime 134, 135, 136, 137, 138–42, 143, 156
    cultural issues 26
    drug trafficking and abuse 138, 139, 140–2, 143, 156
    economic issues 16, 110–11

employment issues 66, 112, 130n
governance issues 66–7
gun ownership 138, 139
homicide rates 66, 138, 139
immigrants 86–8, 87–8
inequality issues 20, 66, 111
mega-urban regions (MURs) 65–6
metropolitanization 51, 58, 64–7, 162, 175
migration 77, 79, 83, 86–7, 96, 97, 99
    migration policies 88
    rural–urban 50, 112
people trafficking 133, 151
police satisfaction 136, 137, 139
population growth 65, 112
security of tenure issues 113
service provision 110, 112
slums 107, 112
social segregation 66
urban economy important 2
urban planning 162–4, 180
urban poverty 59, 66, 102, 111–13, 130n
urbanization 64–6, 112
violence against women 136, 138–9
youth crime 138, 139
    see also individual cities, countries and regions
Latvia 94, 150, 151
Lebanon 67, 89, 113, 114, 143
Leningrad see St Petersburg, Russia
Lesotho 79, 107, 119
Liberia 81, 90, 92, 120
Libya 67, 90, 91, 114, 115
life expectancy 25, 106, 117, 118
Lima, Peru 16, 64, 67
literacy 105, 106, 118
Lithuania 94, 124, 150
Ljubljana, Slovenia 124, 149
local governments
    accountability issues 28, 150
    anti-crime policies 157
    civil society relationship 6, 173, 179, 180
    corporations relationship 33–4, 42, 167–8, 172
    corruption 112, 113, 140, 142, 150
    cultural strategies 5, 26, 33–4, 35, 42, 43
    housing policies 71
    infrastructure responsibility 23, 28, 35
    managing change 26–9
    metropolitan government relationships 55
    national government relationships 74
    planning for the future 27–8, 178, 180
    in public–private partnerships 167–8, 172
    public services responsibility 74, 113
    slum policies 113
    sustainability policies 29, 154
    urban planning responsibility 161, 165, 166, 167–8, 169–70, 172, 181–2
    urban poverty strategies 102
Lodz, Poland 95
London, UK 21, 38, 59, 62, 82, 98, 125
Los Angeles, US 13, 14, 29, 41, 59, 82, 97, 99
Lusaka, Zambia 20, 91
Luxembourg 126

Macedonia, The former Yugoslav Republic of 124, 150
Madagascar 122
Madrid, Spain 96, 153–4
Malaysia 78, 83, 84, 106, 107, 108, 137, 138
Mali 90, 92, 118, 119
Manila, Philippines 16, 20, 110
Marseilles, France 96, 97
Mauritania 118
Mecca, Saudi Arabia 67
media 11, 12, 36, 37, 41, 42, 87, 132
metropolitan governments
    cultural strategies 34–5, 37

financial issues 28, 34–5, *57*, *71*
growth of 55
local government relationship 55
national government relationship 55, *57*, *71*
problems 3, 50–1, 64, *71*
metropolitanization
  business people's role 53
  city users' role 53, 54
  commuters' role 52, 53, 54
  de-metropolitanization 58, 61–2
  differentiation 3, 50, 58–9, 60
  economic dimension 3, 50, 57–8, 60, 61, 63
  employment issues 52, 57–8, 61, *66*
  financial issues 54, *57*
  fragmentation 3, 50, 58, 61, 63, *64*, 74
  globalization relationship 58, 60–2
  governance issues 3, 50–1, 54–5, 72, 73
  inequality 50, 58, 59, 61, *66*
  inhabitants' role 52–3, 54
  mega-urban regions (MURs) 23, *57*, 62, 63, 65–6, 69, 70, 176
  metropolitan expectations 3, 50–1, 60
  population growth relationship 51, *56*, 62, 63, 65, 67–8, 69, 72
  problems caused 3, 50–1, *56–7*, 66
  process of 51, *56*, 61–2
  public services 3, *56*
  relocation of industry 51–2
  social dimension 52–4, 58, 59, 60, 66, 71
  spatial dimension vii, 3, 51–2, 58, 59–60, 61
  urban planning relationship 3, 7, *27*, 50, 55, 175–6
  urban poverty relationship 56–7, 66, 68
  urbanization 62, 63, 64–6, 67–70, 71
Mexico 16, 66, 79, 83, 86, 99
Mexico City, Mexico *16*, 29, 50, 51, 64, 65, 66, 112
Miami, US *26*, *82*, 97, 99
Middle East and Northern Africa (MENA)
  corruption in government 142
  crime 142–3
  drug trafficking and abuse 142–3
  economic issues 113, 114
  governance issues 114, 118, 142
  immigrants *14*, 78, 79, 83, 88–9
  metropolitanization 67–9, 175
  migration 3, 77, 78, 89, 92, 96, *98*
    migration policies 89, 91
    rural–urban 115
  oil industry 67
  population growth 67, 68, 116
  slums *107*, 116
  unemployment 113–14
  urban poverty 68, *102*, 113, 114–16, 130n
  urbanization 67–9, 115, 116, 142
  wars 113–14
  see also individual cities, countries and regions
migration
  economic growth relationship 3, 79, 81, 98
  globalization causes 3, 77
  government policies 82–3, 84, 85–6, 88, 89, 91, 94, 96, 97
  multiculturalism as a result 13, 14, 15, 25–6, 82, 97
  population growth relationship 77–8, 91
  rural to urban 50, 63, 69, 77, 91, 92, 99, 108, 112, 115
  scale of 77–9
  social issues 10, 11, 12, 13–14, 26, 81–2, 85
  spatial dimension 10, *14*
  transit 79, 86, 88–9, *90*, 91, 94, 95
  wars cause 92, 94, 95
  see also immigrants
Millennium Development Goals (MDGs) vii, 1, 108, *153*
Minsk, Belarus 149
Moldova *79*, 124
Mongolia *109*, 150
Morocco 68, *90*, 91, *107*, 113, 115

Moscow, Russia *16*, 72, 73, 95, 123, 166, *167*
Mozambique 93, 94, *120*, 121
multiculturalism 5, 6–7, 10–15, 25–6, 82, 97, 177–8, 182
Mumbai, India 50, 62, 82, 84, 109, *110*, *177*
municipal governments
  anti-crime policies 157
  cultural strategies *34*, *39*, *42*
  financing issues 28
  housing policies *37*
  in metropolitan areas 3, 54–5
  migration policies 84, 94, 97
  urban planning responsibility 162, 166, 167, 175–6
Myanmar 82, 84, 85, 138

Nagoya, Japan 47
Nairobi, Kenya
  corruption in government *148*
  crime 145
  economic issues *16*
  on guns 148, 149
  slums *117*, 119, 120
  traditional crafts 36
  urban planning 164
Nepal 83, 84, *109*, 137
Netherlands 74, 97, *126*, 151, 153, 156, 167–8, 172
networks
  in communities 5, 81–2, 88, 95, 120, *122*
  of immigrants 81–2, 88, *90*, 95
  inter-city 94, 171, 182n
  of NGOs 7n, 88
  in slum communities 82, 103–4, 120, *122*
New York, US
  cultural industries 41, *43*
  demographic change 61
  economic importance 21, 61
  homelessness *129*
  immigrants 12, 13, *14*, 15, 61, 82, 97, 99
  loft living 36, *37*
  metropolitanization 54, 60–1
  as a multicultural city 10
  planning for the future 27, 180
  shopping malls 47
  social segregation 59
  urban poverty 125
New Zealand 6, *11*, 96, 99, 154, 156, *166*
NGOs
  anti-crime initiatives *139*, 143, 157
  failings of 143, 179–80
  on governance norms *133*, 134
  housing initiatives *152*
  immigration work 86, 88
  in networks 7n, 88
  poverty alleviation programmes 179–80
Nicaragua *79*, 82, 86–7, 88, *107*, 111, 112
Niger 90, 92, 119, *122*
Nigeria *56*, *90*, 91, 92, *107*, 119
Northern Africa *see* Middle East and Northern Africa
Northern America 58, 73, 74, 78, 124, 133, 135, 136, 143, 150, 151, 154, 156
see also Canada; United States
Norway 155

Oman 67

Pakistan 78, 83, 95, 106, 108, *109*, *137*, 138
Paraguay 88
Paris, France 5, *33*, 38, *82*, 124, 153–4
Peru 88, 140, *152*
Philippines *79*, 84, 107, 108, 126, 137, *138*, *180*
Poland 73, 95, 96, 123, 124, 151, 154
pollution 7n, 22, 39, 50, 58, 108, 110
population growth
  aging populations 25, 123
  in cities *23*, 24–5, 50

globalization causes 3, *23*, 24–5, 50
  in metropolitan areas 51, *56*, 62, 63, 65, 67–8, 69, 72
  migration relationship 77–8, 91
  slums relationship 104, *106*
  urban poverty relationship 115
Porto Alegre, Brazil 113, *179*, 180
Portugal *126*, 153, 154
Prague, Czech Republic 34, 95, 96, 124, 149
privatization 2, 20–1, 102, 111, 121, 124, 165
public services
  inequality of provision 17, 19, 23, 24, 58–9, 85, 103–4, 111
  local government responsibility 74, 113
  in metropolitan areas 3, *56*
  privatization 2, 20–1
  street maintenance 2, 21, 28, *156*
  waste management 2, 21, 28, 55, *56*
  see also sanitation; water supply
public spaces 4, 5, 6, 10, 12, 32, 46, *156*
Puerto Rico 88, 141

Qatar 67, 89

Rabat, Morocco *90*, 116
rape 4, *117*, *121*, 144, 146, 153
refugees
  defined 100n
  refugee camps 103, 113, *116*, *120*, *122*
  scale of problem *77*, 78–9, *80–1*, 91, 92
  in wars 92, 94, 95, 113, *120*, *121*
Reykjavik, Iceland 34
Riga, Latvia 149
Rio de Janeiro, Brazil *15*, 50, 58, 64, 66–7, 112, 130n, *139*
Riyadh, Saudi Arabia 67, 68
Romania *117*, 122, 124, *125*, 150
Rome, Italy 54, 96
Rotterdam, Netherlands 74, 168, 173, 179
Russia
  aging populations 123
  crime 149, 150, 151
  drug trafficking 151
  economic issues 17
  gender issues *125*
  governance issues 166
  industry 123
  metropolitanization 72–3
  migration 79, 94, 95, 96, 99
  mortality rates 130n
  people trafficking 151
  population growth *123*
  slums 124
  urban planning 165–6, 172
  urban poverty 122, *123*, *125*
Rwanda *121*, *122*

San Francisco, US *82*, 99
San José, Costa Rica 82, 86–7, 88
San Salvador, El Salvador 16
sanitation
  health issues 110
  in slums 3, 103, 104, *106*, 112, *117*, 119
  urban poor lack 103, 108, 116
  in war situations 115
Santa Cruz, Bolivia 55
Santiago, Chile *16*, 64, 66, 162, 163
São Paulo, Brazil
  crime *139*
  employment issues *66*
  governance issues 66, 67
  metropolitanization 50, 51, 58, 64, 65, *66*
  population growth *16*, 50, 112
  urban poverty *111*
Saudi Arabia 67, 89, 116, 142, 143
Scotland 153, 169, 172
Senegal *90*, 91, 92

Seoul, Republic of Korea 50, 62, 107
Serbia and Montenegro 150
Shanghai, China *16*, 47, 51, 108, 175–6
shopping and shopping centres 11, 20, 43, 45–6, 53, 54
Sierra Leone *90*, 92, *107*, 119, *120*
Singapore *36*, 46, 54, 78, 83, 84, 85–6, 106–7
Slovakia *122*, 124
Slovenia 124, 150
slums
    in advanced economies 104, 105
    children affected 107–8, 110
    community networks 82, 103–4, 120–1, *122*
    defined 3–4, 103
    in developing economies 4, 104, 105, *107*, 109
    ethnic spaces *117*, 129
    evictions 104, *117*, 119, *152*
    global estimates 1, 4, *106*, *107*
    government policies 113, *115*, *117*
    health issues 103, 108, 109–10
    HIV/AIDS risks 103, 105, 118, 119, 120
    immigrants inhabit 82, 85, *93*, *117*
    improvement schemes 108, *117–18*
    indicators *103*, *104*, *106*, 130n
    inequality relationship *102*, 104, *107*, 109, *117–18*
    infant mortality rates 104, *116*, 119, *122*
    population growth relationship 104, *106*
    as refugee camps *118*
    sanitation provision 103, 104, *106*, 112, *117*, 119
    in transition economies 105, *107*, 124
    urban poverty relationship vii, 3–4, 20, 68, *102*, 103–5, *106*
    water supply 103, *106*, 110, 119
social issues
    of differentiation 2, 3, 5, 19–20
    of globalization 19–20, 124–5
    of metropolitanization 52–4, 58, 59, 60, 66, 71
    of migration 10, 11, 12, 13–14, 26, 81–2, 85
    segregation 59, 66, 71, 81–2, 93, 99, *177*
    of urban poverty 103, 104, 122
social services 2, 21, 24, 112–13, 123
Sofia, Bulgaria 95, 123, 149
Somalia *80*, 92, *120*
Sotteville, France *37*
South Africa
    crime 134, 144, 145, *156*
    homicide rates 144
    immigrants 14, 79, 91–2, 93, 94
    metropolitanization 70
    slums *107*, 120
    urban planning 165, *166*, 172
    violence against women 146
South America 64, 112, 140
South Asia 61, 63, *90*, 108, 137
Southeast Asia 63, 83, 84, 89, 90, 99, 138
Spain *10*, 97, 126, 153
Sri Lanka 95, *109*, 137
St Petersburg, Russia 72, 73, 95
Stockholm, Sweden 153–4
Stuttgart, Germany 96, 97
sub-Saharan Africa
    corruption in government 146–7, *148*
    crime 134, 135, 136, 137, 143–9
    cultural heritage preservation *44–5*
    economic growth 71, 118, 120
    governance issues 69, 70–1, 146–7
    gun smuggling and ownership 147–9
    HIV/AIDS *11*, 105, 118, 119–20, *147*
    homicide rates 144
    housing issues *117*, 119, *152*
    immigrants 78–9, 91–4
    industrialization 69
    mega-urban regions (MURs) *56*, *57*, 69, 70
    metropolitanization *56*, *57*, 69–71, 175
    migration *15*, 89, 90, 91–2, 97, 111

migration policies 94
    rural–urban 69, 91, 92
people trafficking 133
police satisfaction 137
population growth 69
refugees *121*, *122*
security of tenure issues 6, *117*, 119
service provision *117*, 119
slums 105, *107*, *117–18*, 118, 119, *121*
social segregation 93
urban development 69, *71*, 91
urban planning 164–5, 182n
urban poverty *56–7*, *102*, 105, 118–21, *122*, 130n
urbanization 69–70, 92, 105, 118, 119, 164
violence against women 136, 146, *147*
wars 92, *121*, *122*, 148
xenophobia issues 92, *93*
youth crime 145
see also individual cities, countries and regions
Sudan 67, *90*, 92, *121*
Sweden *126*, 153, 154, 155
Switzerland 96, *166*
Sydney, Australia 99
Syria 89, 113, 143

Tajikistan 124
Tallinn, Estonia 123, 149
Tangiers, Morocco *90*
Tanzania 92, *121*
Tashkent, Uzbekistan 72
Thailand 6, 50, *64*, 85, 106, 107, 108, *109*
Tilburg, Netherlands *172*
Tirana, Albania 149
Tokyo, Japan *21*, 34–5, 99
Toronto, Canada *82*, 97
tourism 18, 35, 36, *42*, 54, *87*
trade and trade liberalization 7n, 16, 17, 57, 102
transition economies
    aging populations 123
    corruption in government 136, 150
    crime 132, 134, 149–51
    drug trafficking 138, 143, 151
    economic issues 102, 122
    governance issues 72–3
    gun ownership 150
    HIV/AIDS 123
    housing issues 72, 123–4
    immigrants 94–6
    inequality issues 123–4
    metropolitanization 71–3
    migration 3, 72, 77, 79, 94–6, 99, 123
    mortality rates 123, 130n
    people trafficking 133, 151
    police satisfaction 135–6, 150
    population growth 72, *123*, *127*
    slums 105, *107*, 124
    unemployment 121–2
    urban planning 165–6
    urban poverty *102*, 105, 121–4, 130n
    urbanization 71
    wars 94, 95, 124
    see also individual cities, countries and regions
Transparency International 134, 136, 137, 140, 147, 155
transport 7n, *21*, 52, 53, 54, *56*, 59, *163*
Trinidad and Tobago 140
Tunisia 68, 113, *115*, *116*, 142
Turkey 16, 89–90, *95*, 98, *109*, 143

Uganda 79, 92, *120*
Ukraine 94, 95, 96, 150, 151
unemployment 102, 113, 115, 116, *117*, 121–2, 126
United Arab Emirates 67, *116*
United Kingdom 33, 74, 97, 126, *166*, 169–70, 172, 175, 179

United States
    civil society 173, 179
    commuting 52
    crime 141–2, 143, 151, 153, 154, 156
    cultural consumption spaces 45
    cultural heritage preservation 33, 36
    drug trafficking and abuse 141–2, 143, 156
    edge cities 52
    gentrification 37–8
    governance issues 74, 155
    HIV/AIDS *129*
    homelessness 125, *126*, 128, *129*
    immigrants 13, *14*, *26*, 79, 83, 96, 97, 99
    metropolitan areas 58, 59
    multicultural cities *26*
    relocation of industry 17, *19*, 126
    shopping 46, 47
    social segregation 59
    unemployment 126
    urban planning 170, 173
    urban poverty 126
urban culture
    arts and crafts 33, 36–7, *42*, *109*, 111
    as built environment 11, *19*, 32
    'cities of culture' vii, 5, 34
    creativity 32, *33*, *34*, 38–9, 47
    cultural districts 34–5, 41–2, 43, 45–7
    cultural heritage preservation *34*, 35–7, *38*
    cultural identities 5–6, 11, 13, 32, *87*, 171, 177
    cultural industries 32, 38–9, 41–2
    defined 4, 10–11
    diversification 11–12
    economic growth relationship vii, 4–5, *18–19*, 32, 35
    financial issues 33, 34
    fusion vii, 5–6, 11, *15*, 42, 43, 45–7
    globalization relationship 4, 10–15, *18–19*
    government strategies 5, 33, 42
    immigrants contribute 11–13, *14*, *26*, 42
    in inclusive cities 6, 47
    language issues 5, 6, 13, 14, 15, 26
    multiculturalism benefits 5, 6, *26*
    museums 33, 34, 41, *42*, 43, 53
    music 11, 13, *15*, 40–1, *141*
    rap/hip-hop 11, *141*
    standardization 11, 12–13, *18*, 34, *40*, 41
    symbolic economy relationship 32, 41, 43
    urban development relationship 4–7, *18–19*, 32
urban development
    cultural dimension 4–7, *18–19*, 32
    endogenous 7, 176–7
    in equality issues 50, 157, 176–7
    globalization affects *18–19*
    inner-city areas 33–5
    public participation 166–7
    urban planning relationship 7, *156*, 157, 165, 172, 175, 181
Urban Governance Index (UGI, UN-Habitat) *134*
urban planning
    civil service responsibility 161, 162
    civil society's role 6–7, 162, 166, 167, 170, 173–4, 178–80, 181–2
    at community level 7, 175–6
    corporations role 167–8, 170, 172, 173, 181–2
    for crime prevention *156*, 157
    economic growth affects 161, 172, 174
    governance relationship 6, 163, 165–7, 169–70, 172, 181–2
    inequality relationship 5, 29, 177–8
    innovative 174–5
    local government responsibility 161, 165, 166, 167–8, 169–70, 172, 181–2
    mega-projects 167–8, 182n
    in metropolitan areas 3, 7, *27*, 50, 55, 175–6
    for multicultural cities 5, 6–7, 177–8, 182

municipal government responsibility 162, 166, 167, 175–6
national government responsibility 6, 160, 161, 166, 167–8, 169–70, 172
planning cultures 6, 160–82
planning for the future 27–8, 162, 172, 174, *178*, 180–1
by public–private partnerships 167–8, 172
for sustainability 27, 170–1, 174, 175
urban development relationship 7, *156*, 157, 165, 172, 175, 181
urban poverty
children affected 59, 107–8, 126, 130n
crime relationship vii, 134, 135
in developing economies 103, 106–21
economic growth relationship 59, 108, 111, 118
financial capital relationship 103, 104
globalization relationship vii, 19, 102, 112, 126
government strategies 102
health issues 20, 24, 103, 107–8
HIV/AIDS relationship 118, 119–20, 123
human capital relationship 103, 104
immigrants affected vii, 88, 102
industry relationship 102, 123, 126
inequality relationship 2, 19, 102, 108, 111, *116*, 123–4
land access issues 6, 112, 113
in metropolitan areas *56–7*, 66, 68
population growth relationship 116
sanitation problems 103, 108, 116
security of tenure issues 6, 82, *103*, 113, *117*, 119, *127*
slums relationship vii, 3–4, 20, 68, *102*, 103–5, *106*
social issues 103, 104, 122
in transition economies 105
unemployment relationship 102, 113, 114, 115, 120–1, *122*, 126
urbanization relationship 104–5, 108
wars affect 113, *121*, 124
water supply problems 103, 108, 116
women affected 102, 107, 115, 124, *125*
young people affected 102

urban spaces
cultural consumption spaces 32, 42–7
enclosed 47
ethnic spaces *12*, 13–15, 25–6, 82, 97, *117*, 129
globalization relationship vii, 2–3, *18*, 21–3, 32, 52, 61
live–work spaces 5, 35, *37*
in metropolitan areas vii, 3, 51–2, 58, 59–60, 61
migration affects 10, *14*
redevelopment 32–8, 43, 45
relocation of industry affects vii, 2–3, 5, *21*, 22, 35
spatial mismatch 3, 58, 59–60
spatial segregation 2, 67, 82, 99, 124, *125*
'splintering' vii, 3, 22
urbanization *24*
in developing economies 15, 105
economic growth relationship 15–16, 50, 71
of metropolitan areas 62, 63, 64–6, 67–70, 71
urban poverty relationship 104–5, 108
Uruguay *87*, 111, 140
Uzbekistan 95, 124

Vancouver, Canada 12, 14, *82*, 97, 99
Vanuatu *79*
Venezuela 86, 88, 138
Venice, Italy 54
Vienna, Austria 96
Viet Nam 14, 84, *85*, 95, 96, 138
Vilnius, Lithuania 149
violence
anti-violence initiatives 139, *151*
domestic 4, *128*, 134, 139, *152*, *153*
guns used 4, 133, 134, 138, 147
inequality relationship 61, 134, 146
sexual 4, *114*, *122*, 136, 146, 154 *see also* rape
against women 4, *128*, 135, 136, 138–9, 146, *147*, *152*
wars 92, 94, 95, 113, 114, *121*, 124, 148
Warsaw, Poland 72, 95, 96, 123, 149
water supply
drinking water 3, 29, *39*, *56*

health issues 23, 110
privatization 21
in slums 103, *106*, *110*, 119
urban poor lack 103, 108, 116
in war situations 113, 114
women
employment 2, 17, 58, 84, *90*, *98*, *118*, *152*
against guns *139*
HIV/AIDS risks 118, *120*, *152*
housing issues *126*, *128*, *152–3*
immigrants 84, *90*, *98*
legislation fails *152–3*
traditional crafts *109*
traffick in 133, 137–8, 151
urban poverty affects 102, 107, 114, 124, *125*
victims of violence 4, *128*, 135, 136, 138–9, 146, *147*, *152*
against violence 139, *151*

xenophobia 3, 11, 12, *81*, 82, 84, 92, *93*

Yemen 67, *79*, 116
young people
aid projects *119*, *145*
crime involvement 135, 138, *139*, *140*, 145, 154–5
drug abuse 123
educational opportunities 59, 114, 154
HIV/AIDS risks 123, *129*
homelessness 127, 128, *129*
homicide rates 138
urban poverty affects 102
youth culture 7n, *11*, 46

Zagreb, Croatia 149
Zambia *122*, 145
Zanzibar, Tanzania 36, *38*
Zimbabwe *120*